AUTOCAD® 2008 AND
AUTOCAD LT® 2008
NO EXPERIENCE REQUIRED™

AUTOCAD® 2008 AND AUTOCAD LT® 2008

NO EXPERIENCE REQUIRED™

David Frey

Jon McFarland

Wiley Publishing, Inc.

Acquisitions Editor: Willem Knibbe
Development Editor: Hilary Powers
Technical Editor: Paul Richardson
Production Editor: Martine Dardignac
Copy Editor: Kim Wimpsett
Production Manager: Tim Tate
Vice President and Executive Group Publisher: Richard Swadley
Vice President and Executive Publisher: Joseph B. Wikert
Vice President and Publisher: Neil Edde
Book Designer and Compositor: Franz Baumhackl
Proofreader: Nancy Riddiough
Indexer: Nancy Guenther
Anniversary Logo Design: Richard Pacifico
Cover Designer: Ryan Sneed
Cover Image: © Dieter Spannknebel, Digital Vision, Getty Images

Dear Reader,

Thank you for choosing *AutoCAD 2008 and AutoCAD LT 2008: No Experience Required*. This book is part of a family of premium-quality Sybex graphics books, all written by outstanding authors who combine practical experience with a gift for teaching.

Sybex was founded in 1976. Now, more than 30 years later, we're still committed to producing consistently exceptional books. With each of our graphics titles we're working hard to set a new standard for the industry. From the paper we print on to the writers and CAD professionals we work with, our goal is to bring you the best books available.

I hope you see all that reflected in these pages. I'm very interested to hear your comments and get your feedback on how we're doing. To let us know what you think about this or any other Sybex book, please send me an email at sybex_publisher@wiley.com. Please also visit us at www.sybex.com to learn more about the rest of our growing graphics line.

Best regards,

Neil Edde
Vice President and Publisher
Sybex, an Imprint of Wiley

David:
To Dr. Schein and his colleagues,
but especially to Dr. Schein

Jon:
To my lovely wife, Lucy,
and our two sons,
Zach and Jacob

ACKNOWLEDGMENTS

I am grateful to the many people who contributed to the publication of this update of the book. For those involved in this project at Sybex and Wiley, I extend my thanks.

Sandy Jaffe clarified the nuances of the contract and patiently gathered answers to my questions, and Janet Chang helped with the logistics of the signing. Thanks to Willem Knibbe who brought me into this project and served as acquisitions editor for this update. He rallied support for its publication and kept me focused on the project, and he maintained a constructive relationship with Jim Quanci and Denis Cadu of the Autodesk Developer Network, which enabled me to get word of release dates and access to the software as early as possible. Thanks also to Jim and Denis for their support.

Thanks to Paul Richardson for lending his expertise to this project as the technical editor. I very much appreciate his lending his teaching and CAD experience in checking the text, figures, and exercises for technical accuracy. Hilary Powers served well as the developmental editor and quickly responded to all issues that arose. The production editor was Martine Dardignac; she kept track of the submissions and all the changes, and, thanks to her, the work progressed at a rate to meet the schedule. Kim Wimpsett served as copy editor and, in doing so, helped update the language and syntax to keep the book very readable; her familiarity with AutoCAD was also an asset in this project.

Finally, I want to thank the production team at Wiley. This is the fourth edition on which Franz Baumhackl has served skillfully as compositor and designer. Nancy Riddiough took on the arduous task of proofreader, and Nancy Guenther has returned to do the index again. Both have performed very well. Everyone involved has been successful in maintaining standards of high quality, and I appreciate their work on this book.

—Jon McFarland

Contents at a Glance

CONTENTS

CHAPTER 17 Materials and Rendering 643

INTRODUCTION

This book was born of the need for a simple yet engaging tutorial that would help beginners step into the world of AutoCAD or AutoCAD LT without feeling intimidated. That tutorial has evolved over the years into a full introduction to the way in which architects and civil and structural engineers use AutoCAD to increase their efficiency and ability to produce state-of-the-art computerized production drawings and designs.

Because AutoCAD and AutoCAD LT are so similar, it makes sense to cover the basics of both programs. For most of the book, the word *AutoCAD* stands for both AutoCAD and AutoCAD LT.

When you come to a section of a chapter that applies to AutoCAD only, an icon (shown here) is displayed in the margin to alert you. Then, at the end of that section, extra information for AutoCAD LT users is provided to give you a workaround or otherwise keep you in step with the tutorial.

Chapters 16 and 17, which are an introduction to drawing in 3D, apply only to AutoCAD, because AutoCAD LT doesn't have the 3D commands and features. But LT users, be assured: Other than the 3D features, LT is much the same program as AutoCAD, with minor differences. You'll be prompted when those differences come along.

This book is directed toward AutoCAD and AutoCAD LT novices—users who know how to use a computer and perform basic file-managing tasks, such as creating new folders and saving and moving files, but who know nothing or little about AutoCAD or LT (as we'll call AutoCAD LT throughout the book). If you're new to the construction and design professions, this book will be an excellent companion as you're learning AutoCAD. If you're already practicing in those fields, you'll immediately be able to apply the skills you'll pick up from this book to real-world projects. The exercises have been successfully used to train architects, engineers, and contractors, as well as college and high-school students, in the basics of AutoCAD.

For those of you in other trades and professions, the project that runs through the book—drawing a small cabin—has been kept simple so that it doesn't require special training in architecture or construction. Also, most chapters have additional information and exercises specifically designed for non-AEC users. Anyone wanting to learn AutoCAD will find this book helpful.

What Will You Learn from This Book?

Learning AutoCAD, like learning any complex computer program, requires a significant commitment of time and attention and, to some extent, a tolerance for repetition. You must understand new concepts to operate the program and to appreciate its potential as a drafting and design tool. But to become proficient at AutoCAD, you must also use the commands enough times to gain an intuitive sense of how they work and how parts of a drawing are constructed.

At the end of most chapters, you'll find one or more additional exercises and a checklist of the tools you have learned (or should have learned!). The steps in the tutorial have a degree of repetition built into them that allows you to work through new commands several times and build up confidence before you move on to the next chapter.

Progressing through the book, the chapters fall into four general areas of study:

- ► Chapters 1 through 3 familiarize you with the organization of the screen, go over a few of the basic commands, and equip you with the tools necessary to set up a new drawing.

- ► Chapters 4 and 5 introduce the basic drawing commands and develop drawing strategies that will help you use commands efficiently.

- ► Chapters 6 through 11 work with AutoCAD's major features.

- ► Chapters 12 through 15 examine intermediate and advanced AutoCAD features.

- ► Chapters 16 and 17 introduce the 3D features of AutoCAD.

In the process of exploring these elements, you'll follow the steps involved in laying out the floor plan of a small, three-room cabin. You'll then learn how to generate elevations from the floor plan and, eventually, how to set up a title block and print your drawing. Along the way, you'll also learn how to do the following:

- ► Use the basic drawing and modify commands in a strategic manner.

- ► Set up layers.

- ► Put color into your drawing.

- ► Define and insert blocks.

- ► Generate elevation views.

- ► Place hatch patterns and fills on building components.

- ► Use text in your drawing.

- ► Dimension the floor plan.

Later chapters in the book touch on more advanced features of AutoCAD, including the following:

- ▶ Drawing a site plan.
- ▶ Using external references.
- ▶ Setting up a drawing for printing with layouts.
- ▶ Making a print of your drawing.
- ▶ Working in three dimensions, for AutoCAD users.

All these features are taught using the cabin as a continuing project. As a result, you'll build up a set of drawings that document your progress through the project and that you can use later as reference material if you find that you need to refresh yourself with material in a specific skill.

At the end of the book is a glossary of terms that are used in the book and are related to AutoCAD and building design, followed by an index.

Files on the Website

If you're already somewhat familiar with AutoCAD and you're reading only some of the chapters, you can pull accompanying files from this book's page on Sybex's website (www.sybex.com/go/acadner2008).

Hints for Success

Because this book is essentially a step-by-step tutorial, it has a side effect in common with any tutorial of this type. After you finish a chapter and see that you have progressed further through the cabin project, you may have no idea how you got there and are sure you couldn't do it again without the help of the step-by-step instructions.

This feeling is a natural result of this kind of learning tool, and you can do a couple of things to get past it. You can work through the chapter again. Doing so may seem tedious, but it offers a great advantage: you gain speed in drawing. You'll accomplish the same task in half the time it took you the first time. If you do a chapter a third time, you'll cut your time in half again. Each time you repeat a chapter, you can skip more and more of the explicit instructions, and eventually you'll be able to execute the commands and finish the chapter by just looking at the figures and glancing at the text. In many ways, this process is like learning a musical instrument. You must go slowly at first, but over time and through practice, your pace picks up.

Another suggestion for honing your skills is to follow the course of the book but apply the steps to a different project. You might draw your own living space or design a new one. If you have a real-life design project that isn't too complex, that's even better. Your chances for success in learning AutoCAD or any computer program are greatly increased when you're highly motivated, and a real project of an appropriate size can be the perfect motivator.

Ready, Set...

When I started learning AutoCAD about 17 years ago, I was at first surprised how long I experienced a level of frustration that I never thought I was capable of feeling. When I finally got over the hump and began feeling that I could successfully draw with this program after all, I told myself that I would someday figure out a way to help others get past that initial frustration. That was the primary motivating force for my writing this book. I hope it works for you and that you too get some enjoyment while learning AutoCAD. As the title says, there is "no experience required," only an interest in the subject and a willingness to learn!

CHAPTER 1

Getting to Know AutoCAD

▶ Opening a new drawing

▶ Getting familiar with the AutoCAD and AutoCAD LT graphics windows

▶ Modifying the display

▶ Displaying and arranging toolbars

Your introduction to AutoCAD and AutoCAD LT begins with a tour of the user interface of the two programs. In this chapter, you'll also learn how to use some tools that help you control the interface's appearance and how to find and start commands. For the material covered in this chapter, the two applications are almost identical in appearance. Therefore, as you tour AutoCAD, I'll point out any differences between AutoCAD and AutoCAD LT. In general, LT is a 2D program, so it doesn't have most of the 3D features that come with AutoCAD, such as solids modeling and rendering. The AutoLISP programming language found in AutoCAD is also absent from LT. The other differences are minor. As mentioned in this book's introduction, when I say AutoCAD, I mean both AutoCAD and AutoCAD LT. I'll also refer to AutoCAD LT as LT throughout this chapter and the rest of the book to specifically refer to that version. Starting AutoCAD is the first task at hand.

Starting AutoCAD

If you installed AutoCAD using the default settings for the location of the program files, start the program by choosing Start ➤ Programs ➤ Autodesk ➤ AutoCAD 2008 ➤ AutoCAD 2008 or by choosing Start ➤ All Programs ➤ Autodesk ➤ AutoCAD LT 2008 ➤ AutoCAD LT 2008, depending on your program. (This command path might vary depending on the Windows scheme you are using.) If you customized your installation, find and click the AutoCAD 2008 icon or the AutoCAD LT 2008 icon on your desktop.

Exploring the New Features Workshop

The New Features Workshop dialog welcome screen opens when you first start AutoCAD and leads to several animated demonstrations and explanations of the new features included in the latest release of AutoCAD (see Figure 1.1). This is a quick and easy way to see how AutoCAD 2008 has improved over AutoCAD 2007 and which tools you can use to augment any skills you already have. Choosing Maybe Later on the left side of the dialog box causes it to reappear every time you start AutoCAD; choosing the No, Don't Show This to Me Again option dismisses the dialog box indefinitely. You must then access the New Features Workshop through the Help menu in the menu bar at the top of the AutoCAD user interface.

Selecting the Yes radio button on the left side of the dialog box opens the New Features Workshop dialog box (see Figure 1.2). Here, you navigate and select the feature you want to investigate in the left pane and observe the selection in the right pane. The drop-down list in the upper-left corner provides access to the New Features Workshops for other Autodesk products installed on your system.

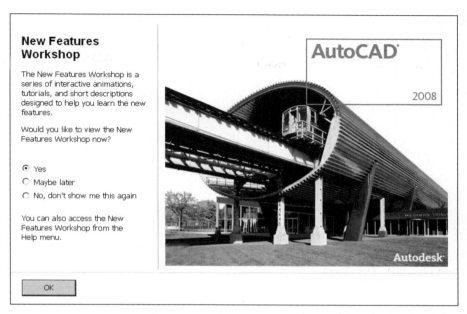

FIGURE 1.1: The AutoCAD welcome screen provides access to the New Features Workshop.

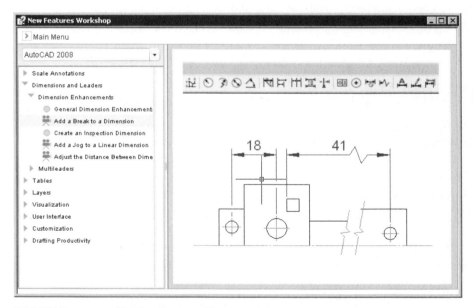

FIGURE 1.2: The New Features Workshop dialog box

The Customer Involvement Program

Nearly all the latest releases of Autodesk products include the opportunity to participate in the customer involvement program (CIP). The CIP is designed to collect nonpersonal information about your Autodesk products and computer system to help the product programmers and developers design software that best meets their customers' needs. If you haven't yet agreed or disagreed to participate, when you first start AutoCAD, you might be prompted to join with the Customer Involvement Program dialog box.

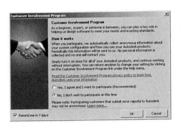

Participation is strictly voluntary, and if you choose to participate, AutoCAD will periodically send a small file to Autodesk containing information such as your software name and version, the commands you use, and your system configuration information. An Internet connection is required, and you must ensure that your firewall settings don't prevent the information from being transmitted.

Exploring the AutoCAD User Interface

AutoCAD and LT offer numerous dialog boxes with various combinations of buttons and text boxes. You'll learn their many functions as you progress through the book.

After bypassing the initial dialog boxes that AutoCAD provides, the program opens to display the AutoCAD user interface, also called the *graphics window*. AutoCAD provides many methods for creating and editing objects, changing the view of a drawing, or executing AutoCAD file maintenance or other utilities. In LT, your screen looks similar to Figure 1.3. For AutoCAD, your monitor displays one of three *workspaces*: the AutoCAD Classic workspace (also similar to Figure 1.3); the 3D Modeling workspace (see Figure 1.4); or the 2D Drafting & Annotation workspace, which is similar to the AutoCAD Classic workspace. You'll be using a variation of the AutoCAD Classic workspace for the first 14 chapters in this book. In the final two chapters, you'll switch to the 3D Modeling workspace, but for now, you need to get your AutoCAD user interface to look like Figure 1.3.

N O T E   The figures and graphics is this book show the drawing area of the AutoCAD user interface with a white background, but the default, and preferred, method is to use a black background to reduce eyestrain. The color choice in the book is simply for readability.

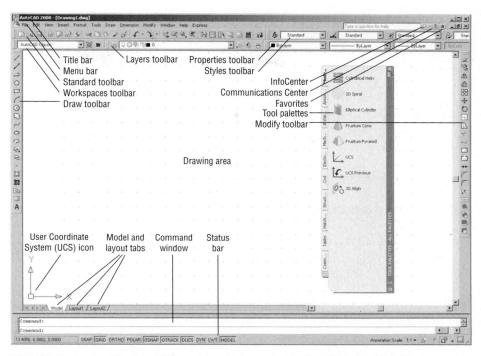

FIGURE 1.3: The AutoCAD graphics window using the AutoCAD Classic workspace

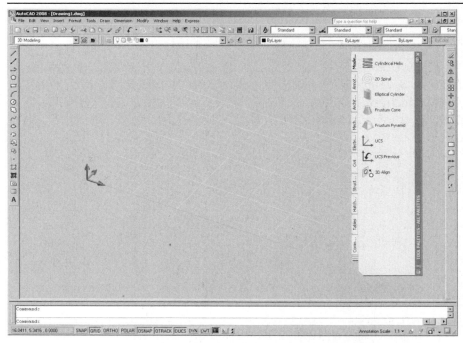

FIGURE 1.4: The AutoCAD graphics window using the 3D Modeling workspace

The toolbars on your screen might not be in the same places as they are shown here. Later in this chapter, you'll see how to move the toolbars, display and place new toolbars, and suppress the toolbars. If your screen looks like Figure 1.4 or isn't at all like Figure 1.3, you need to make a few changes:

1. Click the drop-down arrow in the Workspaces toolbar, and choose Auto-CAD Classic. Alternately, you can choose Tools ➤ Workspaces ➤ AutoCAD Classic. (If AutoCAD Classic already has a check in the box next to it or if you are using LT, this step is unnecessary.)

2. By default, the AutoCAD Classic workspace displays the tool *palettes* on the screen. If the palettes are displayed, you need to turn them off for now by clicking the X in the top-right corner or by choosing Tools ➤ Palettes ➤ Tool Palettes from the menu bar. Your workspace might have different toolbars and palettes displayed than those shown in Figure 1.5. If other palettes are still visible, click the X in the upper-right or upper-left corner of each palette to close it.

    FIGURE 1.5: The tool palettes

3. The large area in the middle of the screen is called the *drawing area*. It might need adjusting. Choose View ➢ Visual Styles ➢ 2D Wireframe.

4. Choose View ➢ 3D Views ➢ Plan View ➢ World UCS. If dots appear in the drawing area, the grid is turned on.

5. Move the cursor to the status bar at the bottom of the screen, and click the Grid readout button so it's in the off (unpushed) position. Be sure all the other readout buttons except Model are in their off (unpushed) positions.

LT users can skip step 3 and move on to step 4.

Your screen should look close enough to Figure 1.3 to continue. You'll arrange the toolbars the way you need them a little later.

Introducing the AutoCAD Graphics Window

At the top of the graphics window sit the title bar, the menu bar, and three toolbars. You might have more or less than three toolbars; if so, you'll change that soon.

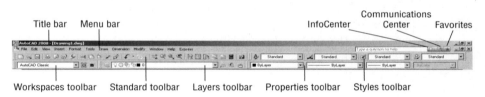

The *title bar* is analogous to the title bar in any Windows program. It contains the program name (*AutoCAD* or *AutoCAD LT*) and the title of the current drawing with its *path*, as long as any drawing other than the default Drawingn.dwg is open. Below the title bar is the *menu bar*, where you'll see the drop-down menus. Among the drop-down menus, File, Edit, Window, and Help are standard Windows menus (meaning that they appear on Windows-compliant applications). These Windows menus also contain a few commands specific to AutoCAD. The rest of the menus contain AutoCAD-specific functions.

The title bar and menu bar at the top of the LT screen are identical to those in AutoCAD except that *AutoCAD LT* appears in the title bar rather than *AutoCAD*.

To the far right of the menus are the InfoCenter, Communications Center, and Favorites buttons. You can enter a question in the field to the left of the Info-Center button to quickly access information from the Help system through the InfoCenter's drop-down panel. With the Communications Center you can determine what type of information, such as software updates, product support, or RSS feeds, Autodesk sends directly to your system.

Below the menus are the *Standard* and *Styles toolbars*. The Standard toolbar contains 25 commonly used command buttons (LT has only 23). Several of these buttons will be familiar to Windows users; the rest are AutoCAD commands. The Styles toolbar to the right defines the appearance of any new objects in the drawing. Just below these toolbars are the *Workspaces*, *Layers*, and *Properties toolbars*, which together contain six command buttons and six drop-down lists.

The blank middle section of the screen is called the *drawing area*. Notice the movable *crosshair cursor*. The crosshairs on your cursor might not extend completely across the screen. Later in this chapter I will show you how to modify the length of the crosshairs as well as make a few other changes. Your screen might or might not display the coordinate tooltips next to the intersection of the crosshairs.

Notice the little box at the intersection of the two crosshair lines. This is one of several forms of the AutoCAD and LT cursor. When you move the cursor off the drawing area, it changes to the standard Windows pointing arrow. As you begin using commands, it will take on other forms, depending on which step of a command you're performing.

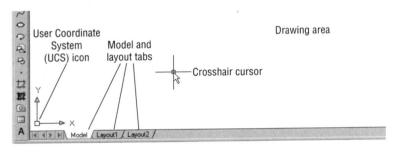

The icon with a double arrow in the lower-left corner of the drawing area is the *UCS icon* (UCS stands for *user coordinate system*). It indicates the positive direction for the X and Y coordinates. You won't need it for most of the chapters in this book, so you'll learn how to turn it off in Chapter 3.

At the bottom of the drawing area are three tabs: a Model tab and two Layout tabs. You use these tabs to switch between viewing modes. (I'll discuss viewing modes in Chapter 13.) This example shows no toolbars floating in the drawing area, but one toolbar is docked on either side of the drawing area. Your screen might or might not have the toolbars, or they might be in different positions. If the toolbars are floating within the drawing area, rather than docked along one edge, they will have a colored title bar. For specifics, see the section "Using the Toolbars" later in this chapter.

Below the drawing area is the *Command window*.

```
Regenerating model.
AutoCAD menu utilities loaded.
Command:
```

When you enter commands, rather than using the menus or buttons, the Command window is where you tell the program what to do and where the program tells you what's happening. It's an important area, and you'll need to learn how it works in detail. Two lines of text should be visible. You'll learn how to increase the number of visible lines later in this chapter in the section "Working in the Command Window."

Below the Command window is the *status bar*.

```
41.0937, 10.0450, 0.0000      SNAP  GRID  ORTHO  POLAR  OSNAP  OTRACK  DUCS  DYN  LWT  MODEL
```

On the left end of the status bar, you'll see a coordinate readout window. In the middle are 10 readout buttons (LT has only 9) that indicate various drawing modes. It's important to learn about the coordinate system and most of these drawing aids (Snap, Grid, Ortho, and Osnap) early on as you learn to draw in AutoCAD or LT. They will help you create neat and accurate drawings. Polar and Otrack are advanced drawing tools and will be introduced in Chapter 5. Ducs stands for *Dynamic User Coordinate System*; it's used in 3D drawings. Dyn is an off/on toggle that activates or suppresses the dynamic display of information next to the crosshair cursor when it's in the drawing area. For now, keep it in the off (unpushed) mode. Lwt (which stands for *lineweight*) will be discussed in Chapter 14. The Model button is an advanced aid that I'll cover in Chapter 13. At the far right of the status bar are tools for controlling the appearance of annotation objects in AutoCAD. The padlock icon controls which types of toolbars and windows are locked in their current positions on the screen. Leave it in the unlocked mode for now.

This has been a quick introduction to the various parts of the graphics window. I didn't mention a couple of items that might be visible on your screen. You might have scroll bars below and to the right of the drawing area; although these can be useful, they can take up precious space in the drawing area. They won't be of any use while working your way through this book, so I suggest you remove them for now.

To temporarily remove these features, follow these steps:

1. Choose Tools ➤ Options to open the Options dialog box (shown in Figure 1.6). It has 10 tabs (LT has only 8) across the top that act like tabs on file folders.

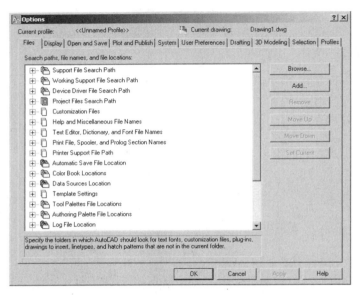

FIGURE 1.6: The Options dialog box

2. Click the Display tab, which is shown in Figure 1.7. Focus on the Window Elements section. If scroll bars are visible on the lower and right edges of the drawing area, the Display Scroll Bars In Drawing Window check box will be selected.

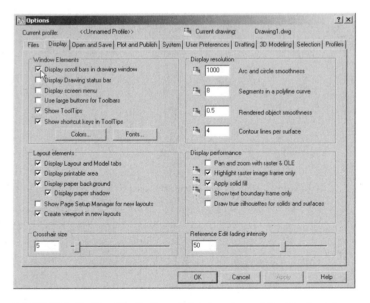

FIGURE 1.7: The Options dialog box open at the Display tab

3. Click the check box to turn off the scroll bars. Also be sure the check box for Display Screen Menu is not selected. Don't click the OK button yet.

Another display setting that you might want to change at this point controls the color of the cursor and the drawing area background. The illustrations in this book show a white background and black crosshair cursor, but you're probably seeing the AutoCAD default, which features a black background and a white crosshair cursor. If you want to change the colors, follow these steps:

1. In the Window Elements area of the Display tab, click the Colors button to open the Drawing Window Colors dialog box (see Figure 1.8). In the upper-left corner of the dialog box, in the Context list box, 2D Model Space should be selected. If it's not, select it.

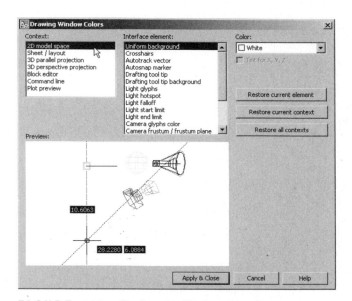

FIGURE 1.8: The Drawing Window Colors dialog box

2. Move to the Color drop-down list, which is in the upper-right corner. If your drawing area background is currently white, a square followed by the word *White* is displayed. Open the Color drop-down list, and select Black (or the background color you want). The drawing area will now be that color, and the cursor color will change to white, as shown in the Preview window below.

3. Click the Apply & Close button to close the Drawing Window Colors dialog box. The background and cursor colors change.

LT doesn't have the Screen menu, so the option to turn it off isn't on LT's Display tab.

4. Don't close the Options dialog box yet.

5. If you want the lines of your crosshair cursor to extend completely across the screen, go to the lower-left corner of the Display tab (the lower-right corner for LT), and move the slider to change the Crosshair Size setting to 100.

6. Click OK to apply any remaining changes and close the Options dialog box.

Your crosshair lines now extend across the drawing area.

 T I P   If you choose a color other than black as the drawing area background color, the color of the crosshair cursor remains the same as it was. To change the crosshair color, in the Drawing Window Colors dialog box, go to the Interface Element list box, and select Crosshairs. Then, select a color from the Color drop-down list.

Working in the Command Window

Just below the drawing area is the Command window. This window is separate from the drawing area and behaves like a Windows window—that is, you can drag it to a different place on the screen and resize it, although I don't recommend you do this at first. If you currently have fewer than three lines of text in the window, you'll need to increase the window's vertical size. To do so, move the cursor to the horizontal boundary between the drawing area and the Command window until it changes to an up-and-down arrow broken by two parallel horizontal lines.

Hold down the left mouse button, drag the cursor up by approximately the amount that one or two lines of text would take up, and then release the mouse button. You should see more lines of text, but you might have to try this a couple of times to display exactly three lines. A horizontal line will separate the top two lines of text from the bottom line of text. When you close the program, AutoCAD will save the new settings; the next time you start AutoCAD, the command window will display three lines of text.

The Command window is where you give information to AutoCAD and where AutoCAD prompts you for the next step in executing a command. It's good practice to keep an eye on the Command window as you work on your drawing. Most errors occur when you aren't looking at it frequently. If the Dyn button on the status bar is in the on position, some of the information in the Command window will appear in the drawing area next to the cursor. I'll cover this feature when you start drawing.

Before you begin to draw, take a close look at the menus, toolbars, and keyboard controls.

N O T E In many cases, you can start AutoCAD commands in a number of ways: from drop-down menus, from the toolbars, from the Command window, and from menus that appear when you right-click. When you get used to drawing with AutoCAD, you'll learn some shortcuts that start commands quickly, and you'll find the way that is most comfortable for you.

Using the Drop-Down Menus

The left end of the menu bar, just below the title bar (see Figure 1.3 earlier in this chapter), consists of an icon and 11 (12 if you have the Express Tools installed) words. Click any of these to display a drop-down menu. The icon and the File and Edit menus are included with all Windows-compliant applications, although they are somewhat customized to work with AutoCAD. The drop-down menu associated with the icon contains commands to control the appearance and position of the drawing area.

Commands in the File menu are for opening and saving new and existing drawing files, printing, exporting files to another application, choosing basic utility options, and exiting the application. The Edit menu contains the Undo and Redo commands, the Cut and Paste tools, and options for creating links between AutoCAD files and other files. The Help menu works like most Windows Help menus and contains a couple of AutoCAD-specific entries as well, including some online resources and a link to the New Features Workshop.

The other eight (or nine) menus contain the most often used AutoCAD commands. You'll find that if you master the logic of how the commands are organized by menu, you can quickly find the command you want. Here is a short description of each of the other AutoCAD drop-down menus:

View   Contains tools for controlling the display of your drawing file.

Insert   Contains commands for placing drawings and images or parts of them inside other drawings.

Format   Contains commands for setting up the general parameters for a new drawing or changing the entities in a current drawing.

Tools   Contains special tools for use while you're working on the current drawing, such as those for finding the length of a line or for running a special macro.

Draw   Contains commands for creating new objects (such as lines or circles) on the screen.

Dimension   Contains commands for dimensioning and annotating a drawing.

Modify   Contains commands for changing existing objects in the drawing.

Window   Contains commands for displaying currently open drawing windows and lists currently open drawing files.

Express   Contains a library of productivity tools that cover a wide range of AutoCAD functions. Express Tools are widely used but unsupported directly by Autodesk. They might or might not be installed on your computer.

Using the Toolbars

Now look at the toolbars on your screen. You'll have two to five toolbars in one or two rows at the top and a couple more on the right and/or left sides of the drawing area. Just below the drop-down menus is the most extensive of the toolbars—the Standard toolbar.

LT has only 23 Standard toolbar buttons. It's missing the Sheet Set Manager and Block Editor buttons because LT doesn't offer these features.

The icons on the AutoCAD toolbars look like flat images and don't appear as raised buttons until you point to them. The Standard toolbar has 25 icons, and they are arranged into 7 logical groups. The icons on the left half of the Standard toolbar are mostly for commands used in all Windows-compatible applications, so you might be familiar with them. The icons on the right half of the Standard toolbar are AutoCAD commands that you use during your regular drawing activities. You use these commands to take care of a number of tasks, including the following:

▶ Changing the view of the drawing on the screen

▶ Changing the properties of an object, such as color or linetype

▶ Borrowing parts of an unopened drawing to use in your current drawing

▶ Displaying a set of palettes that contain objects you can use in your drawing

Accessing the Toolbar Fly-Out Menus

Notice that one icon on the Standard toolbar has a little triangular arrow in the lower-right corner. This arrow indicates that clicking this icon displays more than one command. Follow these steps to see how this special icon works:

1. Move the cursor to the Standard toolbar, and point to the icon that has a magnifying glass with a rectangle in it.

2. Rest the arrow on the button for a moment without clicking. A small window opens just below it, displaying the command the button represents. In this case, the window should say *Zoom Window*. This is a *tool tip*—all buttons have them. Notice the small arrow in the lower-right corner of the icon. This is the multiple-command arrow mentioned earlier.

3. Place the arrow cursor on the button, and hold down the left mouse button. A column of nine buttons opens vertically below the original button (see Figure 1.9). The top button in the column is a duplicate of the button you clicked. This column of buttons is called a *toolbar fly-out menu*. In this example, you're working with the Zoom toolbar fly-out menu.

FIGURE 1.9: Toolbar fly-out menu

4. While still holding down the mouse button, drag the arrow down over each button until you get to the one that has a magnifying glass with a piece of white paper on it. Hold the arrow there until you see the tooltip. It should say Zoom All. Now release the mouse button. The fly-out menu disappears, and AutoCAD executes the Zoom All command. Look in the Command window at the bottom of the screen.

The Zoom All command changes the view of your drawing to include special preset parameters. You'll look at this command in Chapter 3.

```
[All/Center/Dynamic/Extents/Previous/Scale/Window/Object] <real time>: _all
Regenerating model.
Command:
```

At the end of the top line of text is _all. This tells you that you have used the All option of the Zoom command. This fly-out menu is called the *Zoom fly-out menu* because it contains tools for changing views of the drawing, or "zooming around in the drawing."

5. Look at the Standard toolbar where the Zoom Window button was previously. Notice that the Zoom All button has replaced it.

 T I P   On a toolbar fly-out menu, the button you select replaces the button that was on the toolbar. This arrangement is handy if you're going to be using the same command several times, because the button for the command is readily available and you don't have to open the fly-out menu to select it again. The order of the fly-out menu buttons remains the same, so when you open the Zoom fly-out menu again, the Zoom Window button will be at the top of the list. You'll need to become familiar with any fly-out menu buttons you use, because the last one used becomes the representative button on the toolbar.

The behavior of the Zoom fly-out menu on the Standard toolbar is the same as the behavior of fly-out menus in general.

 N O T E   Whenever you start AutoCAD or LT for a new drawing session, the toolbars are reset and contain the original fly-out menu buttons.

The toolbar fly-out menus are regular toolbars that have been attached to another toolbar. AutoCAD has 37 toolbars in all, but only a few have fly-out menus—the Zoom fly-out menu I just discussed and the Insert fly-out menu on the Draw toolbar, for example. You can display the Zoom and Insert fly-out menus as regular toolbars, independent of the Standard and Draw toolbars.

Displaying and Arranging Toolbars

In this section, I'll use the Zoom toolbar to show you some ways you can control and manipulate toolbars. Follow these steps:

1. Be sure the padlock icon in the lower-right corner of your screen is in unlocked mode. Then, right-click any toolbar button on the screen to open the Toolbars menu (see Figure 1.10).

LT has 24 toolbars compared with AutoCAD's 37. The additional toolbars in AutoCAD are almost all for 3D and rendering tools.

3D Navigation
CAD Standards
Camera Adjustment
Dimension
✔ Draw
✔ Draw Order
Inquiry
Insert
✔ Layers
Layers II
Layouts
Lights
Mapping
Modeling
✔ Modify
Modify II
Multileader
Object Snap
Orbit
✔ Properties
Refedit
Reference
Render
Solid Editing
✔ Standard
Standard Annotation
✔ Styles
Text
UCS
UCS II
View
Viewports
Visual Styles
Walk and Fly
Web
✔ Workspaces
Zoom

Lock Location   ▶
Customize...

FIGURE 1.10: The Toolbars menu

2. If you don't see Zoom near the bottom of the list, you should have a down arrow there. Use it to scroll down, if necessary, and then click Zoom to display the Zoom toolbar in the form of a floating box in the drawing area.

Notice that the Zoom toolbar now has a title bar. Toolbars that are positioned on the drawing area are called *floating* toolbars. They have title bars; and by placing the cursor on the title bar and holding down the left mouse button, you can drag the toolbar around the screen. Try this with the Zoom toolbar.

3. Drag the Zoom toolbar to the right side of the screen. You'll notice that as you drag it, the toolbar stays put, and you're dragging a rectangle of the same size as the toolbar (see Figure 1.11). As you drag the rectangle to the right of the drawing area and begin to move it off the drawing area onto the right side of the screen, the rectangle becomes taller and thinner.

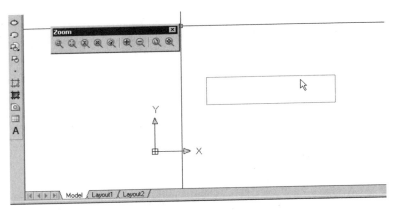

FIGURE 1.11: Dragging the Zoom toolbar

4. Once the rectangle has changed shape, release the left mouse button. The rectangle changes to the Zoom toolbar, which is now positioned off the drawing area without its title bar.

This procedure is called *docking* a toolbar. Notice how the Standard and other toolbars at the top of the drawing area have no title bars—they are docked. Continue with these steps:

1. Drag the Zoom toolbar back onto the drawing area, using the grab bars at the top of the toolbar. You can easily change the shape of any floating toolbar by dragging its edge. Let's change the shape of this toolbar.

2. Move the cursor to the far-right edge of the Zoom toolbar until the crosshair cursor changes to a two-way arrow.

Grab bars are the two lines at the left end of a horizontal toolbar or at the top of a vertical one. They represent the one place to grab a docked toolbar to move it. You can also change a docked toolbar into a floating toolbar by double-clicking its grab bars.

Hold down the left mouse button with the cursor on the right edge of the toolbar, and drag the arrow to the left until the rectangle changes shape. Release the mouse button.

You can reshape and reposition each floating toolbar to fit on the drawing area just as you want it. You won't need the Zoom toolbar just now, so you'll remove it.

3. Move the cursor to the title bar, and click the box with an X in it to close the Zoom toolbar.

Floating toolbars don't affect the size of the drawing area, but they cover your drawing. Each row or column of docked toolbars takes up space that would otherwise be drawing area. You have to decide how many docked and floating toolbars you need on the screen at a time. A good way to start is to leave the Standard, Layers, and Properties toolbars docked on the top of the screen and the Draw and Modify toolbars docked on the left side of the screen.

If your toolbars are positioned as shown in Figure 1.12, continue with the next section. If these toolbars are in another location on the drawing area or not visible, try the steps you used in this section to dock them on the top and left sides of the drawing area. If the toolbars aren't visible, right-click any visible toolbar button, and choose the toolbar you need. Then, drag the toolbar to the left side or top of the drawing area to dock it. Here are the positions I recommend for the five toolbars you should dock on your screen:

▶ At the top, just under the menu bar, dock the Standard toolbar.

▶ Below that, on the left side, dock the Layers toolbar.

▶ To the right of the Layers toolbar, dock the Properties toolbar.

▶ On the left side, dock the Draw toolbar.

▶ Next to the Draw toolbar, dock the Modify toolbar.

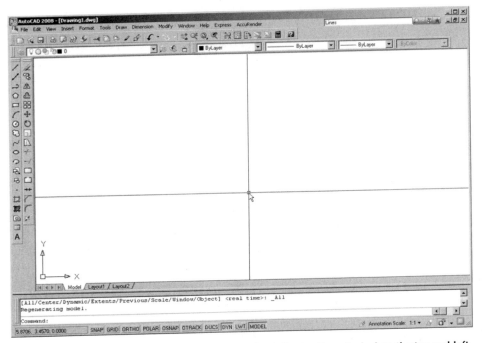

FIGURE 1.12: The AutoCAD user interface with five toolbars docked on the top and left sides of the drawing area

This arrangement of the toolbars will be convenient because you'll often use commands on these five toolbars. When you need other toolbars temporarily, you can use the Toolbars menu to display them in the drawing area and let them float. If you have any other toolbars docked on the screen, use their grab bars to drag them onto the screen. Then, click the Xs in their title bars to close them. Here is a partial list of toolbars that you might have on your screen that need to be turned off:

- ▶ Display Order toolbar

- ▶ Styles toolbar

- ▶ Workspaces toolbar

Customizing Toolbars

You can customize each toolbar, and you can build your own custom toolbars to display only the buttons you use frequently. You can even design your own buttons for commands that aren't already represented by buttons on the toolbars. These activities are for more advanced users, however, and aren't covered in this book. To find out more about how to customize toolbars, see *Mastering AutoCAD 2008 and AutoCAD LT 2008* by George Omura (Wiley, 2007).

Workspaces

Now that you have your screen set up to look like Figure 1.3, you are ready to proceed through the book. I'll direct you to display additional toolbars as needed. For now, though, save this setup as a new workspace because it's a variation of the AutoCAD Classic or LT workspace that comes with the program. Follow these steps:

1. Choose Tools ➤ Workspaces ➤ Save Current As. This opens the Save Workspace dialog box (see Figure 1.13).

FIGURE 1.13: The Save Workspace dialog box

2. Enter 2D Drawing, and click Save. The computer works for a while and then returns you to your workspace. The new 2D Drawing workspace setup will remain as it now is until you change it or until you select a different workspace.

3. Right-click any toolbar, and click the Workspaces entry in the Toolbars list; you'll see the 2D Drawing workspace displayed in the Workspaces toolbar below 2D Drafting & Annotation, 3D Modeling, and AutoCAD Classic (see Figure 1.14). Later in this book, AutoCAD users will switch to the 3D Modeling workspace and make a few adjustments to it.

FIGURE 1.14: The Workspaces menu

4. Close the Workspaces toolbar.

When you make changes to the new workspace—by adding a toolbar or changing the background color of the drawing area—you can easily update the 2D Drawing workspace to accommodate those changes. Follow steps 1 and 2 previously, naming the workspace again to 2D Drawing. You'll get a warning window telling you that a workspace by that name already exists and asking you whether you want the new arrangement to replace the old one. Click Yes.

Using the Keyboard

The keyboard is an important tool for entering data and commands. If you're a good typist, you can gain speed in working with AutoCAD by learning how to enter commands from the keyboard. AutoCAD provides what are called *alias keys*—single keys or key combinations that start any of several often used commands. You can add more or change the existing aliases as you get more familiar with the program.

In addition to the alias keys, you can use several of the F keys (function keys) on the top row of the keyboard as two-way or three-way toggles (switches) to turn AutoCAD functions on and off. Although buttons on the screen duplicate these functions (Snap, Grid, and so on), it's sometimes faster to use the F keys.

Finally, you can activate commands on the drop-down menus from the keyboard, rather than by using the mouse. If you press the Alt key, an underlined letter, called a *hot key*, appears on each menu. Pressing the key for the underlined letter activates the menu. Each command on the menu also has a hot key. Once you activate the menu with the hot-key combination, you can enter the underlined letter of these commands. For a few commands, this method can be the fastest way to start them and to select options.

While working in AutoCAD, you'll need to enter a lot of data, such as dimensions and construction notes; answer questions with "yes" or "no"; and use the arrow keys. You'll use the keyboard constantly. It might help to get into the habit of keeping your left hand on the keyboard and your right hand on the mouse if you're right-handed, or the other way around if you're left-handed.

Using the Mouse

Your mouse most likely has two buttons and a scroll wheel. So far in this chapter, you have used the left mouse button for choosing menus, commands, or options or for holding down the button and dragging a menu, toolbar, or window. The left mouse button is the one you'll be using most often, but you'll also be using the right mouse button.

While drawing, you'll use the right mouse button for the following three operations:

- ▶ To display a menu containing options relevant to the particular step you're in at the moment

- ▶ To use in combination with the Shift or Ctrl key to display a menu containing special drawing aids called *object snaps* (see Chapter 10)

- ▶ To display a menu of toolbars when the pointer is on any icon of a toolbar that is currently open

If you have a three-button mouse, the middle button is usually programmed to display the Object Snap menu, instead of using the right button with the Shift key. If you have a mouse with a scroll wheel, you can use the wheel in several ways to control the view of your drawing. I'll cover those methods in subsequent chapters.

AutoCAD makes extensive use of toolbars and the right-click menu feature. This makes your mouse an important input tool. The keyboard is necessary for inputting numeric data and text, and it has hot keys and aliases that can speed up your work; however, the mouse is the primary tool for selecting options and controlling toolbars.

The next chapter will familiarize you with a few basic commands that will enable you to draw a small diagram. If want to take a break and close AutoCAD, choose File ➤ Exit, and choose not to save the drawing.

Are You Experienced?

Now you can...

☑ recognize the elements of the AutoCAD graphics window

☑ understand how the Command window works and why it's important

☑ use drop-down menus

☑ open and control the positioning of toolbars

☑ save a workspace of your screen setup in AutoCAD

CHAPTER 2

Learning Basic Commands to Get Started

▶ Understanding coordinate systems

▶ Drawing your first object

▶ Erasing, offsetting, filleting, extending, and trimming lines in a drawing

N ow that you've taken a quick tour of the AutoCAD and LT user interface, you're ready to begin drawing. In this chapter, I'll introduce you to a few basic commands used in drawing with AutoCAD and LT. To get you started, I'll guide you through the process of drawing a box (see Figure 2.1).

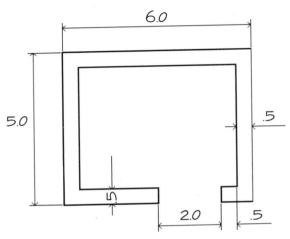

FIGURE 2.1: The box you'll draw

You need to use only five or six commands to draw this box. First you'll become familiar with the Line command and how to make lines a specific length. Then I'll go over the strategy for completing the box.

Using the Line Command

In traditional architectural drafting, lines were often drawn to extend slightly past their endpoints (see Figure 2.2). This is no longer done in CAD except for special effects.

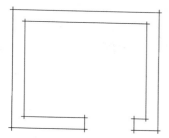

FIGURE 2.2: The box drawn with overlapping lines

The *Line command* draws a straight line segment between locations on existing objects, geometric features, or two points that you can choose anywhere within the drawing area. You can designate these points by clicking them on the screen, by entering the X and Y coordinates for each point, or by entering distances and angles. After you draw the first segment of a line, you can end the command or draw another line segment beginning from the end of the first one. You can continue to draw adjoining line segments for as long as you like. You'll now see how this works.

To be sure you start with your drawing area set up the way it's set up for this book, choose File ➤ Close to close any open drawings. If multiple drawings are open, repeat the Close command for each drawing until you have no drawings open. Your drawing area will be gray and blank with no crosshair cursor, your toolbars will disappear except for four buttons on the Standard toolbar and the informational buttons in the upper-right corner, and you'll have only four drop-down menus. Now, follow these steps:

1. Click the New button at the left end of the Standard toolbar. In the Select Template dialog box, select the `acad.dwt` file, if it's not already selected, and click Open. The menus, crosshair cursor, and toolbars return, and you now have a blank drawing in the drawing area.

N O T E   DWT files are drawing templates with several parameters, such as dimension styles, layers, and plotting settings, already set.

2. Glance at the status bar at the bottom of your screen. All buttons except Model should be off—that is, in an unpushed state. If any of the others appear to be pushed, click them to turn them off.

3. Be sure the Draw and Modify toolbars are docked on the left side of the drawing area, as shown in Figure 2.3. Refer to Chapter 1 if you need a reminder on how to display or move toolbars.

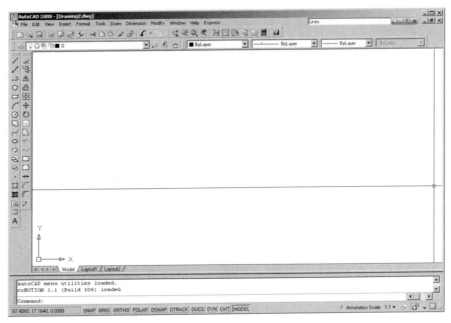

FIGURE 2.3: The Draw and Modify toolbars docked on the left side of the drawing area, and all status bar buttons except Model turned off

You can also start the Line command by choosing Draw ➤ Line or by typing **line** or **l** and pressing the Enter key.

4. Click the Line button at the top of the Draw toolbar. Look at the bottom of the Command window, and see how the Command: prompt has changed.

The prompt now tells you that the Line command is started (Command: _line) and that AutoCAD is waiting for you to designate the first point of the line (Specify first point:).

5. Move the cursor onto the drawing area, and notice that the small box at the intersection of the crosshairs is not there. When you use the cursor to select objects, which is the default condition, the pickbox appears in the cursor. When you use the cursor to designate a point, it does not appear. Using the left mouse button, click a random point to start a line.

6. Move the cursor away from the point you clicked, and notice how a line segment appears that stretches like a rubber band from the point you just picked to the cursor. The line changes length and direction as you move the cursor.

7. Look at the Command window again, and notice that the prompt has changed.

```
Command:
Command: _line Specify first point:
Specify next point or [Undo]: |
```

It's now telling you that AutoCAD is waiting for you to designate the next point (Specify next point or [Undo]:).

8. Continue picking points and adding lines as you move the cursor around the screen (see Figure 2.4). After you draw the third segment, the Command window repeats the Specify next point or [Close/Undo]: prompt; it does this each time you pick another point.

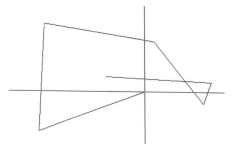

FIGURE 2.4: Drawing several line segments

9. When you've drawn six or seven line segments, press Enter to end the Line command. The cursor separates from the last drawn line segment. Look at the Command window once again.

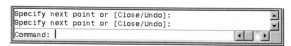

```
Specify next point or [Close/Undo]:
Specify next point or [Close/Undo]:
Command: |
```

T I P The Enter key exits the Line command and several others. Another option is to right-click and choose Enter from the context menu that appears. This might require an extra step but might be faster because your eyes never leave the screen. When you're not entering data, the spacebar also acts like the Enter key and executes a command.

The Command: prompt has returned to the bottom line. This tells you that no command is running.

In this exercise, you used the left mouse button to click the Line button on the Draw toolbar and also to pick several points in the drawing area to make the line segments. You then pressed Enter (↵) on the keyboard to end the Line command.

Note In the exercises that follow, I will use the Enter symbol (↵). When I say to "enter" something, it means to type the data that follows the word enter and then to press the Enter key (↵). For example, rather than writing "enter I and press the Enter key," I'll write "enter I↵."

Using Coordinates

Try using the Line command again, but instead of picking points in the drawing area with the mouse as you did before, this time enter X and Y coordinates for each point using the keyboard. To see how, follow these steps:

1. Click the Erase button on the Modify toolbar.

2. Enter all↵. The objects in the drawing become dashed to indicate that they are selected.

3. Press ↵ to clear the screen.

> You can also start the Erase command by typing e↵ or by choosing Modify ➢ Erase.

Now begin drawing lines again by following these steps:

1. Start the Line command by clicking the Line button on the Draw toolbar.

2. Enter 2,2↵.

3. Enter 6,3↵.

4. Enter 4,6↵.

5. Enter 1,3↵.

6. Enter 10,6↵.

7. Enter 10,1↵.

8. Enter 2,7↵.

9. Press ↵ again to end the command.

These lines are similar to those you drew previously, but this time you know where each point is located relative to the 0,0 point. In the drawing area, every point has an absolute X and Y coordinate. In steps 2–8, you entered the X and Y coordinates for each point. For a new drawing, such as this one, the origin (0,0 point) is in the lower-left corner of the drawing area, and all points in the drawing area have positive X and Y coordinates (see Figure 2.5).

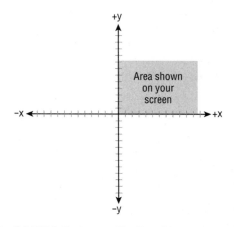

F I G U R E   2 . 5 :   The X and Y coordinates of the drawing area

You'll now explore how the cursor is related to the coordinates in the drawing:

1. At the Command prompt, enter **zoom↵ e↵** to adjust your view to show the extents of the drawing area. There won't be any visible difference in the drawing area.

2. Move the cursor around, and notice the left end of the status bar at the bottom of the screen. This is the coordinate readout, and it displays the coordinates of the cursor's position.

3. Move the cursor as close to the lower-left corner of the drawing area as you can without it changing into an arrow. The coordinate readout should be close to 0.0000, 0.0000, 0.0000.

N O T E   In AutoCAD, you see a readout for the Z coordinate as well, but you can ignore it for now because you'll be working in only two dimensions for the majority of this book. The Z coordinate always says 0 until you work in three dimensions (see the later chapters). LT doesn't have the readout for the Z coordinate because it does not have 3D capabilities.

4. Move the cursor to the top-left corner of the drawing area. The read-out changes to something close to 0.0000, 9.0000, 0.0000, indicating that the top of the screen is 9 units from the bottom.

5. Move the cursor one more time to the upper-right corner of the drawing area. The readout still has a Y coordinate of approximately 9.0000. The X coordinate now has a value from 12.0000 to 16.0000, depending on the size of your monitor and how the various parts of the AutoCAD graphics window are laid out on your screen. (See Chapter 1 for a recap.)

The drawing area of a new drawing is preset to be 9 units high and 12–16 units wide, with the lower-left corner of the drawing at the coordinates 0,0.

N O T E   For the moment, it doesn't matter what measure of distance these units represent. I'll address that topic in Chapter 3. And don't worry about the four decimal places in the coordinate readout. The number of places is controlled by a setting you'll learn about soon.

Using Relative Coordinates

Once you understand the coordinate system used by AutoCAD, you can draw lines to any length and in any direction. Look at the box shown earlier in Figure 2.1. Because you know the dimensions, you can calculate, by adding and subtracting, the absolute coordinates for each *vertex*—the connecting point between two line segments—and then use the Line command to draw the shape by entering these coordinates using the keyboard. But AutoCAD offers you several tools for drawing this box much more easily. Two of these tools are the relative Cartesian and relative polar coordinate systems.

When you're drawing lines, these systems use a set of new points based on the last point designated, rather than on the 0,0 point of the drawing area. They're called *relative* coordinate systems because the coordinates used are relative to the last point specified. If the first point of a line is located at the coordinate 4,6, and you want the line to extend 8 units to the right, the coordinate that is relative to the first point is 8,0 (8 units in the positive X direction and 0 units in the positive Y direction), whereas the actual—or *absolute*—coordinate of the second point is 12,6.

The *relative Cartesian coordinate system* uses relative X and Y coordinates in the manner shown, and the *relative polar coordinate system* relies on a distance and an angle relative to the last point specified. You'll probably favor one system over the other, but you need to know both systems because you'll sometimes find that—given the information you have at hand—one will work better than the other. I'll illustrate a limitation of this nature in Chapter 4.

When entering relative coordinates, you need to enter an at (@) sign before the coordinates. In the previous example, you would enter the relative Cartesian coordinates as @8,0. The @ sign lets AutoCAD know that the numbers following it represent coordinates that are relative to the last point designated.

Using Relative Cartesian Coordinates

The Cartesian system of coordinates, named after the philosopher René Descartes, who invented the X,Y coordinate system in the 1600s, uses a horizontal (X) component and a vertical (Y) component to locate a point relative to the 0,0 point. The relative Cartesian system uses the same components to locate the point relative to the last point picked, so it's a way of telling AutoCAD how far left or right and how far up or down to extend a line or to move an object from the last point picked (see Figure 2.6). If the direction is to the left, the X coordinate will be negative. Similarly, if the direction is down, the Y coordinate will be negative. Use this system when you know the horizontal and vertical distances from point 1 to point 2. To enter data using this system, use this form: @x,y.

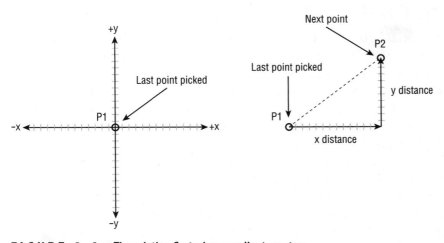

FIGURE 2.6: The relative Cartesian coordinate system

Using Relative Polar Coordinates

This system requires a known distance and direction from one point to the next. Calculating the distance is straightforward; it's always positive and is the distance away from the first point that the second point will be placed. The direction requires a convention for determining an angle. AutoCAD defines right (toward three o'clock) as the default direction of the 0° angle. All other directions are determined from a counterclockwise rotation (see Figure 2.7). On your screen, up is 90°, left is 180°, down is 270°, and a full circle is 360°. To let Auto-CAD know that you're entering an angle and not a relative Y coordinate, use the less-than (<) symbol before the angle and after the distance. So, in the previous example, to designate a point 8 units to the right image of the first point, you would enter @8<0.

N O T E   Remember, use the relative polar coordinates method to draw a line from the first point when you know the distance and direction to its next point. Enter data using this form: **@distance<*angle*.**

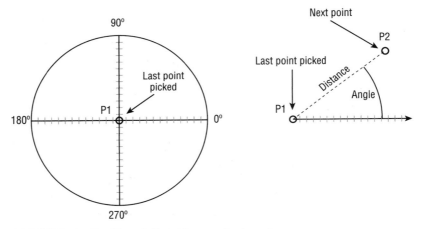

F I G U R E   2 . 7 : The relative polar coordinate system

Using the Direct Distance Method

You can also draw lines by placing the cursor at any angle relative to the last point and entering a distance value at the command prompt. AutoCAD draws the line from the last point toward or through the cursor location at the length specified. The direct distance method is often used when Ortho mode is turned on.

N O T E   When in a drawing command, Ortho mode restricts the cursor to horizontal or vertical movements. You can draw lines, for example, only at 0°, 90°, 180°, and 270°. You toggle on Ortho mode by clicking the Ortho button at the bottom of the user interface or by pressing the F8 key.

Drawing the Box

Now that you have the basics, the following exercises will take you through the steps to draw the four lines that form the outline of the box using both relative coordinate systems.

Using Relative Cartesian Coordinates

To begin drawing the box, use the same drawing:

1. If your drawing is already blank, jump to step 2. If you still have lines on your drawing, start the Erase command, enter all↵, and then press ↵ again.

2. Start the Line command.

3. At the Specify First point: prompt in the Command window, enter 3,3↵. This is an absolute Cartesian coordinate and will be the first point.

4. Enter @6,0↵.

5. Enter @0,5↵.

6. Enter @-6,0↵.

7. Look at the command prompt, which reads Specify next point or [Close/Undo]:. Items enclosed in brackets are additional available options at that particular point of the command that you can enter at the Command prompt. Only the capitalized letters are required to execute the option.

8. Enter c↵. The letter c stands for *close*. Entering this letter after drawing two or more lines closes the shape by extending the next line segment from the last point specified to the first point (see Figure 2.8). It also ends the Line command. Notice that in the Command window the prompt is Command:. This signifies that AutoCAD is ready for a new command.

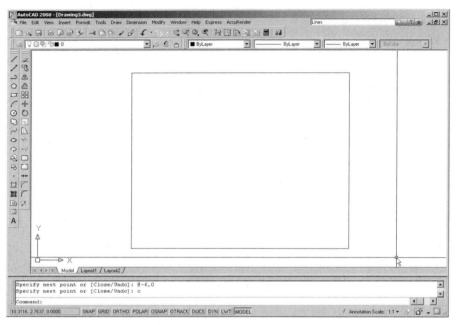

FIGURE 2.8: The first four lines of the box

Erasing Lines

To prepare to draw the box again, use the Erase command to erase the four lines you just drew:

1. Start the Erase command. Notice how the cursor changes from the crosshairs to a little square. This is called the *pickbox*. When you see it on the screen, it's a sign that AutoCAD is ready for you to select objects on the screen. Also notice the Command window; it's prompting you to select objects.

2. Place the pickbox on one of the lines; when it highlights, click. The line changes to a dashed line.

3. Do the same with the rest of the lines.

4. Press ↵. The objects are erased, and the Erase command ends.

N O T E   You've been introduced to two methods of selecting lines to be erased: typing **all**↵ and using the pickbox to select them. Throughout the book, you'll be introduced to several other ways to select objects. The selection process is important in AutoCAD because you need to be able to quickly and precisely select objects.

Controlling How the Selection Tools Are Displayed

When you move the cursor over an object, AutoCAD highlights the object. This is called *rollover highlighting*. It tells you that clicking while the object is highlighted selects that object. You have some choices as to how this highlighting appears:

1. Choose Tools ➣ Options, and then click the Selection tab. Notice the Selection Preview area in the middle of the left side (see the left image of Figure 2.9). Here you can activate or deactivate the check boxes to control whether rollover highlighting occurs when a command is running or when no command is running. If both check boxes are checked, the feature works all the time.

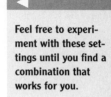

Feel free to experiment with these settings until you find a combination that works for you.

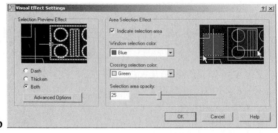

a   b

FIGURE 2.9: The Selection Preview area of the Selection tab in the Options dialog box (a), and the Visual Effect Settings dialog box (b)

2. Click the Visual Effect Settings button below the check boxes to open the Visual Effect Settings dialog box (see the right image of Figure 2.9). You'll see two areas: Selection Preview Effect and Area Selection Effect. The Selection Preview Effect area controls how the rollover highlighting feature appears. Lines dash, lines thicken, and lines both dash and thicken, depending on which radio button is selected.

3. Make any changes you want, and then click OK. Back in the Options dialog box, click OK to return to your drawing.

Using Relative Polar Coordinates

Now draw the box again using the relative polar method by following these steps:

1. Start the Line command. (Click the Line button on the Draw toolbar.)

2. Enter 3,3↵ to start the box at the same point.

3. Enter @6<0↵.

4. Enter @5<90↵.

5. Enter @6<180↵.

6. Enter c↵ to close the box and end the Line command. Your box once again resembles the box shown earlier in Figure 2.8.

You can see from this exercise that you can use either method to draw a simple shape. When the shapes you're drawing get more complex and the amount of available information about the shapes varies from segment to segment, one of the two relative coordinate systems will turn out to be more appropriate. As you start drawing the floor plan of the cabin in Chapters 3 and 4, you'll get more practice using these systems.

Some additional tools make the process of drawing simple *orthogonal* lines like these much easier. I'll introduce these tools in the following three chapters.

Using the Offset Command

The next task is to create the lines that represent the inside walls of the box. Because they're all equidistant from the lines you've already drawn, the *Offset command* is the appropriate command to use. You'll offset the existing lines 0.5 units to the inside.

The Offset command involves three steps:

1. Setting the offset distance

2. Selecting the object to offset

3. Indicating the offset direction

Here's how it works:

1. Be sure the prompt line in the Command window says Command:. If it doesn't, press the Esc key until it does. Then click the Offset button on the Modify toolbar. The prompt changes to Specify offset distance or [Through/Erase/Layer] <1.0000>:. This is a confusing prompt, but it will become clear soon. For now, let's specify an offset distance through the keyboard.

You can also start the Offset command by choosing Modify ➢ Offset or by typing o↵.

W A R N I N G   As important as it is to keep an eye on the Command window, some prompts might not make sense to you until you get used to them.

2. Enter 0.5↵ for a distance, which will offset the lines ½ unit. Now you move to the second stage of the command. Note that the cursor changes to a pickbox, and the prompt changes to Select object to offset or [Exit/Undo] <Exit>:.

3. Place the pickbox on one of the lines; when it highlights, click. The selected line appears dashed to indicate that it is selected (see Figure 2.10), the cursor changes back to the crosshair cursor, and the prompt changes to Specify point on side to offset or [Exit/Multiple/Undo] <Exit>:. AutoCAD is telling you that to determine the direction of the offset, you must specify a point on one side of the line or the other. You make the choice by selecting anywhere in the drawing area on the side of the line where you want the offset to occur.

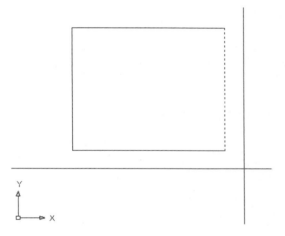

FIGURE 2.10: The first line to be offset is selected.

4. Click a point somewhere inside the box. The offset takes place, and the new line is exactly 0.5 units to the inside of the chosen line (see Figure 2.11). Notice that the pickbox returns. The Offset command is still running, and you can offset more lines the same distance.

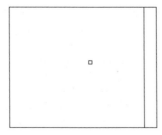

FIGURE 2.11: The first line is offset.

You have three more lines to offset.

5. Click another line; then click inside the box again. The second line is offset.

6. Click a third line, click inside the box, click the fourth line, and then click again inside the box (see Figure 2.12).

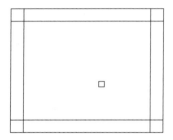

FIGURE 2.12: Four lines have been offset.

N O T E   The offset distance stays set at the last distance you specify—0.5, in this case—until you change it.

7. Press ↵ to end the Offset command.

This command is similar to the Line command in that it keeps running until you stop it. With Offset, after the first offset, the prompts switch between `Select object to offset or [Exit/Undo] <Exit>:` and `Specify point on side to offset or [Exit/Multiple/Undo] <Exit>:` until you press ↵ or the spacebar to end the command.

The inside lines are now drawn, but to complete the box you need to clean up the intersecting corners. To handle this task efficiently, you'll use a tool called the Fillet command.

> You can cancel a command at any time by pressing Esc.

SPECIFYING DISTANCES FOR THE OFFSET COMMAND

The prompt you see in the Command window after starting the Offset command is as follows:

```
Specify offset distance or [Through/Erase/Layer] <1.0000>:
```
This prompt describes several options for setting the offset distance:

▶ Enter a distance using the keyboard.

▶ Select two points on the screen to establish the offset distance as the distance between those two points.

▶ Press ↵ to accept the offset distance that is displayed in the prompt in the angle brackets.

▶ Enter **t**↵ to use the Through option. When you select this option, you're prompted to select the line to offset. You're then prompted to pick a point. The line will be offset to that point. When you pick the next line to offset, you then pick a new point to locate the position of the new line. The Through option allows each line to be offset a different distance.

▶ Enter **e**↵, and then enter **y**↵ to tell AutoCAD to erase the original line that was offset. (After doing this, however, AutoCAD continues erasing offset lines until you reset by entering **e**↵ **n**↵ at the beginning of the Offset command.)

▶ Enter **l**↵ to use the Layer option. (I'll discuss this option in Chapter 6.)

As you become accustomed to using Offset, you'll find uses for each of these options.

Using the Fillet Command

The *Fillet command* lets you round off a corner formed by two lines. You control the radius of the curve, so if you set the curve's radius to 0, the lines form a sharp corner. In this way, you can clean up corners such as the ones formed by the lines inside the box.

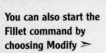

You can also start the Fillet command by choosing Modify ➢ Fillet or by typing f↵.

1. When the Command line just reads Command:, click the Fillet button on the Modify toolbar. Notice how the Command window changes after you've clicked the Fillet button.

```
Command: _fillet
Current settings: Mode = TRIM, Radius = 0.0000
Select first object or [Undo/Polyline/Radius/Trim/Multiple]:
```

The default fillet radius should be 0.0000 units. Like the Offset distance, the fillet radius remains set at whatever length you specify until you change it.

2. If your Command window displays a radius of 0.0000, go on to step 3. Otherwise, enter r↵, and then enter 0↵ to change the radius to zero.

T I P   When the radius value is set to greater than 0, you can temporarily override this by holding down the Shift key while picking the two objects to be filleted. They will be filleted with a radius of 0 while the value set in the Fillet command remains unchanged.

3. Move the cursor—now a pickbox—to the box, and click two intersecting lines, as shown in Figure 2.13. The intersecting lines are both trimmed to make a sharp corner (see Figure 2.14). The Fillet command automatically ends.

When you move the pickbox or the crosshair cursor onto a line, the line highlights. If you click when the line highlights, AutoCAD selects the line.

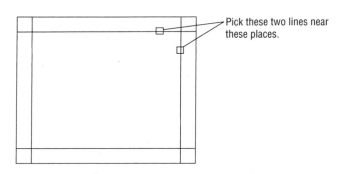

Pick these two lines near these places.

F I G U R E 2 . 1 3 : Pick two lines to execute the Fillet command.

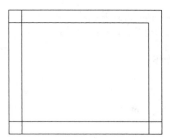

FIGURE 2.14: The first cleaned-up corner

4. Press ⏎ to restart the command, and this time enter **m**⏎ to activate the Multiple option. Multiple repeats the Fillet command until another option is initiated at the Command prompt or the command is terminated with the Enter or Esc key or the spacebar.

5. Fillet the remaining lines for each corner until all the corners are cleaned up (see Figure 2.15).

Once a command has ended, you can restart it by pressing either ⏎ or the spacebar or by right-clicking and choosing Repeat from the context menu.

T I P   In most cases, you'll get the same effect by pressing the spacebar as you get by pressing ⏎. The exception is when you're entering data in a text box in a dialog box or a palette; in those cases, pressing the spacebar makes a space.

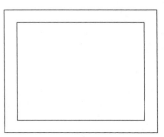

FIGURE 2.15: The box with all corners cleaned up

> **N O T E**   If you make a mistake and pick the wrong part of a line or the wrong line, press Esc to end the command, and then enter u↵. This will undo the effect of the last command.

Used together like this, the Offset and Fillet commands are a powerful combination of tools to lay out walls on a floor plan drawing. Because these commands are so important, you'll now take a closer look at them to see how they work. Both commands are on the Modify toolbar or drop-down menu, both have the option to enter a numeric value or accept the current value (for offset distance and fillet radius), and both hold that value as the default until you change it. However, the Offset command keeps running until you stop it, and the Fillet command stops after each use unless you invoke the Multiple option. These commands are two of the most frequently used tools in AutoCAD. You'll learn about more of their uses in later chapters.

The Fillet command has a sister command, the Chamfer command, that you can use to bevel corners with straight lines. When the distances for the Chamfer command are set to 0, you can use the command to clean up corners the same way you use the Fillet command. Some users prefer to use Chamfer rather than Fillet because they don't bevel corners, but they might at times use Fillet to round off corners. If you use Chamfer to clean up corners, Fillet can have any radius and won't have to constantly be overridden or reset to 0. You'll develop your own preference in time.

Completing the Box

The final step in completing the box (see Figure 2.1 earlier in this chapter) is to make an opening in the bottom wall. From the diagram, you can see that the opening is 2 units wide and set off from the right inside corner by 0.5 units. To make this opening, you'll use the Offset command twice, changing the offset distance for each offset, to create marks for the opening.

Offsetting Lines to Mark an Opening

Follow these steps to establish the precise position of the opening:

1. At the Command: prompt, start the Offset command. Notice the Command window. The default distance is now set at 0.5, the offset distance you previously set to offset the outside lines of the box to make the inside lines. If the distance is different, enter .5↵. You want to use this distance again. Press ↵ to accept this preset distance.

2. Pick the inside vertical line on the right, and then pick a point to the left image of this line. The line is offset to make a new line 0.5 units to its left (see Figure 2.16).

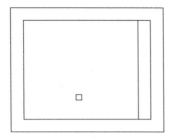

FIGURE 2.16: Offsetting the first line of the opening

3. Press ↵ to end the Offset command, and then press it again to restart the command. This will allow you to reset the offset distance.

4. Enter 2 as the new offset distance, and press ↵.

5. Click the new line, and then pick a point to the left. Press ↵ to end the Offset command (see Figure 2.17).

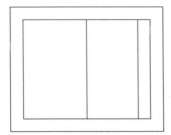

FIGURE 2.17: Offsetting the second line of the opening

You now have two new lines indicating where the opening will be. You can use these lines to form the opening using the Extend and Trim commands.

T I P The buttons you've been clicking in this chapter are also referred to as *icons* and *tools*. When they're in dialog boxes or on the status bar, they have icons (little pictures) on them and look like buttons to click. When they're on the toolbars, they look like icons. But when you move the mouse pointer onto one, it takes on the appearance of a button with an icon on it. I'll use all three terms—*button*, *icon*, and *tool*—interchangeably in this book.

Extending Lines

You use the *Extend command* to lengthen (extend) lines to meet other lines or geometric figures (called *boundary edges*). Executing the Extend command might be a little tricky at first until you see how it works. Once you understand it, however, it will become automatic. The command has two steps: first, you pick the boundary edge or edges; second, you pick the lines you want to extend to meet those boundary edges. After selecting the boundary edges, you must press ↵ before you begin selecting lines to extend.

You can also start the Extend command by choosing Modify ➣ Extend from the drop-down menu or by typing ex↵.

1. To begin the Extend command, click the Extend button on the Modify toolbar. Notice the Command window.

```
Current settings: Projection=UCS, Edge=None
Select boundary edges ...
Select objects or <select all>:
```

The bottom line says `Select objects or <select all>:`, but in this case, you need to observe the bottom two lines of text in order to know that AutoCAD is prompting you to select boundary edges.

2. Pick the very bottom horizontal line (see Figure 2.18), and press ↵.

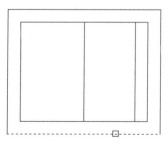

FIGURE 2.18: Selecting a line to be a boundary edge

T I P The Select Objects: prompt would be more useful if it said, "Select objects and press Enter when finished selecting objects." But it doesn't. You have to train yourself to press ↵ when you finish selecting objects in order to get out of selection mode and move on to the next step in the command.

3. Pick the two new vertical lines created by the Offset command. Be sure to place the pickbox somewhere on the lower halves of these lines, or AutoCAD will ignore your picks. The lines are extended to the boundary edge line. Press ↵ to end the Extend command (see Figure 2.19).

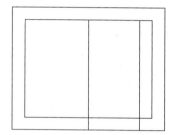

FIGURE 2.19: The lines are extended to the boundary edge.

Trimming Lines

The final step is to trim away the horizontal lines to complete the opening and the unneeded portions of the two most recent vertical lines that you offset. To do this, you use the *Trim command*. As with the Extend command, this requires two steps. The first is to select reference lines—in this case they're called *cutting edges* because they determine the edge or edges to which a line is trimmed. The second step is to pick the lines that are to be trimmed.

1. Click the Trim button on the Modify toolbar to start the Trim command. Notice the Command window. Similar to the Extend command, the bottom line prompts you to select objects or select everything in the drawing, but the second line up tells you to select cutting edges.

You can also start the Trim command by choosing Modify ➤ Trim from the Modify drop-down menu or by typing tr↵.

2. Pick the two vertical offset lines that were just extended as your cutting edges, and then press ↵ (see Figure 2.20).

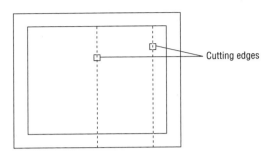

Cutting edges

FIGURE 2.20: Lines selected to be cutting edges

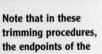

Note that in these trimming procedures, the endpoints of the cutting edge lines, as well as the lines themselves, are used as cutting edges.

3. Pick the two horizontal lines across the opening somewhere between the cutting-edge lines (see Figure 2.21).

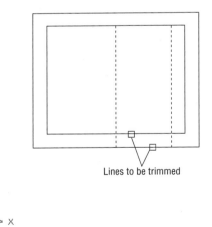

Lines to be trimmed

FIGURE 2.21: Lines selected to be trimmed

This trims away the opening (see Figure 2.22).

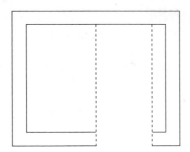

FIGURE 2.22: Lines are trimmed to make the opening.

 NOTE If you trim the wrong line or wrong part of a line, you can click the Undo button on the Standard toolbar. This undoes the last trim without canceling the Trim command, and you can try again.

Now let's remove the extra part of the trimming guidelines:

1. Press ↵ twice—once to end the Trim command and again to restart it. This will let you pick new cutting edges for another trim operation.

2. Pick the two upper horizontal lines next to the opening as your cutting edges, shown in Figure 2.23, and press ↵.

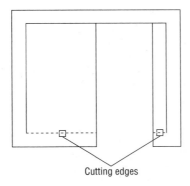

Cutting edges

FIGURE 2.23: Lines picked to be cutting edges

3. Pick the two vertical lines that extend above the new opening. Be sure to pick them above the opening (see Figure 2.24). The lines are trimmed away, and the opening is complete. Press ↵ to end the Trim command (see Figure 2.25).

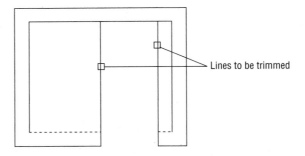

Lines to be trimmed

FIGURE 2.24: Lines picked to be trimmed

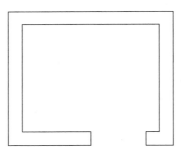

FIGURE 2.25: The completed trim

Congratulations! You've just completed the first drawing project in this book using all the tools covered in this chapter. These skills will be useful as you learn how to work on drawings for actual projects.

A valuable exercise at this time would be to draw this box two or three more times, until you can do it without the instructions. This will be a confidence builder and will get you ready to take on the new information in the next chapter, where you'll set up a drawing for a building.

The box you drew was 6 units by 5 units, but how big was it? You really don't know at this time, because the units could represent any actual distance: inches, feet, meters, miles, and so on. Also, the box was positioned conveniently on the screen so you didn't have any problem viewing it. What if you were drawing a building that was 200 feet long and 60 feet wide or a portion of a microchip circuit that was only a few thousandths of an inch long? In the next chapter, you'll learn how to set up a drawing for a project of a specific size.

You can exit AutoCAD now without saving this drawing. To do so, choose File ➣ Exit. When the dialog box asks whether you want to save changes, click No. Or, you can leave AutoCAD open and go to the following practice section or the next chapter.

If You Would Like More Practice...

Draw the object shown in Figure 2.26.

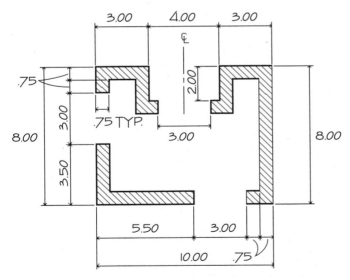

FIGURE 2.26: Practice drawing

You can use the same tools and strategy used to draw the box. Choose File ➤ New to start a new drawing, and then use the acad.dwt template file. Here's a summary of the steps to follow:

1. Ignore the three openings at first.

2. Draw the outside edge of the shape using one of the relative coordinate systems. To make sure the box fits on your screen, start the outline of the box in the lower-left corner at the absolute coordinate of 1,0.5.

3. Offset the outside lines to create the inside wall.

4. Fillet the corners to clean them up. (Lines that aren't touching can be filleted just like lines that intersect.)

5. Use the Offset, Extend, and Trim commands to create the three openings.

Don't worry about trying to put in the dimensions, centerline, or hatch lines. You'll learn how to create those objects later in the book.

Are You Experienced?

Now you can...

☑ **understand the basics of coordinates**

☑ **discern between absolute and the two relative coordinate systems used by AutoCAD**

☑ **use the Line, Erase, Offset, Fillet, Extend, and Trim commands to create a drawing**

CHAPTER 3

THE SKILLS

AutoCAD

FOR SUCCESS

Setting Up a Drawing

- ▶ Setting up drawing units
- ▶ Using AutoCAD's grid
- ▶ Zooming in and out of a drawing
- ▶ Naming and saving a file

I n Chapter 2, you explored the default drawing area that is set up when you open a new drawing. It's probably 9 units high by 12 to 16 units wide, depending on the size of your monitor. You drew a box within this area. If you drew the additional diagram offered as a supplemental exercise, the drawing area was set up the same way.

For most of the rest of this book, you'll be developing drawings for a cabin with outside wall dimensions of 25' × 16', but the tools you use and the skills you learn will enable you to draw objects of any size. In this chapter, you'll learn how to set up the drawing area to lay out the floor plan for a building of a specific size. You'll change the decimal units with which you have been drawing until now to feet and inches, and you'll transform the drawing area so it can represent an area large enough to display the floor plan of the cabin you'll be drawing.

I'll introduce you to some new tools that will help you visualize the area your screen represents and allow you to draw lines to a specified incremental distance, such as to the nearest foot. Finally, you'll save this drawing to a special folder on your hard disk. At the end of the chapter is a general summary of the various kinds of units that AutoCAD supports.

Setting Up the Drawing Units

When you draw lines of a precise length in AutoCAD, you use one of five kinds of linear units. Angular units can also be any of five types. You can select the type of units to use, or you can accept the default decimal units that you used in the previous chapter.

When you start a new drawing, AutoCAD displays a blank drawing called `Drawingn.dwg` with the linear and angular units set to decimal numbers. The units and other basic setup parameters applied to this new drawing are based on a prototype drawing with default settings—including those for the units. This chapter covers some of the tools for changing the basic parameters of a new drawing so you can tailor it to the cabin project or for your own project. Begin by setting up new units:

1. With AutoCAD running, close all drawings, and then click the New button (on the Standard toolbar) to start a new drawing. In the Select Template dialog box, click the arrow to the right of the Open button, and select Open with No Template – Imperial (see Figure 3.1).

   To get started with the steps in this chapter, check to be sure that, for now, all the status bar buttons except Model are clicked to the off position—that is, they appear unpushed. When we get to Chapter 10, you'll see how to use templates to set up drawings.

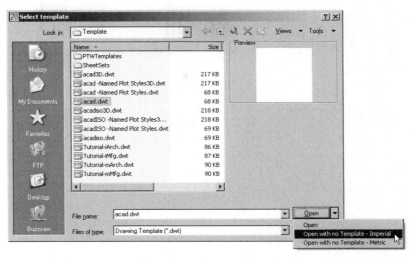

FIGURE 3.1: The Select Template dialog box

2. Choose Format ➤ Units to open the Drawing Units dialog box (see Figure 3.2). In the Length area, Decimal is currently selected. Similarly, in the Angle area, Decimal Degrees is the default.

You can also open the Drawing Units dialog box by typing un↵.

N O T E   You might notice that several items listed in the menus are followed by an ellipsis (...). The ellipsis indicates that the option opens a dialog box, rather than executing a command. The same convention applies to buttons with ellipses included on their labels.

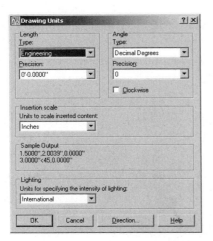

FIGURE 3.2: The Drawing Units dialog box

3. In the Length area, click the arrow in the Type drop-down list, and select Architectural. These units are feet and inches, which you'll use for the cabin project.

Notice the two Precision drop-down lists at the bottom of the Length and Angle areas. When you changed the linear units specification from the Decimal setting to the Architectural setting, the number in the Precision drop-down list on the left changed from 0.0000 to 0'-0 1/16". At this level of precision, linear distances are displayed to the nearest 1/16".

4. Select some of the other Length unit types from the list, and notice the way the units appear in the Sample Output area at the bottom of the dialog box. Then select Architectural again.

N O T E   Drop-down lists are lists of choices with only the selected choice displayed. When you click the arrow, the list opens. When you make another selection, the list closes, and your choice is displayed. When an item on the list is selected and is the focus of the program, indicated by a blue highlight, you can change the available options using the scroll wheel on a mouse or the up and down arrows on the keyboard. You can choose only one item at a time from the list.

5. Click the arrow in the Precision drop-down list in the Length area to display the choices of precision for architectural units (see Figure 3.3). This setting controls the degree of precision to which AutoCAD displays a linear distance. If it's set to 0'-0 1/16", any line that is drawn more precisely—such as a line 6'-3$\frac{1}{32}$" long, when queried, displays a length value to the nearest $\frac{1}{16}$" or, in the example, as 6'-3$\frac{1}{16}$". But the line is still 6'-3$\frac{1}{32}$" long.

If you change the precision setting to 0'-0 1/32" and then use the Distance command (explained in Chapter 7) to measure the line, you'll see that its length is 6'-3$\frac{1}{32}$".

6. Click 0'-0 1/16" to maintain the precision for display of linear units at $\frac{1}{16}$".

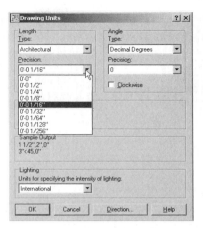

FIGURE 3.3: The Precision drop-down list for architectural units

If you open the Type drop-down list in the Angle area, you see a choice between Decimal Degrees and Deg/Min/Sec, among others. Most AutoCAD users find the decimal angular units the most practical, but the default precision setting is to the nearest degree. This might not be accurate enough, so you should change it to the nearest hundredth of a degree:

1. Click the arrow in the Precision drop-down list in the Angle area.

2. Click 0.00. The Drawing Units dialog box will now indicate that, in your drawing, you plan to use architectural length units with a precision of $\frac{1}{16}$" and decimal angular units with a precision of 0.00 (see Figure 3.4). This doesn't restrict the precision at which you draw, just the values that AutoCAD reports.

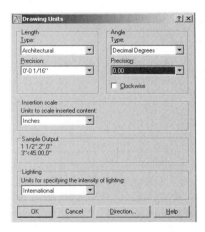

FIGURE 3.4: The Drawing Units dialog box after changes

Clicking the Direction button at the bottom of the Drawing Units dialog box opens the Direction Control dialog box, which has settings to control the direction of 0 degrees. By default, 0 degrees is to the right (east), and positive angular displacement goes in counterclockwise direction. (See Figure 2.7 in Chapter 2 for an explanation.) These are the standard settings for most uses of CAD. You don't need to change them from the defaults. If you want to take a look, open the Direction Control dialog box, note the choices, and then click OK. You won't have occasion in the course of this book to change any of those settings.

N O T E   You'll have a chance to work with surveyor's angular units later in the book, in Chapter 12, when you develop a site plan for the cabin.

3. Click OK in the Drawing Units dialog box to accept the changes and close the dialog box. Notice the coordinate readout in the lower-left corner of the screen: it now displays in feet and inches.

This tour of the Drawing Units dialog box has introduced you to the choices you have for the types of units and the degree of precision for linear and angular measurement. The next step in setting up a drawing is to determine its size.

N O T E   If you accidentally click when the cursor is on a blank part of the drawing area, AutoCAD starts a rectangular window. I'll talk about these windows soon, but for now, just press the Esc key to close the window.

Setting Up the Drawing Size

As you discovered earlier, the default drawing area on the screen for a new drawing is 12 to 16 units wide and 9 units high. After changing the units to architectural, the same drawing area is now 12 to 16 *inches* wide and 9 *inches* high. You can check this by moving the crosshair cursor around on the drawing area and looking at the coordinate readout, as you did in the previous chapter.

T I P   When you change decimal units to architectural units, 1 decimal unit translates to 1 inch. Some industries, such as civil engineering, often use decimal units to represent feet instead of inches. If the units in their drawings are switched to architectural units, a distance that was a foot now measures as an inch. To correct this, you must scale the entire drawing up by a factor of 12.

As you know, the *drawing area* is defined as the part of the screen in which you draw. You can make the distance across the drawing area larger or smaller through a process known as *zooming in* or *zooming out*. To see how this works, you'll learn about a tool called the *grid* that helps you draw and visualize the size of your drawing.

Using the Grid

The AutoCAD *grid* is a pattern of regularly spaced dots used as an aid to drawing. You can set the grid to be visible or invisible. The area covered by the grid depends on the Drawing Limits setting. To learn how to manipulate the grid size, you'll make the grid visible, use the Zoom In and Zoom Out commands to vary the view of the grid, and then change the area over which the grid extends by resetting the drawing limits. Before doing this, however, let's turn off the UCS icon that currently sits in the lower-left corner of the drawing area. You'll display it again and learn how to use it in Chapter 10.

1. At the Command: prompt, enter **ucsicon⏎**, and then type **off⏎**. The icon disappears.

2. At the Command: prompt, move the crosshair cursor to the status bar at the bottom of the screen, and click the Grid button. The button appears to have been pushed down, and dots appear on most of the drawing area (see Figure 3.5). These dots are the grid. They are preset by default to be ½" apart, and they extend from the 0,0 point (the origin) out to the right and up to the coordinate point 1'-0",0'-9".

> You can also control the visibility of the UCS icon by choosing View ➢ Display ➢ UCS Icon ➢ On. If On has a checkmark, clicking it turns off the UCS icon. If it doesn't, clicking turns the icon back on.

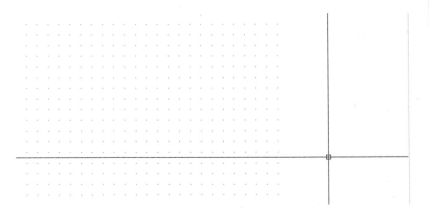

FIGURE 3.5: The AutoCAD grid

3. Right-click the Grid button and then choose Settings from the context menu that appears to open the Drafting Settings dialog box.

T I P   Right-clicking any of the buttons on the status bar (except Ducs, Lwt, Ortho, or Model) and choosing Settings opens the Drafting Settings dialog box to the tab with the parameters that relate to the specific button. You can also open the Drafting Settings dialog box by typing **ds.↵** or by choosing Tools ➤ Drafting Settings from the menu bar.

4. The Snap and Grid tab should be active (see Figure 3.6). If it's not, click the tab. In the Grid Behavior area, be sure Adaptive Grid and Display Grid Beyond Limits are checked. Then click OK. The grid now covers the area only from 0',0" to 1',9", the area defined by the limits of the drawing. (I'll discuss limits in the next section.) The Adaptive Grid options causes AutoCAD to proportionately reduce the number of the grid's columns and rows whenever the zoom factor would cause the grid to become too dense to be effective.

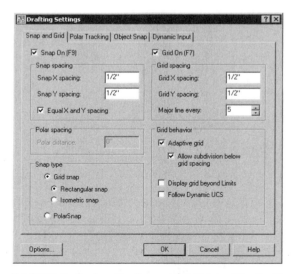

F I G U R E   3 . 6 : The Snap and Grid tab of the Drafting Settings dialog box

Notice that rows of grid dots run right along the left edge, top, and bottom of the drawing area, but the dots don't extend all the way to the right side. The grid dot at the 0'0", 0'0" point is positioned exactly at the lower-left corner of the screen, and the grid dot at 1'-0",0'-9" is on the top edge, not too far from the upper-right corner.

5. For a better view of the entire grid, use the Zoom Out command. Choose View ➤ Zoom ➤ Out or choose Zoom Out from the Zoom fly-out menu on the Standard toolbar. The view changes, and there are fewer grid dots (see Figure 3.7). You might need to perform the zoom twice to see the effect. Move the crosshair cursor to the lower-left corner of the grid, and then move it to the upper-right corner. Notice the coordinate readout in the lower left of your screen. These two points should read as approximately 0'-0",0'-0" and 0'-10",0'-7½", respectively.

FIGURE 3.7: The grid after zooming out

6. On the status bar, next to the Grid button, click the Snap button; then, move the cursor back onto the grid, and look at the coordinate readout again. The cursor stops at each grid point, even those that are no longer displayed because of the zoom factor, and the readout is to the nearest half inch. Now, when you place the crosshair cursor on the lower-left corner of the grid, the readout is exactly 0'-0",0'-0", and it's 0'-10",0'-7½" for the upper-right corner. The Snap tool locks the cursor onto the grid dots; even when the cursor isn't on the grid but somewhere outside it on the drawing area, the cursor maintains the grid spacing and jumps from one location to another.

7. Use the Zoom Out command a few more times.

8. Choose View ➤ Zoom ➤ In or use the scroll wheel on your mouse enough times to bring the view of the grid back to the way it was in Figure 3.5. You aren't changing the size of the grid, just the view of it. It's like switching from a regular lens to a telephoto lens on a camera.

The grid is more a guide than an actual boundary of your drawing. You can change a setting to force lines to be drawn only in the area covered by the grid, but this isn't ordinarily done. For most purposes, you can draw anywhere on the screen. The grid merely serves as a tool for visualizing how your drawing will be laid out.

Because it serves as a layout tool for this project, you need to increase the area covered by the grid from its present size of $1' \times 9"$ to $60' \times 40'$. Because the Drawing Limits setting controls the size of the grid, you need to change it.

Setting Up Drawing Limits

The Drawing Limits setting records the coordinates of the lower-left and upper-right corners of the grid. The coordinates for the lower-left corner are 0,0 by default and are usually left at that setting. You need to change the coordinates only for the upper-right corner:

1. Be sure the Command window displays the Command: prompt; then choose Format ➤ Drawing Limits, or enter limits.⏎. Notice how the Command window has changed.

```
Command: '_limits
Reset Model space limits:
Specify lower left corner or [ON/OFF] <0'-0",0'-0">:
```

The bottom command line tells you that the first step is to decide whether to change the default X and Y coordinates for the lower-left limits, both of which are currently set at 0',0". You don't need to change these.

2. Press ⏎ to accept the 0'0", 0'0" coordinates for this corner. The bottom command line changes and now displays the coordinates for the upper-right corner of the limits. This is the setting you want to change.

3. Enter 60',40'.⏎. Be sure to include the foot sign (').

N O T E AutoCAD requires that, when using architectural units, you always indicate that a distance is measured in feet by using the foot sign ('). You don't have to use the inch sign (") to indicate inches.

The grid now appears to extend to the top-right edge of the drawing area (see Figure 3.8), but it actually extends far past the edges. It was 1 foot wide, and now it's 60 times that, but the drawing area shows only the first foot or so.

F I G U R E 3 . 8 : The same view with the grid extended to 60' × 40'

4. To bring the whole grid onto the screen, use the Zoom command again, but this time use the All option: choose View ➤ Zoom ➤ All, or enter z↵ a↵. The grid fills the screen, but there are fewer dots. The All option zooms the view to display all the objects in the drawing or, in a blank drawing, zooms to the limits.

5. Move the cursor from one dot to another, and watch the coordinate readout. The coordinates are still displayed to the nearest half inch, but the dots are much more than half an inch apart.

By default, when you zoom in or out, AutoCAD adjusts the grid spacing to keep the dots from getting too close together or too far apart. In this case, remember that you found the grid spacing to be ½" by default. If the drawing area is giving you a view of a 60' × 40' grid with dots at ½", the grid is 1,440 dots wide and 960 dots high. If the whole grid were to be shown on the screen, the dots would be so close together that they would be about only 1 pixel in size and would solidly fill the drawing area. So, AutoCAD adjusts the spacing of the dots to keep the grid readable. You need to change that spacing.

For the drawing task ahead, it will be more useful to have the spacing set differently. Remember how you turned on Snap and the cursor stopped at each dot? If you set the dot spacing to 12", you can use Grid and Snap modes to help you draw the outline of the cabin, because the dimensions of the outside wall line are in whole feet: 25' × 16'. Here's how:

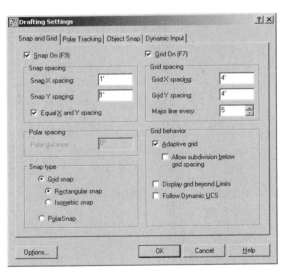

If you set the Grid Spacing to 0, the grid takes on whatever spacing you set for the Snap X Spacing and Snap Y Spacing text boxes. This is how you lock the snap and grid together.

1. Right-click the Grid button on the status bar, and choose Settings from the context menu that opens. The Drafting Settings dialog box opens, and the Snap and Grid tab is active. The settings in both the Grid and Snap areas include X Spacing and Y Spacing settings. Notice that they're all set for a spacing of ½".

2. In the Grid area, click in the Grid X Spacing text box, and change 1/2" to 4'. Then, click the Grid Y Spacing text box. It automatically changes to match the Grid X Spacing text box. If you want different Grid X and Grid Y Spacing values, you must uncheck the Equal X and Y Spacing option in the Snap Spacing area.

3. In the Snap section, change the Snap X Spacing setting to 12. The inch sign isn't required. Then, click the Snap Y Spacing setting. It automatically changes to match the Snap X Spacing setting and changes both text boxes to display 1' instead of 12" (see Figure 3.9).

FIGURE 3.9: New settings on the Snap and Grid tab of the Drafting Settings dialog box

4. In the Snap Type area, be sure Grid Snap and Rectangular Snap are selected.

5. In the Grid Behavior area, only Adaptive Grid should be checked. With the grid set this way, AutoCAD will adjust the number of dots displayed as you zoom in and out but won't add dots between the lowest grid spacing.

6. The Snap On and Grid On check boxes at the top of the dialog box should be selected. If they aren't, click them.

7. Click OK. The new 4' grid is now visible (see Figure 3.10). Move the cursor around on the grid—be sure Snap is on. (Check the Snap button on the status bar; it's pressed when Snap is on.) Notice the coordinate readout. It's displaying coordinates to the nearest foot to conform to the new 12" snap spacing. The cursor stops at three snap points between each grid dot.

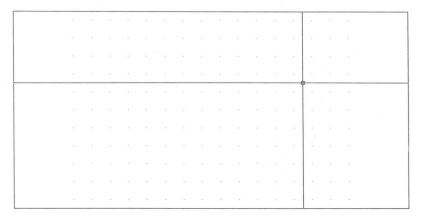

FIGURE 3.10: The new 60' × 40' grid with 4' dot spacing

8. Move the crosshair cursor to the upper-right corner of the grid, and check the coordinate readout. It should display 60'-0", 40'-0", 0'-0". (In LT, you won't have the third coordinate.)

Drawing with Grid and Snap

Your drawing area now has the proper settings and is zoomed to a convenient magnification. You're ready to draw the first lines of the cabin:

1. When the Command window displays the Command: prompt, start the Line command. (Click the Line button on the Draw toolbar, or enter l↵.) Enter 8',8'↵ (see Figure 3.11).

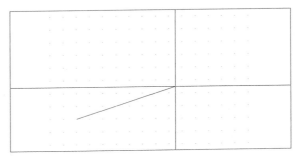

FIGURE 3.11: One point picked on the grid

2. On the status bar, click Dyn to activate dynamic display, and then hold the crosshair cursor above and to the right of the point you just picked. AutoCAD shows dashed linear and angular dimensions that dynamically display the length and angle of the first line segment as the cursor moves, and a tooltip displays the current prompt for the Line command.

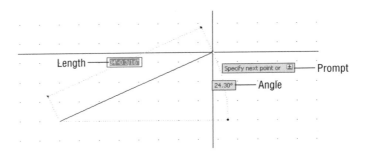

3. Don't click yet. Hold the crosshair cursor directly out to the right of the first point picked, and note how the linear dimension displays a distance in whole feet. The angular dimension should have an angle of 0.00°.

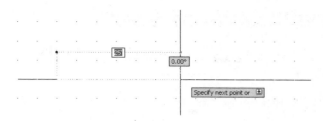

4. Continue moving the crosshair cursor left or right until the dashed linear dimension displays 25'. At this point, click the left mouse button to draw the first line of the cabin wall (see Figure 3.12).

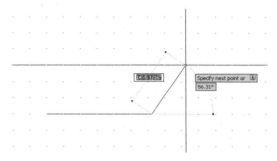

FIGURE 3.12: Drawing the first line of the cabin wall

5. Move the crosshair cursor directly above the last point picked to a position such that the dashed linear dimension displays 16' and the dashed angular dimension displays 90.00°, and pick that point.

6. Move the crosshair cursor directly left of the last point picked until the dashed linear dimension displays 25' and the dashed angular dimension displays 180.00°, and pick that point (see Figure 3.13).

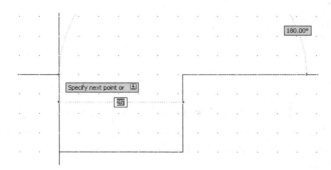

FIGURE 3.13: Drawing the second and third wall lines

7. Finally, enter c↵ to close the box. This tells AutoCAD to draw a line from the last point picked to the first point picked and, in effect, closes the box. AutoCAD then automatically ends the Line command (see Figure 3.14).

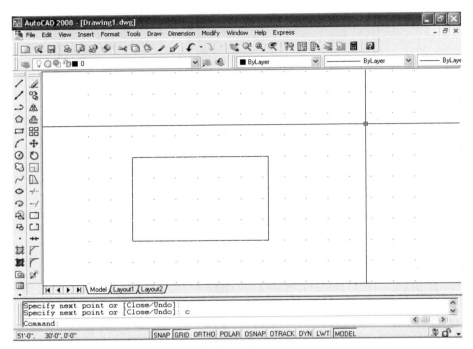

FIGURE 3.14: The completed outside wall lines

This method for laying out building lines by using Snap and Grid and the dynamic display is useful if the dimensions all conform to a convenient rounded-off number, such as the nearest six inches or, as in this case, the nearest foot. The key advantage to this method over just typing the relative coordinates—as you did with the box in Chapter 2—is that you avoid having to enter the numbers. You should, however, assess whether the layout you need to draw has characteristics that lend themselves to using Grid, Snap, and the dynamic display or whether typing the relative coordinates would be more efficient. As you get more comfortable with AutoCAD, you'll see that this sort of question comes up often: which way is the most efficient? This happy dilemma is inevitable in an application with enough tools to give you many strategic choices. In Chapters 4 and 5, you'll learn other techniques for drawing rectangles.

Taking a Closer Look at Dynamic Display

The kind of information shown in dynamic display is similar to that shown in the Command window and the intent of this feature is to keep your eyes on the screen as much as possible. Like the information on the Command line, it depends on what you're doing at the time and on several settings that you access by right-clicking the Dyn button on the status bar and selecting Settings from the shortcut menu. This opens the Drafting Settings dialog box with the Dynamic Input tab activated (see Figure 3.15).

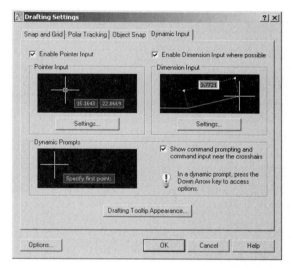

FIGURE 3.15: The Dynamic Input tab of the Drafting Settings dialog box

This tab has three check boxes, two at the top and one near the middle on the right, and three buttons to open three Settings dialog boxes. To make the dynamic input conform to what is shown in the book, do the following:

1. Be sure all three check boxes are selected.

2. In the Pointer Input area, click the Settings button to open the Pointer Input Settings dialog box (see Figure 3.16). In the Format area, the Polar Format and Relative Coordinates radio buttons should be selected. Click OK.

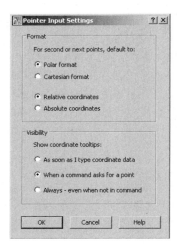

FIGURE 3.16: The Pointer Input Settings dialog box

3. In the Dimension Input area, click the Settings button to open the Dimension Input Settings dialog box (see Figure 3.17).

FIGURE 3.17: The Dimension Input Settings dialog box

4. Be sure the Show 2 Dimension Input Fields at a Time radio button is selected, and then click OK.

5. Below the Dynamic Prompts area of the Drafting Settings dialog box, click the Drafting Tooltip Appearance button to open the Tooltip Appearance dialog box (see Figure 3.18). In the Apply To area at the bottom of the box, be sure the Use Settings Only for Dynamic Input Tooltips radio button is selected. Vary the Colors, Size, and Transparency settings according to your preference. (I used a setting of 1 for Size and 0% for Transparency. Don't worry about Layout Color for now; you'll come back to it in Chapter 13 when you work with layouts.) The model color you choose depends on whether your drawing area has a light or dark background. Experiment. When you're finished, click OK.

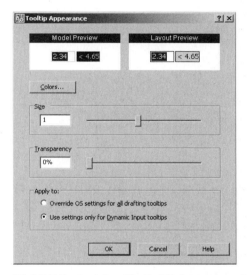

FIGURE 3.18: The Tooltip Appearance dialog box

6. Click OK again to close the Drafting Settings dialog box.

If you decide to disable dynamic display, you can easily do so by clicking the Dyn button in the status bar so that it's in unpushed mode. After this chapter, I'll direct you to turn off Snap and Grid because you won't use them for the rest of the book. I'll also direct you to turn off dynamic display, because it's generally off in the book illustrations. However, you'll turn it back on when you're doing an action in which the feature might be useful. If you prefer to keep it on, feel free to do so.

Saving Your Work

As with all Windows-compliant applications, when you save a file for the first time by choosing File ➤ Save, you can designate a name for the file and a folder in which to store it. I recommend you create a special folder, called something like Training Data, for storing the files you'll generate as you work your way through this book. This will keep them separate from project work already on your computer, and you'll always know where to save or find a training drawing. To save your drawing, follow these steps:

1. In AutoCAD, click the Save button on the Standard toolbar, or choose File ➤ Save. Because you haven't named this file yet, the Save Drawing As dialog box opens, as shown in Figure 3.19.

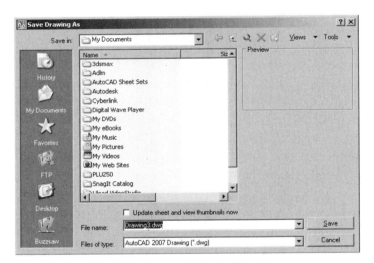

FIGURE 3.19: The Save Drawing As dialog box

The Save button in the Standard toolbar, the Save menu item, and the Ctrl+S key combination actually invoke the QSave (Quick Save) command in AutoCAD. This is evident when you place your cursor over the Save button or menu item and then look at the far left side of the status bar. This area displays the command information regarding the tool the cursor is hovering over (see Figure 3.20).

FIGURE 3.20: The status bar reflecting the command associated with the menu item under the cursor

QSave asks only for a filename when the drawing has not yet been saved for the first time, after which it simply overwrites the existing file with no prompting. Entering the Save command at the command line (**save↵**) always opens the Save Drawing As dialog where you can modify the filename and path.

N O T E   **The actual folders and files might be different on your computer.**

2. In the Save In drop-down list, designate the drive and folder where you want to save the drawing. If you're saving it on the hard drive or server, navigate to the folder in which you want to place the new Training Data folder.

3. Click the Create New Folder button near the top-right corner of the dialog box. The folder appears in the list of folders and is highlighted. It's called New Folder, and a cursor flashes just to the right of the highlighting rectangle.

4. Enter Training Data↵ (or whatever name you want to give the new folder).

5. Double-click the new folder to open it.

6. In the File Name box, change the name to Cabin03. You're not required to enter the .dwg extension.

N O T E From now on when you're directed to save the drawing, save it as Cabinx, with *x* indicating the number of the chapter. This way, you'll know where in the book to look for review, if necessary. Name multiple saves within a chapter Cabinxa, Cabinxb, and so on. To save the current drawing under a different name, used the Save As command (File ≻ Save As or saveas↵).

7. Click Save. Notice that the AutoCAD title bar displays the new name of the file along with its path. It's now safe to exit AutoCAD.

8. If you want to shut down AutoCAD at this time, choose File ≻ Exit. Otherwise, keep your drawing open, and read on.

The tools covered in this chapter are your key to starting a new drawing from scratch and getting it ready for a specific project.

Summarizing AutoCAD's Units

The following is a brief description of each of the linear and angular unit types that AutoCAD offers and how you use them. The example distance is 2'-6½". The example angle is 126°35'10".

Using Linear Units

The linear unit types that AutoCAD uses are as follows:

Architectural This unit type uses feet and inches with fractions. You must use the foot sign ('): for example, 2'-6½". For this distance, enter 2'6-1/2 or 2'6.5. For the most part, these are the units you'll use in this book.

Decimal   This unit type uses decimal units that can represent any linear unit of measurement. You don't use the foot sign, the inch sign, or fractions. For example, if each decimal unit equals 1 inch, then to specify a line to be 2'-6½" long, you must convert feet to inches and enter a length of **30.5**. But if each decimal unit equals 1 foot, you must convert the inches to the decimal equivalent of a foot and enter **2.5417**.

Engineering   This unit is equivalent to architectural units except that inches are displayed as decimals rather than fractions. For a distance of 2'-6½", enter **2'6.5** or **2.5417'**. In either method, the resulting distance is displayed as 2'-6.5".

Fractional   These units are just like architectural units except there is no use of feet. Everything is expressed in inches and fractions. If you enter **30-1/2** or **30.5**, the resulting distance displays as 30½.

Scientific   This unit system is similar to the decimal unit system except for the way in which distances are displayed. If you enter **3.05E+01**, that is what is displayed. The notation always uses an expression that indicates a number from 1 to 10 that is to be multiplied by a power of 10. In this case, the power is 1, so the notation means 3.05×10, or 30.5 in decimal units.

Using Angular Units

The angular unit types that AutoCAD uses are as follows:

Decimal   This type uses 360° in a circle in decimal form, with no minutes and no seconds. All angles are expressed as decimal degrees. For example, you enter an angle of 126°35'10" as **126.586** or **126d35'10"**, and it displays as 126.5861. AutoCAD uses a *d* instead of the traditional degree symbol (°).

Deg/Min/Sec   This is the traditional system for measuring angles. In Auto-CAD's notation, degrees are indicated by the lowercase *d*, the minutes use the traditional ', and the seconds use the traditional ". The system is clumsy. Most users now use decimal angles instead of this system and choose their preference for precision.

Grads   This unit is based on a circle being divided into 400 grads, so 90° equals 100 grads. One degree equals 1.11 grads, and 1 grad equals 0.90 degrees. Auto-CAD uses *g* as the symbol for grads.

Radians   The radian is the angle from the center of a circle made by the radius of the circle being laid along the circumference of the circle. One radian equals 57.3 degrees, and 360 degrees equals 6.28 radians, or 2π radians. AutoCAD uses *r* as the symbol for radians.

Surveyor   These units use bearings from the north and south directions toward the east or west direction and are expressed in degrees, minutes, and seconds. They're discussed in Chapter 12. In this example, 126° 35'10" translates to N 36d35'10" W in bearings, or Surveyor's units.

The next chapter will focus on adding to the drawing, modifying commands you learned as part of Chapter 2, and creating strategies for solving problems that can occur when developing a floor plan.

Are You Experienced?

Now you can...

- ☑ set up linear and angular units for a new drawing

- ☑ make the grid visible and modify its coverage

- ☑ use the Zoom In and Zoom Out commands

- ☑ activate Snap mode and change the Snap and Grid spacings

- ☑ use the Zoom All function to fit the grid on the drawing area

- ☑ draw lines using Grid, Snap, and the dynamic display feature

- ☑ create a new folder on your hard drive from within AutoCAD

- ☑ name and save your file

CHAPTER 4

Gaining Drawing Strategies: Part 1

- ▶ Making interior walls
- ▶ Zooming in on an area using various zoom tools
- ▶ Making doors and swings
- ▶ Using object snaps
- ▶ Using the Copy and Mirror commands

Assuming that you have worked your way through the first three chapters, you have now successfully drawn a box (Chapter 2) as well as the outer wall lines of a cabin (Chapter 3). From here on, you'll develop a floor plan for the cabin and, in Chapter 8, *elevations* (views of the front, back, and sides of the building that show how the building will look if you're facing it). The focus in this chapter is on gaining a feel for the strategy of drawing in AutoCAD and on how to solve drawing problems that come up in the course of laying out a floor plan. As you work your way through this chapter, your activities will include making walls, cutting doorway openings, and drawing doors (see Figure 4.1). In Chapter 5, you'll add steps and a balcony and place fixtures and appliances in the bathroom and kitchen.

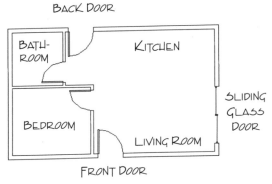

FIGURE 4.1: The basic floor plan of the cabin

Each exercise in this chapter presents opportunities to practice using commands you already know from earlier chapters and to learn a few new ones. The most important goal is to begin to use strategic thinking as you develop methods for creating new elements of the floor plan.

TIP Because you'll be doing quite a bit of drawing in this chapter and the next one, this is a good opportunity to activate the dynamic display feature introduced in Chapter 3. Turn it off and on as you work through the exercises, and notice how the information displayed in the drawing area changes as you move from one command to another. The feature is designed to help you avoid having to continually glance down at the Command window as you work through the steps of a command. Sometimes, however, the information you need appears only in the Command window, so you still have to glance down at it. By the time you finish Chapter 5, you'll know whether you want the feature to be active. I won't illustrate it in the figures unless it becomes important to do so.

Laying Out the Walls

For most floor plans, the walls come first. The first lesson in this chapter is to understand that you won't be putting many new lines in the drawing, at least not as many as you might expect. You'll create most new objects in this chapter from items already in your drawing. In fact, you'll draw no new lines to make walls. You'll generate all the new walls from the four exterior wall lines you drew in the previous chapter.

You'll need to create an inside wall line for the exterior walls (because the wall has thickness) and then make the three new interior walls (see Figure 4.2). The thickness will be 4" for interior walls and 6" for exterior walls, because exterior walls are studier and load bearing and have an additional layer or two of weather protection, such as siding or stucco. Finally, you'll need to cut five openings in these walls (interior and exterior) for the doorways.

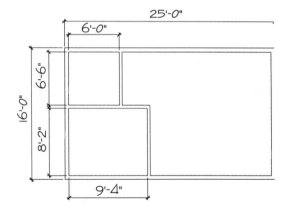

FIGURE 4.2: The wall dimensions

Most of the commands used for this exercise were presented in Chapters 2 and 3. If you need a refresher, glance back at those chapters.

Creating a Polyline

Using the tools you've already learned, you would first offset the existing four wall lines to the inside to make the inside wall lines for the exterior walls. You would then fillet them to clean up their corners, just like you did for the box in Chapter 2. But in this chapter I'll introduce you to the polyline object. Although a line is a single, straight object with no measurable width, polylines are composed of several straight or curved segments that can also maintain a user-defined width. When a polyline is offset, all segments are offset equally and the corners are left sharp, without the need to use the Fillet command to clean them up. You can disassemble any polyline into its component lines and arcs using the Explode command. Using the Pedit command, you can convert several lines and arcs into a single polyline as long as the endpoints of the various segments actually touch one another. Follow these steps:

1. With AutoCAD running, choose File ➤ Open. In the Select File dialog box, navigate to the folder you designated as your training folder, and select your cabin drawing. (You named it Cabin03.dwg at the end of Chapter 3.) Click Open, and you should see the cabin as you left it in Chapter 3 (see Figure 4.3).

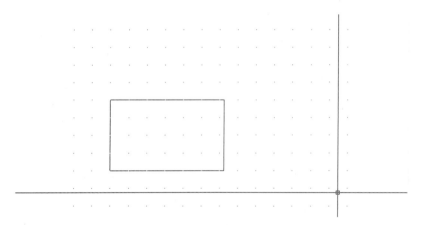

FIGURE 4.3: The cabin as you left it in Chapter 3

2. On the status bar, click the Grid and Snap buttons to turn them off.

3. From the menus, choose Modify ➤ Object ➤ Polyline, or enter pe⏎ to start the Pedit command.

4. Select one of the exterior wall lines. Because this is not a polyline yet, the Command line prompts you to turn it into one, as shown in Figure 4.4.

5. Press the ⏎ key to accept the default Yes option.

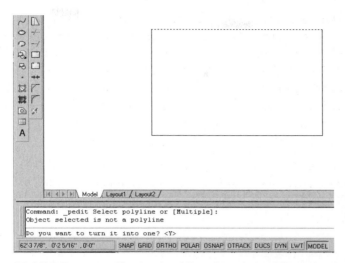

FIGURE 4.4: The Command line when a nonpolyline object is selected

6. The Command line now shows all the possible polyline-editing options: Enter an option [Close/Join/Width/Edit vertex/Fit/Spline/ Decurve/Ltypegen/Undo]:. Enter j↵ to choose the Join option. The intent here is to join the four lines into a single, four-segment, closed polyline.

7. Select all the lines in the drawing including the original line you selected at the beginning of this exercise. Press ↵ when you are done.

8. The second line in the Command window shows 3 segments added to polyline—indicating AutoCAD has added the three subsequent lines selected to the original line that you converted to a polyline. The bottom line indicates that you're still in the Pedit command.

```
Select objects:
3 segments added to polyline
Enter an option [Open/Join/Width/Edit vertex/Fit/Spline/Decurve/Ltype gen/Undo]:
```

9. Press ↵ again to exit the Pedit command.

10. Select one segment of the polyline that forms the perimeter of the box in the drawing area. All four polyline segments are selected, indicating that they exist as a single object, and blue boxes appear at the corners. The blue boxes, called grips, appear because you selected the object outside a command and because they are not exclusive to polylines. I'll explain grips in Chapter 8.

Creating the Exterior Wall Lines

Here, you will use the Offset command to create all four interior lines at one time:

1. Start the Offset command by clicking the Offset button on the Modify toolbar.

2. At the Specify offset distance: prompt, enter 6↵.

N O T E   You don't have to enter the inch sign ("), but you're required to enter the foot sign (') when appropriate.

3. At the Select object to offset: prompt, select the polyline.

4. Click a blank area inside the rectangle. All four segments of the pline are offset 6" to the inside (see Figure 4.5). The Offset command is still running, so press ↵ to terminate it.

F I G U R E   4 . 5 :   All four lines are now offset 6" to the inside.

As you can see, you don't need to fillet the corners, and using polylines can lessen the number of steps and picks required to draw the inside lines. I'll diverge from the cabin exercise briefly to cover the capabilities of the Fillet command when used in conjunction with polylines.

5. Start the Fillet command by clicking the Fillet button on the Modify toolbar.

6. Enter r↵ at the Command prompt then set the radius to 24".

7. Select any two polyline segments that share a corner of the inner box. This shortens the two segments and inserts a curved segment with a 24" radius. The polyline now has five contiguous segments (see Figure 4.6). The Fillet command automatically ends after each fillet.

You can restart the most recently used command by pressing the spacebar or ↵ at the Command: prompt or by right-clicking and choosing the first item on the shortcut menu that opens.

FIGURE 4.6: The first corner is filleted.

8. Press ↵ or the spacebar to restart the Fillet command.

9. Enter p↵ to inform AutoCAD that the fillet is to be performed on all intersections of a polyline. At the `Select 2D polyline:` prompt, select the inner box. All four corners are now filleted (see Figure 4.7).

FIGURE 4.7: The four inside corners are filleted.

10. You can see how the Fillet command, when used with a polyline, can save time. You don't want the objects to remain as polylines for this project, so click the Undo button in the Main toolbar or enter u↵ until all the filleted edges are square again.

11. Click the Explode button in the Modify toolbar or enter ex↵ to start the Explode command. Select both of the polylines, and then press the ↵ key. The two polylines are now eight separate line objects.

OFFSET VS. FILLET

These are characteristics that Offset and Fillet have in common:

▶ Both are on the Modify toolbar and on the Modify drop-down menu.

▶ Both have a default setting—offset distance and fillet radius—that you can accept or reset.

▶ Both require you to select object(s).

These are characteristics that are different in Offset and Fillet:

▶ You select one object with Offset and two objects or polyline segments with Fillet.

▶ Offset keeps running until you stop it. Fillet ends after each fillet operation, so you need to restart Fillet to use it again unless you use the Multiple option.

You'll find several uses for Offset and Fillet in the subsequent sections of this chapter and throughout the book.

Creating the Interior Walls

Create the interior wall lines by offsetting the exterior wall lines:

1. At the Command: prompt, start the Offset command.

2. At the Offset distance: prompt, enter 9'4↵. Leave no space between the foot sign (') and the 4.

N O T E   AutoCAD requires that you enter a distance containing feet and inches in a particular format: no space between the foot sign (') and the inches and a hyphen (-) between the inches and the fraction. For example, if you're entering a distance of 6'-4 ¾", you enter 6'4-3/4". The measurement is displayed in the regular way, 6'-4 ¾", but you must enter it in the format that has no spaces because the spacebar acts the same as the ↵ in most cases.

3. Click the inside line of the left exterior wall (see Figure 4.8).

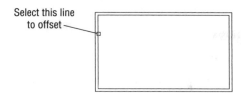

Select this line to offset

FIGURE 4.8: Selecting the wall line to offset

4. Click a blank area to the right of the selected line. The line is offset 9'-4" to the right.

5. Press ↵ twice, or press the spacebar twice. This restarts the Offset command, and you can reset the offset distance.

T I P In the Offset command, your opportunity to change the offset distance comes right after you start the command. So, if the Offset command is already running, and you need to change the offset distance, you must stop and then restart the command. To do so, press ↵ or the spacebar twice.

6. Enter 4↵ to reset the offset distance to 4".

7. Click the new line that was just offset, and then click a blank area to the right of that line. You have created a vertical interior wall (see Figure 4.9). Press ↵ twice to stop and restart the Offset command.

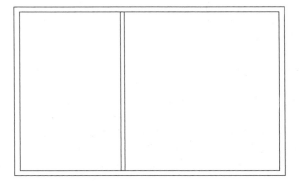

FIGURE 4.9: The first interior wall

8. Enter 6.5'↵ to set the distance for offsetting the next wall.

N O T E   With Architectural units set, you can still enter distances in decimal form for feet and inches, and AutoCAD will translate them into their appropriate form. For example, you can enter 6'-6" as 6.5', and you can enter 4½" as 4.5 without the inch sign.

9. Pick a point on the inside, upper exterior wall line (see Figure 4.10).

Select this line to offset.

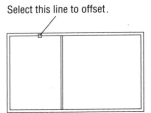

F I G U R E   4 . 1 0 : Selecting another wall line to offset

10. Click a blank area below the line selected. The inside exterior wall line is offset to make a new interior wall line. Press the spacebar twice to stop and restart the Offset command.

11. Enter 4↵. Click the new line, and click again below it. This creates a second wall line, so you now have two interior walls. Press the spacebar to end the Offset command.

These interior wall lines form the bedroom and one side of the bathroom. You need to clean up their intersections with each other and with the exterior walls. If you take the time to do this now, it will be easier to make the last interior wall and thereby complete the bathroom. Refer to Figures 4.1 and 4.2 earlier in this chapter to see where you're headed.

Cleaning Up Wall Lines

Earlier in the book, you used the Fillet command to clean up the corners of intersecting lines. You can use that command again to clean up some of the interior walls, but you'll have to use the Trim command to do the rest of them. You'll see why as you progress through the next set of steps:

1. It will be easier to pick the wall lines if you make the drawing larger on the screen. Enter z↵, and then enter e↵. Press ↵, and then enter

.6x↵. The drawing is bigger. You've just used two options of the Zoom command. First, you zoomed to extents to display all the objects in your drawing. You then zoomed to a scale (.6×) to make the drawing 60 percent the size it was after zooming to Extents. This is a change in magnification on the view only; the building is still 25 feet long and 16 feet wide.

2. Start the Fillet command, set the radius to 0, and click two of the wall lines, as shown in the image at the top of Figure 4.11. Be sure to select the left or lower portions of the lines, as shown, or the opposite ends of the line will remain, creating the corner with the wrong orientation. The lines are filleted, and the results will look like the image at the bottom of Figure 4.11.

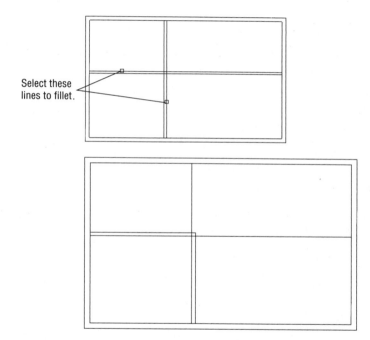

Select these lines to fillet.

FIGURE 4.11: Selecting the first two lines to fillet (top) and the result of the fillet (bottom)

> The best rule for choosing between Fillet and Trim is the following: If you need to clean up a single intersection between two lines, use the Fillet command. For other cases, use the Trim command.

3. Press the spacebar to restart the Fillet command. Select the two lines as shown on the left of Figure 4.12. The results appear on the right of Figure 4.12.

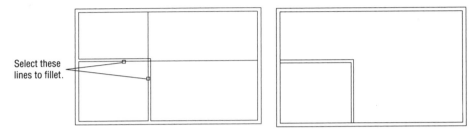

Select these lines to fillet.

FIGURE 4.12: Selecting the second two lines to fillet (left) and the result of the second fillet (right)

The two new interior walls are now the correct length, but you'll have to clean up the areas where they form T intersections with the exterior walls. The Fillet command won't work in T intersections because too much of one of the wall lines gets deleted. You need to use the Trim command in T intersection cases. The Fillet command does a specific kind of trim and is easy and quick to execute, but its uses are limited (for the most part) to single intersections between two lines or multiple intersections on a polyline.

Using the Zoom Command

To do this trim efficiently, you need a closer view of the T intersections. Use the Zoom command to get a better look:

1. Enter z↵. Then, move the crosshair cursor to a point slightly above and to the left of the upper T intersection (see Figure 4.13), and click a blank area outside the floor plan.

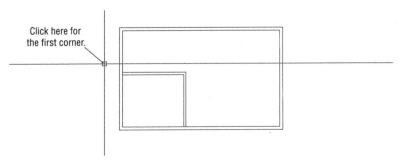

Click here for the first corner.

FIGURE 4.13: Positioning the cursor for the first click of the Zoom command

2. Move the cursor down and to the right, and notice a rectangle with solid lines being drawn. Keep moving the cursor down and to the right until the rectangle encloses the upper T intersection (see the left of Figure 4.14). When the rectangle fully encloses the T intersection, click again. The view changes to a closer view of the intersection of the interior and exterior walls (see the right of Figure 4.14).

When you start the Zoom command by entering z↵ and then picking a point on the screen, a zoom window begins.

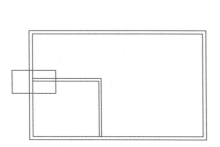

FIGURE 4.14: Using the zoom window option: positioning the rectangle (left) and the new view after the Zoom command (right)

The rectangle you've just created is called a *zoom window*. The area of the drawing enclosed by the zoom window becomes the view on the screen. This is one of several zoom options for changing the magnification of the view. I'll introduce other zoom options later in this chapter and throughout the book.

3. On the Modify toolbar, click the Trim button. In the Command window, notice the second and third lines of text. You're being prompted to select cutting edges (objects to use as limits for the lines you want to trim).

In the Trim command, click the part of the line that needs to be trimmed away at the Select objects: prompt. In the Fillet command, select the part of the line you want to keep.

4. Select the two interior wall lines, and press the spacebar. The prompt changes, now asking you to select the lines to be trimmed.

5. Select the inside exterior wall line at the T intersection, between the two intersections with the interior wall lines that you have just picked as cutting edges (see the top of Figure 4.15). The exterior wall line is trimmed at the T intersection (see the bottom of Figure 4.15). Press the spacebar to end the Trim command.

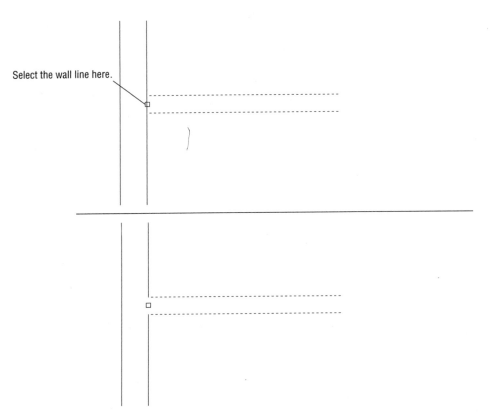

Select the wall line here.

FIGURE 4.15: Selecting a line to be trimmed (top) and the result of the Trim command (bottom)

6. Return to a view of the whole drawing by entering z↵ and then p↵. This is the Zoom command's Previous option, which restores the view that was active before the last use of the Zoom command (see Figure 4.16).

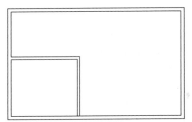

FIGURE 4.16: The result of the Zoom Previous command

Repeat the procedure to trim the lower T intersection. Follow these steps:

1. Enter z↵, and click two points to make a rectangular zoom window around the intersection.

2. Start the Trim command again, select the interior walls as cutting edges, and press the spacebar.

3. Select the inside exterior wall line between the cutting edges.

4. Press the spacebar or ↵ to end the Trim command.

5. Invoke Zoom Previous by typing z↵ p↵.

Figure 4.17 shows the results.

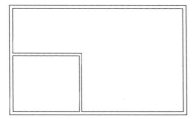

FIGURE 4.17: The second trim is completed.

You need to create one more interior wall to complete the bathroom.

Finishing the Interior Walls

You'll use the same method to create the last bathroom wall that you used to make the first two interior walls. Briefly, this is how you do it:

1. Offset the upper inside line of the left exterior wall 6' to the right; then, offset this new line 4" to the right.

2. Use Zoom Window to zoom into the bathroom area.

 T I P Make a zoom window just large enough to enclose the bathroom. The resulting view should be large enough to allow you to trim both ends of the interior wall without rezooming.

3. Use the Trim command to trim away the short portion of the inter-sected wall lines between the two new wall lines. You can accomplish this in one use of the Trim command: once you select the new wall

lines as cutting edges, you can trim both lines that run across the ends of the selected lines to those same cutting edges.

4. Use Zoom Extents to restore the full view.

The results should look like Figure 4.18.

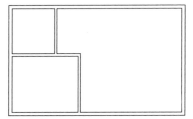

FIGURE 4.18: The completed interior walls

You used Offset, Fillet, Trim, and a couple of zooms to create the interior walls. The next task is to create five doorway openings in these walls. If you need to end the drawing session before completing the chapter, choose File ➤ Save As, then change the name of this drawing to Cabin04a.dwg, and click Save. You can then exit AutoCAD. To continue, do the same save operation, and move on to the next section.

Cutting Openings in the Walls

Of the five doorway openings needed, two are on interior walls and three are on exterior walls (see Figure 4.19). Four of them are for swinging doors, and one is for a sliding-glass door. You won't be doing the hatchings and dimensions shown in the figure—I'll cover those features in future chapters.

The procedure used to make each doorway opening is the same one you used to create the opening for the box in Chapter 2. First, you establish the location of the *jambs*, or sides, of an opening. One jamb for each swinging door opening will be located 6" from an inside wall corner. This allows the door to be positioned next to a wall and out of the way when swung open. When the jambs are established, you'll trim away the wall lines between the edges. The commands used in this exercise are Offset, Extend, and Trim. You'll make openings for the 3'-0" exterior doorways first.

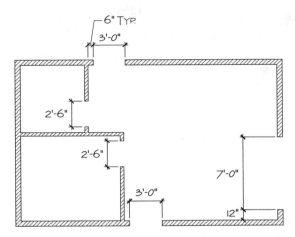

FIGURE 4.19: The drawing with doorway openings

Creating the Exterior Openings

These openings are on the front and back walls of the cabin and have one side set in 6" from an inside corner:

1. Start the Offset command, and then enter **6↵** to set the distance to 6".

2. Click one of the two lines indicated in Figure 4.20, and then click a blank area to the right of the line you selected. Now do the same to the second wall line. You have to offset one line at a time because of the way the Offset command works.

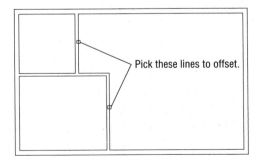

Pick these lines to offset.

FIGURE 4.20: The lines to offset for the 3'-0" openings

3. End and restart the Offset command by pressing the spacebar or ↵ twice; then, enter **3'↵** to set a new offset distance, and offset the new

lines to the right (see Figure 4.21). Next, you need to extend these four new lines through the external walls to make the jamb lines.

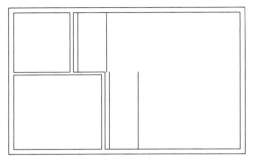

FIGURE 4.21: The offset lines for 3'-0" openings

4. Be sure to end the Offset command by pressing the spacebar or ↵; then, start the Extend command. You use Extend here exactly as you used it in Chapter 2. Select the upper and lower horizontal, outside, external wall lines as boundary edges for the Extend command, and press the spacebar or ↵ (see Figure 4.22). If you had left the exterior rectangle as a polyline, this would have required only a single pick.

T I P   If you start a new command by entering letters on the keyboard, you must first be sure that the previous command has ended. On the other hand, if you start a new command by clicking its icon on a toolbar or by choosing it from the menu bar, it doesn't matter if the previous command is still running. AutoCAD will cancel it.

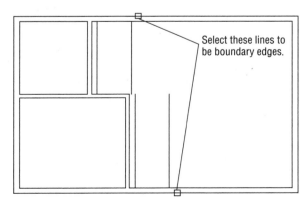

Select these lines to be boundary edges.

FIGURE 4.22: Selecting the boundary edges

5. Click the four jamb lines to extend them. Be sure to pick points on the lines that are near the boundary edges, or the lines will be extended in the opposite direction. The lines are extended through the external walls to make the jambs (see Figure 4.23). End the Extend command by pressing the spacebar or ↵.

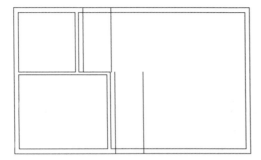

FIGURE 4.23: The lines after being extended through the external walls

T I P The Trim command has the same functionality as the Extend command. While using Trim, select the cutting edges, and then hold the Shift key down at the `Select objects:` prompt. The cutting edges act as boundary edges, and the object is extended, rather than trimmed.

To complete the openings, continue with steps 6 and 7. First you'll trim away the excess part of the jamb lines, and then you'll trim away the wall lines between the jamb lines. You'll use the Trim command the same way you used it in Chapter 2, but this time you'll do a *compound* trim to clean up the wall and jamb lines in one cycle of the command.

6. Enter tr↵ to start the Trim command, and select the three lines at each opening (six lines total), as shown in Figure 4.24. Then, press the spacebar or ↵ to tell AutoCAD you're finished selecting objects to serve as cutting edges.

Select these lines to be cutting edges.

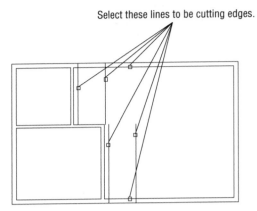

FIGURE 4.24: Selecting the cutting edges

7. Pick the four wall lines between the jamb lines, and then pick the jamb lines—the lines you just extended to the outside exterior walls, as shown in Figure 4.25.

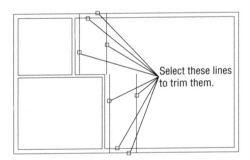

Select these lines to trim them.

FIGURE 4.25: The lines to be trimmed

8. Each time you pick a line, it's trimmed. Press the spacebar or ⌐ to end the command. Your drawing should look like Figure 4.26.

    TIP   When picking lines to be trimmed, remember to pick the lines on the portion to be trimmed away.

You can construct the two interior openings using the same procedure.

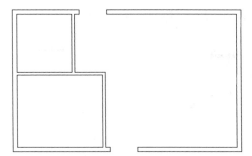

FIGURE 4.26: The finished 3'-0" openings

Creating the Interior Openings

These doorways are 2'-6" wide and also have one jamb set in 6" from the nearest inside corner. Figure 4.27 shows the three stages of fabricating these openings. Refer to the previous section on making openings for step-by-step instructions.

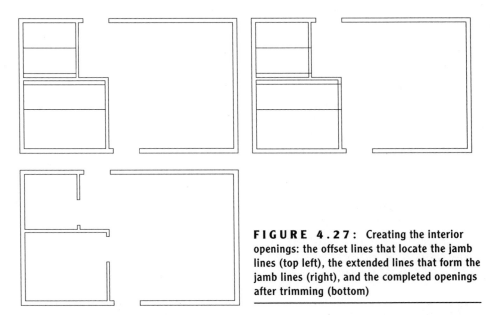

FIGURE 4.27: Creating the interior openings: the offset lines that locate the jamb lines (top left), the extended lines that form the jamb lines (right), and the completed openings after trimming (bottom)

Construct the 7'-0" exterior opening using the same commands and technique.

Creating the 7'-0" Opening

Notice that in Figure 4.19, earlier in this chapter, the opening on the right side of the building has one jamb set in 12" from the inside corner. This opening is for the sliding glass door.

You've done this procedure before, so here's a summary of the steps:

1. Offset the lower interior wall line 12".

2. Offset the new line 7'-0".

3. Extend both new lines through the wall.

4. Trim the new lines and the wall lines to complete the opening.

5. Save this drawing as Cabin04b.dwg.

This completes the openings. The results should look like Figure 4.28.

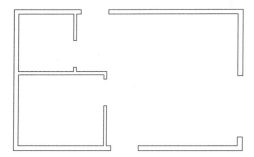

FIGURE 4.28: The completed doorway openings

As you gain more control over the commands you used here, you'll be able to anticipate how much of a task you can do with each use of a command. Each opening required offsetting, extending, and trimming. You constructed these openings two at a time except for the last one, thereby using each of the three commands three times. It's possible to do all the openings using each command only once. In this way, you do all the offsetting, then all the extending, and finally all the trimming. In cutting these openings, however, the arrangement of the offset lines determined how many cycles of the Trim command were most efficient to use. If lines being trimmed and used as cutting edges cross each other, the trimming gets complicated. For these five openings, the most efficient procedure is to use each command twice. In Chapter 8, you'll get a chance to work with more complex multiple trims when you draw the elevations.

Now that the openings are complete, you can place doors and door swings in their appropriate doorways. In doing this, you'll be introduced to two new objects and a few new commands, and you'll have an opportunity to use the Offset and Trim commands in new, strategic ways.

What to Do When You Make a Mistake

When you're offsetting, trimming, and extending lines, it's easy to pick the wrong line. Here are some tips on how to correct these errors and get back on track:

▶ You can always cancel any command by pressing the Esc key until you see the Command: prompt in the Command window. Then, click the Undo button on the Standard toolbar to undo the results of the last command. If you undo too much, click the Redo button. You can click it more than once to redo several undos. Clicking the downward-pointing arrows displays a list of the recent commands executed or undone in reverse order. To undo or redo

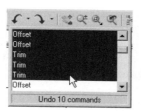

multiple commands, select the last desired command in the list, and Auto-CAD reverts to that point in the drawing. This is similar to the History feature in Adobe Photoshop. Redos must be performed immediately following an undo.

▶ Errors made with the Offset command include setting the wrong distance, picking the wrong line to offset, or picking the wrong side to offset toward. If the distance is correct, you can continue offsetting, end the command when you have the results you want, and then erase the lines that were offset wrong. Otherwise, press Esc to undo your previous offset.

▶ You can sometimes correct errors on the fly made with the Trim and Extend commands, so you don't have to end the command, because each of these commands has an Undo option. If you pick a line and it doesn't trim or extend the right way, you can undo that last action without stopping the command and then continue trimming or extending. You can activate the Undo option used while the command is running in two ways: enter **u**↵, or right-click and choose Undo from the shortcut menu that opens. Either of these actions undoes the last trim or extend, and you can try again without having to restart the command. Each time you activate the Undo option *from within the command*, another trim or extend is undone.

▶ The Line command also has the same Undo option as the Trim and Extend commands. You can undo the last segment drawn (or the last several segments) and redraw them without stopping the command.

Creating Doors

In a floor plan, a rectangle or a line for the door and an arc showing the path of the door swing usually indicate a pivot door. The door's position varies, but it's most often shown at 90° from the closed position (see Figure 4.29). The best rule I have come across is to display the door in such a way that others working with your floor plan will be able to see how far, and in what direction, the door will swing open.

FIGURE 4.29: Possible ways to illustrate pivot doors

The cabin has five openings. Four of them need swinging doors, which open 90°. The fifth is a sliding glass door. Drawing it will require a different approach.

Drawing Swinging Doors

The swinging doors are of two widths: 3' for exterior and 2'-6" for interior (refer to Figure 4.1 earlier in this chapter). In general, doorway openings leading to the outside are wider than interior doors, with bathroom and closet doors usually being the narrowest. For the cabin, you'll use two sizes of swinging doors. You'll draw one door of each size and then copy these to the other openings as required. Start with the front door at the bottom of the floor plan. To get a closer view of the front door opening, use the Zoom Window command. Follow these steps:

1. Before you start drawing, check the status bar at the bottom of the screen, and make sure only the Model button at the far right is on. All other buttons should be in the off position. If any are pressed, click them once to toggle them off. If you want to experiment with the dynamic display options while you work your way through this chapter, leave the Dyn button on. If you decide you don't want it, click the same button to disable this feature.

2. Right-click the Osnap button on the status bar, and choose Settings from the shortcut menu to open the Drafting Settings dialog box. This activates the Object Snap tab (see Figure 4.30).

FIGURE 4.30: The Object Snap tab of the Drafting Settings dialog box

3. Be sure all check boxes are unchecked. If any boxes have check marks in them, click the Clear All button to uncheck them. Then, click OK to close the dialog box.

4. When the Command: prompt appears in the Command window, move the cursor to the Standard toolbar, and click the Zoom Window button. This has the same result as typing z.⌐ with the addition of prompts for the two points.

5. Pick two points to form a window around the front doorway opening, as shown on the top of Figure 4.31. The view changes, and you now have a close-up view of the opening (see the bottom of Figure 4.31). You'll draw the door in a closed position and then rotate it open.

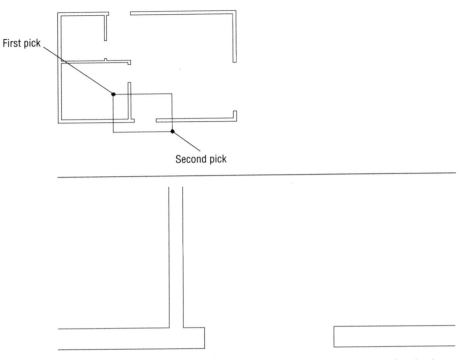

First pick

Second pick

FIGURE 4.31: Forming a zoom window at the front door opening (top) and the result (bottom)

6. To draw the door, click the Rectangle button on the Draw toolbar.

Notice the Command window prompt. Several options are in brackets, but the option Specify first corner point (before the brackets) is the default and is the one you want. You form the rectangle in the same way that you form the zoom window—by picking two points to represent opposite corners of the rectangle. In its closed position, the door will fit exactly between the jambs, with its upper corners coinciding with the upper endpoints of the jambs. To make the first corner of the rectangle coincide with the upper endpoint of the left jamb exactly, you'll use an object snap to assist you. *Object snaps* (or *osnaps*) allow you to pick specific points on objects such as endpoints, midpoints, the center of a circle, and so on. When the Osnap button is active, the cursor will snap to any of the options selected in the Object Snap tab of the Drafting Settings dialog box. These are called *running osnaps*.

You can also start the Rectangle command by choosing Draw ➢ Rectangle or by typing rec.↵ in the Command window.

7. Enter **end**↵. This activates the Endpoint osnap for one pick.

8. Move the cursor near the upper end of the left jamb line. When the cursor gets very close to a line, a colored square, called a *marker*, appears at the nearest endpoint. This shows you which endpoint in the drawing is closest to the position of the crosshair cursor at that moment.

◀

Osnap is short for *object snap*. The two terms are used interchangeably.

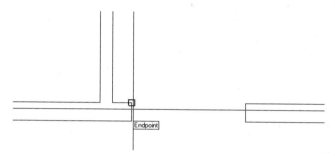

9. Move the cursor until the square is positioned on the upper end of the left jamb line, as shown, and then click that point. The first corner of the rectangle now is located at that point. Move the cursor to the right and slightly down to see the rectangle being formed (see the top of Figure 4.32). To locate the opposite corner, you'll use the relative Cartesian coordinates discussed in Chapter 2.

◀

Because of the way AutoCAD displays the crosshair cursor, both the lines and the crosshair disappear when its lines coincide with lines in the drawing. This makes it difficult to see the rectangle being formed.

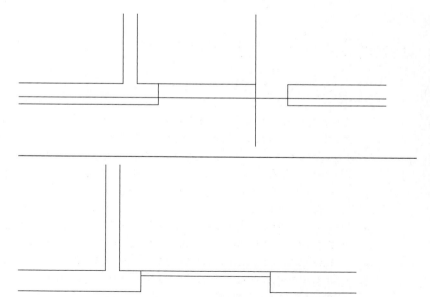

FIGURE 4.32: The rectangle after picking the first corner (left) and the completed door in a closed position (right)

10. When the Command window shows the Specify other corner point or [Area/Dimensions/Rotation]: prompt, enter @3',-1.5↵ in the command line. AutoCAD draws the rectangle across the opening, creating a door in a closed position (see the right of Figure 4.32). You now need to rotate the door around its hinge point to an opened position.

When you used the Rectangle command to draw the swinging doors, you had to use relative Cartesian coordinates because relative polar coordinates would have required you to know the diagonal distance across the plan of the door and the angle of that distance as well.

N O T E   The Rectangle command creates polylines, and you could have used it to lay out the first four wall lines of the cabin in Chapter 3. Then you could have offset all four lines in one step to complete the exterior walls, and the corners would have been automatically filleted. It would have been faster than the method we used, but a rectangle's lines are all one object. To offset them to make the interior walls, they would have to be separated into individual lines using the Explode command.

Rotating the Door

This rotation will be through an arc of 90° in the counterclockwise direction, making it a rotation of positive 90°. By default, counterclockwise rotations are positive, and clockwise rotations are negative. You'll use the Rotate command to rotate the door:

1. Click the Rotate button on the Modify toolbar, or enter ro↵. You'll see a prompt to select objects. Click the door, and then press ↵.

   You're prompted for a base point—a point around which the door will be rotated. To keep the door placed correctly, pick the hinge point for the base point. The hinge point for this opening is the upper endpoint of the left jamb line.

2. Enter end↵.

3. Move the cursor near the upper-left corner of the door. When the marker appears at that corner, click to locate the base point.

4. Check the status bar to be sure the Ortho button isn't pressed. If it is, click it to turn Ortho off. When the Ortho button is on, the cursor is forced to move in a vertical or horizontal direction. This is useful at times, but in this instance such a restriction would keep you from being able to see the door rotate.

5. Move the cursor away from the hinge point, and see how the door rotates as the cursor moves (see the top of Figure 4.33). If the door swings properly, you're reassured that you correctly selected the base point. The prompt says `Specify rotation angle or [Copy/Reference]<0.00>:`, asking you to enter an angle.

6. Enter 90↵. The door is rotated 90° to an open position (see the bottom of Figure 4.33).

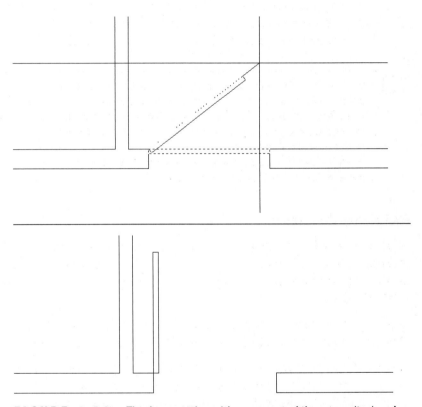

FIGURE 4.33: The door rotating with movement of the cursor (top) and the door after the 90° rotation (bottom)

To finish this door, you need to add the door's swing. You'll use the Arc command for this.

Drawing the Door Swing

The *swing* shows the path that the outer edge of a door takes when it swings from closed to fully open. Including a swing with the door in a floor plan helps resolve clearance issues. You draw the swings using the *Arc command,* in this case using the Endpoint osnap. This command has many options, most of which are based on knowing three aspects of the arc, as you'll see.

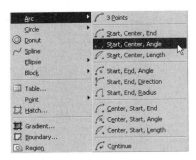

1. Choose Draw ➤ Arc to open the Arc menu. On the menu, 10 of the 11 options have combinations of three aspects that define an arc. You need to draw the arc for this door swing from the upper end of the right jamb line through a rotation of 90°. You know the start point of the arc, the center of rotation (the hinge point), and the angle through which the rotation occurs; therefore, you can use the Start, Center, Angle option on the Arc menu.

THE OPTIONS OF THE ARC COMMAND

You can specify the position and size of an arc using a combination of its components, some of which are starting point, ending point, angle, center point, and radius. The Arc command gives you 11 options, 10 of which use 3 components. With a little study of the geometric information available to you on the drawing, you can choose the option that best fits the situation.

Choosing Draw ➤ Arc on the drop-down menu displays 10 options with their 3 components; an 11th option is used to continue the last arc drawn. For that reason, this is the best way to start the Arc command when you're first learning it.

When you start the Arc command by clicking the Arc button on the Draw toolbar or by typing **a**⏎, you get an abbreviated form of the command in the Command window. You can access all 11 options of the command through this prompt, but you have to select the various components along the way.

2. From the Arc menu, choose Start, Center, Angle. The Command prompt now says _arc Specify start point of arc or [Center]:. The default option is Specify start point of arc. You can also start with the center point, but you have to enter c↵ before picking a point to be the center point.

3. Activate the Endpoint osnap (enter end↵), and pick the upper endpoint of the right jamb line.

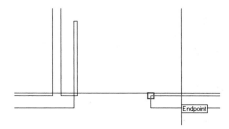

The prompt changes to Specify second point of arc or [Center/End]: _c Specify center point of arc.

This might be confusing at first. The prompt gives you three options: Second Point, Center, and End. (Center and End are in brackets.) Because you previously chose the Start, Center, Angle option, Auto-CAD automatically chooses Center for you. That is the last part of the prompt. You'll need the Endpoint osnap again, but this time you will pick it from a menu.

4. Hold the Shift key down, and then right-click the drawing area to open a context menu containing all the available osnaps. Click the Endpoint osnap, and then select the hinge point. The arc is now visible, and its endpoint follows the cursor's movement (see the top of Figure 4.34). The prompt displays a different set of options and then ends with the Included Angle option.

5. Enter 90↵. The arc is completed, and the Arc command ends (see the bottom of Figure 4.34).

W A R N I N G   In this situation, the arc must be created by selecting the jamb end first and the door end later. Arcs are made in a counterclockwise fashion, so selecting the door end first and the jamb end later would result in a 270° arc that extends behind the door and through the external wall.

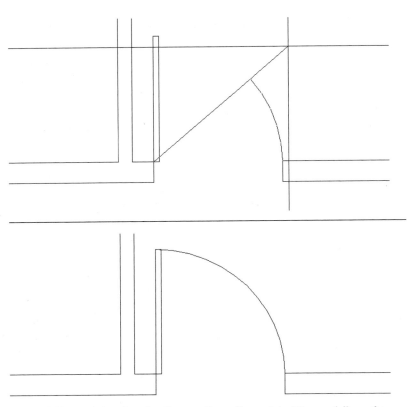

FIGURE 4.34: Drawing the arc: the ending point of the arc follows the cursor's movements (top) and the completed arc (bottom)

The front door is completed. Because the back door is the same size, you can save time by copying this door to the other opening. You'll see how to do that next.

Copying Objects

As you would expect, the Copy command makes a copy of the objects you select. You can locate this copy either by picking a point or by entering relative coordinates from the keyboard. For AutoCAD to position these copied objects, you must designate two points: a base point, which serves as a point of reference for where the copy move starts, and then a second point, which serves as the ending point for the Copy command. The copy is moved the same distance and direction from its original position that the second point is located from the first point. When you know the actual distance and direction to move the copy, the base point isn't critical because you specify the second point with relative polar or relative Cartesian coordinates. But in this situation, you don't know the exact distance or angle to move a copy of the front door to the back door opening, so you need to choose a base point for the copy carefully.

In copying this new door and its swing to the back door opening of the cabin, you must find a point somewhere on the existing door or swing that can be located precisely on a point at the back door opening. You can choose from two points: the hinge point and the start point of the door swing. Let's use the hinge point. You usually know where the hinge point of the new door belongs, so this is easier to locate than the start point of the arc.

1. Click the Copy button on the Modify toolbar, or enter co⏎. The prompt asks you to select objects to copy. Pick the door and swing, and then press ⏎. The prompt says Specify base point or [Displacement/mOde]<Displacement>:.

   Activate the Endpoint osnap, and pick the hinge point. A copy of the door and swing is attached to the crosshair cursor at the hinge point (see Figure 4.35). The prompt changes to Specify second point of displacement or <use first point of displacement>:. You need to pick where the hinge point of the copied door will appear at the back door opening. To do this, you must change the view back to what it was before you zoomed into the doorway opening.

You can also start the Copy command by choosing Modify ➤ Copy on the drop-down menu.

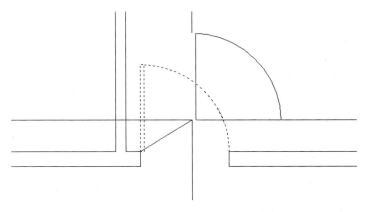

FIGURE 4.35: The copy of the door and swing attached to the crosshair cursor

The Copy command keeps running until you end it. This allows you to make multiple copies of the same object. You'll do that in Chapter 5 when you draw the stovetop.

2. From the Standard toolbar, click the Zoom Previous button to restore the full view of the cabin, or use the scroll wheel on your mouse to zoom out. Move the crosshair cursor with the door in tow to the vicinity of the back door opening. The back door should swing to the

inside and be against the wall when open, so the hinge point for this opening will be at the lower end of the left jamb line.

3. Activate the Endpoint osnap, and pick the lower end of the left jamb line on the back door opening. AutoCAD places the copy of the door and swing in the opening (see Figure 4.36); and by looking at the Command window, you can see that the Copy command is still running. Notice that a copy of the door and swing remains attached to the cursor. Press ↵ to end the command.

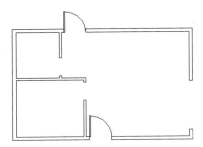

FIGURE 4.36: AutoCAD copies the door to the back door opening.

The door is oriented the wrong way, but you'll fix that next.

When you copy doors from one opening to another, often the orientation doesn't match. The best strategy is to use the hinge point as a point of reference and place the door where it needs to go, as you just did. Then, flip or rotate the door so that it sits and swings the right way. Flipping an object is known as *mirroring*.

Mirroring Objects

You have located the door in the opening, but you need to flip it so that it swings to the inside of the cabin. To do this, you'll use the *Mirror command*.

The Mirror command allows you to flip objects around an axis called the *mirror line*. You define this imaginary line by designating two points on the line. Strategically selecting the mirror line ensures the accuracy of the mirroring action, so it's critical to visualize where the proper line lies. Sometimes you'll have to draw a guideline in order to designate one or both of the endpoints. Follow these steps:

1. Click the Zoom Window icon on the Standard toolbar, and create a window around the back door and its opening.

You were able to use the Zoom command while you were in the middle of using the Copy command. You can use most of the display commands (Zoom, Pan, and so on) in this way. This is called using a command *transparently*.

2. Click the Mirror button on the Modify toolbar. Select the back door and swing, and press ↵. The prompt line changes to `Specify first point of mirror line:`.

3. Activate the Endpoint osnap, and then pick the hinge point of the door. The prompt changes to `Specify second point of mirror line:`, and you'll see the mirrored image of the door and the swing moving as you move the cursor around the drawing area. You're rotating the mirror line about the hinge point as you move the cursor. As the mirror line rotates, the orientation of the mirrored image changes (see Figure 4.37).

<table>
<tr><td>◀</td></tr>
<tr><td>You can also start the Mirror command by choosing Modify ➤ Mirror or typing mi↵.</td></tr>
</table>

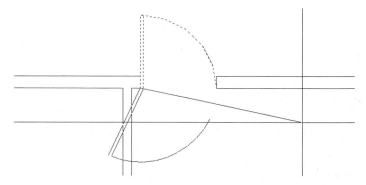

FIGURE 4.37: The mirror image changes as the mirror line rotates.

4. Activate the Endpoint osnap again, and pick the lower end of the right jamb line. The mirror image disappears, and the prompt changes to `Erase source objects? [Yes/No] <N>:`. You have two choices. You can keep both doors by pressing ↵ and accepting the default (No). Or, you can discard the original one by typing y (for Yes) in the command line and pressing ↵.

5. Enter y↵. AutoCAD displays the flipped door and deletes the original one (see Figure 4.38). The Mirror command ends.

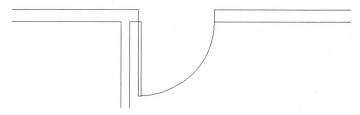

FIGURE 4.38: The mirrored door and swing

It might take some practice to become proficient at visualizing and designating the mirror line, but once you're used to it, you'll have learned how to use a powerful tool. Because many objects—including building layouts, mechanical parts, steel beams, road cross sections, and so on—have some symmetry to them, wise use of the Mirror command can save you a lot of drawing time.

You have two more swinging doors to place in the floor plan.

Finishing the Swinging Doors

You can't copy the existing doors and swings to the interior openings because the sizes don't conform, but you can use the same procedure to draw one door and swing and then copy it to the other opening.

> **N O T E**   You could have used the Stretch command to make the door narrower, but that's an advanced Modify command and won't be introduced until Chapter 11. Besides, you would have to modify the arc to a smaller radius. It's easier to draw another door and swing to a different size. In Chapter 9, I'll demonstrate a *dynamic block* that can serve as a door block for several door sizes.

1. Click the Zoom Previous button on the Standard toolbar. Then zoom in to magnify the view of the interior door openings. Be sure to make the zoom window large enough to leave some room for the new doors to be drawn (see Figure 4.39).

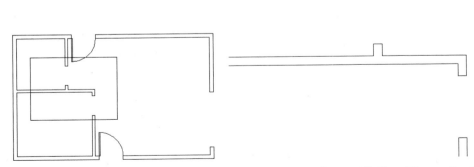

FIGURE 4.39:   A zoom window in the interior door opening area (left) and the results of the zoom (right)

You will need to use the Endpoint osnap a significant amount while creating, copying, rotating, and mirroring the doors. Rather than activating that particular osnap as needed, you will turn on Endpoint as a running osnap.

2. Right-click the Osnap button in the status bar, and then select the Settings option in the context menu.

3. In the Object Snap tab of the Drafting Settings dialog box, check the Endpoint option, and then click the OK button (see Figure 4.40).

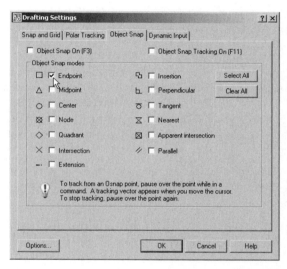

FIGURE 4.40: The Object Snap tab of the Drafting Settings dialog box

4. The osnap is active, but the running osnaps are not turned on. Click the Osnap button to turn on running osnaps. Now, whenever you are prompted to pick a point, a marker will appear over the nearest endpoint of the object the cursor is over.

5. Follow the procedure you used previously for creating the front door to draw the door and swing in the lower opening. Here is a summary of the steps:

   a. Use the Rectangle command and the Endpoint osnap to draw the door from the hinge point to the point @-2'6,-1.5.

► The Start, Center, Angle option and a few other options of the Arc command require that you choose the start point for the arc in such a way that the arc is drawn in a counterclockwise direction. If you progress in a clockwise direction, use a negative number for the angle.

   b. Use the Start, Center, Angle option of the Arc command to draw the door swing, starting at the lower-left corner of the door and using the Endpoint osnap for the two picks and 90° for the angle.

6. Use the Copy command to copy this door and swing to the other interior opening. The base point is the hinge point, and the second point is the left end of the lower jamb line in the upper opening. You should see how the running Endpoint osnap helps you quickly and accurately make both picks.

7. Use the Mirror command to flip up this copy of the door and swing. The mirror line is different from the one used for the back door. The geometrical arrangement at the back opening required that the door and its swing be flipped across the opening. For this one, the door and its swing must flip in a direction parallel to the opening. For this opening, the mirror line is the lower jamb line itself, so pick each end of this line (using the Endpoint osnap) to establish the mirror line.

8. Click the Zoom Previous button or enter z↵ p↵ to see the four swinging doors in place (see Figure 4.41).

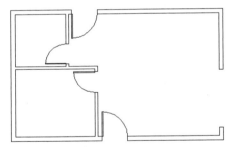

FIGURE 4.41: The four swinging doors in place

    The last door to draw is the sliding-glass door. This kind of door requires an entirely different strategy, but you'll use commands familiar to you by now.

Drawing a Sliding Glass Door

Sliding-glass doors are usually drawn to show their glass panels within the door frames.

To draw the sliding door, you'll apply the Line, Offset, and Trim commands to the 7' opening you made earlier. It's a complicated exercise, but it will teach you a lot about the power of using these three commands in combination:

1. Zoom closely around the 7' opening. In making the zoom window, pick one point just above and to the left of the upper doorjamb and another below and to the right of the lower jamb. This will make the opening as large as possible while including everything you'll need in the view (see Figure 4.42).

FIGURE 4.42: The view when zoomed in as closely as possible to the 7' opening

2. You'll be using several osnaps for this procedure, so it will be convenient to have the Osnap toolbar available. Here's how:

    a. Right-click any button on any of the toolbars on your screen to open the Toolbar menu.

    b. Click Object Snap. The Toolbar menu closes, and the Object Snap toolbar appears in the drawing area. It's in floating mode.

    c. Put the cursor on the colored title bar of the Object Snap toolbar, and, holding down the left mouse button, drag the toolbar to the right side of the drawing area. Dock it there by releasing the mouse button (see Figure 4.43). Now you can easily select all object snaps as needed.

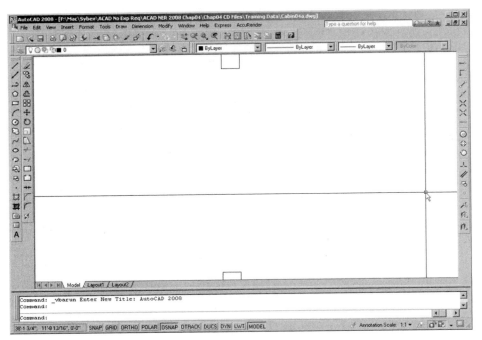

FIGURE 4.43: The Object Snap toolbar docked to the right of the drawing area

3. Offset each jamb line 2" into the doorway opening (see Figure 4.44).

FIGURE 4.44: Jamb lines offset 2" into the doorway opening

4. Enter l↵ to start the Line command. Click the Midpoint Osnap button on the Object Snap toolbar, and then place the cursor near the midpoint of the upper doorjamb line. Notice that the marker, now a triangle, appears when your cursor is in the vicinity of the midpoint. A symbol with a distinctive shape is associated with each osnap. When the triangle appears at the midpoint of the jamb line, click.

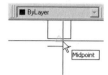

5. Move the cursor over the bottom jamb line, and you'll notice the Endpoint markers appear. The Endpoint running osnap is still active, but typing the first three letters of an osnap or clicking an osnap button from the Object Snap toolbar overrides it. Click the Midpoint Osnap button again, move the cursor to the bottom jamb line, and when the triangle appears at that midpoint, click again. Press ↵ to end the Line command.

6. Start the Offset command, and enter 1.5↵ to set the offset distance. Pick the newly drawn line, and then pick a point anywhere to the right side. Then, while the Offset command is still running, pick the original line again, and pick another point in a blank area somewhere to the left side of the doorway opening (see Figure 4.45). Press ↵ to end the Offset command.

FIGURE 4.45: The offset vertical line between the jambs

7. In the status bar, click Ortho to turn it on. Enter l↵ to start the Line command. Click the Midpoint Osnap button, and then move the cursor near the midpoint of the left vertical line. When the marker appears at the midpoint, click to set the endpoint of the line. Hold the cursor out directly to the right of the point you just selected to draw a horizontal line through the three vertical lines. When the cursor is about 2' to the right of the three vertical lines, pick a point to set the endpoint of this guideline. Press ↵ to end the Line command (see Figure 4.46). Click Ortho off.

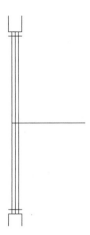

FIGURE 4.46: The horizontal guideline drawn through vertical lines

8. Enter o↵ to start the Offset command. Enter 1↵ to set the offset distance. Select this new line, and then pick a point in a blank area anywhere above the line. Pick the first horizontal line again, and then pick anywhere below it. The new line has been offset 1" above and below itself (see Figure 4.47). Now you have placed all the lines necessary to create the sliding-glass door frames in the opening. You still need to trim back some of these lines and erase others. Press ↵ to end the Offset command.

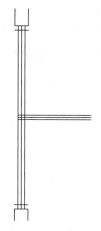

FIGURE 4.47: The offset horizontal guideline

9. Start the Trim command by typing **tr**↵. When you're prompted to select cutting edges, pick the two horizontal lines that you just created with the Offset command. Then, press ↵.

10. Trim the two outside vertical lines by selecting them, as shown on the left of Figure 4.48. The result appears on the right of Figure 4.48.

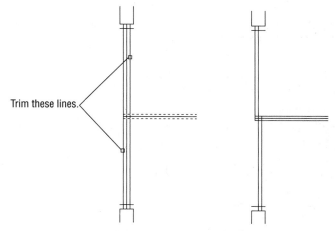

Trim these lines.

FIGURE 4.48: Picking the vertical lines to trim (left) and the result (right)

11. Press ↵ twice to stop and restart the Trim command. When you're prompted to select cutting edges, use a special window called a *crossing window* to select all the lines visible in the drawing. A crossing window selects everything within the window or crossing it. See the sidebar titled "Understanding Selection Windows" for additional information about this feature. Here's how to do it:

a. Pick a point above and to the right of the opening.

b. Move the cursor to a point below and to the left of the opening, forming a semitransparent colored window with dashed boundary lines (see Figure 4.49).

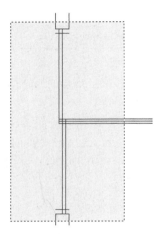

FIGURE 4.49: The crossing window for selecting cutting edges

c. Pick that point. This selects everything inside the rectangle or crossing an edge of it.

d. Press ↵.

12. To trim the lines, pick them at the points noted on the left of Figure 4.50. When you finish trimming, the opening should look like the right of Figure 4.50. Be sure to press ↵ to end the Trim command.

N O T E   If all the lines don't trim the way you expect them to, you might have to change the setting for the Edgemode system variable. Cancel the trim operation, and undo any trims you've made to the sliding-glass door. Enter **edgemode↵**, and then enter **0↵**. Now, start the Trim command, and continue trimming.

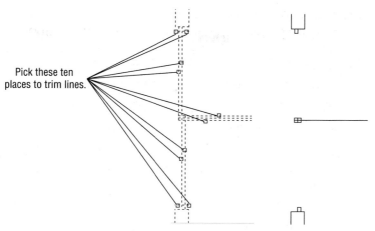

Pick these ten places to trim lines.

FIGURE 4.50: Lines to trim (left) and the result (right)

13. Start the Erase command, and erase the remaining horizontal guideline.

To finish the sliding glass doors, you need to draw two lines to represent the glass panes for each door panel. Each pane of glass is centered inside its frame, so the line representing the pane will run between the midpoints of the inside edge of each frame section.

14. Enter l↵ to start the Line command, and click the Midpoint Osnap button on the Object Snap toolbar.

15. For each of the two sliding door frames, put the cursor near the midpoint of the inside line of the frame section nearest the jamb. When the colored triangle appears there, click.

Click the Perpendicular Osnap button on the Object Snap toolbar, and move the cursor to the other frame section of that door panel. When you get near the horizontal line that represents both the inside edge of one frame section and the back edge of the frame section next to it, the colored Perpendicular osnap marker will appear on that line. When it does, select that point.

16. Press ↵ to end the Line command.

17. Press ↵ to restart the Line command, and repeat the procedure described in step 14 for the other door panel, being sure to start the line at the frame section nearest the other jamb. The finished opening should look like the left of Figure 4.51.

18. Use the Zoom Previous button to see the full floor plan with all doors (see the image on the right side of Figure 4.51).

19. Save this drawing as Cabin04c.dwg.

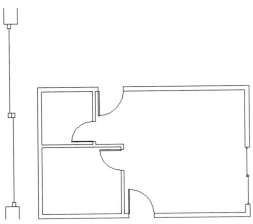

FIGURE 4.51: The finished sliding glass doors (left) and the floor plan with all doors finished (right)

UNDERSTANDING SELECTION WINDOWS

In addition to selecting objects using a direct pick, you can also select objects using a rectangular selection window. To use a selection window at any Select objects prompt, pick a point at a blank spot in the drawing area to define one corner of the window and then a second point to define the opposite corner.

Selection windows come in two styles: *windows* and *crossing windows*. When you use a window selection, all objects must be entirely inside the boundary of the window to be selected. When you use a crossing window, all objects entirely within the boundary as well as any objects that cross the boundary are selected. AutoCAD distinguishes the two types of selection windows visually. Window selection areas are transparent blue and have solid boundary lines, and crossing windows are transparent green with dashed boundary lines.

By default, AutoCAD uses window selections when the boundary is created from left to right, and AutoCAD uses crossing selections when the boundary is created from right to left. You can override the direction default, or create a selection window even when the mouse is clicked when the cursor is over an object, by typing **w**↵ or **c**↵ at the Select objects prompt.

You can even use selection windows to select objects to be trimmed or extended. For instance, visualize a horizontal line with dozens of vertical lines crossing it and each of those lines must be trimmed back to the horizontal line. After designating the horizontal line as the cutting edge, use a crossing selection window to select all the vertical lines on the trim side. All the lines are trimmed with two picks instead of many.

To change settings that control the appearance of the crossing and regular selection windows, choose Tools ➤ Options, and click the Selection tab. In the Selection Preview area, click the Visual Effect Settings button. In the Visual Effect Settings dialog box, in the Area Selection Effect area, are settings for controlling whether the selection windows have color in them, which color will be in each window, and the percentage of transparency of the colors. Experiment with different settings. Click OK twice to return to your drawing, and test the windows to see how they look. This completes the doors for the floor plan. The focus here has been on walls and doors and the strategies for drawing them. As a result, you now have a basic floor plan for the cabin, and you'll continue to develop this plan in the next chapter.

The overall drawing strategy emphasized in this chapter uses objects already in the drawing to create new ones. You started with four lines that constituted the outside wall lines. By offsetting, filleting, extending, and trimming, you drew all the walls and openings without drawing any new lines. For the swinging doors, you made two rectangles and two arcs. Then by copying, rotating, and mirroring, you formed the other two swinging doors. For the sliding-glass door, you drew two new lines; then, you used Offset, Trim, and Erase to finish the door. So, you used four lines and created six new objects to complete the walls and doors. This is a good start in learning to use AutoCAD wisely.

Throughout this chapter, I have indicated several instances when you can press the spacebar instead of the ↵ key. This can be handy if you keep one hand resting on the keyboard while the other hand controls the mouse. For brevity, I'll continue to instruct you to use ↵ and not mention the spacebar; but as you get better at drawing in AutoCAD, you might find the spacebar a useful substitute for ↵ in many cases. At other times—when you're using the Erase tool, for example—right-clicking acts as a ↵ rather than opening a context menu (which will often have Enter as an option). You'll determine your preference. You can substitute the spacebar for ↵ when handling the following tasks:

- ▶ Restarting the previous command

- ▶ Ending a command

- ▶ Moving from one step in a command to the next step

- ▶ Entering a new offset distance or accepting the current offset distance

- ▶ Entering relative or absolute coordinates

- ▶ Entering an angle of rotation

By working with the tools and strategies in this chapter, you now should have an idea of an approach to drawing many objects. In the next chapter, you'll continue in the same vein, learning a few new commands and strategies as you add steps, a balcony, a kitchen, and a bathroom to the floor plan.

If You Would Like More Practice...

If you would like to practice the skills you have learned so far, the following are some extra exercises.

Creating an Alternate Sliding-Glass Door

Here is a simplified version of the sliding-glass door of the cabin. It doesn't include any representation of the panes of glass and their frames.

To draw it, use a technique similar to the one described in the previous section. Copy the jambs for the 7' opening to the right, and draw this door between them.

Creating an Addition to the Cabin

This addition is connected to the cabin by a sidewalk and consists of a remodeled two-car garage in which one car slot has been converted into a storage area and an office (see Figure 4.52). Use the same commands and strategies you have been using up to now to draw this layout adjacent to the cabin. Save this exercise as Cabin04c-addon.dwg.

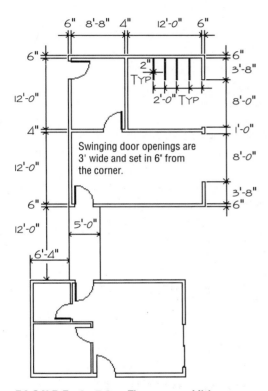

FIGURE 4.52: The garage addition

Refer to this chapter and the preceding one for specific commands. Here is the general procedure:

1. Draw the two lines that represent the walkway between the two buildings.

2. Draw the outside exterior wall line.

3. Use Offset, Fillet, and Trim to create the rest of the walls and wall lines.

4. Use Offset, Extend, and Trim to create the openings.

   5. Use Rectangle and Arc to create a swinging door.

   6. Use Copy, Rotate, and Mirror to put in the rest of the doors.

   7. Use Offset, Line, and Copy to draw the storage partitions.

Drawing Three Views of a Block

Use the tools you have learned in the past few chapters to draw the top, right side, and front views of the block shown in Figure 4.53.

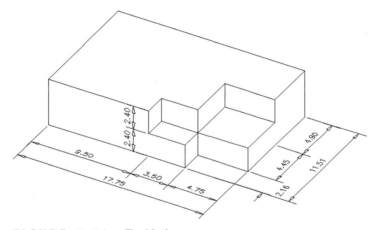

F I G U R E 4 . 5 3 : The block

Figure 4.54 gives you a graphic representation of the 12 steps necessary to complete the exercise.

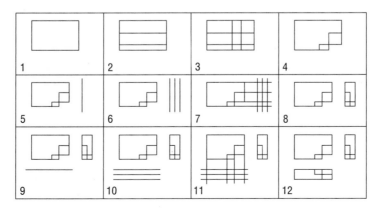

F I G U R E 4 . 5 4 : The 12 steps for creating the block

Here are the 12 steps in summary that correspond to the 12 drawings. Start with the top view:

1. Start a new drawing. Leave all settings at the defaults. Use relative polar or relative Cartesian coordinates and the Line command to draw a rectangle 17.75 wide and 11.51 high. Zoom out if necessary.

2. Offset the bottom horizontal line up 2.16 and the new line up 4.45.

3. Offset the right vertical line 4.75 to the left and the new line 3.50 to the left.

4. Use the Trim command to trim back lines and complete the view.

   Next, do the right side view.

5. Draw a vertical line to the right of the top view. Make it longer than the top view is deep.

6. Offset the vertical line 2.4 to the right, and then offset the new line 2.4 to the right also.

7. Use the Endpoint osnap to draw lines from the corner points of the top view across the three vertical lines.

8. Trim the lines back to complete the side view.

   Finally, draw the front view.

9. Draw a horizontal line below the top view. Make it longer than the top view is wide.

10. Offset this line 2.4 down, and then offset the new line 2.4 down.

11. Use the Endpoint osnap to draw lines from the corner points of the top view, down across the three horizontal lines.

12. Trim the lines back to complete the view.

This ends the exercise. You can rotate and move each view relative to the other views in several ways. We'll look at those commands later in the book and then draw more views in Chapter 8.

Are You Experienced?

Now you can...

- ☑ create polylines
- ☑ offset exterior walls to make interior walls
- ☑ zoom in on an area with the Zoom Window command and zoom back out with the Zoom Previous command
- ☑ use the Rectangle and Arc commands to make a door
- ☑ use the Endpoint, Midpoint, and Perpendicular object snap modes
- ☑ use the Crossing Window selection tool
- ☑ use the Copy and Mirror commands to place an existing door and swing in another opening
- ☑ use the Offset and Trim commands to make a sliding-glass door

CHAPTER 5

Gaining Drawing Strategies: Part 2

▶ Using object snaps

▶ Using polar tracking

▶ Zooming and panning with the Realtime commands

▶ Copying and moving objects

▶ Using direct entry of distances

▶ Creating circles and ellipses

The preceding chapter emphasized using existing geometry (or objects) in a drawing to create new geometry. In this chapter, you'll look at new tools for forming an efficient drawing strategy. Before getting back to the cabin, I'll give you a brief overview of the tools available for starting and running commands.

Developing a drawing strategy begins with determining the best way to start or determining when to start a command. AutoCAD provides several ways to start most of the commands you'll be using. You have seen that you can find the Offset, Fillet, Trim, and Extend commands on either the Modify toolbar or the Modify menu. You can also start them by typing the first letter or two of the command and then pressing ↵.

> **T I P**   Here's a quick recap. To start the Offset command, enter o↵. To start the Fillet command, enter f↵. To start the Trim command, enter tr↵, and to start the Extend command, enter ex↵. You can also start almost all AutoCAD commands by entering the full name of the command; for example, to start the Extend command, enter extend↵. And don't forget that you can access menus and menu items by pressing the Alt key and then the hot key—the letter that becomes underlined in the menu or menu item name when you press the Alt key. For example, to open the Modify menu, press Alt+M.

You'll determine which method to use, to an extent, by what you're doing at the time as well as by your command of the keyboard. When using the abbreviations, keyboard entry is generally the fastest method; but if your hand is already on the mouse and the Modify toolbar is docked on the screen, clicking buttons on the toolbar might be faster. The menus are slower to use because they require more selections to get to a command, but they also contain more commands and command options than the toolbars.

Remember that if you have just ended a command, you can restart that command by pressing ↵, by pressing the spacebar, or by right-clicking. When you right-click, a *shortcut* menu appears near the cursor. The top item on this menu is Repeat *Command*, where *Command* is the last command used. For example, if you just finished using the Erase command and you right-click, the top item of the shortcut menu is Repeat Erase.

I'll introduce the other items on this shortcut menu throughout the rest of the book. The shortcut menu is also called a *context* menu because the items on it depend on the following:

- ▶ Whether a command is running
- ▶ Which command you're using
- ▶ Where you are in a command

In this chapter, I'll introduce you to several new commands and, through the step-by-step instructions, show some alternate methods for accomplishing tasks similar to those you have previously completed. You'll add front and back steps, thresholds, a balcony, and kitchen and bath fixtures to the cabin floor plan (see Figure 5.1). For each of these tasks, the focus will be on noticing which objects and geometry are already in the drawing that can make your job easier and on tools to help you accomplish the tasks more quickly and efficiently. As you work your way through the chapter, try activating the Dyn button on the status bar and working with the dynamic display information shown in the drawing area.

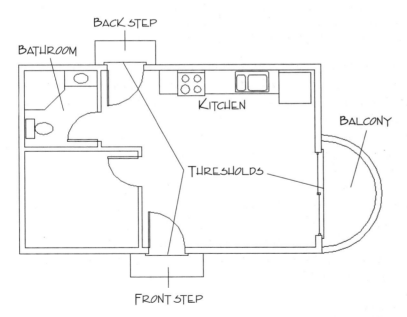

F I G U R E   5 . 1 : The cabin with front and back steps, thresholds, balcony, kitchen, and bathroom

Drawing the Steps and Thresholds

You draw the steps and thresholds each with three simple lines. The trick is to see which part of the drawing you can effectively use to generate and position those lines. Use a width of 2' for the front and back steps, and use a length of 6' for the front step and 5' for the back step. The three thresholds extend 2" beyond the outside wall line and run 3" past either jamb line (see Figure 5.2). These are simple shapes to draw, but you'll learn a few new techniques as you create them.

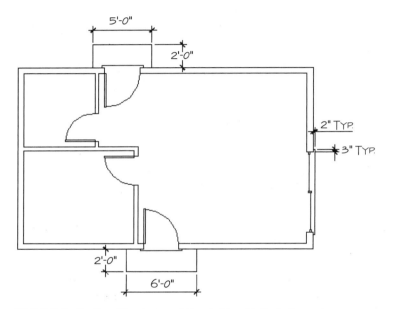

FIGURE 5.2: The steps and thresholds with their dimensions

Drawing the Front Step

As you can see in Figure 5.2, the front step is 2' wide and 6' long. Because you know the width of the doorway opening, you can determine how far past the opening the step extends, assuming it to be symmetrical. You can draw a line from the endpoint of one of the jamb lines down 2' and then offset the proper distance left and right to create the sides of the step. Here's how you do it:

    1. With AutoCAD running, open your cabin drawing (last saved as Cabin04c.dwg), and use the Zoom command options to achieve a view similar to Figure 5.3.

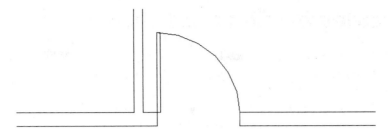

FIGURE 5.3: Zoomed in to the front opening

2. Check to be sure all buttons on the status bar except Model are in their off positions. Start the Line command, activate the Endpoint osnap, and pick a point at the lower end of the left jamb line.

WAYS TO USE THE OBJECT SNAP TOOLS

You can access the object snap tools in several ways:

▶ The Object Snap toolbar might be docked in the drawing area. If not, you can display and dock it.

▶ The Object Snap context menu also contains access to the object snaps. To open this menu, hold down the Shift key or Ctrl key, and right-click.

▶ If you're using a mouse with a scroll wheel or a three-button mouse, you might be able to open the Object Snap menu by clicking on the wheel or the middle mouse button. If this doesn't work, set the mbuttonpan variable to zero. (Enter **mbuttonpan↵ 0↵**.)

▶ In most cases, you can enter the first three letters of any osnap to activate it, as in **end↵** for Endpoint.

3. Right-click the Polar button on the status bar at the bottom of the screen, and then choose Settings from the shortcut menu to open the Drafting Settings dialog box. By default, the Polar Tracking tab is active (see Figure 5.4).

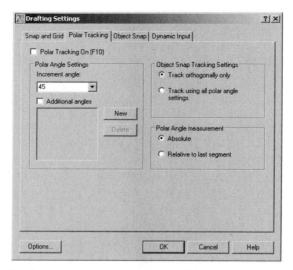

F I G U R E 5 . 4 :   The Polar Tracking tab of the Drafting Settings dialog box

4. In the Polar Angle Settings area, check whether Increment Angle is set to 90.00. If it's not, open the drop-down list, and select 90.00. On the right side, be sure that Absolute is selected in the Polar Angle Measurement area. Finally, in the upper-left corner, click the Polar Tracking On check box. This has the same effect as clicking the Polar button in the status bar. Click OK.

5. Hold the crosshair cursor so that it is below the first point picked. Don't pick a point yet (see Figure 5.5). A dashed line called a *temporary alignment path* is displayed along with a tooltip that identifies the alignment path as a polar path; a relative polar coordinate confirms the angle to be 270°. As you move the cursor from left to right, notice that the alignment path and tooltip disappear when you get too far from a point directly below the first point of the line, and they reappear as you get back close to vertical. If you have dynamic display activated, the tooltip is replaced with an abbreviated command prompt when the cursor varies from the vertical path.

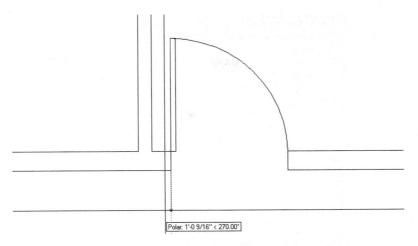

Polar: 1'-0 9/16'' < 270.00"

FIGURE 5.5: The Line command running with polar tracking on

6. While the alignment path and tooltip are visible, create the line using the direct entry method by typing **2'**↵. A vertical line is drawn that is 2 feet long. Because you want the line to be vertical, polar tracking assisted you by producing an alignment path in the vertical direction.

7. Press ↵ to end the Line command. Enter **o**↵ to start the Offset command. Enter **1'6**↵ for an offset distance, and offset this line to the left.

8. Press ↵ twice to stop and restart Offset. Enter **6'**↵, and offset this new line to the right (see Figure 5.6). Press ↵ to end the Offset command.

When Polar Tracking mode is on, temporary alignment paths assist you in drawing lines at angles that are multiples of the increment angle—in this case, 90°.

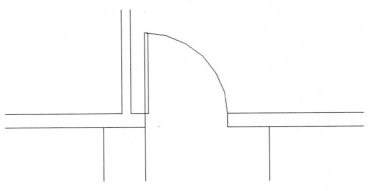

FIGURE 5.6: The sides of the front step after offsetting

9. Erase the original line, and then draw a line from the lower endpoints of these two new lines to represent the front edge of the step. Use the Endpoint osnap for each point picked. Press ↵ to end the Line command. Your drawing should look like Figure 5.7.

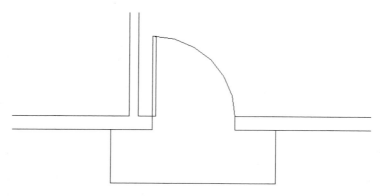

FIGURE 5.7: The completed front step

10. Use Zoom Previous to view the entire floor plan.

The strategy here was to recognize that you can use a line drawn from the jamb line to determine the location of the sides of the step. Using polar tracking to draw is a quick way to enter distances when the lines are at angles that are multiples of the polar tracking increment angle that you set. For the back step, you'll build on this by adding a temporary tracking point to your bag of tools.

Drawing the Back Step

You can apply the method used to draw the front step to the back step as well. The situation is identical; in fact, you'll be working with the same geometry in the drawing and will accomplish the same task. This time, however, you'll use a temporary tracking point to locate the side of the step. This will eliminate the need to use a construction line. Remember that the step in the back is 5' wide.

1. Zoom in to the back step area. Start the Line command, and click the Temporary Tracking Point button on the Object Snap toolbar.

The prompt in the Command window reads _line Specify first
point: _tt Specify temporary OTRACK point:. This is actually
three prompts grouped together:

► _line signifies the start of the Line command.

► Specify first point is the first prompt for the Line command.

► _tt Specify temporary OTRACK point signifies that the Temporary Tracking Point option has been selected.

In this case, because the step is 5' long, you want to begin the side of
the step 1' to the left of the 3'-wide doorway opening. So, the temporary tracking point that you need is the starting point from which
you'll measure the 1' distance—in this case, it is the upper end of the
left jamb line.

2. Select the Endpoint osnap, and pick the upper end of the left jamb line.
A small cross appears at the point you just picked, and the prompt now
has _endp of Specify first point: added to it. This is two more
prompts grouped together:

► _endp signifies that the Endpoint osnap was selected.

► Specify first point is the second prompt for the Temporary
Tracking Point option. AutoCAD has recorded the temporary
tracking point and waits for you to specify the first point of the
line that is to be the left side of the back step. You'll do this by
using polar tracking and direct entry, telling AutoCAD how far
and in what direction from the temporary tracking point you
want to begin the line—in this case, it's 1' to the left.

3. Hold the cursor to the left of the temporary tracking point. When
the temporary alignment path appears with the tooltip, as shown in
Figure 5.8, enter 12↵. A line begins 1' to the left of the opening on
the outside wall line. Hold the crosshair cursor directly above the
beginning of the line, and when you see the vertical alignment path
with the tooltip, enter 2'↵. The side of the step is drawn using the
direct entry technique with polar tracking. The Line command is
still running.

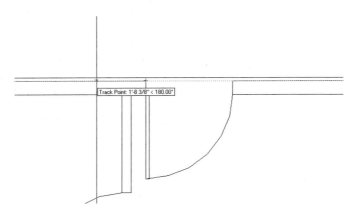

FIGURE 5.8: Using a temporary tracking point with polar tracking and direct entry

4. Hold the crosshair cursor directly to the right from the last point; when you see the alignment path and tooltip, enter 5'↵. AutoCAD draws the front edge of the step. You used direct entry with polar tracking again, and you didn't have to enter either the relative polar or the Cartesian coordinates.

5. Select Perpendicular Osnap from the Object Snap toolbar, and move the cursor to the outside wall line (see Figure 5.9). When the perpendicular icon appears on the wall line, click. AutoCAD draws the right edge of the step, and the back step is complete. Press ↵ to end the Line command.

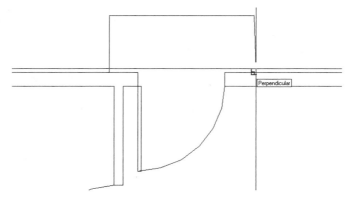

FIGURE 5.9: Completing the back step with the Perpendicular osnap

6. Use Zoom Previous to view the completed back step with the whole floor plan.

Temporary tracking is a handy tool for AutoCAD users. You'll use it a few more times in this book. When you combine it with the technique of using polar tracking to help enter distances, as you have for the back step, you'll be surprised at how quickly you can lay out orthogonal walls in a floor plan. The polar tracking technique, used by itself, powerfully facilitates drawing the footprint of a building. When you work through the next section, you'll get to practice using the temporary tracking tool once more.

I'm sure this seems complicated, but you'll get a chance to try the technique three more times, because you now have to do the thresholds for the three external openings.

Drawing the Thresholds

Thresholds generally are used on doorway openings when the level changes from one side of the opening to the other or to prevent rain and dust from entering the structure. This usually occurs at entrances that open from or to the outside. Although quite different in shape, each threshold for the cabin has the same geometry as the steps. The lip of each threshold is offset 2" from the outside wall, and each edge runs 3" past the doorjamb. (See Figure 5.2 earlier in this chapter.) You'll use a temporary tracking point with polar tracking and direct entry to draw the three thresholds for the cabin.

Here are the steps to draw a threshold for one of the openings. I'll use the front door entry for the illustrations.

1. Zoom in to the opening and its immediate surroundings.

2. Start the Line command, and then click the Temporary Tracking Point button and the Endpoint Osnap button on the Osnap toolbar. If you prefer to use the keyboard, enter the shortcut **tt** for the Temporary Tracking Point osnap.

3. Place the cursor near the outside endpoint of one of the jamb lines, and then move the cursor along the wall line away from the opening until the polar alignment path and Track Point tooltip appear (see the left of Figure 5.10).

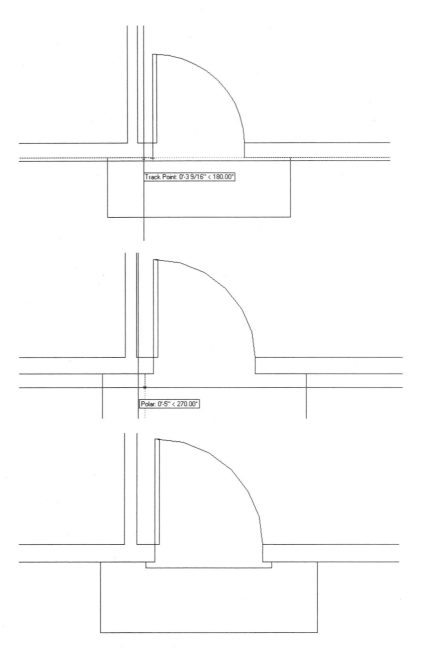

FIGURE 5.10: The tracking path and Track Point tooltip (top), the first threshold line started (middle), and the completed threshold (bottom)

4. Enter the distance that the threshold extends past the jamb. (It's 3".) This begins the first line.

5. Move the crosshair away from the wall line in a horizontal or vertical direction (depending on which opening you're drawing) until the polar alignment path and tooltip appear (see the middle of Figure 5.10).

6. Enter the overhang distance of the threshold. (It's 2".)

7. Move the crosshair in a direction perpendicular to the last segment drawn until the polar alignment line and tooltip appear.

8. Enter the length of the threshold. (It's the length of the opening plus 6".)

9. Invoke the perpendicular osnap, and hold the crosshair back on the wall line; then click. Press ↵ to end the Line command (see the right of Figure 5.10).

10. Use Zoom Previous to view the finished thresholds with the rest of the drawing.

11. Repeat the procedure on the remaining external doors. You can click the Osnap button in the status bar to turn on the running Endpoint osnap if you prefer this over clicking the button every time.

USING DIRECT ENTRY OF DISTANCES

Direct entry is a method used to specify distances for line segments or most other procedures that require distance and direction specifications. You position the crosshair in such a way that the direction from the last point picked indicates the direction for the next line segment. You then enter the distance. You don't need to use either the relative polar or the relative Cartesian coordinates. You primarily use this technique with polar tracking to draw line segments that are oriented at a preset angle—in this case, 90°, 180°, 270°, and 0°. It saves time because you have less data to enter. You can also use direct entry with the Copy and Move commands to specify the displacement of selected objects being moved or copied.

The tracking features in AutoCAD are powerful tools for drawing that you can use in several ways. So far, you have used polar tracking and the Temporary Tracking Point osnap, and you'll use them again along with other tracking features later in this chapter.

Drawing the Balcony: Drawing Circles

A glance back at Figure 5.1 will tell you that the balcony consists of two semicircles. You can draw these in several ways, but here you'll form them from a circle. Often, the easiest way to draw an arc is to draw a circle that contains the arc segment and then trim the circle back:

1. Choose Draw ➤ Circle, and look at the Circle menu for a moment.

   You have six options for constructing a circle. The first two require you to specify a point as the center of the circle and to enter a radius or a diameter. You use the next two when you know two or three points that the circle must intersect. And finally, the last two options use tangents and a radius or just tangents to form a circle.

2. The balcony has a radius of 5', so choose the Center, Radius option. The Command window prompts you to specify a point as the center of the circle. The actual center for the balcony will be 5' above the lower-right corner of the outside wall line, but for this exercise, you'll draw the circle in the living room and move it into position later.

3. Pick a point in the middle of the largest room of the cabin. The center is now established; as you move the cursor, the circle changes size and becomes attached to the crosshair cursor (see Figure 5.11). You could pick a point to establish the radius, but in this case, you know exactly what you want the radius to be.

N O T E   All the Circle creation methods are available at the Command prompt as well.

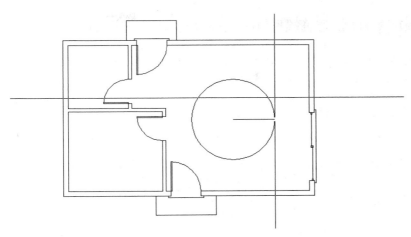

FIGURE 5.11: The circle attached to the crosshair cursor

4. Enter 5'⏎. AutoCAD draws the circle, and the command ends.

5. Click the Move button on the Modify toolbar, or enter m⏎. The cursor changes to a pickbox. Select the circle, and press ⏎.

6. On the Object Snap toolbar or fly-out menu, click the Quadrant button. Quadrant snaps to any of the four points of a circle, arc, or ellipse that project vertically or horizontally from the center point. Select the circle somewhere near its bottom extremity (see the top of Figure 5.12). A dashed image of the circle is attached to the crosshair cursor. Turn off polar tracking by clicking the Polar button on the status bar.

T I P   If an ellipse is rotated, the quadrant points will be located at the two points where the curves are sharpest and the two points where the curves are flattest. The quadrant snaps will always remain at the four points of a circle or arc that project vertically or horizontally from the center point regardless of the object's orientation.

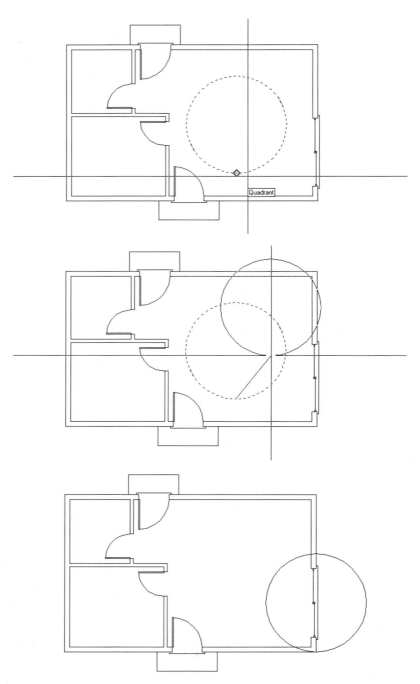

FIGURE 5.12: Selecting the base point with the Quadrant osnap (top), the circle attached to the crosshair cursor at its lowest point (middle), and the circle positioned for the balcony (bottom)

7. Move the crosshair cursor around to see that the lowest point on the circle is attached at the crosshair (see the middle of Figure 5.12). You need to place this point at the lower-right corner of the outside wall line.

8. Select the Endpoint osnap, and then pick the lower-right corner of the cabin. The circle is positioned correctly for the balcony (see the bottom of Figure 5.12). Now you can use the existing wall lines to trim the circle into a semicircle.

9. Zoom in to the area of the balcony, and start the Trim command.

10. Select the two outside wall lines on the far right as the cutting edges, as shown in Figure 5.13, and then right-click or press ↵.

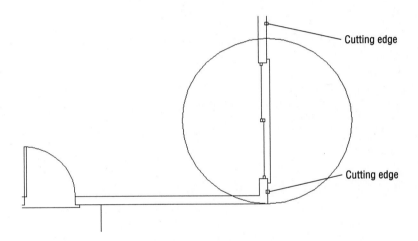

Cutting edge

Cutting edge

FIGURE 5.13: Selecting wall lines to be cutting edges

11. Select the portion of the circle that is inside the cabin. The circle is trimmed into a semicircle. Press ↵ to end the Trim command.

12. Start the Offset command, set the distance for 6", and offset the semicircle to the inside. Press ↵ to end the Offset command. The balcony is complete.

13. Use Zoom Previous to view the floor plan with the completed balcony. Save the drawing as Cabin05a.dwg (see Figure 5.14).

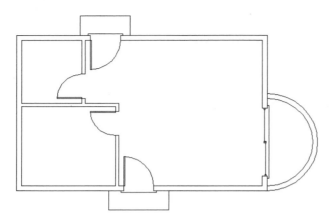

F I G U R E   5 . 1 4 :   The floor plan with the balcony completed

As mentioned at the beginning of this section, you can use several techniques to draw the balcony. The one you used gave you the opportunity to use the Move command and the Quadrant osnap, and it let you see how using the lowest quadrant snap point on the circle is an easy way to locate the balcony on the building. You didn't need to enter any relative coordinates.

In the next section, you'll continue to develop drawing strategies as you focus on laying out a counter and fixtures to complete the kitchen.

Laying Out the Kitchen

The kitchen for the cabin will have a stove, a refrigerator, and a counter with a sink (see Figure 5.15). The refrigerator is set 2" from the back wall. Approaching this drawing task, your goal is to think about the easiest and fastest way to complete it. The first step in deciding on an efficient approach is to ascertain what information you have about the various parts and what geometry in the drawing will be able to assist you. Figure 5.15 gives you the basic dimensions, and you'll get more detailed information about the sink and stove as you progress through the exercise.

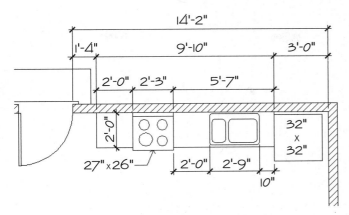

FIGURE 5.15: The general layout of the kitchen

Drawing the Counter

Although the counter is in two pieces, you'll draw it as one piece and then cut out a section for the stove. Try two ways to draw the counter to see which method is more efficient.

Using Polar Tracking and Direct Entry with a Temporary Tracking Point

1. Use a zoom window to zoom your view so it is about the same magnification as Figure 5.16. On the status bar, click the Polar button to turn polar tracking back on if it isn't already on. The Model and Polar buttons should be in their on positions. The rest of the buttons should be off, unless you prefer to have the Dyn button on to dynamically display drawing input information in the drawing area or the running osnaps.

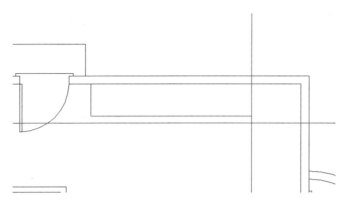

FIGURE 5.16: Drawing the counter using the direct entry technique

2. Start the Line command. Activate the Temporary Tracking Point osnap and then the Endpoint osnap. Next, place the cursor near the lower end of the right rear doorjamb line. A small cross appears on the point you choose.

3. Hold the crosshair cursor directly to the right of that point. When the Track Point tooltip and the dotted-line tracking path appear, enter 1'4.⏎. The line for the left side of the counter begins 16" from the jamb.

4. Hold the crosshair cursor directly below the first point of the line, and enter 2'.⏎. Hold the crosshair cursor to the right, and enter 9'10.⏎ (see Figure 5.16, shown earlier). Select the Perpendicular osnap, and pick the inside wall line again. Press ⏎ to end the Line command. The counter is done.

Using Offset and Fillet

To do the same thing using the Offset command, you'll need to undo the effects of the preceding command. Because all lines were drawn in one cycle of the Line command, one use of the U command will undo the entire counter:

1. Click the Undo button on the Standard toolbar, or enter u.⏎. The counter you just drew should disappear. If you ended the Line command while drawing the counter and had to restart it before you finished, you might have to click the Undo button more than once. If you undo too much, click the Redo button, which is just to the right of the Undo button.

Now draw the counter again, this time using the Offset and Fillet commands.

2. Offset the right inside wall line 3' to the left. Then, offset this new line 9'-10" to the left. Finally, offset the upper inside wall line 2' down (see Figure 5.17).

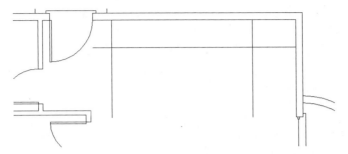

F I G U R E 5 . 1 7 : Offsetting wall lines to create the counter

3. Use the Fillet command with a radius of zero to clean up the two corners.

You can decide which of the two methods is more practical for you. Both are powerful techniques for laying out orthogonal patterns of lines for walls, counters, and other objects.

> If the Fillet command has a nonzero radius setting that you want to keep, hold down the Shift key to set the radius to zero for one use of the command. After the command ends, the radius returns to its nonzero setting.

UNDOING AND REDOING IN AUTOCAD

AutoCAD has two Undo commands, and they operate quite differently:

▶ When you click the Undo button on the Standard toolbar, you're using AutoCAD's U command. You can also start it by typing **u↵**. The U command works like the Undo command for Windows-compliant applications by undoing the results of commands one step at a time.

▶ The Undo command in AutoCAD has many options, and you start it by typing **undo↵**. You use this approach when you want to undo everything you've done since you last saved your drawing or to undo back to a point in your drawing session that you marked earlier. Be careful when you use the Undo command; you can easily lose a lot of your work.

The Oops command is a special undo tool that restores the last objects erased, even if the Erase command wasn't the last command executed.

The Redo command will undo the effect of several undos. So, if you undo a few steps too many, you can still get them back.

Drawing the Stove and Refrigerator

The stove and refrigerator are simple rectangles. Use the Temporary Tracking Point osnap to locate the first corner of each shape:

1. For the refrigerator, click the Rectangle button on the Draw toolbar, and then click the Temporary Tracking Point Osnap option. Use the Endpoint osnap to select a base point by placing the cursor near the upper end of the right side of the counter. Then, hold the cursor directly below that point. When the dotted tracking path and the Track Point tooltip appear, enter 2↵. This starts the rectangle 2" from the back wall, along the side of the counter. To specify the opposite corner of the rectangle, enter @32,-32↵.

2. For the stove, right-click, and choose Repeat Rectangle from the context menu that opens. Use the technique from step 1, but pick the upper end of the left side of the counter as the tracking point. Hold the cursor directly to the right of that point, and enter 2'↵. Then, enter @27,-26↵ to complete the rectangle.

3. Use the Trim command to trim away the front edge of the counter at the stove (see Figure 5.18).

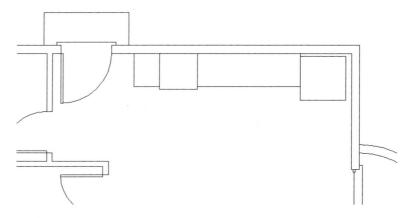

FIGURE 5.18: The stove and refrigerator made with rectangles

 N O T E   Because the stove rectangle is drawn as a *polyline*—a special line in which all segments compose one unique entity—you need to select only one segment of it for all sides of the rectangle to be selected and, in this case, for them to become cutting edges.

Completing the Stove

The stove needs a little more detail. You need to add circles to represent the burners and to add a line off the back to indicate the control panel (see Figure 5.19). You locate the burners by their centers.

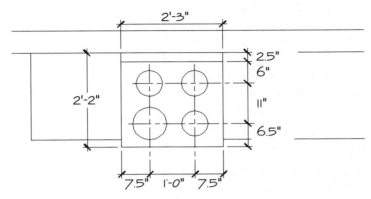

FIGURE 5.19: The details of the stove

1. Zoom in to a closer view of the stove. You need to draw a line along the back of the stove that is 2.5" in from the wall line. Offset seems like the right command to use.

2. Offset the wall line down 2.5". When you pick the line, pick it somewhere to the right or left of the stove—otherwise you might offset the stove rectangle. After it's offset, trim it back to the sides of the stove (see Figure 5.20).

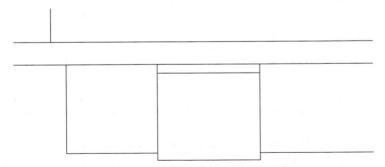

FIGURE 5.20: The stove with the control panel drawn

W A R N I N G   The back segment of the stove coincides with the wall. If you try to pick the wall line where the two lines coincide, you might pick the rectangle of the stove instead. You don't want to offset a line of the stove because it's a polyline. When you attempt to offset any segment of a polyline, all segments are offset, and all corners are filleted automatically. This would be an inconvenience in this situation because only one line segment needs to be offset. When you draw the sink, you'll learn a technique for selecting the line you want when two or more lines overlap or coincide.

3. The next step is to lay out guidelines to locate the centers of the burners. Offset the line you created for the control panel in step 2 down 6". Then, offset this new line down 11". Next you need vertical guidelines. Use tracking to draw the first guideline.

4. Start the Line command, and select Temporary Tracking Point osnap and then Endpoint osnap. Position the cursor near the upper-left corner of the stove.

5. Hold the cursor directly to the right of this point. When the dotted tracking path and the Track Point tooltip appear, enter **7.5↵**. This starts the first guideline.

6. Hold the crosshair cursor below the first point of the guideline, and pick a point just below the stove. Press ↵ to end the Line command.

7. Offset this line 12" to the right (see Figure 5.21). The guidelines are now in place.

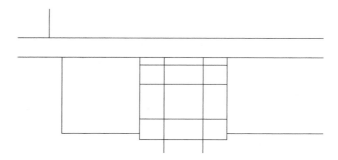

FIGURE 5.21:   The guidelines for the centers of the burner circles

The next step is to draw a circle for one burner, copy it to the other three burner locations, and then change the radius of the left front burner:

1. Use the Circle command and the Intersection osnap to draw a circle with its center at the lower-left intersection of the guidelines and with a radius of 3.5".

2. Start the Copy command. Select the circle, and then press ↵.

3. Choose the Intersection osnap. Select the intersection of the guidelines at the center of the circle as a base point.

4. Select the Intersection osnap again, and pick the intersection of guidelines above the first circle (see Figure 5.22). Select the Intersection osnap again, and pick one of the intersections on the right side. Then, select the Intersection osnap one more time, and pick the fourth intersection of guidelines. Press ↵ to end the Copy command. The burners are in place. Now you need to change the size of the lower-left burner.

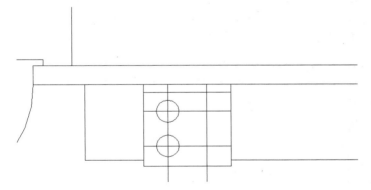

FIGURE 5.22: Copying the first burner

5. Select the lower-left burner. Five grips appear on the circle and at its center.

6. Click the Properties button to the right of the Zoom icons on the Standard toolbar, or right-click the drawing area and select Properties from the context menu, to open the Properties palette. It will fill most of the left part of the screen (see Figure 5.23); you can readjust its size and position. Notice the drop-down list at the top of the Properties palette. This tells you that the currently selected object is a circle.

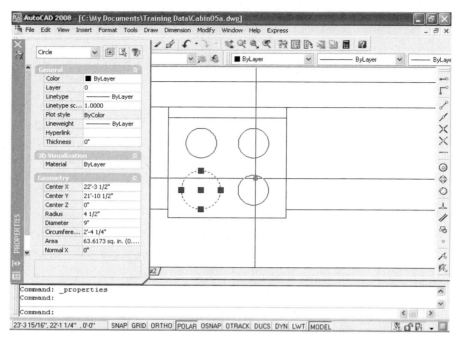

FIGURE 5.23:   The Properties palette and the selected burner

7. Move down the categorized list of properties in the Geometry list, and click Radius.

8. Highlight the 3½" Radius setting. Change it to 4.5", and press ↵. The burner in the drawing is enlarged.

9. Click the X in the upper-left corner of the Properties palette to close it. Then, press the Esc key to turn off the five grips that were on the circle.

10. Erase the guidelines to complete the stove (see Figure 5.24). Use Zoom Previous to see the whole kitchen with the completed stove.

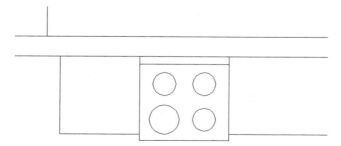

FIGURE 5.24:   The completed stove

With the stove finished, the final task in the kitchen is to draw the sink.

 N O T E   The Properties palette is an important tool for working with objects in a drawing. You'll learn more about it in Chapter 6, and you'll use it throughout the rest of this book.

Drawing the Kitchen Sink

You'll draw a double sink, with one basin larger than the other (see Figure 5.25). You'll use Offset, Fillet, and Trim to create the sink from the counter and wall lines:

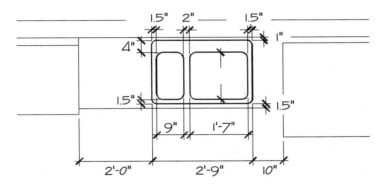

FIGURE 5.25: The sink with dimensions

1. Zoom in to the sink area, keeping the edges of the refrigerator and stove in view. Offset the wall line 1" down and the front edge of the counter 1.5" up.

2. Restart the Offset command, and set the offset distance to 10". You're going to offset the right side of the counter 10" to the left, but it coincides with the left side of the refrigerator. Hold down the Shift key and the spacebar as you pick that line. If the refrigerator becomes dashed, pick the same line again. The selected line switches to the line representing the edge of the counter. When the counter edge is selected, release the Shift key and the spacebar. Press ↵, and then complete the offset by picking a point to the left of the selected line. This selection technique is called *cycling*. It allows you to select a line that might coincide with another line.

3. Offset this new line 2'-9" to the left. This forms the outside edge of the sink (see the top of Figure 5.26).

When you drew the detail onto the stove, you could have used selection cycling to select the wall line where it coincided with the stove outline. You didn't need to because you could easily select the wall line at a point where the stove outline wasn't interfering.

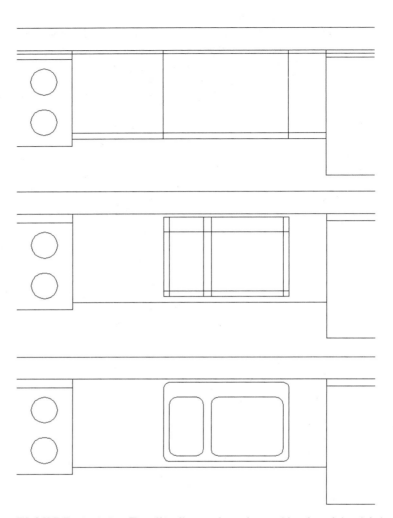

FIGURE 5.26: The offset lines to form the outside edge of the sink (top), the offset lines to form the inside edges of the sink (middle), and the finished sink (bottom)

4. Fillet the corners of this rectangle to clean them up, using a radius of zero.

5. Offset the left side, bottom, and right sides of the sink 1.5" to the inside. Offset the top side 4" to the inside. Then, offset the new line on the left 9" to the right and again 2" farther to the right. This forms the basis of the inside sink lines (see the middle of Figure 5.26).

6. Trim away the horizontal top and bottom inside sink lines between the two middle vertical sink lines. Then, fillet the four corners of each sink with a 2" radius to clean them up.

7. Fillet all four outside sink corners with a 1.5" radius. This finishes the sink (see the bottom of Figure 5.26). Use Zoom Previous to view the whole kitchen with the completed sink.

This completes the kitchen area. You drew few new lines to complete this task because you created most of them by offsetting existing lines and then trimming or filleting them. Keep this in mind as you move on to the bathroom.

Constructing the Bathroom

The bathroom has three fixtures: a sink, a shower, and a toilet (see Figure 5.27). When drawing these fixtures, you'll use a few object snaps over and over again. You can set one or more of the osnap choices to be continually running until you turn them off. That way, you won't have to select them each time.

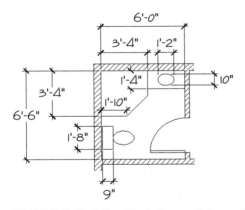

FIGURE 5.27: The bathroom fixtures with dimensions

Setting Running Object Snaps

You'll set three osnaps to run continually for now, until you get used to how they work:

1. Right-click the Osnap button on the status bar, and choose Settings from the shortcut menu to open the Drafting Settings dialog box. By default, the Object Snap tab is on top (see Figure 5.28).

FIGURE 5.28: The Object Snap tab of the Drafting Settings dialog box

Each of the 13 osnap options has a check box and a symbol next to it. The symbol appears as a marker in the drawing when you select a particular osnap and the cursor is near a point where you can use that osnap. You can select any number of osnaps to be running at a time.

N O T E   **You can choose a different color for the markers if you want. If you're using a dark background in the drawing area, use a bright color, such as yellow. For a white background, try blue.**

2. In the lower-left corner of the Drafting Settings dialog box, click Options to open the Options dialog box (see Figure 5.29); the Drafting tab should be on top. Then, on the left side in the AutoSnap Settings area, click the Colors button to open the Drawing Window Colors dialog box. 2D Model Space and AutoSnap Marker will be selected. Open the Color drop-down list in the upper-right corner, and select a color. Then click Apply & Close. While you're in the Autosnap Settings area of the Drafting tab, make sure the Marker, Magnet, and Display AutoSnap Tooltip check boxes are selected. Also make sure that the Display AutoSnap Aperture Box is unchecked. You can change the size of the markers using the slider in the AutoSnap Marker size area, but don't make them so large that they become cumbersome to work with. Click OK.

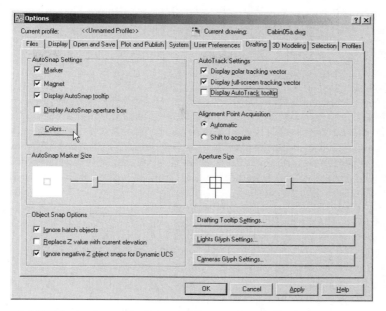

FIGURE 5.29: The Drafting tab of the Options dialog box

3. Back on the Object Snap tab of the Drafting Settings dialog box, click the check boxes next to Endpoint, Midpoint, and Intersection. Then, above the list and to the left, be sure the check box next to Object Snap On is selected. Click OK to close the dialog box. These osnaps will now be active anytime you're prompted to select a point on the drawing. You can deactivate them by turning off Osnap mode in the status bar.

Now you're ready to begin drawing the three fixtures for the bathroom. The shower determines the placement of the other two, so let's start there.

Drawing a Shower Unit

You'll start the shower unit with a rectangle and then trim away one corner. As you start this exercise, check the status bar. The Polar, Osnap, and Model buttons should be in their on positions. The rest of the buttons should be off. Follow these steps:

1. Enter z↵e↵ to zoom to the drawing's extents. Then, use the zoom window to view the bathroom close-up. Start the Rectangle command. For the first point, move the cursor to the upper-left inside corner of the room. Notice the square that appears at the corner.

This is the AutoSnap marker for the running Endpoint osnap. As soon as it appears on the endpoint you want to snap to, click. This places the first corner of the rectangle at the endpoint. For the second point, enter @40,-40↵.

T I P   If you don't get the rectangle you want after entering the relative coordinates for the second corner, choose Tools ➤ Options to open the Options dialog box. Click the User Preferences tab. In the upper-right corner, in the Priority for Coordinate Data Entry area, be sure that the button next to Keyboard Entry Except Scripts is active. Then, click OK. Try the rectangle again.

2. Start the Line command, and move the cursor near the midpoint of the bottom line of the rectangle. Notice that a triangle, the Midpoint AutoSnap symbol, appears when you get near the midpoint of the line. When you see the triangle on the midpoint you want, click.

3. Move the cursor near the midpoint of the right side of the rectangle until you see the triangle appear at the midpoint location (see Figure 5.30). Click again. Press ↵ to end the Line command.

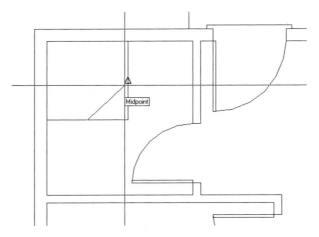

FIGURE 5.30: Using the Midpoint osnap to complete a line across the corner of the shower

4. Start the Trim command, and using the last line you created as a cutting edge, trim away the lower-right corner of the shower rectangle. The trimming requires only one pick because you're trimming a

polyline. Press ↵ to stop the Trim command. This completes the shower.

You want to offset the shower inward evenly on all sides, but the perimeter now consists of an open polyline and a line. To close the polyline, you could use the Polyedit command's Join option, as you did in an earlier exercise, or delete the line and direct the polyline to create a segment that closes its perimeter. For this exercise, you will do the latter.

5. Select and erase the diagonal line you used as a cutting edge to trim the shower.

6. Choose Modify ➤ Object ➤ Polyline from the menu, or enter pe↵. At the `Select polyline or [Multiple]:` prompt, select any segment of the shower polyline. Enter c↵ to choose the Close option. The Close option closes an open polyline by creating a straight segment between the open endpoints.

7. Offset the shower polyline inward 1½", as in Figure 5.31.

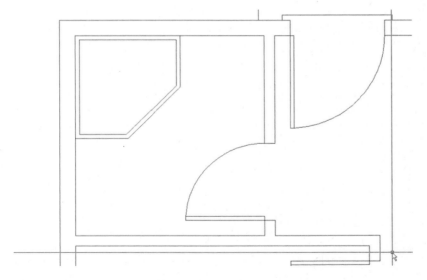

FIGURE 5.31: The offset shower polyline

Next, draw the sink to the right of the shower.

Drawing the Bathroom Sink

You'll offset a line and draw an ellipse for this fixture while practicing using the Temporary Tracking Point osnap option in the process. The Endpoint and Midpoint osnaps are still running.

1. Zoom in to the sink area with a zoom window. Offset the top inside wall line down 16". Then, use the outside shower wall as a cutting edge, and trim back the line.

2. Click the Ellipse button on the Draw toolbar, or enter el↵. Enter c↵ to select the Center option.

3. Activate the Temporary Tracking Point osnap, and then move the cursor near the midpoint of the newly offset line. When the small cross appears in the AutoSnap marker, the tracking point is established.

4. Move the crosshair cursor directly above the tracking point. When the dotted tracking path and the Track Point tooltip appear, enter 8↵ to locate the center of the counter. The Command window will prompt you for the location of the ends of two perpendicular axes. Start with the left/right axis, and enter the distance using direct entry and polar tracking, as you did for the steps earlier in this chapter.

5. Hold the crosshair cursor directly to the right of the center point. Enter 7↵. Hold the crosshair cursor directly above the center, and enter 5↵. The ellipse is constructed, and the sink fixture is complete (see Figure 5.32). Leave the view on your screen as it is for a moment.

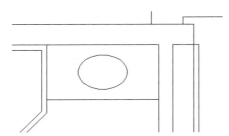

FIGURE 5.32: The completed sink fixture

Drawing the toilet is the final task in this chapter. You'll use the Ellipse command again, along with the Rectangle command. You'll also learn about a couple of new display options.

Positioning a Toilet

The toilet consists of a rectangle and an ellipse centered between the shower and the wall. The tank is offset 1" from the back wall and is 9" × 20". The ellipse representing the seat measures 18" in one direction and 12" in the other.

1. On the Standard toolbar, click the Pan Realtime button. The cursor changes to a small hand when you return it to the drawing area. Position it in the lower-left corner of the drawing area with the view still zoomed in on the sink.

2. Hold down the left mouse button, and drag the hand up and to the right. When the toilet area comes into view, release the mouse button. The drawing slides along with the movement of the cursor. If necessary, do this again until you have the toilet area centered in the drawing area.

With Zoom Realtime, moving the cursor to the left or right has no effect on the view. The magnification is controlled solely by the up-and-down motion.

T I P   **You can also perform a _pan_, a lateral change in the viewing area with no change in zoom factor, by holding down the middle mouse button or scroll wheel. The mbuttonpan variable must be set to one (enter mbuttonpan⏎ 1⏎) for this functionality to be available. Now that most people use a wheel mouse, this manner of panning is becoming the preferred method. Rolling the wheel to zoom is also common.**

3. Right-click, and choose Zoom from the shortcut menu that opens. Back on the drawing, the cursor changes to a magnifying glass with a plus and minus sign.

4. Position the Zoom Realtime cursor near the top of the drawing, and hold down the left mouse button. Drag the cursor down, and watch the view being zoomed out in real time. Move the cursor up, still holding down the mouse button. Position the cursor in such a way that you have a good view of the toilet area, and then release the mouse button. Right-click again, and choose Exit from the context menu to end the Zoom Realtime command.

These zooming options are convenient tools for adjusting the view of your drawing. Let's move on to the toilet. You need to find a way to position the toilet accurately, centering it between the wall and shower. The midpoint of the left wall line isn't useful because the wall line runs behind the shower. You'll have to construct a guideline:

1. With the Rectangle command, draw the 9" × 20" toilet tank a few inches to the right of the wall, not touching any lines. Then, offset

the left wall line 1" to the right to make a guideline. Use the shower as a cutting edge, and trim this guideline down to the shower (see the top of Figure 5.33).

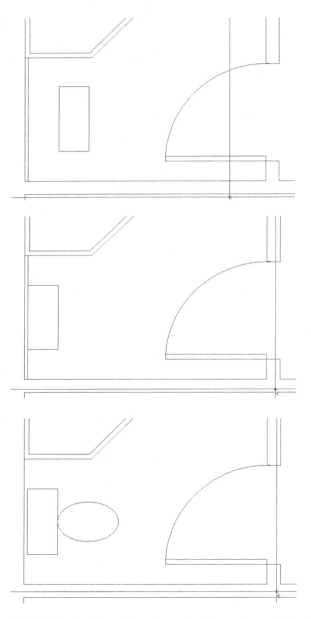

FIGURE 5.33: The toilet tank with an offset guideline (top), the tank correctly positioned (middle), and the cursor controlling the size of the second axis for the toilet seat (bottom)

2. Start the Move command, select the tank, and then press ↵.

3. For the base point, move the cursor to the middle of the left side of the tank. When you see the triangle at the midpoint, click.

4. For the second point, move the cursor onto the guideline. When it gets closer to the midpoint than the endpoint, the triangle appears at the midpoint. At this point, click. The rectangle is accurately positioned 1" from the left wall and centered between the shower and lower wall (see the middle of Figure 5.33).

5. Erase the guideline.

6. Start the Ellipse command. The Command window displays a default prompt of `Specify axis endpoint of ellipse or [Arc/Center]:`. Using the Specify Axis Endpoint option, you can define the first axis from one end of the ellipse to the other. This will help you here.

7. Move the cursor near the midpoint of the right side of the tank, and when the triangle shows up there, click. This starts the ellipse.

8. Hold the crosshair cursor out to the right of the rectangle, and enter 1'6↵. This positions the first axis. Now, as you move the crosshair cursor, you'll see that a line starts at the center of the ellipse, and the cursor's movement controls the size of the other axis (see the bottom of Figure 5.33). To designate the second axis, you need to enter the distance from the center of the axis to the end of it, or half the overall length of the axis.

9. Hold the crosshair cursor directly above the center point, and enter 6↵. The ellipse is complete, so you've finished the toilet.

10. Before you save this drawing, use the Pan and Zoom tools to zoom out and pan your drawing until the whole floor plan fills the drawing area, except for a thin border around the outside of the plan (see Figure 5.34). Save this drawing as `Cabin05b.dwg`.

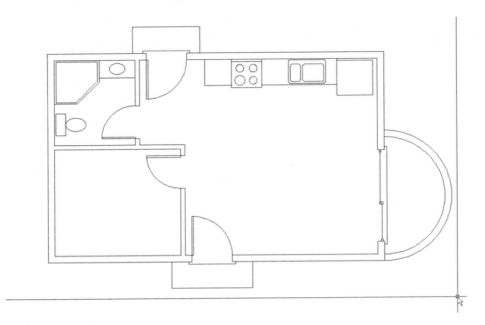

FIGURE 5.34: The completed floor plan zoomed and panned to fill the screen

The bathroom is complete, and you now have a fairly complete floor plan for the cabin. While completing the drawing tasks for this chapter, you were exposed to several new commands and techniques to add to those introduced in Chapter 4. I hope you have experimented with the dynamic display feature (the Dyn button on the status bar) and know whether you want it to be active and, if so, when. You now have a set of tools that will take you a long way toward being able to lay out a drawing of any size.

Chapters 1 through 5 fill out the basic level of skills in AutoCAD that allow you to draw on the computer approximately as you would with pencil and vellum, although you might already see some of the advantages CAD offers over traditional board drafting. Beginning with the next chapter, I'll introduce you to concepts of AutoCAD that don't have a counterpart in board drafting. These features will take you to a new level of knowledge and skill, and you'll start to get an idea of what sets computer drafting apart.

USING PAN REALTIME AND ZOOM REALTIME

The Pan Realtime and Zoom Realtime buttons are next to each other on the Standard toolbar. You can start Pan Realtime by typing **p**↵. You can start Zoom Realtime by typing **z**↵↵. You can also start Pan Realtime or Zoom Realtime by right-clicking at the Command: prompt and then choosing Pan or Zoom from the shortcut menu. If you try this, you'll find that it's easier than clicking the Pan Realtime or Zoom Realtime button.

Once one of these Realtime commands is running, you can switch to the other one by clicking the other Realtime button or by right-clicking and choosing the other one from the shortcut menu. This shortcut menu also has other options that help make Pan Realtime and Zoom Realtime quite useful commands:

Exit   Ends the Zoom Realtime or Pan Realtime command.

Pan   Switches to Pan Realtime from Zoom Realtime.

Zoom   Switches to Zoom Realtime from Pan Realtime.

3D Orbit   Is a special viewing tool for 3D that is covered in later chapters.

Zoom Window   Allows you to make a zoom window without first ending Pan Realtime or Zoom Realtime. You pick a point, hold down the left mouse button, and then drag open a window in your drawing. When you release the button, you're zoomed into the window you made, and Pan Realtime or Zoom Realtime resumes.

Zoom Original   Restores the view of your drawing that you had when you began Pan Realtime or Zoom Realtime.

Zoom Extents   Zooms to the drawing extents.

To end Pan Realtime or Zoom Realtime, press the Esc key, press ↵, or right-click and choose Exit from the context menu.

When Pan Realtime or Zoom Realtime is running, AutoCAD is in a special mode that makes the status bar invisible and therefore unusable.

If You Would Like More Practice...

The following are several additional exercises that will give you the opportunity to practice the skills and techniques you have learned up until now.

Drawing the Cabin Again

As is true for almost any skill, the key to mastery is practice. Redrawing the entire cabin might seem daunting at this point when you think of how long it took you to get here. But if you try it all again, starting with Chapter 3, you'll find that it will take about half the time it did the first time, and if you do it a third time, it'll take half that time. Once you understand the techniques and how the commands work, feel free to experiment with alternative techniques to accomplish tasks and with other options on the commands.

Drawing Something Else

If you have a specific project in mind that you would like to draw in AutoCAD, so much the better—try it.

Drawing Some Furniture for the Cabin

Once you put some furniture in the cabin, you'll quickly see how small it is! But it can still accept some basic furniture without seeming too cramped. You should be able to add the following:

- ▶ Kitchen—a table and chairs
- ▶ Living room—a short couch or love seat, coffee table, and easy chair
- ▶ Bedroom—a double bed, dresser, and nightstand

Use a tape measure, and go around your office or home to determine the approximate dimensions of each piece. The goal here is not so much to ensure accuracy of scale but to practice drawing in AutoCAD. Figure 5.35 shows the floor plan with these items of furniture. If you draw the bed shown here, try using the Spline tool for the curved, turned-down sheets. It's in the middle of the Draw toolbar. You'll see how it works after a little experimentation.

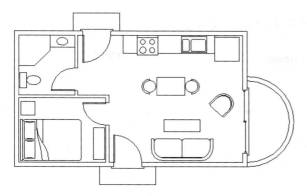

FIGURE 5.35: The floor plan with furniture

Drawing a Gasket

Figure 5.36 shows a gasket that is symmetrical around its vertical and horizontal axes. This symmetry will allow you to use the Mirror command to create much of the drawing.

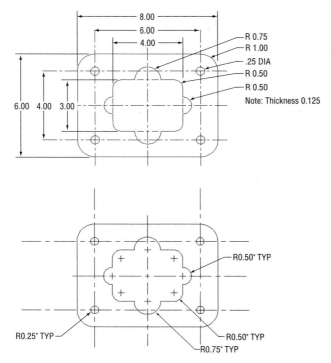

FIGURE 5.36: A gasket

The diagrams in Figure 5.37 summarize the steps.

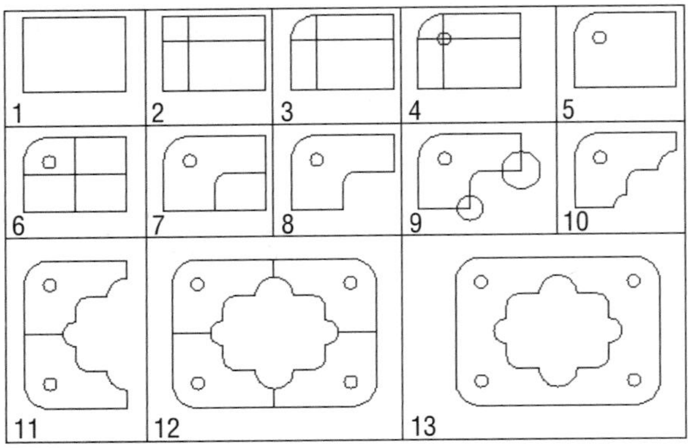

FIGURE 5.37: The 13 steps to creating the gasket

To draw the gasket, set Linear Units to Engineering with a precision of 0'-0.00". Set Angular Units to Decimal with a precision of 0.00. Now, follow these steps:

1. Use the Line command to draw a rectangle 4" wide and 3" high.

2. Offset the upper horizontal line and the left vertical line 1" to the inside of the rectangle.

3. Use Fillet with a radius set to 1" on the upper-left corner of the original rectangle.

4. Draw the circle with the 0.25" radius, using the intersection of the two offset lines as the center.

5. Erase the offset lines.

6. Offset the right vertical line 2" to the left and the bottom horizontal line 1.5" up.

7. Use Fillet with a radius of 0.50" on the intersection of these two lines, retaining the right and lower segments.

8. Trim back the lower-right corner of the original rectangle.

9. Draw circles with 0.50" and 0.75" radii on the bottom and right sides of the shape.

10. Use Trim to remove unneeded lines.

11. Use Mirror to flip the shape down.

12. Use Mirror again to flip the shape to the right.

13. Erase unneeded lines. (Each line to be erased is really two lines.)

If you choose to save this drawing, name it `Gasket-05.dwg`.

Drawing a Parking Lot

Figure 5.38 shows a parking lot partially bordered by sidewalks and streets.

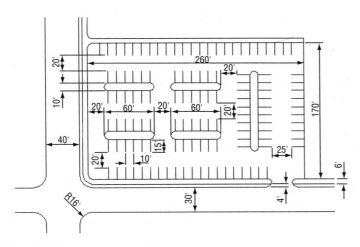

FIGURE 5.38: A parking lot

You'll get a lot of practice using the Offset and Fillet commands while completing this drawing. Guidelines will help you, so don't be afraid to use them. Note the tip at the end of this section. Here's a summary of the steps:

1. Set Linear and Angular units to Decimal, each with a precision of 0. Assume that 1 linear decimal unit equals 1'. Set Polar Tracking to 90°, and turn it on. Set the Endpoint and Midpoint osnaps to be running. Set Snap to 10, Grid to 0, and Drawing Limits to 400, 250. Zoom All.

2. Use Grid and Snap to draw the large 260' × 170' rectangle using the Line command and relative Cartesian coordinates as you did in Chapter 3. Turn off the Grid and Snap. Offset three of the lines 6' to the outside to make the sidewalk.

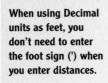

When using Decimal units as feet, you don't need to enter the foot sign (') when you enter distances.

3. On two sides, offset the outer sidewalk line 4' to the outside to make the curb. Then, offset the curb lines 30' and 40' to make the street.

4. Draw extra lines to make the street intersection.

5. Fillet and Trim lines to create the curved corners of the intersection and sidewalks.

6. Offset the lines of the inner rectangle to the inside to make guidelines for the parking strips and islands.

7. Use Fillet and Trim to finish the drawing.

8. If you choose to save this drawing, name it Parking Lot-05.dwg.

T I P   Using Fillet on two parallel lines creates a semicircle to connect them. Try it on the islands in the parking area.

Are You Experienced?

Now you can...

☑ use the Temporary Tracking Point option to create and use tracking points

☑ use the Quadrant and Intersection osnaps

☑ set up and use running osnaps

☑ move around the drawing area with Zoom Realtime and Pan Realtime

☑ use the Circle and Ellipse commands

☑ move and duplicate objects with the Move and Copy commands

☑ use a circle and the Trim command to make a semicircle arc

☑ use guidelines to locate the center of circles for a stovetop

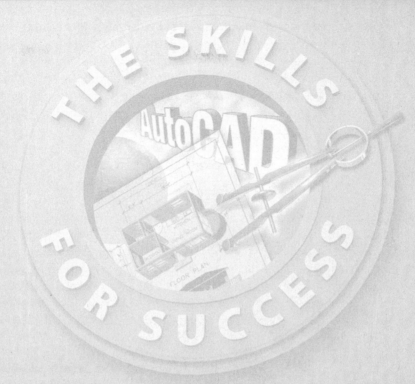

CHAPTER 6

Using Layers to Organize Your Drawing

▶ Creating new layers

▶ Assigning a color and a linetype to layers

▶ Moving existing objects onto a new layer

▶ Controlling the visibility of layers

▶ Working with linetypes

▶ Creating layer states

I n precomputer days, drafters used sets of transparent overlays on their drafting tables. These were sheets that stacked on top of one another, and the drafters could see through several at a time. Specific kinds of information were drawn on each overlay, with all related spatially so that several overlays might be drawn for the same floor plan. Each discipline, such as plumbing, electrical, or HVAC, as well as charts and tables, were drawn on separate overlays so that the floor plans were not required to be reproduced for every type of drawing produced. Each overlay had small holes punched near the corners so the drafter could position the overlay onto buttons, called *registration points*, that were taped to the drawing board. Because all overlays had holes punched at the same locations with respect to the drawing, information on the set of overlays was kept in alignment.

To help you organize your drawing, AutoCAD provides you with an amazing tool, called *layers*, which is a computerized form of the transparent overlays, only much more powerful and flexible. In manual drafting, you could use only four or five overlays at a time before the information on the bottom overlay became unreadable (copying the drawing meant sending all the layers through the blueprint machine together). In AutoCAD, you aren't limited in the number of layers you can use. You can have hundreds of layers, and complex CAD drawings often do.

Using Layers as an Organization Tool

To understand what layers are and why they are so useful, think again about the transparent overlay sheets used in hand drafting. Each overlay is designed to be printed. The bottom sheet might be a basic floor plan. To create an overlay sheet for a structural drawing, the drafter traces over only the lines of the floor plan that the overlay needs and then adds new information pertinent to that sheet. For the next overlay, the drafter performs the same task again. Each sheet, then, contains some information in common, in addition to data unique to that sheet.

In AutoCAD, using layers allows you to generate all the sheets for a set of overlays from a single file (see Figure 6.1). Nothing needs to be drawn twice or traced. The wall layout is on one layer, and the rooflines are on another. Doors are on a third. You can control the visibility of layers so that you can make all objects residing on a layer temporarily invisible. This feature lets you put all information keyed to a particular floor plan in one .dwg file and from that drawing produce a series of derived drawings, such as the foundation plan, the second floor plan, the reflected ceiling plan, and the roof plan, by making different combinations of layers visible for each drawing. When you make a print, you decide which layers will be visible. Consequently, in a set of drawings, each sheet based on the floor plan displays a unique combination of layers, all of which are in one file.

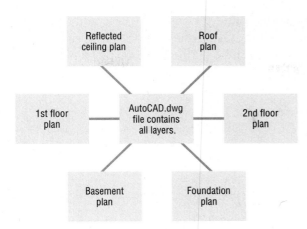

FIGURE 6.1: A diagram of several drawings coming from one file

Layers, as an organization tool, allow you to classify the various objects in a computerized drawing—lines, arcs, circles, and so on—according to the component of the building they represent, such as doors, walls, and windows. Each layer is assigned a color, and all objects placed on the layer take on that assigned color unless you specify a different color for the objects. This lets you easily distinguish between objects that represent separate components of the building (see Figure 6.2). And you can quickly tell which layer a given object or group of objects is on.

FIGURE 6.2: Separate layers combined to make a drawing

First, you'll look at the procedure for achieving this level of organization, which is to set up the new layers and then move existing objects onto them. Following that, you'll learn how to create new objects on a specific layer.

Setting Up Layers

All AutoCAD drawings have one layer in common—layer 0. Layer 0 is the default layer in all new drawings. If you don't add any new layers to a drawing, everything you create in that drawing is on layer 0. Everything so far in the cabin drawing has been drawn on layer 0.

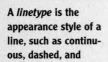

Objects and layers are analogous to people and countries; just as all people must reside in some country, so must all objects be on some layer.

All objects in AutoCAD are assigned a layer. In this book, I'll refer to objects assigned to a particular layer as *being on* that layer. You can place objects on a layer in two ways: you can move them to the layer, or you can create them on the layer in the first place. You'll learn how to do both in this chapter. But first you need to learn how to set up layers. To see how you do this, you'll create seven new layers for your cabin drawing—Walls, Doors, Steps, Balcony, Fixtures, Headers, and Roof—and then move the existing objects in your drawing onto the first five of these layers. After that, you'll create new objects on the Headers and Roof layers. You'll begin by creating a few new layers:

1. Open AutoCAD, and then open Cabin05b.dwg. The Layers toolbar should be just above the drawing area on your screen on the left; it contains four buttons and a drop-down list for controlling layers. (The LT Layers toolbar has only two buttons.)

A *linetype* is the appearance style of a line, such as continuous, dashed, and dash-dot.

To the right is the Properties toolbar with four drop-down lists for controlling linetypes, colors, and other layer properties. These are the default positions for these toolbars, but your screen might have a different arrangement.

 2. Click the Layer Properties Manager button on the left end of the Layers toolbar to open the Layer Properties Manager dialog box (see Figure 6.3). Notice the large open area in the middle right of the dialog box with layer 0 listed at the top. This is the Layer List box. All the layers in a drawing are listed here, along with their states and properties. Cabin05b.dwg has only one layer so far.

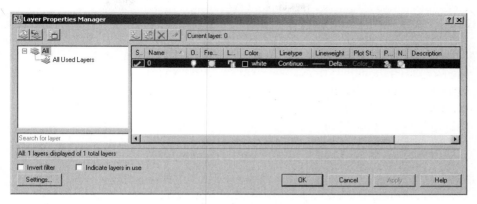

FIGURE 6.3: The Layer Properties Manager dialog box

To the left of the Layer List box is the Layer Filters tree view box where you can define which layers to display in the Layer List box. The Layer Properties Manager dialog box has seven buttons at the top to perform layer and filter management tasks. You'll see two check boxes and five buttons at the bottom of the dialog box including a Settings button for defining the actions AutoCAD takes when you introduce a new layer into the drawing. Before setting up new layers, look for a moment at the Layer List box.

> You'll look more closely at the Layer Filters tree view box in Chapter 12.

Using the Layer List Box

Each layer has four properties—Color, Linetype, Lineweight, and Plot Style—that determine the appearance of the objects on that layer. Look at the layer 0 row in the list, and notice the square and the word *white* in the Color column. The square is black (or white if you have a black background for your drawing area), but the name of the color is White whether the square is black or white. Continuous is in the Linetype column. This tells you that layer 0 has been assigned the setting White (meaning black or white) and the Continuous linetype by default.

N O T E   If you set up your drawing area so that the background is white, AutoCAD automatically changes the color assigned to White in the Layer List box to black, so lines that would ordinarily appear as white on a black background now appear as black on the white background. When you then switch to a black background, the black lines change to white lines. This allows the lines to be visible regardless of the background color, and AutoCAD doesn't have to assign a new color to a layer that has been assigned the White setting when you switch background colors.

The five columns to the left of the Color column are Status, Name, On, Freeze, and Lock. They have icons or text in the layer 0 row. These columns represent some of the status modes—or *states*—of the layer, and they control whether objects on a layer are visible, whether they can be changed, or on which layer new objects are created. I'll discuss the visibility and status of layers later in this chapter, and I'll discuss the columns to the right of the Linetype column—Lineweight, Plot Style, Plot, and Description—in Chapter 15. Don't worry about them right now.

Creating New Layers and Assigning Colors

Let's create a few new layers, name them, and assign them colors:

1. Just above the Status column, click the New Layer icon. A new layer named Layer1 appears in the list. The layer's name is highlighted, which means you can rename it by typing another name now.

2. Enter **Walls**↵. Layer1 changes to Walls. The row for the Walls layer should still be highlighted (see Figure 6.4).

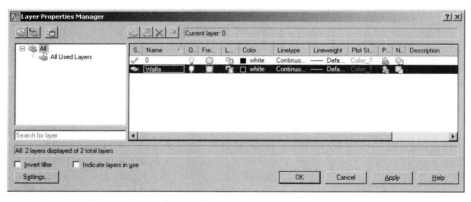

FIGURE 6.4: The Layer Properties Manager dialog box with a new layer named Walls

For LT users, your Select Color dialog box has only one tab—the Index Color tab—which is the one you'll use in this book.

3. Click White in the Color column for the Walls row to open the Select Color dialog box (see Figure 6.5). Notice the three tabs at the top—Index Color, True Color, and Color Books. Each has a different selection of colors available to AutoCAD. Be sure the Index Color tab is selected. You have three sets of color swatches and two buttons for making color choices. In the row of 9 color swatches, below the large group of 240 choices, click the cyan (turquoise) square. In the Color text box, White changes to Cyan, and the front rectangle in the lower-right corner takes on the color cyan.

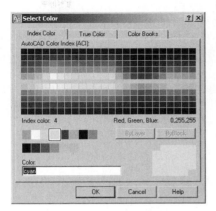

FIGURE 6.5: The Index Color tab in the Select Color dialog box

  T I P As you move the cursor over the available color swatches, the index color number, from 1 through 255, appears beneath the large field of 240 choices.

  4. Click OK to close the Select Color dialog box. In the Layer List box of the Layer Properties Manager dialog box, you can see that the color square for the Walls layer has changed to cyan.

As you create your new list of layers and assign them colors, notice how each color looks in your drawing. Some are easier to see on a screen with a light background, and others do better against a dark background. In this book, I'll assign colors that work well with a black background. If your system has a white background, you might want to use darker colors, which you can find in the array of 240 color swatches in the upper half of the Index Color tab.

You'll now continue creating new layers and assigning them colors. You'll master this procedure as you add a new layer or two in each chapter throughout the rest of the book:

  1. In the Layer Properties Manager dialog box, click the New Layer button, or right-click in the Layer List box and choose New Layer from the list.

  2. Enter **Doors**↵ to change the name of the layer.

  3. Pick the color square in the Doors row. When the Select Color dialog box opens, click the red square in the same row of color swatches where you previously found cyan. Click OK.

  4. Repeat these steps, creating the following layers with their assigned colors. Pick the colors from the same row of color swatches that you have been using.

W A R N I N G   In the row of 9 colors, the ninth swatch might not be clearly visible when it is close to the background color of the dialog box.

Layer Name	Color
Steps	9 (Light Gray)
Balcony	Green
Fixtures	Magenta
Headers	Yellow
Roof	Blue

 T I P   Blue might or might not read well on a black background. If you don't like the way it looks, try picking a lighter shade of blue from the array of 240 colors on the Index Color tab.

When finished, the layer list should have eight layers with their assigned colors in the color squares of each row (see Figure 6.6). All layers are assigned the Continuous linetype by default. This is convenient because most building components are represented in the floor plan by continuous lines, but the roof—because of its position above the walls—needs to be represented by a dashed line. Later you'll assign a Dashed linetype to the Roof layer.

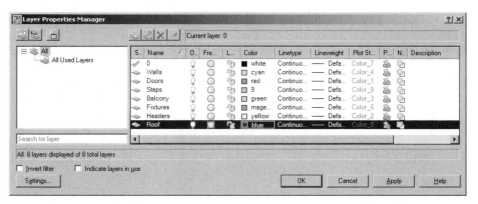

F I G U R E   6 . 6 : The Layer List box, in the Layer Properties Manager dialog box, with the seven new layers and layer 0

NAMING LAYERS

You can name layers in a variety of ways. With their different color assignments, layers make it possible for you to easily distinguish which objects in your drawing represent walls or other parts of your building. Most offices follow a standard for organizing layers by name, color, and linetype. The American Institute of Architects (AIA) publishes layering standards, which are often adapted by architecture firms and customized to fit their specific needs. Before AutoCAD version 2000, lineweights in AutoCAD drawings were controlled only by color, so the layer standards were developed around this determining factor. Since version 2000, this is no longer the case. As a result, you can expect that layering standards used for years will be changing. With the cabin drawing, you'll start developing a basic set of layers. Once you learn how to manage the set you're using here, tackling more complex layering systems will come naturally.

N O T E   When you name layers, you can use uppercase and lowercase letters, and AutoCAD will preserve them. But AutoCAD doesn't distinguish between them and treats *Walls*, *WALLS*, and *walls* as the same layer.

USING AUTOCAD'S TRADITIONAL COLORS

The traditional set of 255 colors for AutoCAD is set up in such a way that the first 7 colors are named (Blue, Red, and so on) and numbered (1 through 7), whereas the other 248 colors have only numbers.

As you saw on the Index Color tab of the Select Color dialog box, AutoCAD has three groupings of colors: a large array of swatches in the top half and two rows of swatches below. Moving the cursor over a swatch displays its AutoCAD number below the array as well as its red, green, blue (RGB) values. Click a swatch to assign it to the layer that has been selected in the Layer Properties Manager dialog box.

You should avoid using colors that resemble the background color, such as colors 250 or 18 with a black background. The objects with these colors could become visually lost in the drawing area. Be aware of this if your drawings might be sent to someone who doesn't use your color standards so that they can work efficiently with the drawings.

Continues

In more complex drawings, you might need several layers for variations of the same building component, landscape element, or machine part. You might replace the Walls layer, for example, with several layers, such as Existing Walls to Remain, Walls to Be Demolished, and New Walls. Once you acquire the skills presented here, you'll have no difficulty progressing to a more complex layering system.

USING AUTOCAD'S TRADITIONAL COLORS *(Continued)*

The array of 240 colors   In the top half of the dialog box are colors numbered 10 through 249, arranged in an array of 24 columns, each having 10 swatches.

The row of 9 standard color swatches   This group includes colors 1 through 9. The first 7 colors in this group also have names: Red (1), Yellow (2), Green (3), Cyan (4), Blue (5), Magenta (6), and White/Black (7). Colors 8 and 9 have numbers only. Color 7 is named White, but it will be black if you're using a white background color.

The row of 6 gray shades   These colors are often assigned screening values (such as 50 percent, 75 percent, and so on) numbering 250 through 255. As pure color assignments, they range from almost black to almost white.

These 255 colors, plus the background color, make up the traditional Auto-CAD 256-color palette. Two additional colors are in a group by themselves, Logical Colors, and are represented by buttons on the Index Color tab.

The two buttons in this grouping—ByLayer and ByBlock—represent two ways you can assign a color to objects—such as lines, circles, text, and so on—via the layer they are on or via the *block* they are part of, rather than to the objects themselves. (I'll cover blocks in the next chapter.) When you assign cyan to the Walls layer and place all objects representing walls on that layer, all wall objects are automatically assigned the color ByLayer and take on the color of their layer—in this case, cyan.

You can change the color of an object to one other than the layer color by selecting the object and choosing a color from the Color Control drop-down list in the Properties toolbar. Setting an object's color directly is not always best practice, however, and you should try to maintain color assignments by layer whenever practical.

Looking at the Other Tabs in the Select Color Dialog Box

AutoCAD also supports a True Color palette and various Pantone, DIC, and RAL color groups. Although I won't cover these features in any depth in this book, you'll take a quick look at them before moving on.

The True Color Tab   With the Layer Properties Manager dialog box open, click one of the color swatches in the Layer List box to open the Select Color dialog box again. Then, click the True Color tab. In the upper-right corner, the Color

Model drop-down list displays either RGB or HSL. The RGB color model looks like the left of Figure 6.7, and the hue, saturation, luminance (HSL) model looks like the right of Figure 6.7.

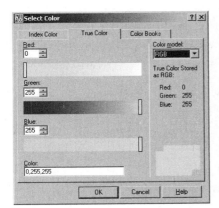 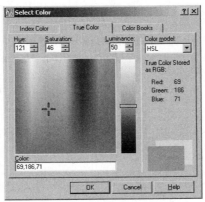

F I G U R E   6 . 7 :   The True Color tab with the RGB color model (left) and the HSL color model (right)

The RGB screen shows three horizontal color bands, one for each of the three primary colors. Move the sliders on each band to set a number from 0 to 255, or enter a number in the box for each color. The three primary color values that combine to make up the final color appear at the bottom and on the right side, and the rectangles in the lower-right corner show the currently selected and previously selected color.

The HSL screen displays a rectangle of colors and a vertical band with a slider. Drag the crosshairs around on the rectangle. The color in the front rectangle in the lower-right corner changes as you move the crosshairs. Moving it left or right takes the hue through a range of 360 values. Moving it up or down changes the percentage of saturation, or *intensity*, with the top of the rectangle representing 100 percent.

The slider to the right of the rectangle controls the luminance, which, like saturation, varies from 0 percent—representing black—to 100 percent, or white. A luminance of 50 percent maximizes a color's brightness.

The Color text box displays the currently selected color's three RGB numbers. You can also specify a color by entering numbers in the individual boxes for Hue, Saturation, and Luminance—or the boxes for Red, Green, and Blue in the RGB screen. And you can use the up and down arrows in these boxes to scroll through the possible settings.

If you select a color using the RGB or HSL screen, it appears in the Layer List box of the Layer Properties Manager dialog box by its three RGB numbers.

The Color column might be compressed in such a way that the names of colors in the list are abbreviated. You can widen the column by dragging the divider at the right of the title farther to the right.

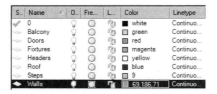

With the combination of 255 values for each of the three primary colors, you now have more than 16 million colors to choose from in AutoCAD.

The Color Books Tab   The Color Books tab displays the colors of the selected color book (see the left of Figure 6.8). AutoCAD has 20 color books. Each book appears in the Color Book drop-down list at the top of the tab; the current book appears in the box. Below that, a set of colors that corresponds to the position of the slider is displayed in bars. Moving the slider to a new position displays another set of colors. Click a displayed color bar to select it, and then click OK. The color appears in the Layer Properties Manager Layer List box by its identifying name and number (see the right of Figure 6.8).

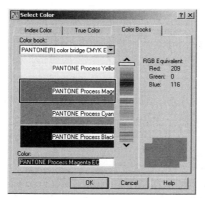

FIGURE 6.8:   The Color Books tab in the Select Color dialog box (left) and the layer list with an assigned Pantone number (right)

Later in the book, you'll be asked to create new layers and assign them colors of your choice. Use this opportunity to explore the True Color and Color Books tabs of the Select Color dialog box, and try using some of these colors in your drawing. Keep the Layer Properties Manager dialog box open. You'll use it to assign linetypes in the next section.

You can delete selected layers using the Delete Layer button, shaped like a red X, in the Layer Properties Manager dialog box. You can delete only *empty* layers—those containing no objects. Empty layers are identifiable in the Layer Properties Manager by the grayed-out icon in the Status column. Deleted layers are not immediately removed from the list; they are only marked with an X in the Status column but are removed when the Layer Properties Manager is closed and then reopened.

Assigning Linetypes to Layers

When you assign a color to a layer, you can choose any color supported by your system. This is not so with linetypes. Each new drawing has only one linetype loaded into it by default (the Continuous linetype). You must load any other linetypes you need from an outside file:

1. In the Layer Properties Manager dialog box, click Continuous in the column for the Roof layer to open the Select Linetype dialog box (see Figure 6.9). In the Loaded Linetypes list, only Continuous appears. No other linetypes have been loaded into this drawing.

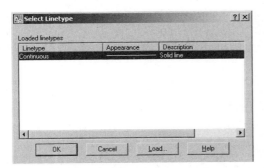

FIGURE 6.9: The Select Linetype dialog box

2. Click Load to open the Load Or Reload Linetypes dialog box. Scroll down the list to the Dashed, Dashed2, and DashedX2 linetypes (see Figure 6.10). Notice how, in this family, the dashed lines are different sizes.

Dashed linetype family

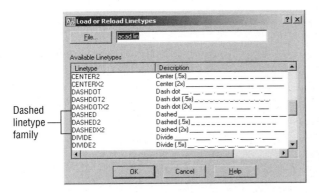

FIGURE 6.10: The list scrolled to the three Dashed linetypes

3. Click Dashed in the left column, and then click OK. You're returned to the Select Linetype dialog box. The Dashed linetype has been added to the Linetype list under Continuous (see Figure 6.11). Click Dashed to highlight it, and click OK. In the Layer Properties Manager dialog box, the Roof layer has been assigned the Dashed linetype (see Figure 6.12).

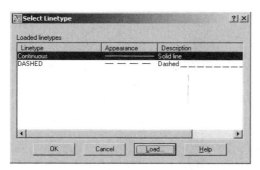

F I G U R E   6 . 1 1 :   The Select Linetype dialog box with the Dashed linetype loaded

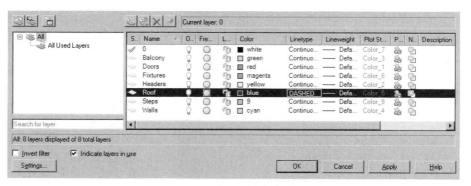

F I G U R E   6 . 1 2 :   The Layer Properties Manager dialog box with the Roof layer assigned the Dashed linetype

AutoCAD's Linetypes

The Available Linetypes list in the Load Or Reload Linetypes dialog box lists 45 linetypes. They fall into three groups:

Acad_ISO   The first 14 linetypes are in the Acad_ISO family (ISO is the International Organization for Standardization). They are set up to be used in metric drawings and have *lineweight*, or pen-width, settings.

Standard   Below the ISO linetypes are eight families of three linetypes each, mixed with seven special linetypes that contain graphic symbols. Each family has one basic linetype and two that are multiples of it: one has dashes twice the size (called, for example, Dashed × 2), and one has dashes half the size (called Dashed2). (See Figure 6.10, shown earlier.) Having an assortment of different sizes of one style of linetype is helpful for distinguishing between building components, such as foundation walls and beams, which, in addition to rooflines, might also need dashed lines.

Complex   Mixed in with the Standard linetypes are seven linetypes that contain symbols, letters, or words. You can use these linetypes to indicate specific elements in the drawing, such as fences, hot-water lines, railroad tracks, and others.

It isn't difficult to create or acquire your own custom linetypes. You can do so in three ways:

Using Notepad   Start the Notepad program, and navigate to the Support folder for AutoCAD 2008, usually found at this location: C:\Documents & Settings*your name*\Application Data\Autodesk\AutoCAD 2008\R18.0\enu\support. (LT users will see AutoCAD LT instead of AutoCAD 2008.)

Open the file named acad.lin whose type is listed as AutoCAD Linetype Definition. It contains the definition codes for all the linetypes; they are easy to figure out. Copy an existing pattern, and create your own. It's recommended that you back up the acad.lin file before making any modifications to it.

Using the Linetype command   Type **-linetype↵**, and then type **c↵** for the Create option. You'll be guided through the steps to create your own .lin file or add to an existing file. To use the Linetype command, you need to know the definition codes. Use Notepad until you get a feel for the codes.

Use existing linetypes   You can often find an acceptable linetypes that other AutoCAD users have created on the Internet or in various industry publications. Many are free, and some are available at a reasonable cost. The line code is simply appended to the acad.lin file on your system.

Learning More About Lineweight

In the Layer Properties Manager dialog box is a column for the Lineweight property. When you first create a layer, it's assigned the default lineweight. Just as you assigned a color and a linetype for each new layer in the cabin drawing, you can also assign a lineweight. Once assigned, lineweights can be displayed so you can see how your drawing will look when printed. In Chapter 14, you'll learn more about lineweights, about how to assign them to layers, and about how to view your drawing as it will look when printed or in What-You-See-Is-What-You-Get (WYSIWYG) mode.

Using the Current Layer as a Drawing Tool

Now is a good time to look at what it means for a layer to be current. Notice the green check mark above the Layer List box in the Layer Properties Manager dialog box. The name of the current layer, in this case, 0, appears just above the Layer List box next to the green check mark. The same green check mark appears in the Status column in the layer 0 row.

At any time, one, and only one, layer is set as the current layer. When a layer is current, all objects you draw will be on the current layer and will take on the properties assigned to that layer unless directed otherwise. Because layer 0 is current—and has been current so far in this book—all objects that you have drawn so far are on layer 0 and have the linetype and color that are specified by default for layer 0: Continuous and White (or Black), respectively. If you make the Walls layer current, any new lines you draw will be Cyan and Continuous. If the Roof layer is current, any new lines will be Blue and Dashed. Here's how to make the Walls layer the current layer:

1. Click the Walls layer in the Layer List box to highlight it, and then click the Set Current green check mark above the Layer List box. Alternately, you can double-click the Walls layer. The Walls layer replaces layer 0 as the current layer and then appears in the text box next to the green check mark. The green check mark also appears next to the Walls layer in the Layer List box.

2. Click OK to close the Layer Properties Manager dialog box and return to your drawing.

3. Look at the Layer Control drop-down list on the Layers toolbar. Most of the symbols you saw in the Layer List box, in the Layer Properties Manager dialog box, are on this drop-down list. The Walls layer is the visible entry on the list and has a cyan square (the color you assigned

to the Walls layer earlier). The layer visible in this list when it's closed and no objects are selected is the current layer.

4. Now look at your drawing. Nothing has changed because the objects in the drawing are still on layer 0.

You need to move the objects in the drawing onto their proper layers. To do this, you'll use the Layer Control drop-down list on the Layers toolbar to assign each object to one of the new layers.

Assigning Objects to Layers

When assigning existing objects in the drawing to new layers, your strategy will be to begin by selecting all the objects that belong on the same layer and that are easiest to select. You'll reassign them to their new layer using the Layer Control drop-down list. You'll then move to a set of objects that belong on a different layer and are slightly more difficult to select, and so on.

1. In the drawing, pick the two arcs of the balcony. Grips appear on the arcs, and the lines ghost. This signals that the lines have been selected (see Figure 6.13).

The grips that appear on the arcs include squares as well as triangles. It makes the drawing look complicated, but don't worry about the triangles for now.

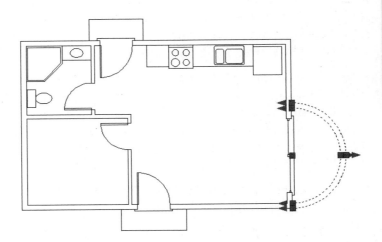

FIGURE 6.13: The balcony arcs, selected and displaying their grips

Notice also that in the Layer Control drop-down list, the layer being displayed now is layer 0 rather than Walls, the current layer. When objects are selected with no command running, the Layer Control drop-down list displays the layer to which the selected objects are currently assigned. If selected objects are on more than one layer, the Layer Control drop-down list is blank.

2. Click the Layer Control drop-down list to open it (see Figure 6.14).

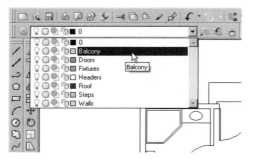

FIGURE 6.14: The opened Layer Control drop-down list

3. Click the Balcony layer. The list closes. The Balcony layer appears in the Layer Control drop-down list. The balcony arcs have been moved to the Balcony layer and are now green.

4. Press Esc to deselect the arcs and remove the grips. The current layer, Walls, returns to the Layer Control drop-down list.

This is the process you need to go through for each object so it will be placed on the proper layer. In the next section, you'll move the threshold and steps to the Steps layer. You'll select the threshold and steps by using a selection window.

Selecting Objects with Windows

The crossing window is represented by dashed lines, and its interior is, by default, a semitransparent light green color. The regular window is represented by solid lines, and its interior is a semitransparent lavender color when using a white background and blue when using a black background.

By default, AutoCAD is set up so that whenever no command is running and the prompt in the Command window is Command:, you can pick objects one at a time or start a regular or crossing window. If you pick an object, it's selected, and its grips appear. If you select a blank area of the drawing, this starts a selection window. If you then move the cursor to the right of the point just picked, this starts a regular window. If you move the cursor to the left, this starts a crossing window.

You'll use a crossing window to select the sliding-glass door threshold, and you'll use two regular windows to select the front and back steps and those thresholds:

1. Zoom into the sliding-glass door area. Click the Osnap button on the status bar to turn it off, if it isn't already off.

2. Hold the crosshair cursor above and to the right of the upper-right corner of the balcony threshold—still inside the balcony wall—as shown in the left of Figure 6.15. Click that point, and then move the cursor down and to the left until you have made a tall, thin crossing window that completely encloses the right edge of the threshold and is crossed on its left edge by the short horizontal connecting lines, as shown in the right of Figure 6.15. Then, click again. The three lines that make up the threshold are selected. Click the Layer Control drop-down list to open it, and then click the Steps layer. The balcony threshold is now on the Steps layer.

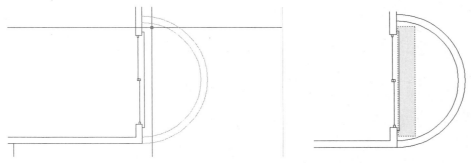

When you zoom or pan with the Zoom or Pan tool, the grips are deselected. When you zoom or pan using the scroll wheel, they are not.

FIGURE 6.15: Starting the crossing selection window (left) and completing it (right)

3. Use Zoom Previous to return to a view of the entire drawing. Make two regular selection windows to select the front and back steps and their thresholds. Be sure your first pick starts a window at the left and finishes to the right of each step so the window completely encloses the horizontal and vertical lines that make up each step and threshold. Figure 6.16 illustrates the two regular selection windows and the points to pick to create them. Once selected, the objects display their grips. For lines, grips appear at each endpoint and at the midpoint of each segment. When endpoints of lines coincide, their grips overlap. When lines are very short, their grips might appear to overlap, but this is just the result of the zoom factor.

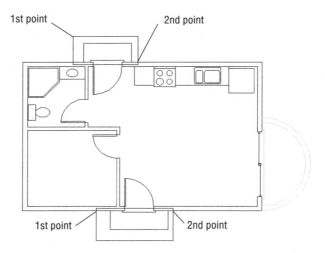

FIGURE 6.16: The two regular selection windows used to select the front and back steps and thresholds

4. Click the Layer Control drop-down list, and then click the Steps layer. The front and back steps and their thresholds are now on the Steps layer.

5. Press the Esc key to deselect the objects and remove the grips.

Selecting the Doors and Swings

Grips have uses other than signaling that an object has been selected. You'll learn about some of these as you progress through the chapters.

To select the doors and swings, you can use crossing windows. Let's examine this task closely to learn more valuable skills about how to select objects:

1. Place the crosshair cursor in a clear space below and to the right of the back door, and then pick that point to start the selection window. Move the cursor up and to the left until the crossing window crosses the back door and swing but doesn't cross the wall line, as shown in the top of Figure 6.17.

2. When you have the crossing window sized and positioned correctly, click again to select the back door and its swing.

3. Move to the bathroom, and position the crosshair cursor in the clear space directly above the swing. When the crosshairs is positioned, click. Then, move the cursor down and to the left until the window you're creating crosses the bathroom door and swing, without crossing any wall lines (see the middle of Figure 6.17). Click in a clear space again. The bathroom door and swing are selected.

4. Continue this procedure to select the other two doors and their swings. For the bedroom door, start the crossing window directly below the door swing. For the front door, start a crossing window above and to the right of the door. The bottom of Figure 6.17 shows the two crossing windows that will select the bedroom and front doors.

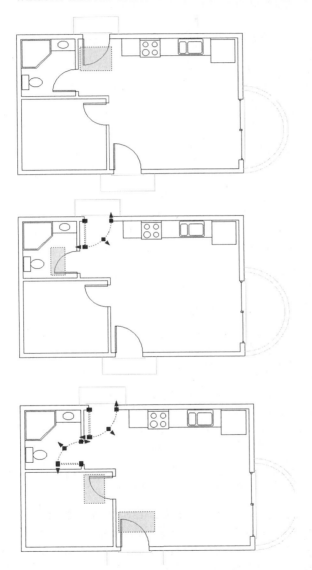

FIGURE 6.17: Using a crossing window to select the doors and swings: the back door (top), the bathroom door (middle), and the bedroom and front doors (bottom)

5. Open the Layer Control drop-down list, and select the Doors layer. Then, press Esc to remove the grips. The swinging doors are now red and on the Doors layer.

For the sliding-glass door, it's awkward to create a crossing window from left to right because it might be difficult to position the pickbox between the threshold lines and the sliding door. In this situation, use a regular window to select the objects:

1. Zoom in to the sliding-glass door area. Pick a point to the left of the balcony opening, just above the upper jamb line. Move the crosshairs down and to the right until the right edge of the window sits inside the wall but just to the right of the sliding-glass window frames, not encompassing the entire jamb. When your window is positioned as shown in Figure 6.18, click. The entire sliding-glass door assembly is selected but not the jambs, walls, threshold, or balcony. Many grips appear: 13 lines make up the sliding-glass door, and each has 3 grips, a grip at each endpoint and a grip at each midpoint. Many of the grips overlap.

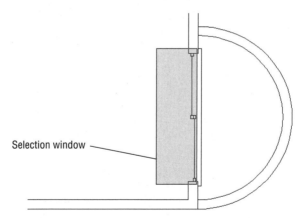

Selection window

FIGURE 6.18: Using a regular selection window to select the sliding-glass door

2. Open the Layer Control drop-down list, and select the Doors layer.

3. Press Esc to remove the grips, and then use Zoom Previous. You have a full view of the floor plan, and all doors are red and reside on the Doors layer.

The next task is to move the kitchen and bathroom counters and fixtures onto the Fixtures layer. In doing this, you'll learn how to deselect some objects from a group of selected objects.

Selecting the Kitchen and Bathroom Fixtures

Sometimes it's more efficient to select more objects than you want and then deselect those you don't want. You'll see how this is done when you select the kitchen and bathroom fixtures:

1. Pick a point in the kitchen area just below the refrigerator to start a crossing window.

2. Move the cursor to the left and up until the upper-left corner of the crossing window is to the left of the left edge of the counter and inside the back wall, as shown in the left of Figure 6.19. When you have it correct, click that point. The entire kitchen counter area and the back wall line are selected.

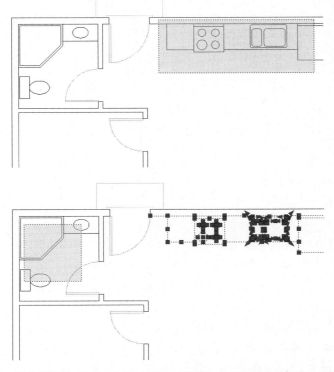

FIGURE 6.19: A crossing window to select the kitchen objects (top), another crossing window to select the bathroom objects (bottom), and the completed selection set after removing the door swing and back wall line (next page)

Continues

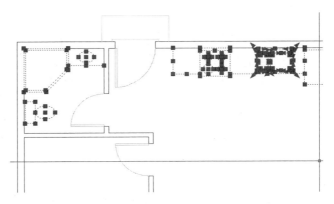

FIGURE 6.19 *(Continued)*

3. Move over to the bathroom, and pick a point in the middle of the bathroom sink, being careful not to touch any lines with the crosshair cursor.

4. Move the crosshair cursor down and to the left until the lower-left corner of the crossing window is in the middle of the toilet tank (see the middle of Figure 6.19). When you have it positioned this way, click that point. All the bathroom fixtures and the door swing are selected.

5. Hold down the Shift key, and then pick the selected door swing in the bathroom and the back wall line in the kitchen. Be careful to not pick a grip. As you pick them, their lines become solid again and their grips disappear, letting you know they have been deselected, or removed, from the selection set (see the right of Figure 6.19). Be sure to pick the back wall line in the kitchen where it doesn't coincide with the stove.

6. Release the Shift key. Open the Layer Control drop-down list, and select the Fixtures layer. The fixtures are now on the Fixtures layer and are magenta.

7. Press the Esc key to deselect the objects.

The last objects to move onto a new layer are the wall lines. As the drawing is now, it won't be easy to select the wall lines because so many other objects in the drawing are in the way. However, these other objects are now on their own layers, whereas the wall lines are still on layer 0. If you make all your layers temporarily invisible except for the 0 and Walls layers, selecting the wall lines will be easy.

Before you do that, let's pause and look at the selection process. The sidebar "Selecting Objects in Your Drawing" summarizes the selection process and the tools I have covered so far.

SELECTING OBJECTS IN YOUR DRAWING

As you select objects in the cabin drawing to move them onto their pre-scribed layers, you use various selection tools. These tools are important, and mastering them will greatly enhance your performance as an AutoCAD user. As you select objects by picking them and windowing them, you're building a *selection set*. You might later want to remove objects from that selection set. Here is a summary of the basic selection tools that you have used so far, with a couple of additions:

Picking   This is the basic, bottom-line selection tool. Click the line, circle, or other object to select it. If no command is running, grips appear on the selected object, and the object becomes dashed. If a command is running and you're being prompted with `Select objects:`, grips don't appear, but the object is selected and ghosts. In AutoCAD you can select objects and then issue a command, or you can issue the command first and then select the objects as directed.

Selecting a window automatically   To start a window, click a location that is in an empty portion of the screen, where there are no objects. To form a regular window, move your cursor to the right. To form a crossing window, move your cursor to the left. This feature is called *implied window-ing*, and it works this way if no command is running or if one is running and the prompt says `Select objects:`.

If the geometry of your drawing makes forming a crossing or regular selec-tion window difficult because of the need to move from right to left (cross-ing) or from left to right (regular), you can force one or the other by typing **c↵** or **w↵**, respectively, but only if a command is running.

Removing objects from a selection set   At some point, you'll find it more efficient to select more objects than you want and then remove the unwanted ones. You can do this in two ways:

▶ To remove a couple of objects, hold down the Shift key, and pick the objects.

▶ To remove many objects from the selection set, hold down the Shift key, and use one of the selection window types.

▶ If a command is running, enter **r↵**, and then use the selection tools (picking, windows, and so on) without the Shift key to remove objects from the selection set.

If you are in a command and need to add objects back to the selection set after removing some, enter **a↵**. This puts you back into selection mode, and you can continue adding objects to the set.

Turning Off and Freezing Layers

You can make layers invisible either by turning them off or by *freezing* them. When a layer is turned off or frozen, the objects on that layer are invisible. These two procedures operate in nearly the same way and perform about the same function, with one significant difference: objects on frozen layers cannot be selected with the All option, while objects on layers that are off can. For example, if you enter e↵ a↵↵ to erase all objects, all the visible and invisible objects on the layers turned off are deleted, while the objects on frozen layers remain in the drawing but are still invisible. Here is a good rule to follow: If you want a layer to be invisible for only a short time, turn it off; if you prefer that it be invisible semipermanently, freeze it.

For the task at hand, you'll turn off all the layers except layer 0 and the Walls layer. You'll then move the wall lines onto the Walls layer:

Layers beginning with numbers appear first, in numeric order. Following those are the rest of the layers, listed alphabetically.

1. Click the Layer Properties Manager button on the Layers toolbar to open the Layer Properties Manager dialog box. Notice that layer 0 is still first in the list and that the other layers have been reorganized alphabetically (see the left of Figure 6.20). Also, notice the icons in the Status column: a green check mark signifies that the Walls layer is current; the light blue layer icons signify that those layers (0, Balcony, Doors, Fixtures, and Steps) now have objects on them; and the light gray layer icons tell you that those layers (Headers and Roof) don't have any objects on them.

N O T E   Because the Walls layer is current and has a green check mark in the Status column, you can't tell whether it has any objects on it. You have to make another layer current and then check whether the Walls icon is blue or gray.

2. Click the Balcony layer to highlight it. Then, hold down the Shift key, and click the Steps layer. All layers are selected except layer 0 and the Walls layer.

3. Move the arrow cursor over to the On column, which has a lit lightbulb as a symbol for each layer row.

4. Click one of the lightbulbs of the selected layers. The lit lightbulb symbols all change to unlit bulbs except the ones for layer 0 and the Walls layer (see the right of Figure 6.20).

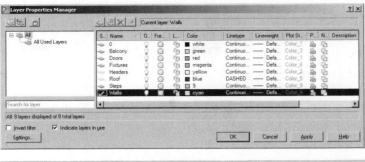

FIGURE 6.20: The layers, now listed alphabetically (top) and newly turned-off layers (bottom)

5. Click OK. All objects in your drawing are invisible except the wall lines (see Figure 6.21). The wall lines are still on layer 0.

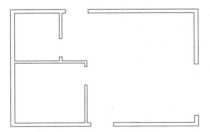

FIGURE 6.21: The floor plan with all layers turned off except the Walls layer and layer 0

6. Start a regular selection window around the cabin by clicking the upper-left corner of the drawing area, above and to the left of any lines. Then, click the lower-right corner in the same way. All the wall lines are selected, and grips appear on all of them.

7. Open the Layer Control drop-down list, and then click the Walls layer. The walls move to the Walls layer and are now cyan. Press Esc to deselect the objects.

8. Click the Layer Properties Manager button on the Layers toolbar. In the Layer Properties Manager dialog box, right-click any layer, and choose Select All from the shortcut menu. All layers are highlighted.

9. Click one of the unlit bulbs in the On column. All unlit bulbs become lit. Click OK. Back in your drawing, all objects are now visible and on their correct layers (see Figure 6.22).

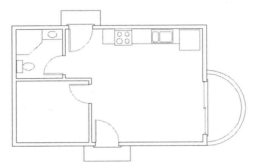

FIGURE 6.22: The floor plan with all layers visible and all objects on their correct layers

10. Save this drawing in your training folder as Cabin06a.dwg.

Two of your layers, Roof and Headers, still have no objects on them because these components haven't been drawn yet. You'll draw the headers now.

Drawing the Headers

Most door and window openings don't extend to the ceiling. The portion of the wall above the opening and below the ceiling is the *header*. The term comes from the name of the beam inside the wall that spans the opening. In a floor plan, wall lines usually stop at the door and window openings, but you need lines across the gap between jamb lines to show that an opening doesn't extend to the ceiling; hence, you'll create the header.

To draw headers directly onto the correct layer, you need to make the Headers layer current. As you've seen, you can use the Layer Properties Manager dialog box. But you can also use a shortcut, the Layer Control drop-down list, which you have just been using to move objects from one layer to another:

1. Click anywhere on the drop-down list, or click the down-arrow button on the right end. The drop-down list opens, displaying a list of the layers in your drawing. If you have more than 10 layers, a scroll bar becomes operational, giving you access to all the layers.

2. Click the Headers layer. The drop-down list closes. Headers is now in the box; this tells you that the Headers layer has replaced Walls as the current layer.

3. Turn on the Osnap button on the status bar if necessary. The End-point, Midpoint, and Intersection osnaps are now active. If not, then choose Settings from the shortcut menu to open the Drafting Settings dialog box at the Object Snap tab. Check the Endpoint, Midpoint, and Intersection are the only Object Snap modes with a check mark, and then click OK.

4. The doors and steps might be in your way. Click the Layer drop-down list. When the list of layers appears, click the lightbulb icons for the Doors and Steps layers to turn them off. Then, click Headers. The drop-down list closes; the Headers layer is still current. The doors, steps, and thresholds have temporarily disappeared.

   You need to draw two parallel lines across each of the five openings, from the endpoint of one jamb line to the corresponding endpoint of the jamb on the opposite side of the opening.

5. To start the Line command, enter l↵. Move the cursor near the upper end of the left jamb for the back door until the colored square appears at the upper endpoint of the jamb line, and then click.

6. Move the cursor to the upper end of the right jamb, and repeat the preceding step.

7. Right-click once to open a context menu near your cursor (see Figure 6.23).

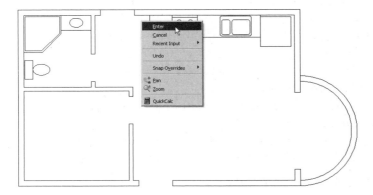

FIGURE 6.23: A right-click context menu

8. Choose Enter from the menu, and then right-click again to open another context menu at the cursor, as shown in Figure 6.24.

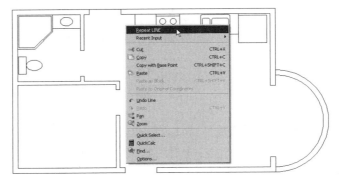

FIGURE 6.24: A second right-click context menu

9. Choose Repeat Line.

10. Move to the lower endpoint of the right jamb line for the back door and—with the same technique used in steps 5 through 9—draw the lower header line across the opening. You can see the results in the bottom of Figure 6.25.

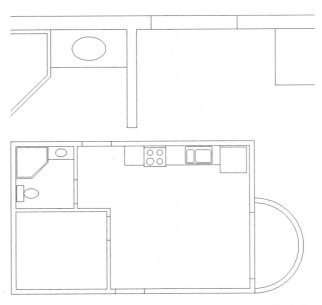

FIGURE 6.25: The header lines drawn for the back door opening (top) and for the rest of the doorway openings (bottom)

11. Keep using the same procedure to draw the rest of the header lines for the remaining four doorway openings. Use a click, click, right-click, click, right-click, click pattern that repeats for each header line. Here are the steps:

   a. Click one of the jamb corners.

   b. Click the opposite jamb corner.

   c. Right-click to open a context menu.

   d. Choose Enter on the menu to end the Line command.

   e. Right-click again to open another context menu.

   f. Choose Repeat Line.

   g. Click one of the jamb corners.

   h. And so on.

The floor plan will look like the right of Figure 6.25.

N O T E   Context menus—also called *shortcut menus* and *right-click menus*—contain frequently used tools. The specific tools on a menu depend on what you're doing when you right-click. It was not terribly efficient to use them to draw the header lines, but it was a good way to introduce them to you. It's also a way to draw without using the keyboard.

The Layer drop-down list box is a shortcut that allows you to quickly pick a different layer as the current layer and to turn off or turn on individual layers. To create new layers or to turn off many layers at a time, use the Layer Properties Manager dialog box. (Click the Layer Properties Manager button on the Layers toolbar, or enter la↵.) You'll learn about another tool for changing the current layer as you draw the rooflines.

Drawing the Roof

Before you start to draw the rooflines, refer to Figure 6.26, and note the lines representing different parts of the roof:

► Four *eaves lines* around the perimeter of the building, representing the lowest edge of the roof

► One *ridgeline*, representing the peak of the roof

► Four *hip lines*, connecting the endpoints of the eaves lines to an endpoint of the ridgeline

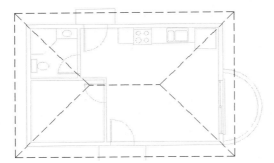

F I G U R E 6 . 2 6 : The floor plan with the rooflines

The roof for the cabin is called a *hip roof* because the end panels slope down to the eaves just as the middle panels do. The intersections of the sloping roof planes form the hip lines. You'll start with the eaves.

Creating the Eaves

Because the roof is cantilevered out beyond the exterior walls the same distance on all sides of the building, you can generate the eaves lines by offsetting the outside wall lines:

1. Open the Layer drop-down list, and select Roof to make it current. Then, start the Offset command. The second prompt line from the bottom of the command window says Layer=Source, meaning the objects created by the Offset command will be on the same layer as the object offset. Enter l↵ to use the Layer option. Enter c↵ to select Current. Then, enter 1'6↵ to set the offset distance. Pick the left out-side wall line, and then pick a point to the left of that line to offset it to the outside. The offset line is on the Roof layer.

2. Move to another side of the building, pick one of the outside wall lines, and offset it to the outside.

3. Repeat this process for the other two sides of the building until you have offset one outside wall line to the outside of the building on each side of the cabin (see Figure 6.27). Press ↵ to end the Offset command. Be sure you have only one line offset on each side of the building. If you offset two lines on one side, erase one. Start the Off-set command again, enter l↵, and then enter s↵ to reset the Layer setting to Source. Press Esc to end the Offset command.

4. Enter f↵ to start the Fillet command. Make sure the radius is set to zero. If it is, go to step 5. If it isn't, enter r↵, and then enter 0↵ to reset the radius (or use the Shift key to override the radius value).

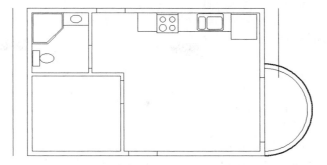

FIGURE 6.27: One outside wall line is offset to each side of the building.

5. Click any two of these newly offset lines that are on adjacent sides of the building. Click the half of the line nearest the corner where the two selected lines will meet (see the left of Figure 6.28). The lines extend to meet each other and form a corner (see the right of Figure 6.28). The Fillet command ends.

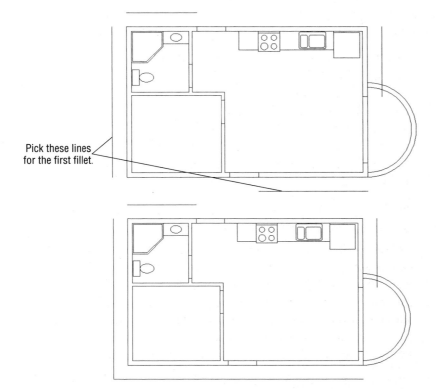

Pick these lines for the first fillet.

FIGURE 6.28: Picking lines to fillet one of the eaves' corners (top) and the result (bottom)

6. Press ↵ to restart the Fillet command, and then enter m↵ to select the Multiple option. Pick the remaining three pairs of adjacent lines that will meet at the corners, and then press the Esc key to terminate the command. The result is a rectangle that represents the eaves of the roof surrounding the building, offset 1'-6" from the outside exterior walls (see Figure 6.29).

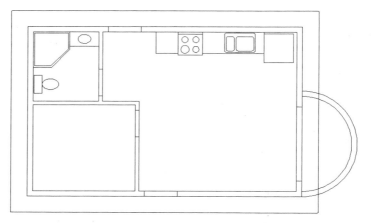

FIGURE 6.29: The eaves lines after filleting

Setting a Linetype Scale Factor

By default, the dashes in the Dashed linetype are set up to be ½" long with ¼" spaces. This is the correct size for a drawing that is close to actual size on your screen, like the box you drew in Chapter 2. But for something that is the size of your cabin, you must increase the linetype scale to make the dashes large enough to see. If the dashes were 12" long with 6" spaces, they would at least be visible, although possibly not exactly the right size. To make such a change in the dash size, ask what you must multiply ½" by to get 12". The answer is 24—so that's your scale factor. AutoCAD stores a Linetype Scale Factor setting that controls the size of the dashes and spaces of noncontinuous linetypes. The default is 1.00, which gives you the ½" dash, so you need to change the setting to 24.00:

1. Enter ltscale↵ or lts↵. The prompt in the Command window says New scale factor <1.0000>:.

2. Enter 24↵ to set the linetype scale factor to 24. Your drawing changes, and you can see the dashes (see Figure 6.30).

   If you aren't satisfied with the dash size, restart the Ltscale command, and increase the scale factor for a longer dash or decrease it for a shorter one. This linetype scale factor is global, meaning that it affects every noncontinuous line in the drawing. There is also an individual scale factor for linetypes. You'll see that in the next section.

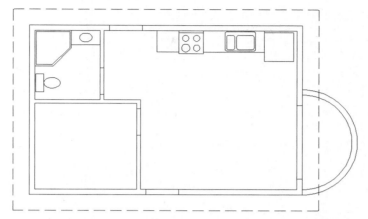

FIGURE 6.30: The eaves lines on the Roof layer with visible dashes

Assigning an Individual Linetype Scale Factor

Although the Ltscale command sets a linetype scale factor for all noncontinuous lines in the drawing, you can adjust the dash and space sizes for individual lines. To change the dash and space size for one of the eaves lines of the roof to make them larger, follow these steps:

1. Select an eaves line.

2. Click the Properties button on the Standard toolbar, or right-click and choose Properties from the context menu, to open the Properties palette.

3. Click Linetype Scale. Highlight the current scale of 1.0000, and enter 3↵.

4. Close the Properties palette, and press Esc to deselect the objects. The dashes and spaces of the previously selected eaves line are three times larger than those for the rest of the rooflines.

5. Click the Properties button, and use the same procedure to change the current linetype scale factor for the eaves line back to 1.

> **N O T E**   If no objects are selected and you set Linetype Scale in the Prop-
> erties palette to a number other than 1.000, any noncontinuous lines that are
> subsequently drawn will be controlled by this new Linetype Scale setting.

This feature allows you to get subtle variations in the size of dashes and spaces for individual noncontinuous lines. But remember that all lines are controlled by an individual linetype scale factor and by the global linetype scale factor. The actual size of the dashes and spaces for a particular line is a result of multiplying the two linetype scale factors together. This additional flexibility requires you to keep careful track of the variations you're making.

To find out the current linetype scale value for new objects and the global linetype scale factor, follow these steps:

1. Enter **linetype**↵ to open the Linetype Manager dialog box.

2. Make sure the Details area is visible at the bottom of the dialog box. If it isn't, click Show Details in the upper-right corner.

3. Note the bottom-right corner. The current global and object linetype scales appear here (see Figure 6.31). You can also modify them here.

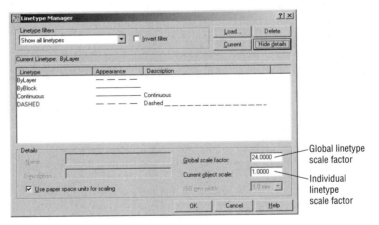

FIGURE 6.31: The Linetype Manager dialog box

4. For now, click Cancel.

Drawing the Hip Lines and Ridgelines

Next, you'll draw two of the diagonal hip rooflines and then use the Mirror command to create the other two. Look at the Linetype Control drop-down list on the Properties toolbar. A dashed line with the name ByLayer appears there. ByLayer tells you that the current linetype will be whatever linetype has been assigned to the current layer. In the case of the Roof layer, the assigned linetype is Dashed. You'll read more about ByLayer later in this chapter.

First, make a few setting adjustments. Then you'll draw the rooflines:

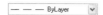

1. The Endpoint osnap should still be running. How can you tell? Enter os.↵ to open the Drafting Settings dialog box to the Osnap tab. You can easily see which osnaps are checked. Next, click the Polar Tracking tab (see Figure 6.32).

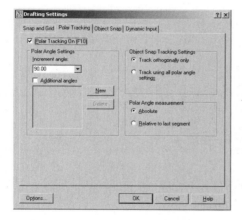

FIGURE 6.32: The Polar Tracking tab in the Drafting Settings dialog box

2. At the top, click the Polar Tracking On (F10) check box to turn on polar tracking.

3. In the Polar Angle Settings area, open the Increment Angle drop-down list, and select 45.

4. Click OK to close the Drafting Settings dialog box.

5. Start the Line command. Move the crosshair cursor to the lower-left corner of the rectangle representing the roof until the square appears on the corner, and then click. This starts a line.

6. Move the crosshair cursor up and to the right at a 45° angle from the lower-left corner of the roof. When the angle of the line being drawn approaches 45°, a tracking path and a Polar tooltip appears, along with a small *x* near the crosshair cursor (see the top of Figure 6.33).

7. While the tracking path is visible, enter 15'.↵↵. This draws the first hip line, and the Line command ends (see the bottom of Figure 6.33). The line is a bit longer than you need, but you'll trim it shortly.

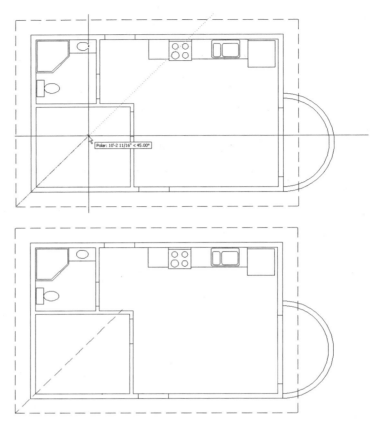

Polar: 10'-2 11/16" < 45.00°

FIGURE 6.33: The 45° tracking path for the first hip line of the roof (top) and the completed first hip line (bottom)

Use the same procedure to draw another hip line from the upper-left corner of the roof. Here's a summary of the steps:

1. Restart the Line command, and start a line at the upper-left corner of the roof.

2. Hold the crosshair cursor down and to the right at an angle of approximately 45° until the polar tracking path with its tooltip appears. (The tooltip confirms that the actual angle is 315°.)

3. Enter 15'⌐⌐. This completes the second hip line.

You need to fillet the two hip lines together at their intersection:

1. Start the Fillet command, and then fillet the two hip lines with a radius of zero (see the left of Figure 6.34). Now you need to mirror these two diagonal lines to the right side of the roof.

2. Start the Mirror command. At the prompt to select objects, select the two diagonal lines, and then press ↵. At the Specify first point of mirror line: prompt, use the Midpoint osnap to place the cursor at the middle of the top horizontal eaves line above the cabin. When the triangle appears at the midpoint of the eaves line, click.

3. Move the crosshair cursor down into the living room, keeping it directly below the point just picked; when the tracking line and Polar tooltip appear, click a clear space. Press ↵ when asked whether to delete old objects. The diagonal lines from the left are mirrored to the right (see the bottom of Figure 6.34). The Mirror command automatically ends. To finish the roof, you'll draw the ridgeline.

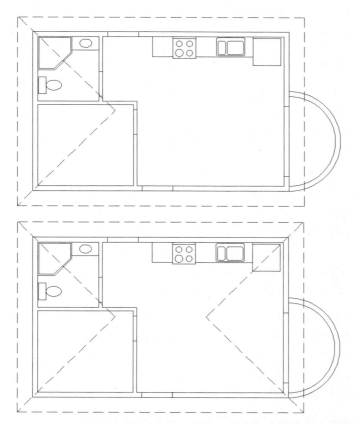

F I G U R E 6 . 3 4 : The first two hip lines are filleted together (top) and then mirrored to the right (bottom).

4. Start the Line command. The Endpoint osnap is still running. Pick the two intersections of the diagonal lines, and then press ⏎. Open the Layer Control drop-down list, and turn on the Doors and Steps layers. Then, click the Roof layer to close the drop-down list. This completes the ridgeline and finishes the roof (see Figure 6.35).

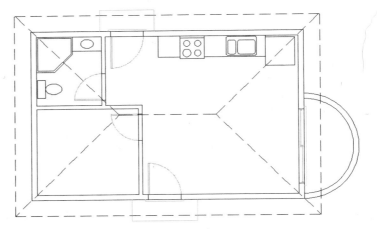

FIGURE 6.35: The completed roof

Making the Doors Layer Current

Before saving this drawing, use the Make Object's Layer Current button to make the Doors layer current:

 1. Click the Make Object's Layer Current button on the Layers toolbar, just to the right of the Layer Control drop-down list. You'll get the `Select object whose layer will become current:` prompt.

2. Pick one of the door or swing lines. The Doors layer replaces Roof in the Layer drop-down list, telling you the Doors layer is now the current layer.

3. Save this drawing as `Cabin06b.dwg`.

 T I P   The Make Object's Layer Current button works two ways. You can click the button and then select the object whose layer will become current, or you can select an object with the target layer and then click the button. If the latter method is used and multiple objects are selected, they must all reside on the current layer, or the tool will prompt you for a layer.

By drawing the rooflines, you have completed the exercises for this chapter. The cabin floor plan is almost complete. In the next chapter, you'll complete the floor plan by placing windows in the external walls using a new grouping tool called a *block*. The rest of this chapter contains a short discussion about color, linetypes, and lineweights and how they work with layers and objects.

Setting Properties of Layers and Objects

Here are a few concepts to consider when assigning properties to layers and objects.

Selecting Colors for Layers and Objects

First, you must decide whether you prefer a light or dark background color for the drawing area. This is generally a personal preference, but the lighting in your work area can be a contributing factor. Bright work areas usually make it difficult to read monitors easily, and with a dark background color on your screen in a brightly lit room, you'll often get distracting reflections on the screen. Eyestrain can result. Darkening your work area will usually minimize these effects. If that's not possible, you might have to live with a lighter background.

Next, look at the colors in your drawing. If the background of your drawing area is white, notice which colors are the easiest to read. For most monitors, yellow, light gray, and cyan are somewhat faded, while blue, green, red, and magenta are read easily. If your drawing area background is black, the blue is sometimes too dark to read easily, but the rest of the colors that you have used so far usually read well. This is one reason that most users prefer the black or at least a dark background color.

Assigning a Color or a Linetype to an Object Instead of a Layer

You can also assign properties of layers, such as color, linetype, and lineweights, to objects. So, for example, think about the Roof layer. It's assigned the Dashed linetype. A line on the Roof layer can be assigned the Continuous linetype, even though all other lines on the Roof layer are dashed. The same is true for color and lineweights. Occasionally, this makes sense, especially for linetypes, but that is the exception, rather than the rule. To make such a change, select the line, open the Properties palette, and change the linetype from ByLayer to the linetype of your choice. You can also use the Properties toolbar to make quick changes to an object's appearance.

In this chapter, you have seen how to assign colors and linetypes to layers in order to control the way objects on those layers appear. That is the rule to follow. When objects are assigned properties that vary from those of their layer, the result can be confusing to someone working with your drawing file, because the objects don't appear to be on their assigned layer. If the object's properties match those of another layer, you can mistakenly think the object is on that layer.

Making a Color or a Linetype Current

If you look at the Properties toolbar for a moment, you'll see, to the right of the Layer Control drop-down list, more such lists. The first three are the Color, Linetype, and Lineweight controls. You use these tools to set a color, linetype, or lineweight to be current. When this is done, each object subsequently created will be assigned the current linetype, lineweight, and/or color, regardless of which linetype, lineweight, and color have been assigned to the current layer. If, for example, the Doors layer is set as the current layer and the Dashed linetype and green color are also assigned as current, any lines drawn are dashed and green but still on the Doors layer. This isn't a good way to set up the system of layers, linetypes, and colors because of the obvious confusion it will create in your drawing, but beginners often accidentally do this.

The best way to maintain maximum control of your drawing is to keep the current linetype, lineweight, and color set to ByLayer, as they are by default. When you do this, colors and linetypes are controlled by the layers, and objects take on the color and linetype of the layers they are on. If this configuration is accidentally disturbed and objects are created with the wrong color or linetype, you can correct the situation without too much trouble. First, reset the current color, lineweight, and linetype to ByLayer by using the Property Control drop-down list on the Properties toolbar. Second, select all problem objects; then click the Properties button to change the linetype, lineweight, or color of the ByLayer. They will then take on the color, lineweight, and linetype of the layer to which they have been assigned, and you can quickly tell whether they are on their proper layers.

Creating Layer States

Although they might read well when printed, drawings might get cluttered in the viewports, and it can get difficult to properly execute the command. This was evident earlier when the door swing made it harder than it should have been to trim the hip lines. Often, you will find yourself freezing or turning off the same layers to execute a specific task and then making them visible again. In the course of your workday, you might issue the same sequence of layer commands dozens of time. To make this task more efficient, layer states are available. *Layer states* are named settings where you can save the conditions of the layers, such as On, Frozen, or Current, and restore them through the Layer States Manager dialog box. The following exercise demonstrates how to create a layer state that shows only the floor plan and not the roof or fixtures:

1. Make layer 0 the current layer.

2. From the Layer Control drop-down list or the Layer Properties Manager dialog box, freeze the Roof and Fixtures layers.

3. From the Layers toolbar, click the Layer States Manager button. This button is also available on the toolbar in the Layer Properties Manager dialog box. The Layer States Manager dialog box opens (see Figure 6.36).

FIGURE 6.36: The Layer States Manager dialog box

4. Click the New button to create a new saved layer state. In the New Layer State to Save dialog box, enter **Floor Plan** in the New Layer State Name field. If you like, enter a description for the layer state as well. Click the OK button when you are done.

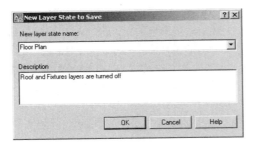

5. The new layer state appears in the Layer States Manager dialog box, as shown in Figure 6.37. Click the Close button to close the Layer States Manager dialog box.

FIGURE 6.37: The Layer States Manager dialog box showing the new layer state

6. Thaw the Roof and Fixtures layers. The objects on those layers become visible again.

7. Open the Layer States Manager dialog box again. Click the More Restore Options button, the right-facing arrow at the bottom-right corner, to display additional options. The items shown in the Layer Properties to Restore section are, when checked, the features of the layer state that are affected when it is restored. It is important to note that if you make changes to a layer's color or lineweight, those changes are lost when the layer state is restored if those features are checked here.

8. Uncheck the Color, Linetype, and Lineweight options (see Figure 6.38), and then click the Restore button.

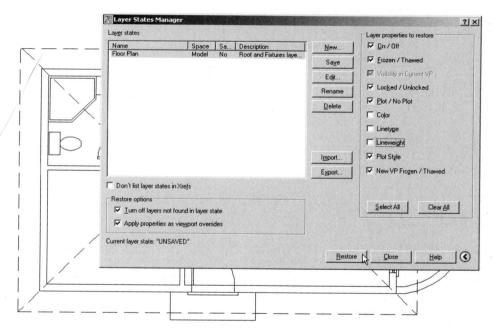

FIGURE 6.38: The Layer States Manager dialog box with the restore options selected

9. The Roof and Fixtures layers are frozen again (see Figure 6.39).

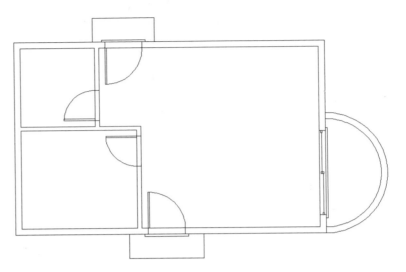

FIGURE 6.39: The cabin with the Roof and Fixtures layers frozen

10. Save this drawing as Cabin06c.dwg.

As you can see, saving layer states can reduce the number of steps it takes to restore a specific set of layer properties. In a complex drawing, it isn't uncommon to have a dozen or more saved layer states.

If You Would Like More Practice...

All trades and professions that use AutoCAD have their own standards for naming and organizing layers. The following suggestions urge you to apply this chapter's concepts to your individual use of the program.

Experimenting with Linetypes and Linetype Scales

Choose Save As to save Cabin06b.dwg to a new file called Cabin06b_Linetype.dwg. Then, experiment with the linetypes and linetype scales (Global and Object) to get a feel for how the linetypes look and how the scales work. You won't be using this practice file again, so feel free to draw new objects that will make it convenient for you to work with linetypes. Here are some suggestions for linetypes to experiment with:

- ▶ Dashed2 or Dashed (0.5×)
- ▶ Dashed×2 or Dashed (2×)
- ▶ Hidden (as compared to Dashed)
- ▶ Phantom
- ▶ DashDot
- ▶ Fenceline2
- ▶ Hot_Water_Supply

Here is a summary of the steps to get a new linetype into your drawing:

1. Create a new layer, or highlight an existing layer.
2. Click linetype name in the Linetype column for the chosen layer.
3. Click the Load button.
4. Highlight a linetype in the list, and click OK.
5. Highlight the new linetype in the Linetype Manager dialog box, and click OK.
6. Make the layer with the new linetype the Current layer, and then click OK to close the Layer Properties Manager dialog box.
7. Draw objects.

Once you have a few linetypes represented in the drawing, open the Linetype Manager dialog box, and experiment with the Global and Object linetype scale factors.

Setting Up Layers for Your Own Trade or Profession

Open a new drawing, and set up approximately 10 layers that you might use in your own profession. Assign them colors and linetypes. Most activities that use CAD have some layers in common, such as Centerline, Border or Titleblock, Drawing Symbols, Dimensions, and Text or Lettering.

Are You Experienced?

Now you can...

- ☑ create new layers and assign them a color and a linetype
- ☑ load a new linetype into your current drawing file
- ☑ move existing objects onto a new layer
- ☑ turn layers off and on
- ☑ make a layer current and create objects on the current layer
- ☑ reset the linetype scale factor to make noncontinuous lines visible
- ☑ use polar tracking to draw a diagonal line
- ☑ create layer states
- ☑ use the individual linetype scale factor to adjust the size of one dashed line

CHAPTER 7

Combining Objects into Blocks

- ▶ Creating and inserting blocks

- ▶ Using the Wblock command

- ▶ Detecting blocks in a drawing

- ▶ Working with AutoCAD's DesignCenter

- ▶ Controlling the appearance of palettes on your screen

C omputer drafting derives much of its efficiency from a feature that makes it possible to combine a collection of objects into an entity that behaves as one object. AutoCAD calls these combined objects a *block*. The AutoCAD tools that work specifically with blocks make it possible to do the following:

► Create a block in your current drawing.

► Repeatedly place copies of a block in precise locations in your drawing.

► Share blocks between drawings.

► Create .dwg files either from blocks or from portions of your current drawing.

► Store blocks on a palette for easy reuse in any drawing.

In general, objects best suited to becoming part of a block are the components that are repeatedly used in your drawings. In architecture and construction, examples of these components are doors, windows, and fixtures or drawing symbols, such as a "north" arrow or labels for a section cut line (see Figure 7.1). In your cabin drawing, you'll convert the doors with swings into blocks. You'll then create a new block that you'll use to place the windows in the cabin drawing. To accomplish these tasks, you need to learn two new commands:

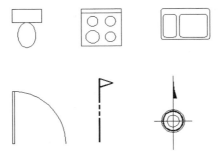

FIGURE 7.1: Examples of blocks often used in architectural drawings

Making a Block for a Door

When making a block, you create a *block definition*. This is an invisible entity that is stored in the drawing file and consists of the following:

► The block name

► An insertion point to help you place the block in the drawing

► The objects to be included in the block

You specify each of these in the course of using the Block command. When the command is completed, the objects are designated as a single block, and the block definition is stored with the drawing file. You then insert additional copies of the block into the drawing using the Insert command.

N O T E   In general, I'll refer to a command by the tooltip that appears when you place the cursor on the command's icon on the toolbar or the command as you enter it at the Command line. If the command doesn't have an icon on a toolbar, I'll refer to its name on the drop-down menu. In the rare case that the command doesn't appear in either place, I'll tell you what you need to enter in the Command window. You can start all commands by entering their name or an alias in the Command window.

Before you create a block, you must consider the layers on which the objects to be blocked reside. When objects on layer 0 are grouped into a block, they take on the color and linetype of the layer that is current when the block is inserted. Objects on other layers retain the properties of their original layers, regardless of which color or linetype has been assigned to the current layer. This characteristic distinguishes the 0 layer from all other layers.

As you define a block, you must decide which—if any—of the objects to be included in the block need to be on the 0 layer before they are blocked. If a block will always be on the same layer, the objects making up the block can remain on that layer. On the other hand, if a block might be inserted on several layers, the objects in the block need to be moved to the 0 layer before the block definition is created in order to avoid confusion of colors and linetypes.

The objects that compose blocks can reside on more than one layer.

As you learn to make blocks for the doors, you'll also see how layers work in the process of creating block definitions. You'll create a block for the exterior doors first, using the front door, and call it door3_0 to distinguish it from the smaller interior door. For the insertion point, you need to assign a point on or near the door that will facilitate its placement as a block in your drawing. The hinge point makes the best insertion point.

For this chapter, the Endpoint osnap should be running most of the time, and polar tracking should be off. Follow these steps to set up your drawing:

Feel free to activate the Dyn button on the status bar for this chapter.

1. If you're continuing from the preceding chapter, skip to step 2. If you're starting a new session, once AutoCAD is running, click the Open button on the Standard toolbar. In the Select File list, highlight Cabin06c.dwg, and click Open. If this .dwg file isn't in the list, click the arrow to the right of the Look In drop-down list at the top of the dialog box, navigate to your Training Data folder, and then select the file.

You're using the Freeze option for layers this time because you won't need to see the lines on the Roof and Headers layers for a while. This might be a good situation to consider creating another layer state.

2. Click the Layers drop-down list, and click the sun icons for the Roof and Headers layers to freeze them. The suns turn into snowflakes. Then, click the Doors layer to close the list. The Doors layer is now current, and the headers and rooflines are no longer visible in the drawing (see Figure 7.2).

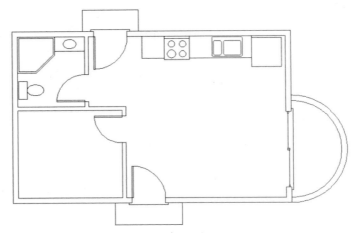

F I G U R E 7 . 2 : The floor plan with the Headers and Roof layers frozen

3. Check the status bar, and make sure the Osnap button is in the on position. Right-click the Osnap button, and choose Settings from the shortcut menu.

4. On the Object Snap tab of the Drafting Settings dialog box, be sure the Endpoint check box is selected.

5. Click OK. In the status bar, turn Polar off if it's on, and be sure only the Model and Osnap buttons are in their on positions. (The Dyn button can also be in the on position if you prefer working with the dynamic display feature.)

Now you're ready to make blocks.

You can also start the Block command by choosing Draw ➢ Block ➢ Make or by typing b↵.

1 Click the Make Block button on the Draw toolbar to open the Block Definition dialog box. Notice the flashing cursor in the Name text box. Enter **door3_0**, but don't press ↵ (see Figure 7.3).

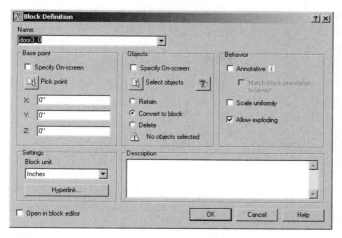

FIGURE 7.3: The Block Definition dialog box

2. Click the Pick Point button in the Base Point area. The dialog box temporarily closes, and you're returned to your drawing.

3. Zoom in to the front door area in your drawing.

4. Move the cursor to the front door area, and position it near the hinge point of the door. When the Endpoint marker appears on the hinge point (see the top of Figure 7.4), click. This selects the insertion point for the door, and the Block Definition dialog box returns. The insertion point is the location, relative to the cursor, that the block references when it is inserted.

5. Click the Select Objects button in the Objects area. You're returned to the drawing again. The cursor changes to a pickbox, and the Command window displays the Select objects: prompt.

6. Select the door and swing, and then press ↵. You're returned to the Block Definition dialog box. At the bottom of the Objects area, the count of selected objects appears. Just above that are three radio buttons. Click the Delete radio button if it's not already selected. The Delete option erases the selected objects after the block definition is created, while the Convert To Block option substitutes the objects with a block definition. In this situation, the Convert To Block option would be a better choice, but you want to get some practice using the Insert command.

7. At the bottom of the dialog box, be sure the Open in Block Editor check box is not selected, and then click OK to close the dialog box. The door and swing disappear (see the bottom of Figure 7.4).

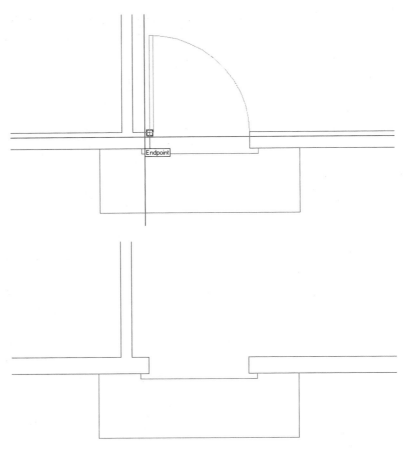

Endpoint

FIGURE 7.4: The front door opening when picking the hinge point as the insertion point (top) and after creating the door3_0 block and deleting the door and swing (bottom)

You have now created a block definition, called door3_0. Block definitions are stored electronically with the drawing file. You need to insert the door3_0 block (known formally as a *block reference*) into the front door opening to replace the door and swing that were just deleted when the block was created.

Inserting the Door Block

You'll use the Insert command to place the door3_0 block back into the drawing.

1. On the Draw toolbar, click the Insert Block button to open the Insert dialog box. At the top, the Name drop-down list contains the names of the blocks in the drawing. Open the list, and select door3_0. A preview of the block appears in the upper-right corner (see Figure 7.5). Below the Name list are three areas with the Specify On-Screen option. These are used for the insertion procedure.

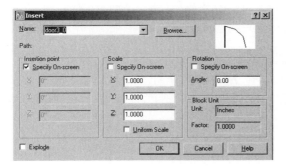

FIGURE 7.5: The Insert dialog box

2. Check the Specify On-Screen options for the Insertion Point and Rotation options, but leave Scale unchecked. (The scale of the door should not change unless it is used to flip the door, as shown in the next exercise.) Also, make sure the Explode check box in the lower-left corner is unchecked. Explode disassembles the block into its component parts upon insertion into the drawing.

3. Click OK. You're returned to your drawing, and the door3_0 block is now attached to the cursor, with the hinge point coinciding with the intersection of the crosshairs (see Figure 7.6). The Command window says Specify insertion point or [Basepoint/Scale/X/Y/Z/Rotate]:.

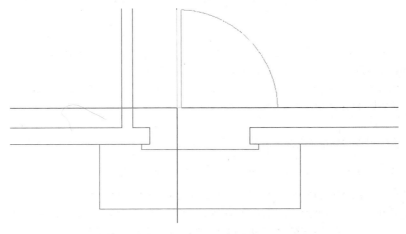

FIGURE 7.6: The door3_0 block attached to the cursor

4. With the Endpoint osnap running, move the cursor toward the upper end of the left jamb line in the front door opening. When the Endpoint marker appears at the jamb line's upper endpoint, click.

5. The door3_0 block is no longer attached to the cursor, and its insertion point has been placed at the upper end of the left jamb line. The block now rotates as you move the cursor (see the top of Figure 7.7). At the Specify rotation angle <0.00>: prompt, press ↵ again to accept the default angle of 0°. The door3_0 block properly appears in the drawing (see the bottom of Figure 7.7).

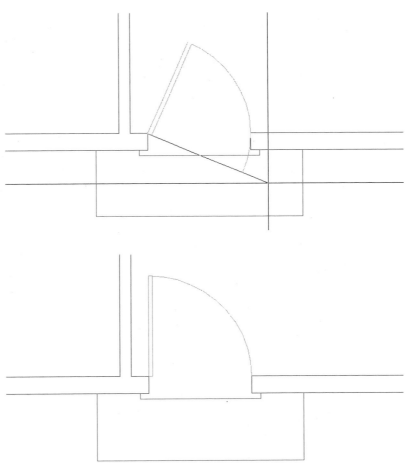

FIGURE 7.7: The rotation option (top) and the final placement (bottom)

Each time a block is inserted, you can specify the following on the screen or in the Insert dialog box:

- ► The location of the insertion point of the block
- ► The X and Y scale factors
- ► The Z scale factor in the dialog box (used for 3D drawings, in Auto-CAD only)
- ► The rotation angle

As you insert blocks, you can stretch or flip them horizontally by specifying a negative X scale factor or vertically by specifying a negative Y scale factor, or you can rotate them from their original orientations. Because you created the door3_0 block from the door and swing that occupied the front door opening and the size was the same, inserting this block back into the front door opening required no rotation; so, you followed the defaults. When you insert the same block into the back door opening, you'll have to change the Y scale factor, because the door will be flipped vertically.

Flipping a Block While Inserting It

The X scale factor controls the horizontal size and orientation. The Y scale factor matches the X scale factor unless you explicitly change it. For the next insertion, you'll make such a change:

1. Click the Zoom Previous button on the Standard toolbar to zoom back out to a full view of the floor plan.

2. Click the Zoom Window button, and make a window around the back door area, including plenty of room inside and outside the opening so that you can see the door3_0 block as it's being inserted. You'll be zoomed into a close view of the back door (see Figure 7.8).

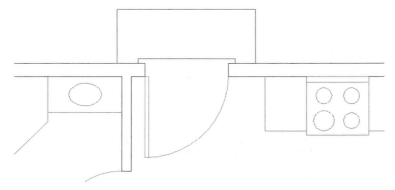

FIGURE 7.8: The result of the zoom

3. Use the Erase command to erase the door and swing from the back door opening.

4. Choose Insert ➤ Block, or enter i↵. In the Insert dialog box, door3_0 should still be in the Name drop-down list. Check the Specify On-Screen option for the Scale option.

5. Click OK. You're returned to your drawing, and the door3_0 block is attached to the cursor.

6. Move the cursor to the lower end of the left jamb line. When the osnap marker appears at that endpoint (see the top of Figure 7.9), click. AutoCAD places the insertion point, and the prompt is now `Enter X scale factor, specify opposite corner, or [Corner/XYZ]<1>:`.

7. Press ↵ to accept the default X scale factor of 1. The prompt changes to `Specify Y scale factor <use X scale factor:`. To flip the door down to the inside of the cabin, you need to give the Y scale factor a value of –1.

8. Enter -1↵. Then, press ↵ again to accept the default rotation angle of 0°. The Insert command ends, and the door3_0 block appears in the back door opening (see the bottom of Figure 7.9).

   The bottom of Figure 7.9 looks exactly like Figure 7.8.

9. Click the Zoom Previous button on the Standard toolbar, or enter z↵ p↵ to zoom back out to a full view of the floor plan.

> Nothing has changed about the geometry of the door, but it's now a different kind of object. Before it was a rectangle and an arc; now it's a block reference made up of a rectangle and an arc.

N O T E   When inserting a block, giving a value of –1 to the X or Y scale factor has the effect of flipping the block, much like the Mirror command did in Chapter 4, when you first drew the doors. Because you can flip or rotate the door3_0 block as it's inserted, you can use this block to place a door and swing in any 3'-0" opening, regardless of its orientation.

Doors are traditionally sorted into four categories, depending on which side the hinges and doorknob are on and which way the door swings open. To be able to use one door block for all openings of the same size, you need to know the following:

▶ How the door and swing in the block are oriented

▶ Where the hinge point is to be in the next opening

▶ How the block has to be flipped and/or rotated during the insertion process to properly fit in the next doorway opening

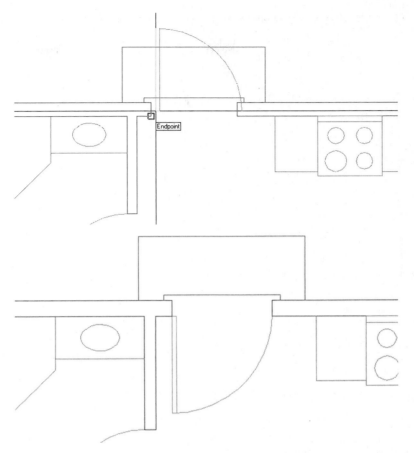

FIGURE 7.9: Placing the door3_0 insertion point (top) and the block after insertion (bottom)

Blocking and Inserting the Interior Doors

Because the interior doors are smaller, you need to make a new block for them. You could insert the door3_0 block with a ⅚ scale factor, but this would also reduce the door thickness by the same factor, and you don't want that.

On the other hand, for consistency, it's a good idea to orient all door blocks the same way, and the bath and bedroom doors are turned relative to the door3_0 block. You'll move and rotate the bathroom door and its swing to orient it like the front door:

1. Use Zoom Window to define a window that encloses both the bathroom doors and the bedroom doors. The view changes to a close-up of the area enclosed in your window (see top left of Figure 7.10).

◄

After you finish the swinging doors, I'll go into some detail about AutoCAD's *dynamic block*, which you can use for all swinging doors.

2. Use the Move command to move the bathroom door and swing to the right, and then use the Rotate command to rotate them −90° (see the bottom of Figure 7.10).

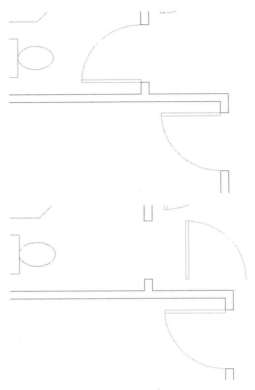

FIGURE 7.10: The result of a zoom window (top) and the bathroom door and swing moved and rotated (bottom)

3. Repeat a procedure similar to the one you used to make a block out of the front door and swing to make a block out of the bathroom door and swing. Here is a summary of the steps:

a. Start the Block command. (Click the Make Block button on the Draw toolbar.)

b. In the dialog box, enter **door2_6** to name the new block. Don't press ↵.

c. Click the Pick Point button, and pick the hinge point of the bathroom door.

    d. Click the Select Objects button, and pick the door and swing. Then, press ↵.

    e. In the Objects area, make sure the Delete radio button is selected.

    f. Click OK. The door and swing disappear.

4. Insert the door2_6 block in the bathroom doorway opening. Follow the steps carefully. Here's a summary:

    a. Start the Insert command.

    b. Open the Name drop-down list, select door2_6, and then click OK.

    c. Pick the left end of the lower jamb line.

    d. Accept the default of 1 for the X scale factor.

    e. Accept the default of <use X> for the Y scale factor.

    f. Enter 90↵ for the rotation.

N O T E   If all your doors are at 90° angles, you can turn on Ortho mode to speed up the rotation process. With Ortho active, wherever you move the cursor at the `Specify rotation angle <0.00>:` prompt, the rotations are restricted to 90° increments.

5. Erase the bedroom door and swing, restart the Insert command, and insert the door2_6 block in the bedroom door opening. Here are the parameters:

    ► Check Specify On-Screen for Insertion Point, Scale, and Rotation.

    ► The insertion point is at the left endpoint of the upper jamb line.

    ► The X scale factor is –1.

    ► The Y scale factor is 1.

    ► The rotation is 90.

6. Use Zoom Previous (see Figure 7.11).

7. Save your drawing as `Cabin07a.dwg`.

T I P   If you have trouble anticipating how a block such as the door block needs to be flipped or rotated during insertion, don't worry about it; just be sure to locate the insertion point accurately in the drawing. Then, after the block is inserted, you can flip or turn it by using the Mirror and Rotate commands.

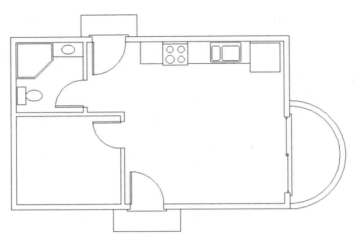

FIGURE 7.11: The floor plan with all swinging doors converted into blocks

THE FATE OF OBJECTS USED TO MAKE A BLOCK

The three radio buttons in the Objects area of the Block Definition dialog box represent the options you have for objects transformed into a block:

Retain   The objects remain unblocked. Click this if you want to make several similar blocks from the same set of objects.

Convert To Block   The objects become the block reference. Click this if the first use of the block has geometry identical to that of the set of objects it's replacing.

Delete   The objects are automatically erased after the block has been defined. Click this if the first use of the block will be at a different scale, orientation, or location from the set of objects it's replacing.

This view looks the same as the view you started with at the beginning of this chapter; see Figure 7.2, shown earlier. Blocks look the same as other objects, and you can't detect them by sight. They're useful because you can use them over and over again in a drawing or in many drawings and because the block is a combination of two or more (and sometimes many more) objects represented as a single object. Your next task is to learn how to detect a block; but first, I'll discuss AutoCAD's dynamic block feature.

Using Dynamic Blocks

Dynamic blocks are blocks whose appearance can be changed in a variety of ways, depending on how they are set up. Any block can be transformed into a dynamic block, and AutoCAD offers several sample dynamic blocks that have already been set up. Take the door3_0 block, for example. By adding extra information to the block, you could use it for openings in a variety of preset sizes. And the thickness of the door remains the same.

After you insert the dynamic block, click it. Arrows appear at opposite sides of the opening.

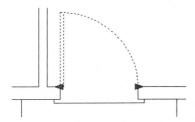

When you click the right arrow, the dynamics begin, and markers appear below the opening, indicating the preset sizes to which the door and swing can be changed. In this example, you can use the door for openings from 2'-0" to 3'-6", at 6" intervals.

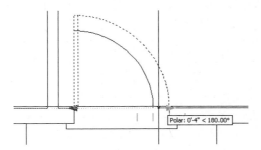

Once you set a new size, the door and swing take on that size, whereas the door thickness remains the same. Now you can move this door to a smaller opening.

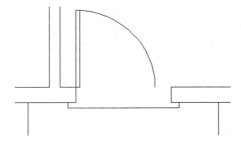

Later in this chapter, when I introduce *palettes*, I'll show you where to find AutoCAD's sample dynamic blocks. For instructions on creating and using dynamic blocks, see Chapter 9.

Finding Blocks in a Drawing

You can detect blocks in a drawing in at least three ways: by using grips, by using the List command, and by looking at the Properties palette.

Using Grips to Detect a Block

Grips appear on objects that are selected when no command is started. When an object that isn't a block is selected, grips appear at strategic places. But if you select a block, by default, only one grip appears, and it's always located at the block's insertion point. Because of this, clicking an object when no command is started is a quick way to see whether the object is a block:

1. At the Command: prompt, click one of the door swings. The door and swing turn into dashed lines, and a square blue grip appears at the hinge point.

2. Press Esc to clear the grip.

3. Choose Tools ➢ Options to open the Options dialog box, and then click the Selection tab. The Grips area is on the right side. Enable Grips Within Blocks is unchecked by default. If this option is checked, grips appear on all objects in the block as if they weren't blocked when you click a block with no command running. Leave this setting unchecked.

   You can also change the size of the grip and any of the three color states. By default, unselected grips are blue, grips that you click to select are red, and grips that you hover the cursor over are green.

4. Click OK to close the Options dialog box.

We'll look at grips in more detail in Chapter 12. You might need to know more about a block than just whether something is one. If that is the case, you'll need to use the List command.

Using the List Command to Detect a Block

You can use the List command to learn more about a block:

1. Choose Tools ➢ Inquiry ➢ List, or enter li↵ at the Command prompt.

2. Click the front door block, and then press ↵. The AutoCAD Text Window temporarily covers the drawing (see Figure 7.12). In the Text Window, you can see the words BLOCK REFERENCE Layer: "DOORS", followed by 13 lines of text. These 14 lines describe the block you selected.

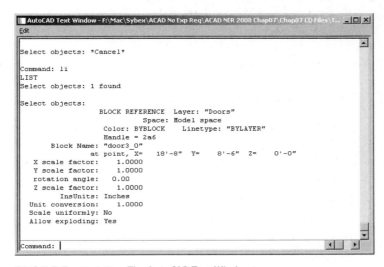

FIGURE 7.12: The AutoCAD Text Window

The information stored in the Text Window includes the following:

▶ What the object is (block reference)

▶ The layer the object is on (Doors layer)

▶ The name of the block (door3_0)

▶ The coordinates of the insertion point in the drawing

▶ The X and Y scale factors

▶ The rotation angle

3. Press F2. The AutoCAD Text Window closes.

T I P The AutoCAD Text Window isn't exclusively for use with the List command. Instead, it is a constantly scrolling history of the command prompt. The F2 key acts as a toggle to turn the window on and off. You can even copy information from all but the bottom line for use inside or outside AutoCAD. The Text Window displays only one page of information at a time and then pauses while the Press ENTER to continue: prompt appears at the Command line. Press ↵ to continue. If you need to see information that has scrolled off the window, use the scroll bar on the right side to bring it back into view.

4. Right-click, and choose Repeat List from the shortcut menu.

5. At the Select objects: prompt, click one of the arcs that represents the balcony, then click one of the wall lines, and finally press ⏎.

6. The Text Window appears again, and you can see information about the arc that you selected, followed by information about the selected wall line.

7. Press F2, and then slowly press it a few more times. As you switch back and forth between the Text Window and the drawing, notice that the last two lines in the Text Window appear in the Command window of the drawing (see Figure 7.13). The Command window displays a strip of text from the Text Window, usually the last two lines.

8. Press F2 to close the Text Window.

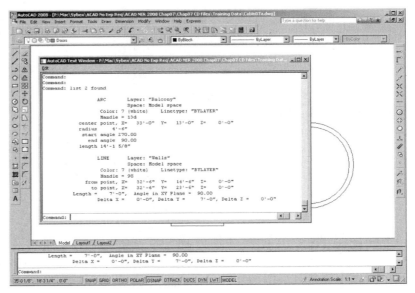

FIGURE 7.13: Toggling between the Text Window (above) and the drawing with its Command window (next page)

Continues

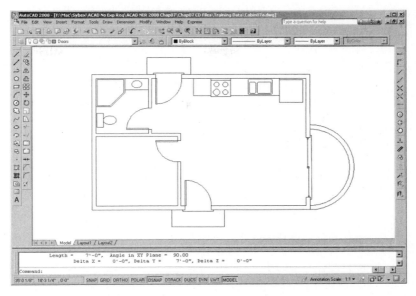

FIGURE 7.13: *(Continued)*

Using the Properties Palette to Examine a Block

In Chapter 6, you used the Properties palette to change the individual linetype scale for the ridgeline of the roof. It can also be a tool for investigating objects in your drawing. When the Properties palette is open and only one object is selected, it displays data specific to the selected object. If multiple objects are selected, it shows only the data shared by those objects.

1. Click one of the door blocks.

2. Click the Properties button on the Standard toolbar, or right-click and choose Properties from the context menu. The Properties palette opens.

   The data displayed on the palette is similar to that displayed when you used the List command, but it's in a slightly different form (see Figure 7.14). At the top of the dialog box, a drop-down list displays the type of object selected—in this case, a block reference. The fields that are white signify items that you can change directly in the palette, and items that are grayed out cannot be changed. You can't change any values in the AutoCAD Text Window.

Block insertion means the same thing as *block reference*, and both are casually called *blocks*.

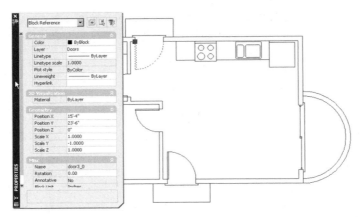

FIGURE 7.14:   The Properties palette with a door block selected

3. Close the Properties palette by clicking the X in the upper-left or upper-right corner; then, press Esc to deselect the door block.

T I P   The X you click to close the Properties palette is in the upper-left or upper-right corner of the palette if it's floating and in the upper-right corner if it's docked.

If you're ever working on a drawing that you didn't draw, these tools for finding out about objects will be invaluable. The next exercise on working with blocks involves placing windows in the walls of the cabin.

Creating a Window Block

You can create all the windows in the cabin floor plan from one block, even though the windows are four different sizes (see Figure 7.15). You'll create a window block and then go from room to room to insert the block into the walls:

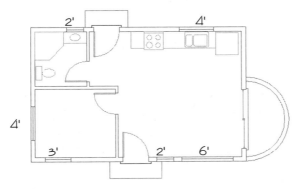

FIGURE 7.15:   The cabin windows in the floor plan

1. Click the Layers list on the Layers toolbar to open the drop-down list, and click the layer 0 in the list to make it current.

2. Right-click the Osnap button on the status bar, and choose Settings from the shortcut menu. Add check marks to the Midpoint and Perpendicular osnaps, and uncheck Intersection. Click OK.

3. Zoom in to a horizontal section of wall where there are no jamb lines or intersections with other walls by clicking the Zoom Window button on the Standard toolbar and picking two points to be opposite corners of the zoom window (see Figure 7.16). Because the widths of the windows in the cabin are multiples of 12", you can insert a block made from a 12"-wide window for each window, and you can apply an X scale factor to the block to make it the right width. The first step is to draw a 12"-wide window inside the wall lines.

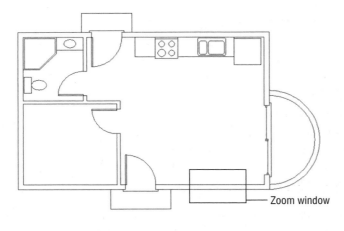

Zoom window

FIGURE 7.16: Making a zoom window (top) to zoom in to a section of straight length of wall (bottom)

Use the **Nearest** osnap when you want to locate a point somewhere on an object but aren't concerned exactly where on the object the point is located.

4. Start the Line command, and then click the Nearest osnap button on the Object Snap toolbar or enter **nea↵**. The Nearest osnap will allow you to start a line on one of the wall lines; it snaps the cursor to any part of any object under the cursor and guarantees that the objects form an intersection but do not cross.

5. Move the cursor to the upper wall line, a little to the left of the center of the screen, and with the hourglass-shaped marker displayed, click. A line begins on the upper wall line.

6. Move the cursor to the lower wall line. The perpendicular marker appears directly below the point you previously picked. When it's displayed, click. The line is drawn between the wall lines. Press ↵ to end the Line command.

7. Start the Offset command. Enter 12↵ to set the offset distance to 12". Pick the line you just drew, and then pick a point to the right of that line. The line is offset 12" to the right. Press ↵ to end the Offset command.

8. Start the Line command again. Move the cursor near the midpoint of the line you first drew. When the Midpoint marker appears, click. Move the cursor near the midpoint of the line that was just offset. When the Perpendicular or Midpoint symbol appears, click. Press ↵ to end the Line command. Your drawing should look like Figure 7.17.

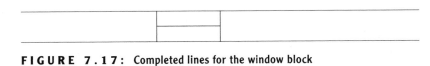

FIGURE 7.17: Completed lines for the window block

The three lines you've drawn will make up a window block. They represent the two jamb lines and the glass (usually called *glazing*). By varying the X scale factor from 2 to 6, you can create windows 2', 3', 4', and 6' wide. This is a single-line representation, with no double lines to indicate the frames, so there is no thickness issue, regarding scaling the blocks, like there was with the doors.

Before you create the block, you need to decide the best place for the insertion point. For the doors, you chose the hinge point because you always know where it will be in the drawing. Locating a similar strategic point for the window is a little more difficult but certainly possible. You know the insertion point shouldn't be on the horizontal line representing the glazing, because it will always rest in the middle of the wall. There is no guideline in the drawing for the middle of the wall, and this would require a temporary tracking point every time a window is inserted. Windows are usually dimensioned to the midpoint of the glazing line rather than to either jamb line, so you don't want the insertion point to be at the endpoint of a jamb line. The insertion point needs to be positioned on a wall line but also lined up with the midpoint of the glazing line.

To locate this point, draw a guideline from the midpoint of the glazing line straight to one of the wall lines. The line will not be included in the window block:

1. Press ↵ to restart the Line command. Move to a point near the midpoint of the glazing line. When the Midpoint marker appears, click.

2. Move to the bottom wall line. When the Perpendicular marker appears, click. A guideline is drawn from the midpoint of the glazing line that is perpendicular to the lower wall line (see Figure 7.18). The lower endpoint of this line is the location of the window block insertion point. Press ↵ to end the Line command. Now you're ready to define the window block.

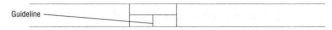

Guideline

FIGURE 7.18: The guideline is completed

3. Enter **b**↵ to start the Block command. In the dialog box, enter **win-1** for the block name, and then click the Pick Point button.

4. Back in the drawing, with the Endpoint, Midpoint, and Perpendicular osnaps running, move the cursor to the lower end of the guideline you just drew. When the Endpoint marker appears at that location, click.

If only the Perpendicular osnap marker appears, click Endpoint on the Object Snap toolbar, and then try again.

5. In the dialog box, click the Select Objects button.

6. Back in the drawing, select the two jamb lines and the glazing line, but don't select the guideline whose endpoint locates the insertion point. Press ↵.

7. Back in the dialog box, be sure the Open in Block Editor check box at the bottom is unchecked and the Delete radio button is selected, and then click OK. The win-1 block has been defined, and the 12" window has been erased.

8. Erase the guideline using the Erase command.

9. Use Zoom Previous to zoom out to a view of the whole floor plan.

This completes the definition of the block that will represent the windows. The next task is to insert the win-1 block where the windows will be located and scale them properly.

UNDERSTANDING GROUPS

Another method for causing several objects to act as one is to use the Group command. Groups differ from blocks in that they do not replace separate objects with a single definition but instead associate several objects by name so they react as if they are a single object. Some similar programs use the term *named selection set* to represent what AutoCAD calls a group. Selecting one member object from the group selects all the members. Unlike with objects in a block, you can add or remove members of a group and toggle the group to allow the individual members to be selected. Use groups when you know the association between the objects is not permanent, and use blocks when it might be. The procedure for creating a group is as follows:

1. Enter **Group**⏎ at the Command line to open the Object Grouping dialog box.

2. Enter a name for the group in the Group Name field.

3. Click the New< button in the Create Group area. The dialog box closes temporarily.

4. Select the objects to be added to the group, and then press ⏎. The Object Grouping dialog box reopens, and the group name appears in the field at the top. Select the group name.

Continues

UNDERSTANDING GROUPS *(Continued)*

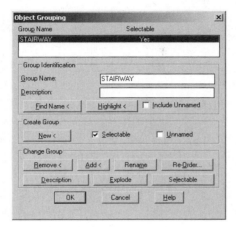

Clicking the Selectable button in the Change Group section (not the Selectable check box in the Create Group section) acts as a toggle that causes the group members to react to selection picks as if they are not members of a group. The Add< and Remove< buttons increase or decrease the membership of the group, and Explode destroys the group, leaving its member objects as individuals again.

Inserting the Window Block

Several factors come into play when deciding where to locate windows in a floor plan:

- ▶ The structure of the building

- ▶ The appearance of windows from outside the building

- ▶ The appearance of windows from inside a room

- ▶ The location of fixtures that might interfere with placement

- ▶ The sun angle and climate considerations

For this exercise, you'll work on the windows for each room, starting with the bedroom.

Rotating a Block During Insertion

The bedroom has windows on two walls: one 3' window in the front wall and one 4' window centered in the left wall (see Figure 7.19).

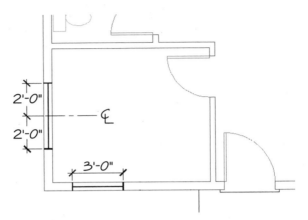

FIGURE 7.19: The bedroom windows

You'll make the 4' window first:

1. Use a zoom window to zoom in to a view of the bedroom similar to that in Figure 7.19. Click the Polar button on the status bar to turn on polar tracking. Polar, Osnap, and Model should now be in their on positions.

2. Create a new layer by clicking the Layer Properties Manager button and then clicking the New Layer button in the Layer Properties Manager dialog box. The new Layer1 appears and is highlighted. Enter **Windows** to rename Layer1.

3. Click the color square in the Windows row to open the Select Color dialog box, with the white swatch highlighted and *white* listed in the Color text box. Enter **30** to change the color to a bright orange. (If you don't have 256 colors available, choose any color.) The Select Color dialog box closes.

4. With Windows still highlighted in the Layers Properties Manager dialog box, click the Set Current button, or double-click the name of the layer, to make the Windows layer current. Then, click OK. You're returned to your drawing, and Windows is the current layer.

5. Start the Insert command (click the Insert Block button on the Draw toolbar). Open the Name drop-down list in the Insert dialog box. In

the list of blocks, click win-1. Be sure all three Specify On-Screen check boxes are selected, and then click OK.

6. In your drawing, the 12" window block is attached to the cursor at the insertion point (see Figure 7.20). Note that it's still in the same horizontal orientation that it was in when you defined the block. To fit it into the left wall, you'll need to rotate it as you insert it.

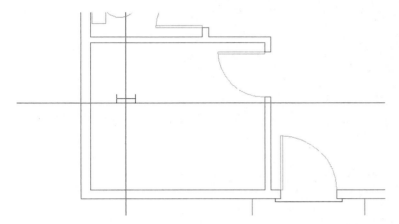

FIGURE 7.20: The win-1 block attached to the cursor

7. Move the cursor near the midpoint of the left inside wall line. When the midpoint marker appears, click.

8. You're prompted for an X scale factor. This is a 4' window, so enter 4↵. For the Y scale factor, enter 1↵.

9. You're prompted for the rotation angle. The window block is now 4' wide and rotates with the movement of the cursor. Move the cursor so that it's directly to the right of the insertion point. The polar tracking lines and tooltip appear (see the top of Figure 7.21). They show you how the window will be positioned if the rotation stays at 0°. Obviously, you don't want this.

10. Move the cursor so that it's directly above the insertion point. Another tracking line and tooltip appear. They show what position a 90° rotation will result in (see the middle of Figure 7.21). The window fits nicely into the wall here.

11. With the tracking line and tooltip visible, click. The win-1 block appears in the left wall. The Insert Block command ends (see the bottom of Figure 7.21).

◄

The Y scale factor will be 1 for all the win-1 blocks because all walls that have windows are 6" wide— the same width as the win-1 block.

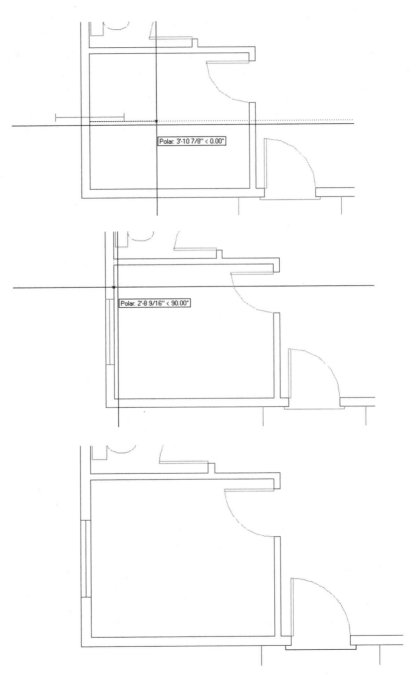

FIGURE 7.21: Rotating the win-1 block 0° (top) and 90° (middle) and the final position (bottom)

Using Guidelines When Inserting a Block

The window in the front wall of the bedroom is 3' wide and 6" from the center of the bedroom wall (refer to Figure 7.19, shown earlier). You can use a guideline to locate the insertion point for this window:

1. Start the Line command, and locate the cursor on the inside, horizontal exterior wall line near its midpoint. When the triangular marker appears at the midpoint of this line, click. A line starts.

2. Hold the cursor at a point a few feet below the first point of the line. When the polar tracking line and tooltip appear, click. Press ↵ to end the Line command. This establishes a guideline at the center of the wall. The insertion point for the window is at its center. The distance between the center of the wall and the insertion point is half the width of the window plus the distance to the guideline—in other words, 2'.

3. Offset the line that you just drew 2' to the left (see Figure 7.22). Now you have established the location for the insertion point of the win-1 block, and you're ready to insert it.

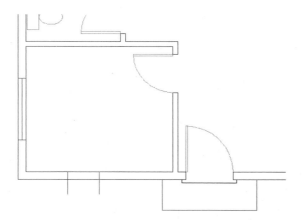

FIGURE 7.22: Guidelines for the window block

4. Start the Insert command. In the Insert dialog box, the win-1 block is still displayed in the Name drop-down list because it was the last block inserted. Click OK.

5. Back in the drawing, the win-1 block is again attached to the cursor. To locate the insertion point, you can choose the upper endpoint of the left guideline or the intersection of this guideline with the exterior outside wall line. Which one would be better? The second choice requires no rotation of the block, so it's easier and faster to use that intersection.

6. Click the Intersection Osnap button on the Object Snap toolbar, and position the cursor on the outside wall without touching any other lines (see the top of Figure 7.23). A colored *x* appears with three dots to its right, along with an Extended Intersection tooltip. Click.

Now hold the crosshair cursor on the lower portion of the leftmost off-set guideline, again without touching any other lines. The *x* appears, this time at the intersection of this guideline with the outside wall line and without the three dots. The tooltip now says Intersection (see the bottom of Figure 7.23). Click again. The insertion point is set at the intersection of the guideline and the outside wall line. You could have easily clicked directly on the desired intersection, but this method showed you how you can select an intersection when it is in a congested area of the drawing.

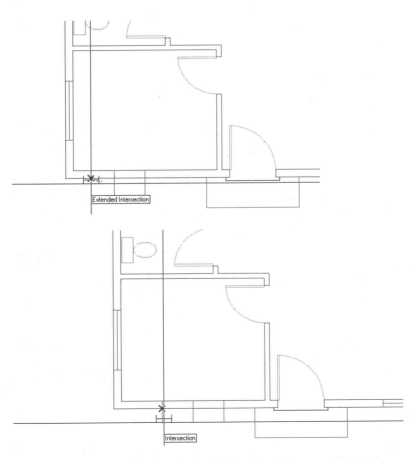

FIGURE 7.23: Selecting the first line (top) and the second (bottom)

7. Enter 3↵ for the X scale factor, and then enter 1↵ for the Y scale factor. At the rotation angle prompt, press ↵ to accept the default of 0°. This inserts the 3' window on the left in the front wall.

8. Erase the guidelines.

Because you chose to locate the insertion point on the lower of the two wall lines, the block needed no rotation. When finished, the bedroom looks like Figure 7.24.

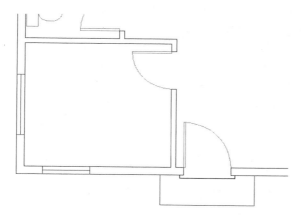

FIGURE 7.24: The bedroom with both windows inserted

Using Object Snap Tracking and Polar Tracking to Insert a Block

The next room to work on is the bathroom, which has one small window over the sink. Follow these steps:

1. Click the Pan button on the Standard toolbar, or hold down the middle mouse button or scroll wheel. The cursor changes to a hand.

2. Position the hand on the wall between the bedroom and the bathroom, and then hold down the left mouse button and drag the drawing down. When the bathroom is in the middle of the drawing area, release the mouse button. Press Esc or ↵, if necessary, to cancel the Pan command.

You want to create one 2' window, centered over the sink. This time, you'll insert the block without using guidelines. Be sure the Endpoint and Midpoint osnaps are running, and turn off the Perpendicular osnap. On the status bar, click the Otrack button to turn on object snap tracking. Polar and Osnap should also be in their on positions.

3. Start the Insert command. Be sure win-1 is in the Name drop-down list, and check that all Specify On-Screen check boxes are marked. Click OK.

4. At the `Specify insertion point:` prompt, position the crosshair cursor near the midpoint of the line representing the front edge of the sink counter. When a marker appears at the midpoint of that line, put the crosshairs near the triangle momentarily, *without clicking*. Look closely, and you'll see a small + appear at the midpoint of the line (see the top of Figure 7.25). When it does, move the crosshair cursor up to the point where the right side of the shower meets the wall line. When the square box appears at the intersection, place the cursor near the square box momentarily, again without clicking. Another + appears there (see the middle of Figure 7.25). You have set—or *acquired*—two temporary tracking points without using the Temporary Tracking Point osnap.

> When Otrack is turned on and the + appears at the object snap symbol, a tracking point has been *acquired*. It remains acquired until you place the cursor directly on the object snap symbol a second time or until that part of the command is done.

5. Move the cursor to the right, along the lower outside wall line, just in back of the sink. A horizontal tracking line appears and coincides with the wall line. When the crosshair reaches a point directly above the first tracking point, a vertical tracking line appears, and the tooltip identifies the intersection of the two tracking lines as `Endpoint: <0.00°, Midpoint: <90.00°` (see the bottom of Figure 7.25). When you see this tooltip, click. This places the insertion point on the inside wall line, centered over the sink.

6. At the X scale factor prompt, enter 2⏎. Then, at the Y scale factor prompt, enter 1⏎. Press ⏎ again to accept the default rotation angle of 0°. The 2' window is inserted into the wall behind the sink (see Figure 7.26).

T I P   When using object snap tracking, you'll inevitably acquire a tracking point that you don't need or want. To remove it, place the crosshair cursor on it momentarily. The tracking point will disappear.

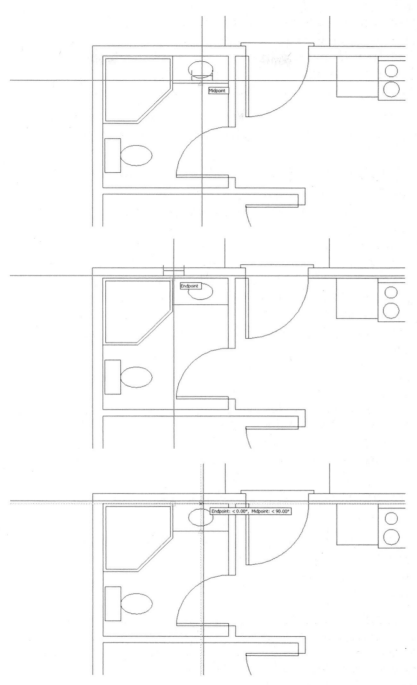

FIGURE 7.25: Setting a temporary tracking point (top), setting a second tracking point (middle), and using the intersection of the two tracking lines to locate the insertion point (bottom)

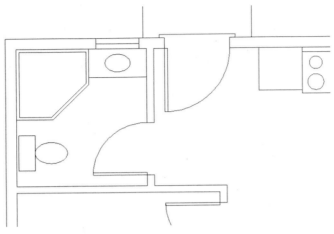

FIGURE 7.26: The 2' window after insertion

You're more than halfway done with the windows. Just three remain to be inserted: one in the kitchen and two in the living room. You'll use object snap tracking again on the kitchen window:

1. Pan and zoom in to the sink area, leaving enough of the counter visible to see the line where the right edge of the counter meets the upper wall line.

2. You need to insert a 4' window in the back wall, centered behind the sink (see Figure 7.15, shown earlier). Start the Insert command to open the Insert dialog box, and then click OK. The win-1 block appears on the cursor.

3. At the Specify insertion point: prompt, move the cursor near the lower edge of the sink. When the Midpoint triangle symbol appears, place the cursor directly on it until the + appears (see the top of Figure 7.27).

4. Move the cursor to the point where the right edge of the counter meets the wall line. When the Endpoint square symbol appears, place the cursor directly on the square until the + appears.

5. Move the cursor to the left, along the wall line. A tracking line appears and coincides with the wall line. When the cursor reaches a point directly above the first tracking point, a vertical tracking line appears and intersects the horizontal one, and the tooltip says Midpoint: <90.00°, Endpoint: <180.00° (see the bottom of Figure 7.27). When this happens, click. The insertion point for the win-1 block is established.

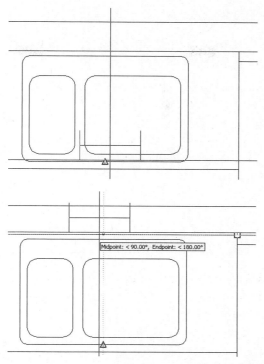

FIGURE 7.27: The first tracking point is established (top), and the intersection of the two tracking lines is the location of the insertion point (bottom).

6. Enter 4↵ for the X scale factor. Then, enter 1↵ for the Y scale factor. For the rotation angle, press ↵ again to accept the default angle of 0°. The window is placed in the back wall, centered behind the sink.

7. Zoom out until you can see the entire kitchen (see Figure 7.28).

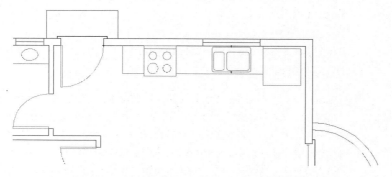

FIGURE 7.28: The inserted window behind the sink

Finishing the Windows

The last two windows to insert are both in the front wall of the living room. You'll use skills you've already worked with to place them:

1. Use the Pan command to adjust your view of the drawing down to the front wall of the living room. One window is 6' wide. Its right jamb is 12" to the left of the inside corner of the wall. The other one is a circular window, 2' in diameter, positioned halfway between the 6' window jamb and the front door jamb (see Figure 7.29). You don't know that distance yet.

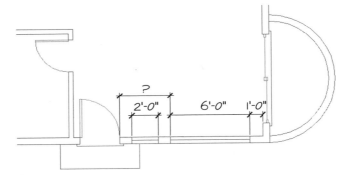

FIGURE 7.29: The windows in the front wall of the living room

2. Set the osnaps so that only Endpoint is running. (To review how to do this, return to the "Creating a Window Block" section in which you created the win-1 block.) Start the Insert command, and click OK in the Insert dialog box to select the win-1 block.

3. Click the Temporary Track Point osnap button. Then, with the Endpoint osnap running, pick the lower-right inside corner of the cabin. The insertion point is positioned to the left of this corner at a distance of 12" in plus half the width of the 6' window—in other words, 4' from the corner.

4. Hold the crosshair cursor directly to the left of the point just picked. When the tracking path and tooltip appear, enter 4'↵. This sets the insertion point 4' to the left of the corner, on the inside wall line.

5. For the scale factors, enter 6↵, and then enter 1↵.

6. For the rotation angle, hold the cursor directly to the right of the insertion point to see the position of the window at 0° rotation. Then, hold the cursor directly above the insertion point to see how a 90° rotation would look. Finally, hold the cursor directly to the left for a view of the effect of a 180° rotation. The 180° view is the one you want.

7. Enter 180↵. The 6' window is placed in the front wall.

Finally, you need to locate the 2' circular window halfway between the left jamb of the 6' window and the right jamb of the front door opening. Use the Distance command to find out the distance between the two jambs. Then, offset one of the jambs half that distance to establish the location of the insertion point on the wall lines. Of the two jamb lines, you must offset the door jamb because the window jamb is part of the window block and can't be offset. Follow these steps:

1. Enter di↵ to start the Distance command. With the Endpoint osnap running, pick the upper end of the front doorjamb, and then pick the upper end of the left window jamb. In the Command window, the distance is displayed as 3'-10". You need to offset the doorjamb half that distance to locate the insertion point for the 2' window.

2. Start the Offset command, and then enter 1'-11↵ to set the offset distance.

3. Pick the door jamb, and then pick a point to the right of the door jamb. Press ↵ to end the Offset command.

T I P   **In a cluttered area, you can enter non↵ at any** Select Point **or** Select Objects **prompt to disable osnaps for the duration of a single pick.**

4. Start the Insert Block command. Click OK to accept the win-1 block. Pick the bottom endpoint of the offset jamb line to establish the insertion point.

5. Enter 2↵ for the X scale factor. Enter 1↵ for the Y scale factor.

6. For the rotation angle, press ↵ to accept the default of 0°. This inserts the last window in the front wall, and the Insert command ends. Erase the offset jamb line (see Figure 7.30).

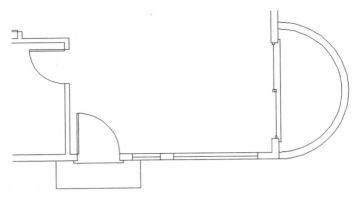

F I G U R E   7 . 3 0 :   The two windows inserted in the front wall of the living room

**Zoom Extents is one
of the zoom options
and is the bottom
button of the Zoom
fly-out menu on the
Standard toolbar.**

7. Enter z↵ e↵ to zoom out to the Extents view of the drawing. This
    changes the view to include all the visible lines. The view fills the
    drawing area.

8. Enter z↵ 0.85x↵ to zoom out a little from the Extents view so all objects
    are set in slightly from the edge of the drawing area (see Figure 7.31).

9. Save this drawing as Cabin07b.dwg.

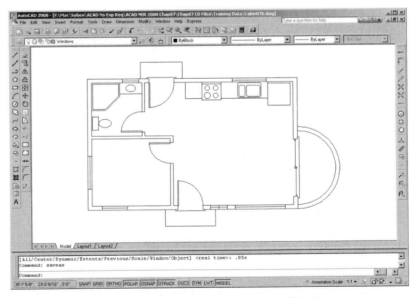

F I G U R E   7 . 3 1 :   Zooming to .85x after zooming to Extents

You have inserted six windows into the floor plan, each generated from the win-1 block. You created the win-1 block on the 0 layer and then made the Windows layer current, so each window block reference took on the characteristics of the Windows layer when it was inserted.

> **T I P**   All your windows are in 6" thick walls, so they are all 6" wide. But what if you want to put a window block in the 4" wall between the bedroom and the living room? You can still use the win-1 block. During insertion, you change the Y scale factor to ⅔ to reflect the change in thickness of the wall.

You can disassociate the components of blocks by using the Explode command. It's the bottom button on the Modify toolbar. Exploding a block has the effect of reducing the block to the objects that make it up. Exploding the win-1 block reduces it to three lines, all on the layer 0. If you explode one of the door blocks, it's reduced to a rectangle and an arc, with both objects on the Doors layer because these components of the door block were on the Doors layer when you defined the block.

You can also start the Explode command by choosing Modify ➤ Explode or by entering ex↵.

Revising a Block

If you need to revise a block that has already been inserted in the drawing several times, choose a block whose X and Y scale factors are the same. You inserted all the windows using different X and Y scale factors, so to revise the win-1 block, you'll need to insert that block one more time, this time using the same X and Y scale factors. You can then make changes to the objects that make up the win-1 block reference. When finished with the changes, you can save the changes to the block definition. This redefines the block and updates all associated block references.

Let's say that the client who's building the cabin finds out that double glazing is required in all windows. So, you want the windows to show two lines for the glass. If you revise the win-1 block definition, the changes you make in one block reference will be made in all six windows.

> **N O T E**   Using standard commands, you can move, rotate, copy, erase, scale, and explode blocks. All objects in a block are associated and behave as if they were one object.

LT users should skip to the Revising a Block with LT sidebar for information regarding modifying blocks.

1. Start the Insert command, select the win-1 block if necessary, and click OK.

2. Pick a point in the middle of the living room. This establishes the insertion point location.

3. Press ↵ three times to accept the defaults for the X and Y scale factors and the rotation angle. The win-1 block is inserted in the living room (see Figure 7.32).

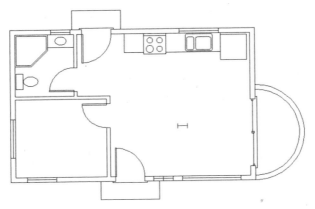

FIGURE 7.32: The win-1 block inserted into the living room

4. Choose Tools ➤ Xref And Block In-Place Editing ➤ Edit Reference In-Place, or enter **refedit**↵ at the Command prompt.

5. Select the new block reference in the middle of the living room to open the Reference Edit dialog box (see Figure 7.33). The win-1 block is identified, and a preview appears.

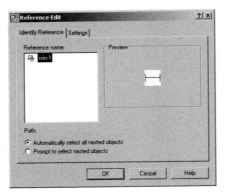

FIGURE 7.33: The Reference Edit dialog box

6. Click OK. In the drawing, the rest of the windows have disappeared, the other objects in the drawing have faded slightly, and the Refedit toolbar appears.

7. Zoom in to a closer view of the window you just inserted.

8. Use the Offset command to offset the glazing line 0.5" up and down. Then, erase the original horizontal line (see Figure 7.34). This window block now has double glazing.

F I G U R E 7 . 3 4 : The result of the modifications to the win-1 block

9. On the Refedit toolbar, click the rightmost button, the one with the Save Reference Edits tooltip.

10. An AutoCAD warning window appears. Click OK. The Refedit toolbar closes, and the block definition has been revised.

11. Erase this block reference; you don't need it anymore.

12. Use Zoom Previous to view the entire drawing. All windows in the cabin now have double glazing.

13. Zoom in to a closer look at the bedroom in order to view some of the modified window block references (see Figure 7.35).

14. Use Zoom Previous to a view of the entire floor plan. Save this drawing as Cabin07c.dwg.

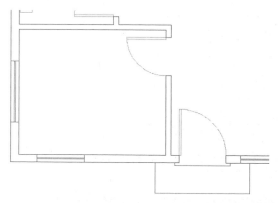

F I G U R E 7 . 3 5 : Zooming in to see the revised window blocks with double glazing

Revising a Block with LT

LT users should follow these steps to revise a block:

1. Start the Insert command, and click OK to accept the win-1 block to be inserted.

2. Pick a point in the middle of the living room. This establishes the insertion point location.

3. Press ↵ three times to accept the defaults for the X and Y scale factors and the rotation angle. This inserts the win-1 block in the living room (see Figure 7.32, shown earlier).

4. Zoom in to a closer view of this window. Start the Line command. On the Object Snap toolbar, click the SnapTo Insert button. (This button has a yellow rectangle and a circle.) Put the cursor anywhere on the window, and click. This starts a line from the insertion point of the block.

5. Pick another point a foot or so below the insertion point, and then end the Line command. This creates a marker for the insertion point. You'll use it shortly.

6. Click the Explode button at the bottom of the Modify toolbar. Select the new block reference, and press ↵. Doing so de-blocks the window; it's now just three lines.

7. Use the Offset command to offset the glazing line 0.5" up and down. Then, erase the original horizontal line (see Figure 7.34, shown earlier). This window now has double glazing.

8. Start the Make Block command. For the name, enter **win-1**. For the insertion point, pick the upper endpoint of the marker line you just drew. For the objects, select the two glazing lines and the two jamb lines but not the marker line. Click the Delete option in the Objects area, and then click OK.

9. A warning box appears, telling you that a block by this name already exists and asking whether you want to redefine it. ClickYes.

10. Erase the marker line.

Continue with step 12 in the Revising a Block exercise.

Sharing Information Between Drawings

You can transfer most of the information in a drawing to another drawing. You can do so in several ways, depending on the kind of information that you need to transfer. You can drag blocks and lines from one open drawing to another when both drawings are visible on the screen. You can copy layers, blocks, and other *named objects* from a closed drawing into an open one using the Design-Center. I'll demonstrate these two features—and touch on three others—as I finish this chapter.

Dragging and Dropping Between Two Open Drawings

In AutoCAD, several drawings can be open at the same time, just like files in a word-processing program. You can control which one is visible, or you can tile two or more to be visible simultaneously. When more than one drawing is visible, you can drag objects from one drawing to another:

1. With Cabin07c.dwg as the current drawing, click the QNew button on the Standard toolbar. In the Select Template dialog box, click the arrow next to the Open button, and then click the Open With No Template – Imperial option. These actions open a blank drawing.

2. Choose Window ➤ Tile Vertically. The new blank drawing (called Drawing1.dwg) appears alongside Cabin07c.dwg (see Figure 7.36).

   Each drawing has a title bar, but only one drawing can be active at a time. At this time, the blank drawing (Drawing1, Drawing2, and so on) should be active. If it is, its title bar is dark blue or some other color, and the Cabin07c.dwg title bar is grayed out. If your Cabin07c.dwg drawing is active instead, click once in the blank drawing.

3. Choose Format ➤ Units. In the Drawing Units dialog box, change the type of units in the Length area to Architectural, and then click OK.

4. Click the Cabin07c.dwg drawing to make it the active drawing.

5. Use Zoom Extents, and then use Realtime Zoom to zoom out a little.

6. Use the Layer Control drop-down list to make the Walls layer current, and then turn off the Doors, Fixtures, Steps, and Windows layers. The walls and balcony should be the only lines visible.

7. Form a selection window to surround the cabin with its balcony. Grips appear on all lines.

Named objects are, quite simply, AutoCAD objects with names, such as blocks and layers. Lines, circles, and arcs don't have individual names, so they aren't named objects.

Like most Windows-based programs, AutoCAD 2008 can have multiple drawing files open in a session. When you open the Window menu, the bottom of the menu contains a list of AutoCAD files currently open. Click the file you want active.

The new drawing might be called Drawing2.dwg or Drawing3.dwg. This doesn't affect how the exercise works.

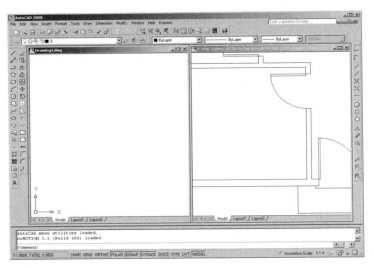

FIGURE 7.36: The user interface with two drawings tiled

8. Place the cursor on one of the wall lines at a point where there are no grips, and then click and hold down the left mouse button. Drag the cursor across the drawing to the center of the blank drawing, and then release the mouse button. The blank drawing is now active and contains the lines for the walls and balcony.

9. Use Zoom to Extents in this drawing, use Realtime Zoom to zoom out a little, and then enter **ucsicon**↵ **off**↵ (see Figure 7.37).

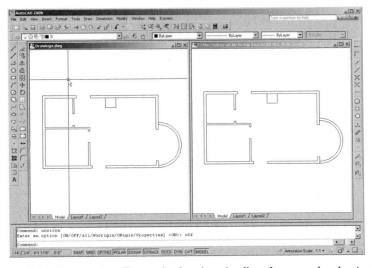

FIGURE 7.37: The result after dragging lines from one drawing to another

10. Open the Layer Control drop-down list, and note that the new drawing (Drawing4.dwg in the example) now has the Balcony and Walls layers.

In this fashion, you can drag any visible objects from one drawing into another, including blocks. If you drag and drop a block, its definition is copied to the new drawing, along with all layers used by objects in the block. If you drag with the right mouse button, you get a few options as to how to place the objects in the receiving drawing.

If you don't choose to have both open drawings visible at the same time, you can always use the Copy and Paste tools available in most Windows-based programs. Here's the general procedure:

1. Click the Maximize icon in the upper-right corner of the new drawing. The new drawing fills the screen.

2. Click Window in the drop-down menu bar. When the menu opens, notice at the bottom that the open drawings are displayed and the active one is checked (see Figure 7.38).

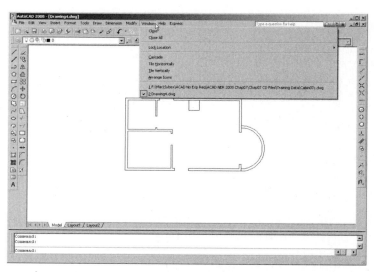

FIGURE 7.38: The Window menu with **Drawing4.dwg** active

3. Click the Cabin07c.dwg drawing. It replaces the new drawing as the active drawing and fills the screen. Turn on the layers you turned off previously. Leave the Headers and Roof layers frozen.

4. Select the fixtures in the kitchen and bath from this drawing, using the selection tools you have learned, and then right-click and choose Copy With Base Point from the shortcut menu. You're prompted to specify a base point in the Cabin07c.dwg drawing. Click the upper-left corner of the building with the Endpoint osnap. Press Esc to deselect the objects.

5. Click Window in the drop-down menu bar. When the menu opens, click Drawing1.dwg to make it active.

6. Click the Paste button on the Standard toolbar, or press Ctrl+V. Pick the upper-left corner of the building with the Endpoint osnap. The fixtures are accurately positioned in the new drawing. If you check the layers, you'll see that the new drawing now has a Fixtures layer, in addition to the Walls and Balcony layers.

Using AutoCAD's DesignCenter

The DesignCenter is a tool for copying named objects (blocks, layers, text styles, and so on) to an opened drawing from an unopened one. You can't copy lines, circles, and other unnamed objects unless they are part of a block. You'll see how this works by bringing some layers and a block into your new drawing from Cabin07c.dwg:

1. Make Cabin07c.dwg current, and then close it. Don't save changes. Maximize the window for your new drawing if it isn't already maximized.

2. Click the DesignCenter button on the Standard toolbar, or enter dc↵ at the Command prompt. It's just to the right of the Properties button. The DesignCenter appears on the drawing area. It can be docked, floating, or, if floating, hidden (see Figure 7.39). Your screen might not look exactly like the samples shown here. The tree diagram of file folders on the left might or might not be visible. Also, your Design-Center might be wider or narrower.

> To hide the DesignCenter, leaving only its title bar, right-click its title bar, and choose Auto-Hide.

3. Click the Tree View Toggle button at the top of the DesignCenter (the fourth button from the right) a few times to close and open the file folder tree diagram. You can resize the DesignCenter horizontally (and vertically as well, if it's floating), and you can resize the

subpanels inside. If Auto-Hide is on, the DesignCenter hides behind the title bar until you put your cursor on it. Leave the tree view open.

4. Click the Load button in the upper-left corner of the DesignCenter palette to open the Load dialog box. Navigate to your Training Data folder, and open it.

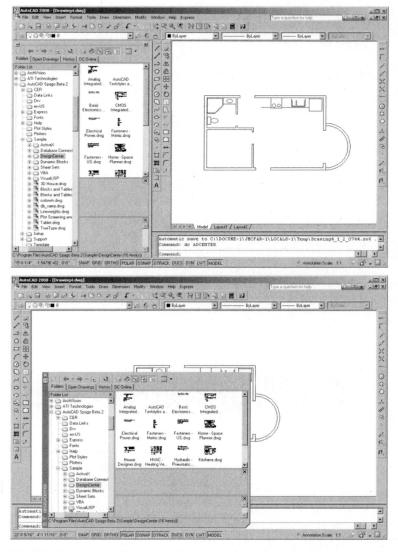

FIGURE 7.39: The DesignCenter docked (top), floating (bottom), and hidden (next page)

Continues

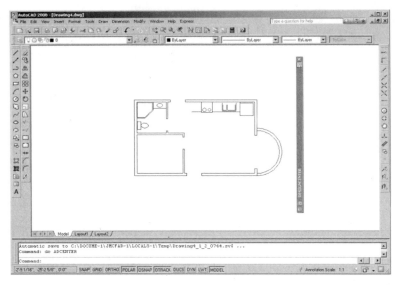

FIGURE 7.39: (*Continued*)

5. Highlight Cabin07c.dwg, and click Open. The Load dialog box closes, and you are returned to your drawing. Now the left side of the DesignCenter lists your drawings in the Training Data folder and Cabin07c.dwg is highlighted; the right side of the DesignCenter shows the types of objects in Cabin07c.dwg that are available to be copied into the current drawing—in this case, Drawing4.dwg (see the left of Figure 7.40).

6. On the left side once again, click the + symbol to the left of Cabin07c.dwg. The list of named objects in the right panel now appears below Cabin07c.dwg in the tree view on the left. Click the Layers icon on the left side. The list of layers in Cabin07c.dwg appears in the panel on the right (see the right of Figure 7.40).

7. Click the Views button above the right window of the DesignCenter (the button on the far right). Choose List in the menu that opens. This changes the view of layers displayed into a list.

8. Use the Shift and Ctrl keys to help you select all the layers except 0, Balcony, Fixtures, and Walls (see Figure 7.41).

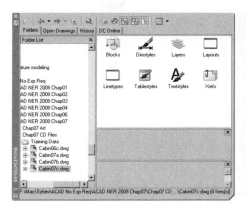 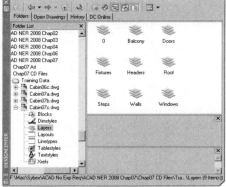

FIGURE 7.40: The DesignCenter displaying the files in the Training Data folder on the left and accessible objects on the right (left) and types of accessible objects on the left (right)

FIGURE 7.41: The DesignCenter with the layers to grab highlighted

9. Right-click somewhere on the highlighted layers in the right window, and choose Add Layers from the shortcut menu.

10. Open the Layer Control drop-down list on the Object Properties toolbar. It now displays all the layers of the Cabin07c.dwg drawing, including those you just transferred to the Drawing4.dwg drawing.

Now let's see how this process works when you want to get a block from another drawing:

1. On the left side of the DesignCenter, click Blocks in the list under the Cabin07c.dwg drawing. On the right side, the list of blocks in that drawing appears (see the left of Figure 7.42).

If you prefer dragging and dropping, click and hold the left mouse button, drag the cursor onto the drawing, and then release.

2. Click door3_0 in the right panel, and then click the Preview button at the top of the DesignCenter. A picture of the block appears in the lower-right corner of the DesignCenter (see the right of Figure 7.42). You can resize the preview pane vertically.

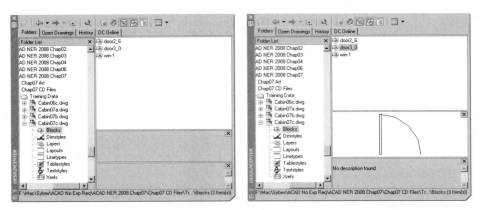

FIGURE 7.42: The DesignCenter with Blocks selected (left) and with the door3_0 block selected and preview on (right)

3. Open the Layer Control list, and make Doors the current layer.

4. Dock the DesignCenter on the left side of the drawing area if it's not already there, and then zoom in to the front door area of the drawing (see Figure 7.43). The Endpoint osnap should be running.

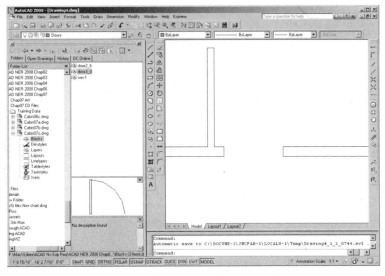

FIGURE 7.43: Zoomed in to the front door area with the DesignCenter docked

5. In the DesignCenter, click and drag door3_0 from the list to the drawing. As the cursor comes onto the drawing, the door3_0 block appears. Use the Endpoint osnap to locate the block at the opening, as you did earlier in this chapter (see Figure 7.44).

6. Click the Close icon in the upper-right corner of the DesignCenter to close it.

7. Keep your new drawing open in case you want to use it in the first few practice exercises at the end of this chapter. Otherwise, close it without saving it.

You can also right-click and drag a block from the DesignCenter into the current drawing. If you do this, a shortcut menu appears. Click Insert Block. This opens the Insert dialog box, and you can complete the insertion procedure.

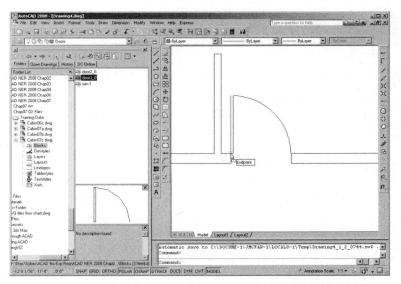

FIGURE 7.44: Dragging the door3_0 block into `Drawing1` from the DesignCenter

By doing this insertion, door3_0 block is now a part of your new drawing, and you can reinsert it in that drawing without the DesignCenter.

At the top of the DesignCenter window, the buttons on the left are tools for navigating through drives and folders to find the files you need to access; the buttons on the right give you options for viewing the named objects in the window.

DESIGNCENTER OPTIONS

Here's a brief description of the functions of the DesignCenter buttons, from left to right:

Load   Opens the Load dialog box, which you use to navigate to the drive, folder, or file from which you want to borrow named AutoCAD objects.

Back   Moves you one step back in your navigation procedure.

Forward   Moves you one step forward in the navigation procedure that you have been using.

Up   Moves up one level in the folder/file/named objects tree.

Search   Opens a Search dialog box in which you can search for a file.

Favorites   Displays a list of files and folders that you have previously set up.

Home   Navigates to the `DesignCenter` folder in the AutoCAD program. This folder has subfolders of sample files that contain libraries of blocks and other named objects to import through the DesignCenter.

Tree View Toggle   Opens or shuts the left panel that displays the logical tree of folders, files, and unnamed objects.

Preview   Opens or shuts a preview window at the bottom of the right palette window. When you highlight a drawing or block in the palette window, a preview appears. You can resize the preview pane.

Description   Displays or hides a previously written description of a block or drawing. You can resize the description pane.

Views   Controls how the items in the palette window are displayed. There are four choices: Large Icons, Small Icons, List, and Details.

Using Other Ways to Share Information Between Drawings

You can transfer information between drawings in several other ways. You'll look at three of them. First, you can use the Wblock command to take a portion of a drawing and create a new drawing file from the selected objects. Second, you can insert any .dwg drawing file into any other drawing file. Finally, you can create *palettes* of blocks that can be accessed for any drawing.

Using the Wblock Command

To perform a Wblock operation, you create a new file and then tell AutoCAD which elements of the current drawing you want in the new file. Let's say you want to create a new .dwg file for the bathroom of the cabin. Here are the steps:

1. Open Cabin07c.dwg, and then pan to see the bathroom. Enter w↵ to open the Write Block dialog box.

2. At the top, under Source, click the Objects radio button (see Figure 7.45).

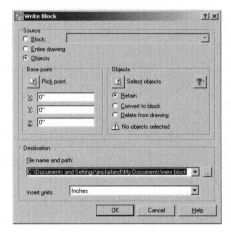

FIGURE 7.45: The Write Block dialog box

3. In the middle portion, the Base Point and Objects areas are similar to those for creating a block. For the Base Point, the default is 0,0. Click the Pick Point button, and in the drawing, pick the point at the inside left corner of the bathroom. For the Objects, click Select Objects, use a window to select everything you want to include, and then press ↵. Click the Retain radio button in this area so that the selected objects aren't deleted from the current drawing.

When you select with a crossing window here, you'll get more than you need, but you can clean up the new drawing later.

4. In the Destination area, enter a filename—say, **bath**—for the new drawing, and choose a folder in which to save it.

5. In the Insert Units drop-down list, select Inches, in case the new drawing is used in a drawing that has units other than Architectural.

6. Click OK. A preview widow briefly appears, the command ends, and the selected material is now a new drawing file located in the folder that you specified.

7. Close the Cabin07c.dwg drawing without saving any changes.

You can use the Wblock command in three ways. They appear as radio buttons at the top of the Write Block dialog box. Here's a brief description of each:

Block   To make a drawing file out of a block that's defined in the current drawing, select the name of the block from the drop-down list at the top, and then follow the procedure in steps 4 through 6 in the preceding exercise. When you follow this procedure, the objects in the new drawing are no longer a block. Wblocking a block has the effect of exploding it.

Entire Drawing   Click this button to *purge* a drawing of unwanted objects such as layers that have no objects on them and block definitions that have no references in the drawing. You aren't prompted to select anything except the information called for in the preceding steps 4 through 6. You can keep the same drawing name or enter a new one. A preferable way to accomplish the same task is to use the Purge command. Enter **purge⏎** to open the Purge dialog box, and select which features to purge.

Objects   You select which objects to use to create a new file, as in the preceding steps 1 through 6.

Inserting a Drawing into a Drawing

When you insert a drawing into another drawing, it comes in as a block. You use the same Insert Block command that you use to insert blocks, in a slightly different way. For example, say you have Wblocked a portion of `Cabin07c.dwg` and made a new file called `bath.dwg` (see the preceding section). Now you want to insert `bath.dwg` into a drawing that you'll call `DrawingC.dwg`. Use this procedure:

1. Make `DrawingC.dwg` current.

2. Start the Insert command.

3. In the Insert dialog box, click the Browse button, and then navigate to the folder containing `bath.dwg`.

4. Open that folder, highlight `bath.dwg`, and then click Open to return to the Insert dialog box. The drawing file that you selected is now displayed in the Name drop-down list. At this point, a copy of `bath.dwg` has been converted to a block definition in `DrawingC.dwg`.

5. Set the insertion parameters, and then click OK.

6. Finish the insertion procedure as if you were inserting a block.

You transfer blocks between drawings by dragging and dropping or by using the DesignCenter. You can also convert them into .dwg files by using the Wblock command, and you can insert them back into other .dwg files as blocks by using the Insert command. They become disassociated when they leave the drawing and can be inserted as a block when they enter another drawing.

Exploring AutoCAD's Palettes

AutoCAD provides a tool called *palettes* to make blocks and other features immediately accessible for any drawing. You'll now take a brief look at the sample palettes that come with AutoCAD and see how to manage them on the screen:

1. Open the Cabin07c.dwg drawing, and use Zoom to Extents. Then, use Zoom Realtime to zoom out a little.

2. If palettes aren't already visible in the drawing area, choose Tools ➢ Palettes ➢ Tool Palettes to display the palettes (see Figure 7.46). You can also open the tool palettes by clicking the Tool Palettes button in the Standard toolbar or by using the Ctrl+3 shortcut keys. They can be floating or docked on either side of the drawing area, and the navigation bar can be on the left or right side.

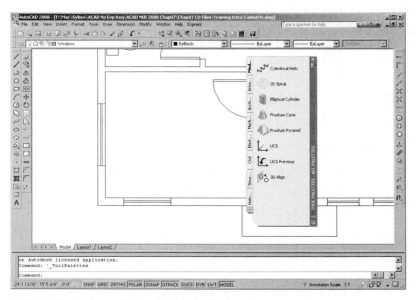

FIGURE 7.46: The tool palettes displayed on the screen

Your palettes might appear different from those shown in a couple of ways. The ones shown here are positioned on the right side but aren't docked there. Yours might be transparent, showing your drawing beneath them, or your palettes might be hidden and show only the title bar. In Figure 7.46, several tabs are on the left side, indicating the available palettes. On the right side is the palette title bar with control icons at the top and bottom.

On each palette is its content. The Hatches sample palette has hatch patterns and fills (discussed in Chapter 11), and the Draw and Modify palettes contain commands from the Draw and Modify toolbars, respectively.

3. Click the Architectural tab to display its content on the palette. Its tab might be abbreviated to read Arch....

Notice the scroll bar next to the title bar. This appears when there is more content than the palette can show. The palettes eclipse part of the right side of the drawing; if you make the palettes transparent, you can see the drawing underneath them.

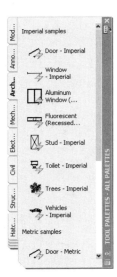

FIGURE 7.47: The tool palettes with the Architectural tab active

4. Move the cursor to the title bar. Right-click, and choose Transparency from the shortcut menu to open the Transparency dialog box (see Figure 7.48). Here you can toggle transparency on and off and adjust the degree of transparency for the palettes.

W A R N I N G AutoCAD might display a notification dialog box, rather than the Transparency dialog box, if your video driver and operating system combination is unable to display palette transparency.

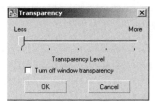

F I G U R E 7 . 4 8 : The Transparency dialog box

5. Be sure the Turn Off Window Transparency check box is not selected, and be sure the Transparency Level slider is at mid-position or on the More side. Click OK. Now the drawing is visible through the palettes (see Figure 7.49).

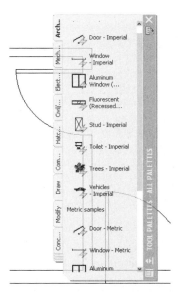

F I G U R E 7 . 4 9 : The palettes in transparent mode

6. Put the cursor back on the palettes' title bar. Right-click, and choose Transparency from the shortcut menu to open the Transparency dialog box again. Select the Turn Off Window Transparency check box, and then click OK.

7. Right-click the palettes' title bar, and choose Auto-Hide from the shortcut menu. When the menu closes, move the cursor off the palettes. The palettes disappear except for the title bar (see Figure 7.50). When you move the cursor back onto the title bar, the palettes reappear—a handy feature.

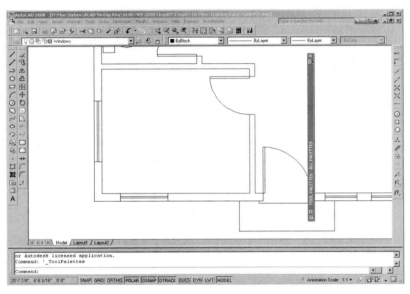

FIGURE 7.50: The palettes title bar with Auto-Hide on

8. Close the Cabin07c.dwg drawing without saving any changes.

With both Transparency and Auto-Hide active, the palettes are less intrusive and take up less screen area, but they remain easily accessible. In Chapter 11, you'll learn more about palettes and their properties and how to set up new palettes and change existing ones.

T I P When they are in floating mode, the Properties palette and Design-Center also have the Auto-Hide option.

This chapter has outlined the procedure for setting up and using blocks, the Wblock command, and AutoCAD's DesignCenter. Blocks follow a set of complex rules, some of which are beyond the scope of this book. For a more in-depth discussion on blocks, see *Mastering AutoCAD 2008 and AutoCAD LT 2008* by George Omura (Wiley, 2007).

If You Would Like More Practice...

Here are some suggestions that will give you some practice in working with blocks, drag-and-drop procedures, and the DesignCenter:

- ▶ Make blocks out of any of the fixtures in the bathroom or kitchen. Try to decide on the best location to use for the insertion point of each fixture. Then, insert them back into the Cabin07c.dwg drawing in their original locations. Create them on the 0 layer, and then insert them on the Fixtures layer. Here's a list of the fixtures:

  - ▶ Shower
  - ▶ Bath sink
  - ▶ Toilet
  - ▶ Oven/range
  - ▶ Kitchen sink
  - ▶ Refrigerator

- ▶ At the end of Chapter 5, I suggested creating pieces of furniture for the kitchen, living room, and bedroom of the cabin. If you did that, it will be good practice to make blocks out of those pieces and insert them into the cabin floor plan. If you didn't do that exercise, you can do so now and then convert the pieces of furniture into blocks.

- ▶ Drag some of the dynamic blocks on the Civil/Structural, Electrical, Mechanical, Architectural, and Annotation sample palettes into the Cabin07c.dwg drawing, and experiment with them to see how they work.

▶ If you work in a profession or trade not directly concerned with architecture or construction, develop a few blocks that you can use in your own work:

▶ Electrical diagrams consist of many simple symbols, each of which can be a block.

▶ Cams and gears—or gear teeth—and other engine parts that have been made into blocks can be assembled into a mechanical drawing.

▶ Plumbing diagrams, like electrical ones, use a variety of symbols repetitively—valves, meters, pumps, joints. You can easily make them into blocks and then reassemble them into the diagram.

In each of these examples, choosing the most useful location for the insertion point will determine whether the block that you create will be a handy tool or a big frustration.

Are You Experienced?

Now you can...

☑ **create blocks out of existing objects in your drawing**

☑ **insert blocks into your drawing**

☑ **vary the size and rotation of blocks as they are inserted**

☑ **detect blocks in a drawing**

☑ **use point filters to locate an insertion point**

☑ **revise a block**

☑ **drag and drop objects from one drawing to another**

☑ **use AutoCAD's DesignCenter**

☑ **use the Wblock command**

☑ **open palettes and control their appearance**

CHAPTER 8

Controlling Text in a Drawing

► Setting up text styles

► Placing new text in the drawing

► Modifying text in a drawing

► Working with grid lines

► Managing single-line and multiline text

► Adding hyperlinks

Y ou have many uses for text in your drawings, including titles of views, notes, and dimensions. It's not uncommon for the majority of a page to be covered with text outlining pertinent information including legal and code requirements, construction or manufacturing information, and contact information for companies or individuals involved in the project. Each of these might require a different height, orientation, justification, and style of lettering. To control the text, you'll need to learn how to do the following:

- ▶ Determine how the text will look by setting up text styles.
- ▶ Specify where the text will be, and enter it in the drawing.
- ▶ Modify the text already in your drawing.

AutoCAD offers two types of text objects: single-line and multiline. *Single-line text* makes a distinct object of each line of text, whether the line is one letter or many words. This type of text is useful for titles of drawings, titles of views within a drawing, room labels, and schedules. You use multiline text for dimensions, tables, and longer notes. With *multiline text*, AutoCAD treats a whole body of multiline text as one object, whether the text consists of one letter or many paragraphs.

The two types of text share the same text styles, but each has its own command for placing text in the drawing. When you modify text, you can use the same commands for either type of text, but the commands operate differently for multiline text than for single-line text. AutoCAD handles any text used in *dimensioning*—a process by which you indicate the sizes of various components in your drawing—differently from other text; I'll cover dimensioning in Chapter 12.

You'll progress through this chapter by first looking at the process of setting up text styles. You'll then start placing and modifying single-line text in the cabin drawing. Finally, you'll look at the methods for creating and controlling multiline text as it's used for notes and tables. If you work in a non-AEC profession or trade, be assured that the features presented in this chapter will apply directly to your work. The basic principles of working with text in AutoCAD and LT "cross the curriculum" (an educational metaphor) and apply universally.

Setting Up Text Styles

In AutoCAD, a text style consists of a combination of a style name, a text font, a height, a width factor, an oblique angle, and a few other, mostly static settings. You specify these text style properties with the help of a dialog box that opens when you start the Style command. You'll begin by setting up two text styles—one for labeling the rooms in the floor plan and the other for putting titles on the two views. You'll need a new layer for text:

1. Open the Cabin07c.dwg drawing.

2. Zoom out so that you can see the entire drawing.

3. Create a new layer named Text1. Assign it a color, and make it current.

4. Thaw and turn on all the other layers.

5. Display the Styles toolbar, dock it next to the Standard toolbar at the top of the AutoCAD window, and save the file as `Cabin08a.dwg`. Your drawing should look like Figure 8.1.

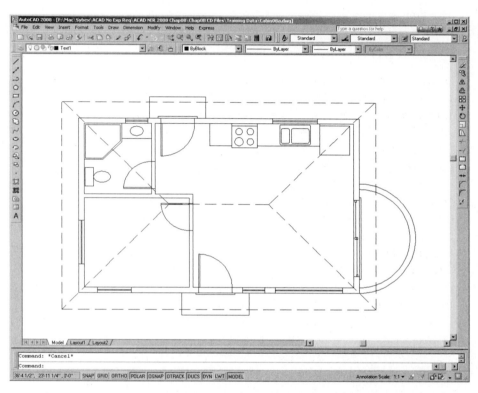

F I G U R E   8 . 1 : The `Cabin08a` drawing with all layers displayed and the Styles toolbar docked

Determining Text and Drawing Scale

When you set up text styles for a drawing, you have to determine the height of the text letters. To make this determination, you first need to decide the scale at which the final drawing will be printed.

In traditional drafting, you can ignore the drawing scale and set the actual height of each kind of text. This is possible because, although the drawing is to a scale, the text doesn't have to conform to that scale and is drawn full size.

A *layout* is a drawing environment that has been overlaid on the drawing of your project. The layout and the drawing are part of the same file.

In AutoCAD, a feature called *layouts* makes it possible to set the height of text in the same way—that is, at the height at which it will be printed. You'll learn about using layouts in Chapter 14. In that chapter, you'll place text on layouts; in this chapter, I'll demonstrate how you use text without layouts. You'll place text in the cabin drawing. The drawing is actual size, but the text has to be much larger than actual size because both the drawing and its text will be scaled down by the same factor in the process of printing the drawing.

In this drawing, you'll use a final scale of ⅛" = 1'-0". This scale has a true ratio of 1:96 and a scale factor of 96. (See Table 8.1.) If you want text to be ⅛" high when you print the drawing at ⅛-inch scale, multiply ⅛" by the scale factor of 96 to get 12" for the text height. You calculate the scale factor by inverting the scale fraction and multiplying it by 12. You can check that calculated text height by studying the floor plan for a moment and noting the sizes of the building components represented in the drawing. You can estimate that the room label text should be about half as high as the front step is deep, or 1 foot.

TABLE 8.1: Standard Scales and Their Corresponding Ratios

Scale	True Scale Factor
1" = 1'-0"	12
½" = 1'-0"	24
¼" = 1'-0"	48
⅛" = 1'-0"	96
1/16" = 1'-0"	192

Defining a Text Style for Room Labels

Now that you have a good idea of the required text height, it's time to define a new text style. Each new AutoCAD .dwg file comes with one predefined text style named Standard. You'll add two more. Follow these steps:

You can also start the Style command by choosing Format ➢ Text Style.

1. Enter st↵ to start the Style command, and open the Text Style dialog box (see Figure 8.2). In the Styles area, you'll see the default Standard text style as well as the Annotative text style.

2. Click New to open the New Text Style dialog box. You'll see a Style Name text box set to style1 in it, highlighted. When you enter a new style name, it will replace *style1*.

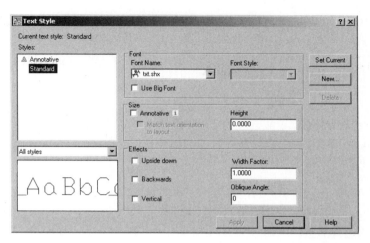

FIGURE 8.2: The Text Style dialog box, in which text styles are set up

3. Enter Label↵. The New Text Style dialog box closes, and in the Text Style dialog box, Label appears in the Style Name drop-down list. You've created a new text style named Label. It has settings identical to those of the Standard text style, and it's now the current text style. Next, you'll change some of the settings for this new style.

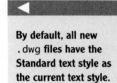

By default, all new .dwg files have the Standard text style as the current text style.

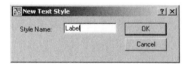

4. Move down to the Font area, and click the Font Name drop-down list to open it. A list of fonts appears; the number of choices depends on what software is installed on your computer. AutoCAD can use both its native .shx font files as well as Windows .ttf (TrueType font) files.

A *font* is a collection of text characters and symbols that all share a characteristic style of design and proportion.

5. Scroll through the list until you find romans.shx, and then click it. The list closes, and in the Font Name text box, the romans.shx font replaces the txt.shx font that was previously there. In the Preview area in the lower-left corner, a sample of the romans.shx font replaces that of the txt.shx font.

6. Press the Tab key a few times to move to the next text box. The Height setting is highlighted at the default of 0'-0".

7. Enter 12, and then press Tab again. A height of 1'-0" replaces the default height.

8. You won't need to change any of the other parameters that define the new text style. They can all stay at their default settings.

9. Click Apply at the bottom of the dialog box, and then click Close. The Label text style is saved with the current drawing and becomes the current text style. The current text style appears in the Text Style Control drop-down list in the Styles toolbar.

 N O T E   The current text style is similar to the current layer. All text created while a text style is current will follow the parameters or settings of that text style.

When you define a new text style, you first name the new style. This has the effect of making a copy of the current text style settings, giving them the new name, and making the new text style current. You then change the settings for this new style and save the changes by clicking Apply.

Defining a Second Text Style

Before you close the dialog box, define another text style:

1. Click the New button.

2. In the New Text Style dialog box, enter Title, and click OK. A new text style called Title is created and is now the current text style. Its font, height, and other settings are a copy of the Label text style. Now you'll make changes to these settings to define the Title text style.

3. Click the current font, romans.shx. The drop-down list of fonts opens. Scroll up one font, and click romand.shx. The list closes, and romand.shx appears as the chosen font.

4. Press Tab until the Height text box is highlighted, enter 18, and then press Tab again. This changes the height to 1'-6".

 T I P   If you press ↵ after entering the height, the new style is automatically applied, meaning it's saved and made the current text style. Don't do this if you need to change other settings for the style.

5. Click Apply, and then click Close.

Of the many fonts available in AutoCAD, you'll use only a few for your drawings. Some are set up for foreign languages or mapping symbols. Others would appear out of place on architectural or technical drawings but might be just right for an advertising brochure or a flier. Later in this chapter, you'll have a chance to experiment with the available fonts.

Refer to Figure 8.2 for a moment, and note that the Standard text style has a height of 0'-0". When the current text style has a height set to 0, you're prompted to enter a height each time you begin to place single-line text in the drawing. The default height will be ³⁄₁₆" (or 0.20 for decimal units and 2.5 for metric). Multiline text will use the default height of ³⁄₁₆" unless you change it.

Now that you have two new text styles, you can start working with single-line text.

SHX AND TTF FONTS

AutoCAD text styles can use either the AutoCAD .shx files or the Windows .ttf (TrueType font) files on your system. The .shx fonts are older files that were originally designed for use with pen plotters that required the pen tip to follow a precise vector. When you zoom into an AutoCAD font or print it large on a drawing, the straight line segments that comprise it become apparent. Two more fonts in the roman font family—romant (triplex) and romanc (complex)—have multiple, closely set lines and are used for larger text.

TrueType fonts are mathematical representations of vector formats and are common in most Windows applications. Many fonts are available, and you can use them with no loss of crispness regardless of the size of the font or the zoom factor in the drawing.

The .shx fonts are small files designed specifically to work with AutoCAD and do not significantly affect your system's performance. TrueType fonts usually look better but can affect workflow, especially when panning or zooming the view. If you must use .ttf fonts, such as in a large field of text where the serifs would make reading easier, turn off or freeze the text's layer when necessary. In either case, anybody opening your drawing file must have all the included fonts on their system in order to see the drawing properly.

Using Single-Line Text

Your first task is to put titles in for the floor plan using the new Title text style.

Placing Titles of Views in the Drawing

The titles need to be centered approximately under each view. If you establish a vertical guideline through the middle of the drawing, you can use it to position the text. Here are the steps:

1. Pan the drawing up to create a little more room under the floor plan.

2. Set up your osnaps and status bar such that Polar and Osnap are on and Endpoint and Midpoint osnaps are running. Drop a line from the midpoint of the ridgeline in the floor plan to a point near the bottom of the screen.

3. Offset the bottom line of the front step in the floor plan down 4'.

4. Choose Draw ➤ Text ➤ Single Line Text or enter dt↵ to start the Dtext command—the command used for single-line text.

5. The bottom line of text in the Command window says Specify start point of text or [Justify/Style]:. The line above it displays the name of the current text style and the style's height setting. The bottom line is the actual prompt, with three options. By default, the justification point is set to the lower-left corner of the text. You need to change it to the middle of the text to be able to center it on the guideline.

6. Enter j↵. All the possible justification points appear in the prompt.

7. Enter c↵ to choose Center as the justification.

8. Hold down the Shift key, and right-click to open a menu of osnap options next to where the cursor was just positioned.

9. Choose Intersection, and pick the intersection of the guideline and the offset line.

> The *justification point* for the text functions like the insertion point for blocks.

> The Osnap Cursor menu (Shift+right-click) contains all the object snap tools, access to the Osnap Settings dialog box to allow you to set running osnaps, and a Point Filters menu.

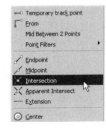

10. For the rotation, press ↵ to accept the default angle of 0°, or enter 0↵ if 0° is not the default. A flashing I-shaped cursor superimposed over a narrow box appears at the intersection (see Figure 8.3).

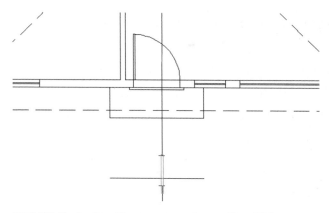

FIGURE 8.3: The text cursor sits on the guidelines.

11. With Caps Lock on, enter **FLOOR PLAN**↵. The text is centered at the intersection as you enter it, and the cursor moves down to allow you to enter another line (see the left of Figure 8.4).

12. Press ↵ again to end the Dtext command. The text is centered relative to the vertical guideline and sits on the offset line (see the right of Figure 8.4).

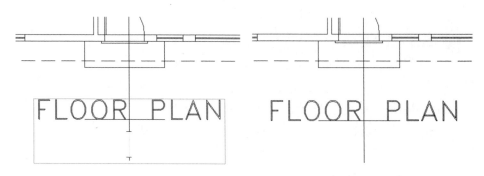

FIGURE 8.4: The first line of text is entered (left) and placed (right).

13. Erase the offset line and the vertical guideline. Your drawing will look like Figure 8.5.

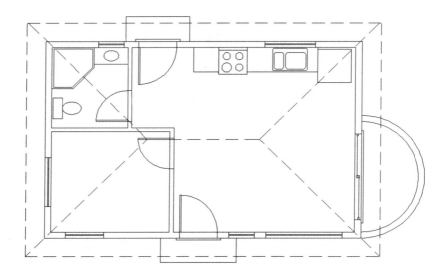

FLOOR PLAN

FIGURE 8.5: The drawing with the title complete

You specified a location for the text in two steps: first, you set the justification point of each line of text to be centered horizontally; second, you used the Intersection osnap to position the justification point at the intersection of the two guidelines. I'll discuss justification in more depth a little later in this chapter.

Next you'll move to the interior of the cabin floor plan and place the room labels in their respective rooms.

Placing Room Labels in the Floor Plan

Text for the room labels will use the Label text style, so you need to make that style current before you start placing text. You can accomplish this from the Styles toolbar:

1. Click the Polar and Osnap buttons on the status bar to turn off these features.

2. Expand the Text Style Control list on the Styles toolbar to display a list of all the text styles in the drawing. Click Label, as shown in Figure 8.6, to make Label the current style.

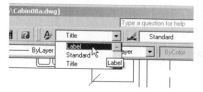

FIGURE 8.6: Selecting a new current text style from the Styles toolbar

3. Start the Dtext command, and notice that the FLOOR PLAN text shows as dashed lines. If you press ↵ at the Specify start point of text or [Justify/Style]: prompt, the new text will be placed just below the last text created.

4. Pick a point in the kitchen a couple of feet below and to the left of the oven.

5. Press ↵ at the rotation prompt. The text cursor appears at the point you picked.

6. With Caps Lock on, enter **KITCHEN**↵ **LIVING ROOM**↵ **BEDROOM**↵ **BATH**↵↵. The Dtext command ends. You have four lines of text in the kitchen and living room area (see Figure 8.7).

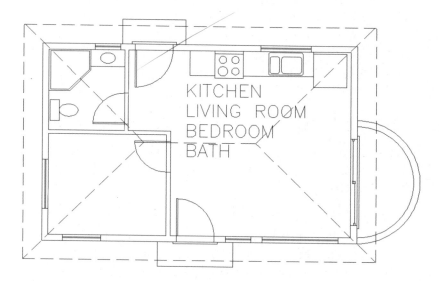

FIGURE 8.7: The four room labels placed in the cabin

For this text, you used the default Left justification, and each line of text was positioned directly below the previous line at a spacing set by AutoCAD. In many cases, it's more efficient to enter a list of words or phrases first and then move the text to its appropriate location. That's what you're doing for this text. When you know the location of the insertion point for the next line, you can click that point, instead of pressing ↵ at the end of the current line. This starts the next line of text at the selected location.

Moving Text

You'll eyeball the final position of this text because it doesn't have to be exactly centered or lined up precisely with anything. It should just sit in the rooms in such a way that it's easily readable:

1. Click the BATH text. One grip appears, at the justification point of the text.

2. Click the grip to activate it. The BATH text is attached to the cursor and moves with it (see the top of Figure 8.8). The Stretch command automatically starts. Because text can't be stretched, the Stretch command functions like the Move command.

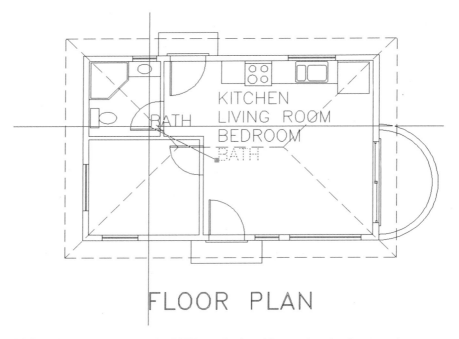

FIGURE 8.8: Moving the BATH text (top) and its new location (next page)

Continues

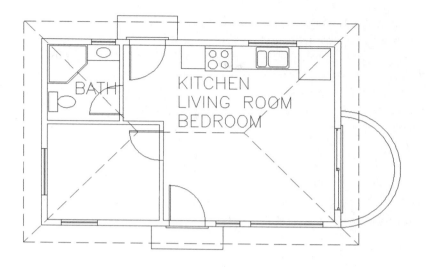

FLOOR PLAN

FIGURE 8.8 *(Continued)*

3. Be sure that Ortho, Polar, and Osnap (and, for AutoCAD only, Otrack) are turned off. Move the cursor to the bathroom, and click a location to place the word in such a way that the letters—although they might be on top of the door swing and the roofline—don't touch any fixtures or walls.

4. Press Esc to deselect the text and remove the grip (see the bottom of Figure 8.8). Then, select the BEDROOM text.

5. Click the grip for the newly selected text.

6. Pick a point in the bedroom so that the BEDROOM text is positioned approximately at the center of the bedroom and is crossing only the roofline. Press Esc to remove the grip.

7. Repeat this process to move the LIVING ROOM and KITCHEN text into their appropriate locations (see Figure 8.9). You might not have to move the KITCHEN text.

When you move text in this way, you're actually using the Stretch option of the grips feature. Because text can't be stretched, it just moves with the cursor.

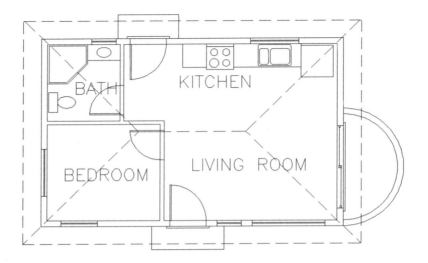

FLOOR PLAN

FIGURE 8.9: The BEDROOM, LIVING ROOM, and KITCHEN text moved to their positions

As you've seen, you can easily move text around the drawing. Often, however, you'll be unable to position it without it sitting on top of a line or other object. In the cabin, three of the room labels are crossing the roofline, and BATH is crossing a door swing. You need to erase parts of these lines around the text. To do this, you'll use the Break command.

Breaking Lines

The Break command chops a line into two lines. When you're working with text that intersects a line, you'll usually want a gap between the lines after the break. The Break command provides this option as well as others. Follow these steps:

You can also start the Break command by choosing Modify ➤ Break or by entering br↵.

1. Be sure no osnaps are running, and click the Break button on the Modify toolbar.

2. Move the cursor near the roofline that crosses through the LIVING ROOM text. Place the pickbox on the roofline just above the text, and click. The line ghosts, and the cursor changes to the crosshair cursor.

3. Put the crosshair cursor on the roofline just below the text, and pick that point. The line is broken around the text, and the Break command ends.

4. Press ↵ to restart the Break command, and do the same operation on the roofline that crosses the BEDROOM text.

5. The arc representing the door swing is part of the door2_6 block and, as such, can't be broken. You must explode the block to be able to break the arc, but we need the door block intact for a later exercise. Move the BATH text to where it just fits above the door swing and between the shower and the wall.

6. Start the Break command again, and break the roofline around the BATH text. Your drawing should look like Figure 8.10.

7. Save your drawing as Cabin08b.dwg.

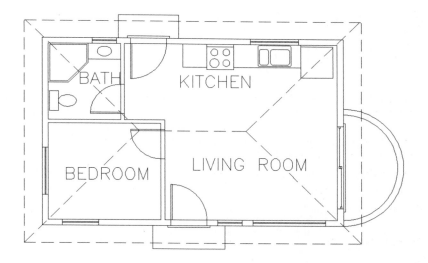

FLOOR PLAN

FIGURE 8.10: Lines are broken around the room labels.

T I P The multiline text objects have a mask feature that creates an envelope over and around the text that hides the objects behind it. Unlike the breaking-lines approach, the masked objects reappear when you move the text. Masking is not supported for single-line text, but the Text Mask utility is available in the Express Tools.

Taking a Closer Look at the Break Command

Use your own judgment to determine how far from the text a line has to be broken back. You have to strike a balance between making the text easy to read and keeping what the broken line represents clear. In the bathroom, I directed you to keep the text away from any fixtures because if any lines of the fixtures had to be broken to accommodate the text, this might have made it difficult for a viewer to recognize that those lines represent a shower or a toilet.

Here are some other options for the Break command:

▶ Ordinarily, when you select a line to be broken, the point where you pick the line becomes the beginning of the break. If the point where the break needs to start is at the intersection of two lines, you must select the line to be broken somewhere other than at a break point. Otherwise, AutoCAD won't know which line you want to break. In that case, after selecting the line to break, enter **f↵**. You'll be prompted to pick the first point of the break, and the command continues. Now that AutoCAD knows which line you want to break, you can use the Intersection osnap to pick the intersection of two lines.

▶ To break a line into two segments without leaving a gap, click the Break at Point button, which is just above the Break button in the Modify toolbar. You might want to do this to place one part of a line on a different layer from the rest of the line. To break the line this way, start the command, select the line to break, and then pick the point on the line where the break is to occur, using an osnap if necessary. AutoCAD makes the break and ends the command.

Using Text in a Grid

AutoCAD provides a grid of dots or lines, which you worked with in Chapter 3. The grid is a tool for visualizing the size of the drawing area and for drawing lines whose geometry conforms to the spacing of the dots or lines. Many floor plans have a separate *structural* grid, created specifically for the project and made up of lines running vertically and horizontally through key structural components of the building. At one end of each grid line, a circle or a hexagon is placed, and a letter or number is centered in the shape to identify it. This kind of grid is usually reserved for large, complex drawings, but you'll put a small grid on the cabin floor plan to learn the basic method for laying one out:

1. Create a new layer called Grid. Assign it a color, and make it current.

2. Enter z↵ .6x↵ to make more room around the floor plan.

3. Offset the upper roofline up 10'. Offset the left roofline 10' to the left. Offset the lower roofline down 2'. Offset the right roofline to the right 4'. Pan and zoom as necessary.

4. Turn Osnap on if it's off, set the Endpoint and Perpendicular osnaps to be running, and then start the Line command.

5. Draw lines from the upper-left and upper-right corners of the exterior walls up to the horizontal offset line. Then, draw lines from the left upper and lower corners of the exterior walls to the vertical offset line on the left (see Figure 8.11).

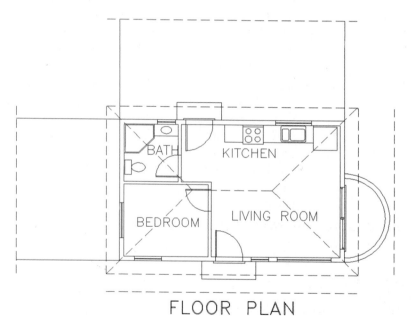

FIGURE 8.11: The first grid lines

6. Now you need to draw grid lines through the middle of the interior walls. Zoom in to the bathroom area, and draw a short guideline across the interior wall between the bathroom and bedroom, where this wall meets the exterior wall (see Figure 8.12).

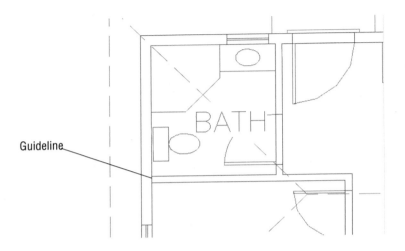

FIGURE 8.12: A guideline for drawing a grid line through one of the interior walls

7. Use Zoom and Pan to set up the view so that it contains the bathroom and the offset rooflines above and to the left of the floor plan.

8. Draw two vertical lines and one horizontal line from the middle of the interior walls out to the offset rooflines. Select Midpoint from the Osnap toolbar (or enter **mid.┘** at the Specify first point: prompt), and pick one of the jamb lines or the guideline to start each line from the middle of a wall (see Figure 8.13).

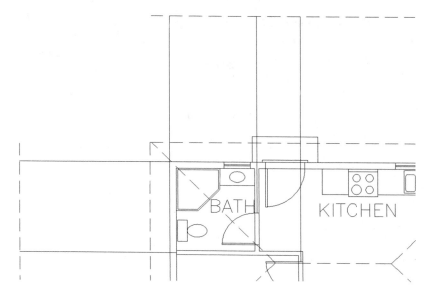

FIGURE 8.13: Drawing the grid lines

T I P   Because the Endpoint osnap is already running and the guideline is so short, it's easier to select Midpoint from the Object Snap toolbar than to have it running. If it's running along with the Endpoint osnap, it's hard to control which of the osnaps will be activated on the jamb lines and on the guideline. When you select Midpoint from the Object Snap toolbar, you cancel all running osnaps for the next pick.

9. Erase the guideline you drew in step 6, and then zoom out to a view that includes the floor plan, the grid lines, and all the offset rooflines (see the top of Figure 8.14).

10. Use the Extend command to extend the seven grid lines to the right or down, and use the offset rooflines on those sides of the floor plan as boundary edges (see the bottom of Figure 8.14).

T I P   When erasing the guideline, select it with a regular selection window.

When several osnaps are running, the marker for only one (and not necessarily the correct one) appears at a time. You can cycle through all the running osnaps for every object your cursor is over or near by pressing the Tab key.

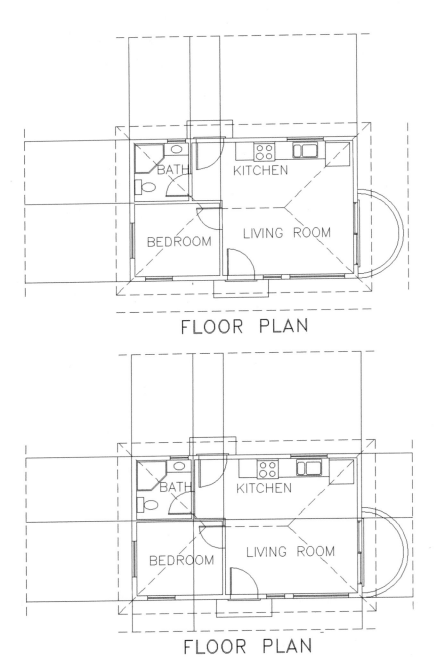

FIGURE 8.14: The zoomed view for completing the grid lines (top) and the completed grid lines (bottom)

This completes the grid lines. To finish the grid, you need to add a circle with a letter or a number in it to the left or upper end of the lines. You'll use letters across the top and numbers running down the side:

1. Erase the four offset rooflines. Zoom out a little.

2. Choose Draw ➤ Circle ➤ 2 Points, and then pick the upper end of the leftmost vertical grid line.

3. Enter @2'<90↵. This places a circle 2' in diameter at the top of the grid line (see the top of Figure 8.15).

4. Click the KITCHEN text. A grip appears.

5. Click the grip; enter c, for *copy*; and press ↵.

6. Select the Center osnap, and click the circle on the grid. The KITCHEN text appears on the circle, with the lower-left corner of the text at the center of the circle (see the bottom of Figure 8.15). Press Esc twice, once to end the Stretch function and again to clear the grip.

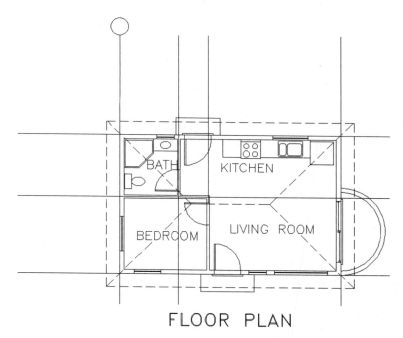

FLOOR PLAN

FIGURE 8.15: The circle on the grid line (top) and the KITCHEN text copied to the circle (next page)

Continues

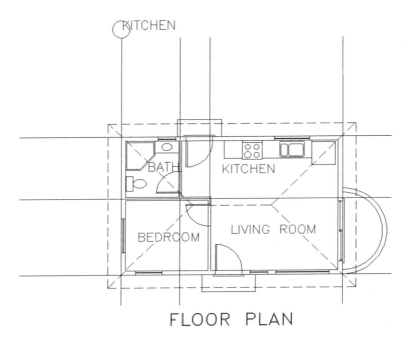

FLOOR PLAN

FIGURE 8.15   *(Continued)*

This might seem like a roundabout way to generate letters for the grid symbols, but this exercise is meant to show you how easy it is to use text from one part of the drawing for a completely different text purpose. It's a handy technique, as long as you want to use a font that has been chosen for a previously defined text style. A faster way to do this is to use the Single Line Text command with the Justify setting set to Middle, use the Center osnap to place the text cursor at the center of the circle, and then enter A↵↵.

▶

7. Click the copy of the KITCHEN text that is now on the grid, and then click the Properties button on the Standard Properties toolbar to open the Properties palette. Text appears on the drop-down list at the top, telling you that you've selected a text object.

8. Use the Properties palette to change the KITCHEN text as follows:

   a. Change Layer from Text1 to **Grid**.

   b. Change Contents from KITCHEN to **A**.

   c. Change the Justify setting from Left to **Middle**.

For each change, follow these steps in the Properties palette:

   1. Click the category in the left column that needs to change. If the setting is on a drop-down list, an arrow appears in the right column.

   2. Click the down arrow to open the list. In the case of the KITCHEN text, just highlight it, because there is no drop-down list.

   3. Click the new setting, or enter it.

   4. When you're finished, close the Properties palette, and press Esc to remove the grip.

The KITCHEN text changes to the letter *A*, is centered in the grid circle, and moves to the Grid layer (see Figure 8.16).

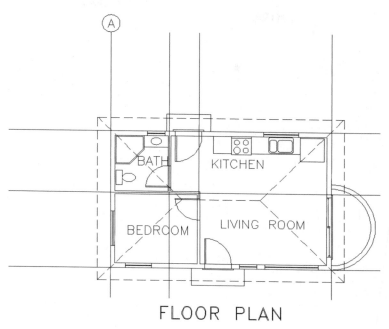

FLOOR PLAN

FIGURE 8.16: The grid circle with the letter *A*

You used the Center osnap on the KITCHEN text to position its justification point at the center of the circle. You then modified the justification point from the Left position (which is short for Lower Left) to the Middle position (short for Center Middle). The Middle position is the middle of the line of text, horizontally and vertically. So, what you did had the effect of centering the text in the circle. You'll now look at text justification briefly.

Justifying Text

Each line of single-line text is an object. It has a justification point, which is similar to the insertion points on blocks. When drawing, you can use the Insert osnap to precisely locate the justification point of text (or the insertion point of blocks) and thereby control the text's position on the drawing. When you use the Dtext command, the default justification point is the lower-left corner of the line of text. At the Dtext prompt (`Specify start point of text or [Justify/Style]:`), if you enter j↵, you get the prompt `Enter an option [Align/Fit/Center/Middle/Right/TL/TC/TR/ML/MC/MR/BL/BC/BR]:`. These are your justification options.

Figure 8.17 shows most of these options. The dots are in three columns—left, center, and right—and in four rows—top, middle, lower, and base. The names of the justification locations are based on these columns and rows. For example, you have TL for Top Left, MR for Middle Right, and so on. The third row down doesn't use the name Lower; it simply goes by Left, Center, and Right. Left is the default justification position, so it's not in the list of options. The Middle position sometimes coincides with the Middle Center position, but not always. For example, if a line of text has *descenders*—lowercase letters that drop below the baseline such as *j* and *p*—the Middle position drops below the Middle Center position. Finally, the lowest row, the *Base row*, sits just below the letters at the lowest point of any descenders.

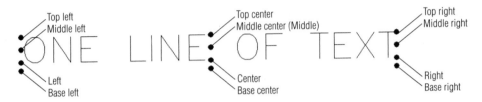

FIGURE 8.17: The justification points on a line of text

Finishing the Grid

To finish the grid, you need to copy the grid circle with its text to each grid line and then change the text:

1. Be sure the Endpoint osnap is still running. Then, at the Command prompt, select the letter *A*, and click the circle. Grips appear.

2. Click the grip at the bottom of the circle to activate it.

3. Right-click, and choose Move; right-click again, and choose Copy to activate the copy option.

4. Pick the top end of each vertical grid line; then right-click, and choose Enter to terminate the command (see Figure 8.18).

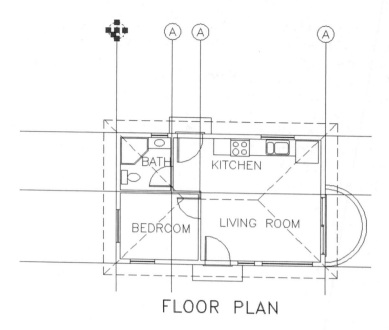

FLOOR PLAN

FIGURE 8.18: The grid circle and letter are copied to the top of all three vertical lines.

5. Move back to the original grid circle, and select the grip on the right side of the circle to activate it.

6. Repeat steps 3 and 4 to copy the original grid circle and letter to the left end of each horizontal grid line.

7. Press Esc to remove the grips. Now you'll use the Ddedit command to change the text in each circle.

8. Be sure Caps Lock is on. Enter **ddedit**↵ or the aliase **ed**↵. At the `Select an annotation object or [Undo]:` prompt, select the letter *A* in the second grid circle from the left on the top row.

9. With Caps Lock on, enter B↵. The *A* changes to *B*, and the command remains active.

10. Click the *A* in the next circle to the right, and then enter C↵. The *A* changes to a *C*.

11. Repeat this process for the remaining four grid circle letters, changing them to *D*, *1*, *2*, and *3*. Press ↵ to end the Edit Text command. The letters and numbers are all in place, and the grid is complete (see Figure 8.19).

You can also start the ddedit command by choosing Modify ➢ Object ➢ Text ➢ Edit or by double-clicking the text that you want to modify.

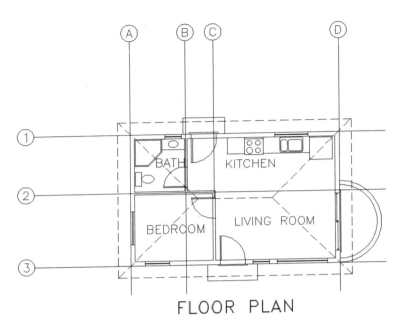

FIGURE 8.19: The completed grid

> **12.** Save this drawing as Cabin8c.dwg.

Often it's easier to copy existing text and modify it than to create new text, and grips are a handy way to copy text. Using the Edit Text command (technically called Ddedit) is a quick way to modify the wording of short lines of text, meaning those that consist of a word or a few letters. The Properties palette is useful for changing all aspects of a line of text.

For the next exercise with text, you'll get a chance to set up some more new text styles, place text precisely, and use the Ddedit command again to modify text content. You'll do all this while you develop a title block for your drawing.

Creating a Title Block and Border

The first step in creating a title block and border for the cabin drawing is deciding on a sheet size for printing the final drawing. Because many people have access to 8.5" × 11"–format printers, you'll use that sheet size. So if you print the drawing at a scale of ⅛" = 1'-0", will it fit on the sheet?

To answer that question, you have to ask, how big an area will fit on an 8.5" × 11" sheet at ⅛" = 1'-0" scale? The answer is quite simple: if every inch on the sheet represents 8', you multiply each dimension of the sheet in inches by 8' per inch. For this sheet, you multiply 8.5" × 8' per inch to get 68'. And you multiply 11" × 8' per inch to get 88'. So, the 8.5" × 11" sheet represents a rectangle with dimensions of 68' × 88' at a scale of 1" = 8'-0" (usually called *eighth-inch scale*). Even when you account for the unprintable area around the perimeter of the sheet, that should be plenty of room for your cabin drawing. This is the information you need to start creating the title block.

Drawing the Border

The border of the drawing will be set in from the edge of the sheet. Here are the steps:

1. Create a new layer called Tblk1. Leave the default color assigned, and make this layer current.

2. Start the Rectangle command (used in Chapter 4 to make the doors).

3. At the prompt, enter 0,0↵. Then, enter 68',88'↵. This draws a rectangle that extends off the top of the screen (see Figure 8.20).

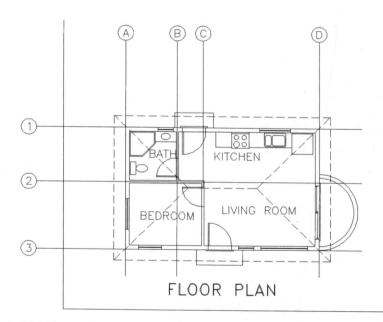

FIGURE 8.20: Creating the rectangle

4. Use Zoom Realtime to zoom out until the entire rectangle is visible in the drawing area (see Figure 8.21). You need to fit the drawing into the rectangle as if you were fitting it on a sheet of paper—the easiest and safest way to do this is to move the rectangle over to enclose the drawing. You'll leave plenty of room for the elevation that you will draw in a later chapter.

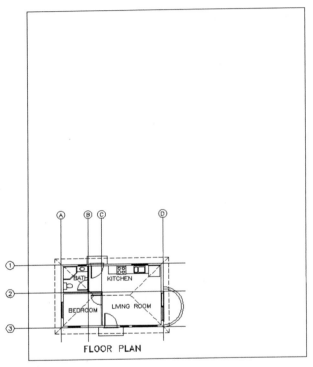

FIGURE 8.21: Zooming out to include the entire rectangle

5. At the Command prompt, click the rectangle to select it. Grips appear at the corners of the rectangle.

6. Click the lower-left grip. Press the spacebar once. Then move the rectangle over the drawing (see the top of Figure 8.22).

7. When the rectangle is approximately in the position shown in the bottom of Figure 8.22, click. Press Esc to turn off the grips. The rectangle is positioned around the drawing and represents the edge of the sheet.

Once you activate a grip and the Stretch function begins, pressing the spacebar toggles through the other four commands in this order: Move, Rotate, Scale, Mirror.

▶

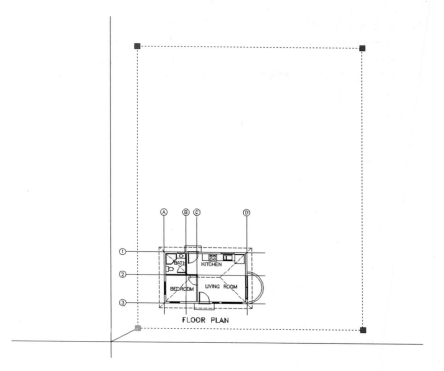

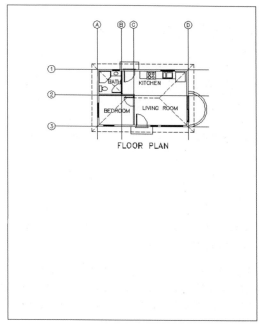

F I G U R E   8 . 2 2 : Moving the rectangle with grips (top) and the results (bottom)

8. You need a border set in from the edge. Offset the rectangle 3' to the inside. (With a scale of 1" = 8'-0", which is another way of expressing the scale of ⅛" = 1'-0", each 1'-0" on the drawing will be represented by ⅛" on the sheet. So, a 3' offset distance will create an offset of ⅜" on the printed sheet.)

9. Double-click the inside rectangle to start the Pedit command.

10. Enter w↵ 3↵↵. This command sets the width of the inside rectangle's lines to 3". (When printed at ⅛ inch scale, the lines will be ¹⁄₃₂" thick.)

11. Use Zoom to Extents, and then zoom out a little to create a view in which the drawing with its border nearly fills the screen (see Figure 8.23). The outer rectangle represents the edge of the sheet of paper, and the thicker, inner rectangle is the drawing's border.

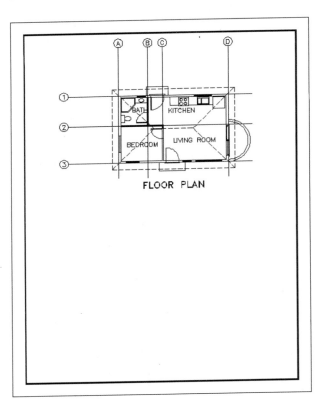

FIGURE 8.23: The drawing with its border

Constructing a Title Block

The *title block* is a box that contains general information about a drawing, such as the name of the project, the design company, and the date of the drawing. It will be set up in the lower-right corner of the border and will use the same special line—the *polyline*—that is created when the Rectangle command is executed.

You first used the Rectangle command in Chapter 4 for drawing the doors. At that time, I mentioned that rectangles created with the Rectangle command consist of a polyline whose four segments are grouped as one object. In step 10 of the previous section, you saw that these segments could have varying widths.

The *Polyline command*, nicknamed the Pline command, allows you to draw continuous straight and curved line segments of varying widths, with all segments behaving as if they were one object.

When you explode a polyline using the Explode command, the segments lose any width they have and become independent lines. The ability of a polyline to have a width makes it useful in constructing title blocks. You'll use the Pline command to draw the various lines that make up the title block, and then you'll fill in the text:

1. Zoom in to a view of the lower third of your drawing, including the bottom of the border. Be sure the Endpoint and Perpendicular osnaps are running.

2. Click the Polyline icon on the Draw toolbar. The `Specify start point:` prompt appears in the Command window.

3. Click Polar on the status bar to turn on polar tracking. Then, select the Temporary Tracking Point osnap. Click the lower-left corner of the border, and hold the cursor directly above that point. When the vertical tracking path appears along the left boundary line, enter 12'↵. This starts a polyline on the left side of the border 12' above the lower-left corner.

4. Notice the bottom two lines of text in the Command window. The upper one tells you the current width set for polylines. The lower one displays the options for the Polyline command, with the default option being to pick a second point. This is the time to set the line width.

5. Enter w↵, and then enter 3.↵↵. This sets the starting and ending widths of polyline segments to 3". The original polyline command prompt returns.

You can also start the Polyline command by entering pl↵ or by choosing Draw ➤ Polyline.

6. Hold the crosshair cursor on the right side of the border. When the Perpendicular osnap marker appears on the border line, click. Then, press ↵ to terminate the command. The first polyline segment is drawn (see Figure 8.24). The 3" width setting will stay until you change it and will be saved with the drawing file.

FIGURE 8.24: Drawing a polyline for the title bar

7. Restart the Polyline command. Choose the Midpoint osnap, and start a new segment at the midpoint of the line you just drew.

8. Move to the bottom of the border near its midpoint. When the running Perpendicular osnap is activated, click. The left edge of the title block is drawn (see the top of Figure 8.25). Press ↵ to end the Polyline, or Pline, command.

9. Trim the left half of the upper horizontal pline drawn back to the pline just drawn.

10. Offset the horizontal pline down 4', offset this new line down 3', and then offset this new line down 2'-6" (see the middle of Figure 8.25).

11. Start the Pline command. Using Midpoint osnap, start a pline at the midpoint of the third horizontal line down. Then, end the segment at the bottom of the border, taking advantage of the running Perpendicular osnap. Press ↵ to end the Pline command.

12. Trim the right side of the line just above the bottom of the border, back to the line you just drew (see the bottom of Figure 8.25).

FIGURE 8.25: Building the title block: the left edge (top), the horizontal lines (middle), and the last line trimmed (bottom)

The lines for the title block are almost done. Some of the plines might look wider than others. The monitor distorting the picture at the current view almost certainly causes this. By zooming in, you can assure yourself that everything is correct:

1. Zoom in to a close view of the title block. Notice that the intersection of the outer lines in the upper-left corner doesn't seem clean.

2. Zoom in to that corner using a zoom window (see the top of Figure 8.26). The lines don't intersect in a clean corner because they are two separate polylines. You need to join them as one.

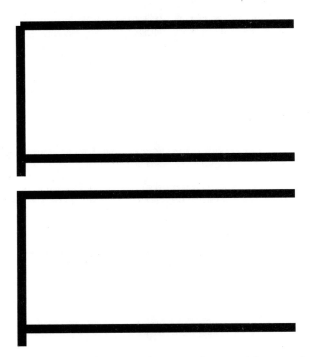

FIGURE 8.26: Zoomed in to the upper-left corner (top) and the corner corrected (bottom)

3. Enter **pe**↵ to start the Polyline Edit (Pedit) command, and select one of the two lines. When a pline is thicker than the pickbox, you must place the pickbox on the edge of the polyline to select it, not over the middle of it.

4. Enter **j**↵ to activate the Join option, then select the other pline, and finally press ↵. This corrects the corner (see the bottom of Figure 8.26). Enter **x**↵ or ↵ to end the Pedit command.

5. Use Zoom Previous once. Then, use Zoom Realtime to zoom out enough to see the entire title block (see Figure 8.27).

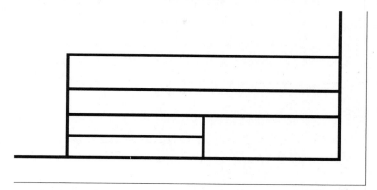

FIGURE 8.27: The completed lines of the title block after zooming out

Putting Text in the Title Block

The title block has five boxes that will each contain distinct pieces of information. The large one at the top will contain the name of the project. Below that will be the name of the company producing the drawing—your company. (If you don't have a company name, make one up.) Below that on the left will be the initials of the person—you—who drew this drawing and, below that, the date. In the lower-right corner will be the sheet number, in case more than one sheet is required for this project. This follows a standard format. Most title block layouts contain this information and more, depending on the complexity of the job.

You need to put labels in some of the boxes to identify what information will appear there. For this, you need to set up a new text style:

1. Choose Format ➤ Text Style to open the Text Style dialog box. The Label text style should still be current. If not, then select it.

2. Click New, enter **Tblk-label**, and then click OK. Leave the font set to `romans.shx`, but change the height to 8". Click Apply & Close. Tblk-label is the current text style.

3. Be sure Caps Lock is on, and enter **dt↵** to start the Dtext command. Click the Snap to None osnap button, or enter **non↵**. Then, pick a point in the upper-left corner of the upper box of the title block. It doesn't have to be the perfect location now; you can fix it after you see the text.

4. Press ↵ at the rotation prompt. Enter **PROJECT:↵↵**. PROJECT: appears in the upper box (see the left of Figure 8.28).

If you press ↵ after changing the height, the Apply button turns gray and unselectable. Pressing ↵ at this point has the same effect as clicking the Apply button.

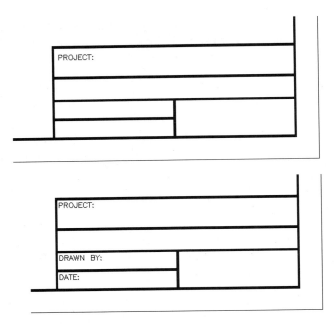

FIGURE 8.28: One line of text placed (top) and the text changed to the correct wording (bottom)

The closer you zoom in, the more precisely you'll be able to fine-tune the location of the text. You then need to zoom out to check how it looks.

5. If necessary, move this text to the upper-left corner, as far as possible, while still allowing it to be readable. It will help if Polar and Osnap are temporarily turned off.

T I P   If you have running osnaps and need to have them off for one pick, you can click the Snap to None osnap button. Doing so cancels all running osnaps for the next pick. If you need running osnaps turned off for several picks, click the Osnap button on the status bar. Click it again when you want the running osnaps to become active.

6. Use the Copy command to copy this text to the bottom two boxes on the left, using the endpoint of the horizontal lines above each of the boxes as the base and displacement points. This keeps each piece of text in the same position relative to the upper-left corner of each box.

7. Enter ed↵ to start the Ddedit command. Then, click the upper of the two copies of text. You can also double-click the text to edit it.

8. Enter **DRAWN BY:**, and press ↵. Pick the lower copy of text. The Edit Text dialog box returns.

9. Enter **DATE:**, and press ↵. Press ↵ to end the Ddedit command. This changes the text, so three of the boxes have their proper labels (see the bottom of Figure 8.28).

Using the Ddedit command is a quick way to change the wording of text and to correct spelling. You have to change one line at a time, but the command keeps running until you stop it.

The next area to work on is the lower-right box. This is where the sheet number appears, and it's usually displayed in such a way that the person reading the drawing can tell not only the page number of the current sheet but also the number of sheets being used for the project. You'll create a new text style for this box:

1. Start the Style command. In the Text Style dialog box, click New.

2. Turn off Caps Lock, then enter **Sheet_No**, and finally click OK. For the font, select `romand.shx`. Change the height to 1'-3". Click Apply, and then click Close. Sheet_No is now the current text style.

3. You need to center the text horizontally in the box. Doing so requires breaking the horizontal line running across the top of this box at the upper-left corner of the box. To do this, click the Break at Point button on the Modify toolbar. Then, select the line to break at a point where no other lines are touching it.

4. Use the Endpoint running osnap to pick the upper-left corner of the box. AutoCAD breaks the line at that point without leaving a gap and ends the command.

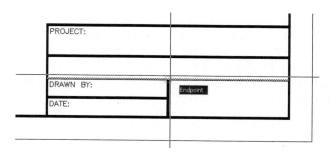

5. Start the Dtext command, and enter **j**↵. Then, enter **tc**↵ to set the justification to the top center of the text. Select the Midpoint osnap, and pick a point on the line across the top of the box.

6. Press ↵ at the rotation prompt. Turn Caps Lock back on, and then enter **SHEET NO.:**↵ **1 of 1**↵↵. (When you get to the *of*, turn off Caps Lock, or hold down the Shift key while typing.) This inserts the text into the box and centers it horizontally (see the top of Figure 8.29).

7. With polar tracking on, use the Move command to move the text down and center it vertically in the box (see the bottom of Figure 8.29). Remember, when you select the text to move it, you have to pick each line because they are two separate objects.

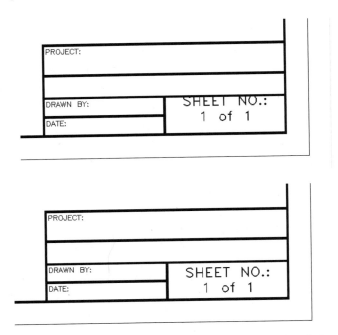

FIGURE 8.29: The text after being inserted (top) and after centering vertically (bottom)

Now it's time for you to experiment. Use the techniques you just learned to fill in the text for the other four boxes. Feel free to try other fonts, but you'll have to adjust the height for each text style so that the text fits in its box. Some guidelines for height follow:

Box	Recommended Height of Text
Project	2'-6"
Company	1'-3"
Drawn By	1'-0"
Date	1'-0"

You can use the same style for all text with the same properties, but you'll have to set up a new style for each new font or height you choose unless you set up a style with a height of 0'-0". In that case, you'll be prompted for the height each time you start to place text in the drawing. This is the recommended way to operate for the top two boxes because it will give consistency to the text even when heights vary. You might try several fonts and then come back to this technique at the end. I also recommend you use a relatively simple font for the text in the Drawn By and Date boxes.

Try these fonts:

- ▶ `romant.shx` or `romanc.shx`
- ▶ Any of the swis721 series
- ▶ Times New Roman
- ▶ Technic
- ▶ SansSerif
- ▶ CityBlueprint or CountryBlueprint
- ▶ Arial

In the top two boxes, you can center the text vertically and horizontally if you draw a line diagonally across the box, choose Middle as a justification for the text, and use the Midpoint osnap to snap to the diagonal line when you start the text. For the Drawn By and Date boxes, centering the text horizontally isn't advisable because the label text already in the boxes takes up too much space. However, you can use the diagonal line to center it and then move the text to the right until it makes a good fit. Using polar tracking will keep the new text vertically centered.

Be careful in your use of running osnaps as you position text. If you're eyeballing the final location, it's best to have no running osnaps. On the other hand, if you're precisely locating justification points by snapping to lines and other objects, you might try having the following osnaps running: Endpoint, Intersection, Perpendicular, and Insertion, with Midpoint optional. When you finish, your title block should look something like Figure 8.30.

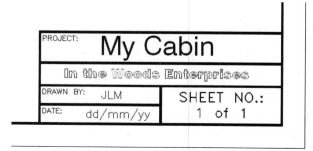

FIGURE 8.30: The completed title block

If you're going to design your own company title block, be ready to spend a little time setting it up and deciding which fonts will give the look that best reflects the image you want to project. You can then use this title block on all your subsequent projects.

Use Zoom to Extents, and then zoom out a little to view the entire drawing. Save this drawing as Cabin8d.dwg (see Figure 8.31).

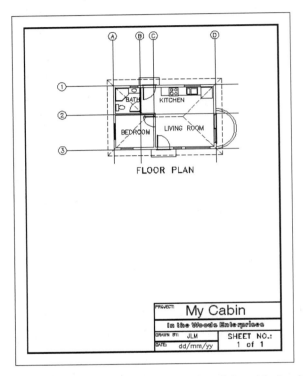

FIGURE 8.31: The latest version of the cabin drawing

Looking at AutoCAD's Title Blocks

Now that you've created a title block and a border, you'll briefly look at the title blocks and borders that AutoCAD provides in its template files and see how you can use these files to set up a new drawing. Follow these steps:

1. Click the QNew icon on the Standard toolbar to open the Select Template dialog box.

2. Double-click `Tutorial-iArch.dwt`. The new drawing appears with a title block and border (see Figure 8.32). In addition, this sheet has extra lines, arrows, and a section near the upper edge for listing revisions to the drawing.

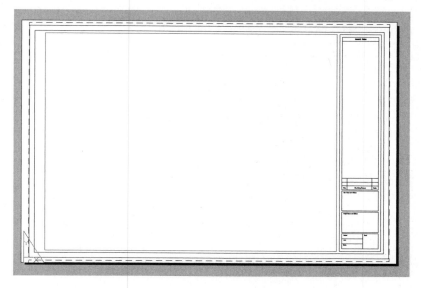

F I G U R E   8 . 3 2 : A new drawing made from the Tutorial-iArch template

3. Zoom in to the title block on the lower part of the drawing. Notice that it has spaces for the scale and sheet number, among other information, and that some areas are left blank.

4. Close this drawing, and click the QNew button again to look at some of the other template files on the list. Don't worry about the part of the template name that identifies plot style types. I'll cover this in Chapter 15. The background for the template files is gray because they use *layouts*, which I'll introduce in Chapter 14.

When you open a new drawing by selecting a template file, AutoCAD uses the template file as the basis of your new drawing. It copies the information in the template file onto the new drawing file and names the new drawing `Drawing1`, `Drawing2`, and so on. You can convert any drawing into a template file. Simply choose File ➢ Save As, and in the Files Of Type drop-down list at the bottom of the Save Drawing As dialog box, select AutoCAD Drawing Template (*.dwt). The new file will have the `.dwt` extension. You can store it in AutoCAD's `Template` folder or any folder you choose. When you click Save, the Template Options dialog box opens, giving you the option of writing a description of the new template file and choosing whether the template will use metric or English units (see Figure 8.33).

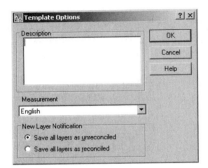

FIGURE 8.33: The Template Options dialog box

The final part of this chapter introduces you to multiline text, which you'll also work with as you learn about dimensions in the next chapter, and introduces you to tables.

Using Multiline Text

Multiline text (often referred to as *Mtext*) is more complex than single-line text. You can use it in the same way you used single-line text in this chapter, and it can do more. If you have several lines of text or if you need certain words within a line of text to appear differently than the adjacent words, multiline text is the best feature to use.

A paragraph of multiline text is a single entity. The text wraps around, and you can easily modify the length of a line after you place the text in the drawing. Within the multiline text entity, all text can be edited and behaves as if it were in a word processor. You can give a special word or letter of the text its own text style or color. Everything you learned about defining a new text style applies to multiline text, because both kinds of text use the same text styles. Just as polylines become lines when exploded, multiline text is reduced to single-line text when exploded.

Dimensions use multiline text, and any text that is imported into an AutoCAD drawing from a word-processing document or text editor becomes multiline

Use the Explode command to turn multiline text into single-line text, to unblock objects in a block reference, and to convert a polyline into regular lines. Click the Explode button on the Modify toolbar to start the command.

text in the drawing. In this section, you'll learn how to place a paragraph of multiline text in the cabin drawing and then modify it. In Chapter 12, you'll work with dimension text and text with leader lines, both of which use multiline text.

T I P   If you have the Express Tools installed, the Txt2mtxt command (Express ➤ Text ➤ Convert Text to Mtext) changes the selected Dtext objects into Mtext objects. When multiples lines of Dtext are selected, they are converted into a single Mtext object.

You'll start by adding a note in the lower-left corner of the Cabin8d drawing, using the Multiline Text command:

1. Click the Make Object's Layer Current button just to the right of the drop-down Layer Control list on the Layers toolbar. Then, click the FLOOR PLAN text to make the Text1 layer current. Zoom in to the blank area to the left of the title block in the lower-left corner of the cabin drawing.

2. Click the Osnap button on the status bar to temporarily disable any running osnaps. Then, click the Multiline Text button on the Draw toolbar. The Command window displays the name of the current text style and height and prompts you to specify a first corner.

3. Select a point near the left border line in line with the top of the title block. The prompt now says Specify opposite corner or [Height/Justify/Line spacing/Rotation/Style/Width/ Columns]:. These are all the options for the Multiline Text command.

4. If the current style is Label, go on to step 5. Otherwise, enter s⏎ for the Style option, and enter label⏎.

T I P   Entering ?⏎⏎ at the Enter style name or [?] <style name>: prompt displays a list of saved text styles in the AutoCAD Text Window.

5. Drag open a window that fills the space between the left border and the left side of the title block. This defines the line length for the multiline text (see Figure 8.34). Click to finish the window.

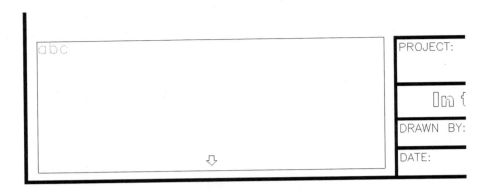

FIGURE 8.34: Making a multiline text window

6. The Text Formatting toolbar appears, and, below it, the Multiline Text Editor opens where you made the window in step 5. This is where you'll type the text. In the drop-down lists on the toolbar, you can see the current text style and its font and height.

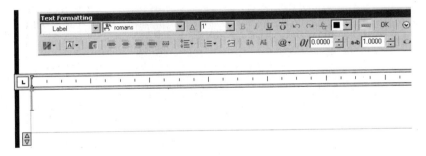

7. Enter the following text, using single spacing and pressing ↵ only at the end of the first line and at the end of each note. Lines that are longer than the window that you dragged out will wrap automatically.

GENERAL NOTES:

All work shall be in accordance with the 2000 Ed. Uniform Building Code and all local ordinances.

Roof can be built to be steeper for climates with heavy snowfall.

Solar panels available for installation on roof.

All windows to be double-paned.

When you're finished, click OK in the Text Formatting toolbar, or click a blank spot in the drawing area. The text appears in the drawing (see the top of Figure 8.35). The window you specified was used only to define the line length. Its height doesn't control how far down the text comes; that is determined by how much text you enter. Before you adjust the text to fit the area, you will have AutoCAD add numbering to the notes.

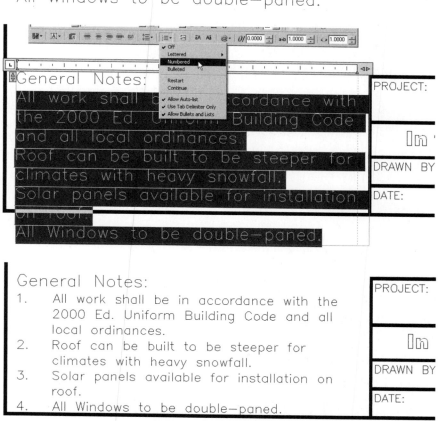

FIGURE 8.35: Mtext in the drawing (top), adding the note numbers (middle), and modified to be smaller (bottom)

You can expand the Multiline Text Editor typing area to the right and down to accommodate more lines of text and greater line length.

8. Double-click anywhere on the new text to display the Multiline Text Editor and the Text Formatting toolbar.

9. Move the cursor to the upper-left corner of the window containing the text and in front of the *A* in the first word (*All*) of the first note. Hold down the left mouse button, and drag to the right and down until all the remaining text is highlighted. Release the mouse button. Click and hold the Numbering button in the Text Formatting toolbar, and then choose Numbered from the menu that pops up (see the middle of Figure 8.35).

10. The note numbers appear. Select all the text including the "General Notes" line. The actual numbers don't appear to be selected, but they are. In the rightmost drop-down list on the Text Formatting toolbar, change Text Height from 1' to 9", and click OK. AutoCAD redraws the text smaller, and now it fits better within the space available (see the bottom of Figure 8.35).

11. Double-click the Mtext again. The Multiline Text Editor opens and displays the text you just clicked.

12. Highlight all the text again. In the middle drop-down list on the Text Formatting toolbar, select SansSerif as the current font. The selected text changes to the new font.

13. Click OK. The Mtext in the drawing becomes more compact, and there is room for more notes (see Figure 8.36).

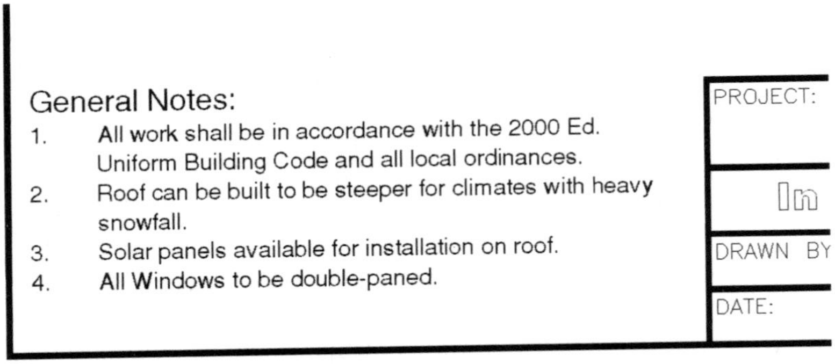

General Notes:
1. All work shall be in accordance with the 2000 Ed.
    Uniform Building Code and all local ordinances.
2. Roof can be built to be steeper for climates with heavy
    snowfall.
3. Solar panels available for installation on roof.
4. All Windows to be double-paned.

PROJECT:

DRAWN BY

DATE:

FIGURE 8.36: The results of a font modification

SansSerif is a TrueType font supported by Windows. When used in Auto-CAD drawings, it can be italic or bold. To see how to change individual words within the text, you'll underline and use bold for the "Uniform Building Code" text:

1. Double-click the Mtext again to open the Multiline Text Editor dialog box.

2. Use the same technique as earlier to highlight just the "Uniform Building Code" text. Then, click the Bold and Underline buttons on the Text Formatting toolbar. This underlines the selected text and adds bold.

3. Click OK. AutoCAD redraws the text with the changes (see Figure 8.37).

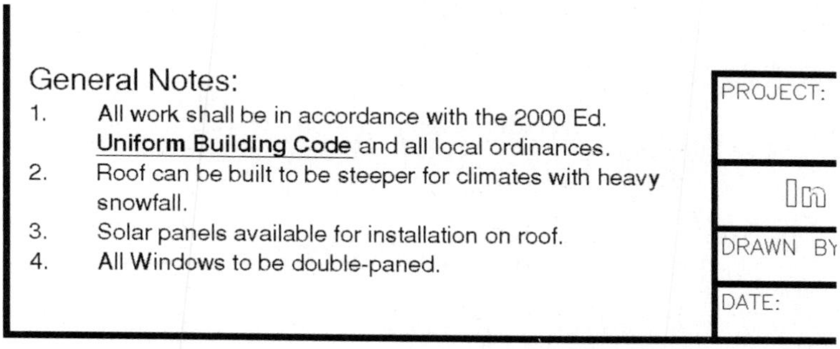

General Notes:
1.   All work shall be in accordance with the 2000 Ed.
      Uniform Building Code and all local ordinances.
2.   Roof can be built to be steeper for climates with heavy
      snowfall.
3.   Solar panels available for installation on roof.
4.   All Windows to be double-paned.

PROJECT:

DRAWN BY

DATE:

FIGURE 8.37: The Mtext with individual words modified

You can also italicize individual words and give them a different color or height from the rest of the Mtext by using the other tools on the Text Formatting toolbar. I encourage you to experiment with all these tools to become familiar with them.

You can easily alter the length of a line to make the Mtext fit more conveniently on the drawing. Let's say you've decided to put your company logo to the left of the title block. You need to squeeze the text into a narrower space. You have some extra room at the bottom, so you should be able to do it:

1. At the Command prompt, click the Mtext to select it. Four grips appear at the corners of the body of Mtext.

2. On the status bar, be sure Polar and Osnap are off. (For AutoCAD users only, Otrack should also be off.) Then, click the lower-right grip to activate it.

3. Slowly move the cursor down and to the left. Note when the bottom line of text gets close to the bottom line of the border (see the top of Figure 8.38).

4. When that happens, click the mouse, and then press Esc. The text is squeezed into a narrower space but still fits on the page (see the bottom of Figure 8.38).

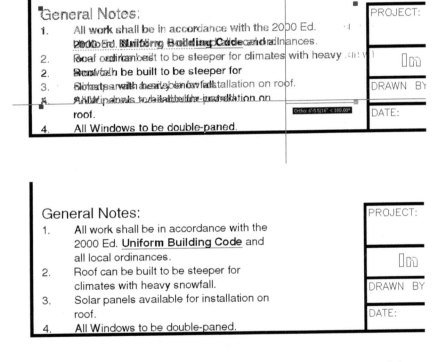

FIGURE 8.38: Modifying the Mtext line length with grips (top) and the results (bottom)

The ruler at the top of the Mtext Editor window has two sliding indicators for setting indentions. The top indicator is for the first line in the Mtext object and the first line after each ↵. The bottom indicator is for the rest of the text. You set that one in a little to make the note numbers stand out. Follow these steps:

1. Double-click the text again.

2. In the Mtext Editor window, highlight the four notes.

3. Use the mouse to slide the bottom indicator on the ruler one notch to the left (see Figure 8.39). Click OK. The notes are now a bit closer to the numbers.

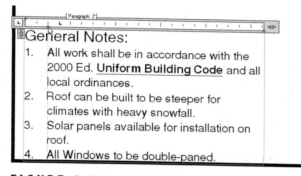

FIGURE 8.39: Adjusting the paragraph slider on the ruler and the results

Adding a Hyperlink

You have the ability to add *hyperlinks*, links to web pages or files, to the body of an Mtext object. When a hyperlink to a URL exists, anyone with the drawing open can hold down the Ctrl button and click the link to open the associated page in their web browser. Hyperlinks can also point to local or network files, causing the file's associated application to open when they are clicked. Here is the procedure for adding a hyperlink:

1. Double-click the Mtext object.

2. Highlight the text where you want the hyperlink to appear.

3. Right-click, and choose Insert Field from the context menu (see Figure 8.40).

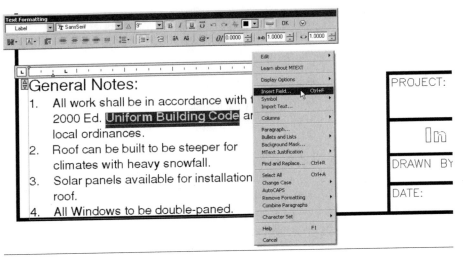

FIGURE 8.40: Inserting a field into an Mtext object

4. In the Field Names section of the Field dialog box that opens, select Hyperlink. In the Text to Display field, enter the text that you want to appear in the Mtext line (see Figure 8.41).

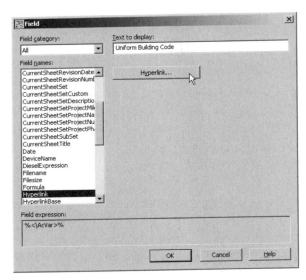

FIGURE 8.41: The Field dialog box

5. In the Edit Hyperlink dialog box, you can do any of the following:

> ▶ Enter the web page or filename and path in the Type the File or Web Page Name box.

> ▶ Click the File button under Browse For to select a file to which to link the text.

> ▶ Click the Web Page button under Browse For to navigate to the web page to which you want to link the text.

Perform one of these options, click the OK button to close this dialog box, and then click the OK button to close the Field dialog box (see Figure 8.42).

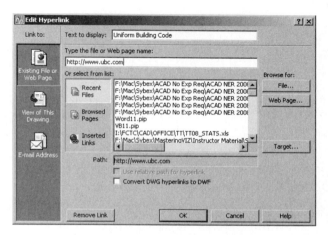

FIGURE 8.42: The Edit Hyperlink dialog box

6. Click OK to close the Text Formatting toolbar. The link appears as text with a gray background; the background doesn't appear in a printed drawing.

7. Hold the Ctrl key down, and hover the cursor over the gray background (see Figure 8.43). The cursor changes to the hyperlink cursor, and instructions to follow the link appear on a tooltip. With Ctrl still pressed, click the background. This minimizes AutoCAD, opens your browser, and navigates to the selected web page.

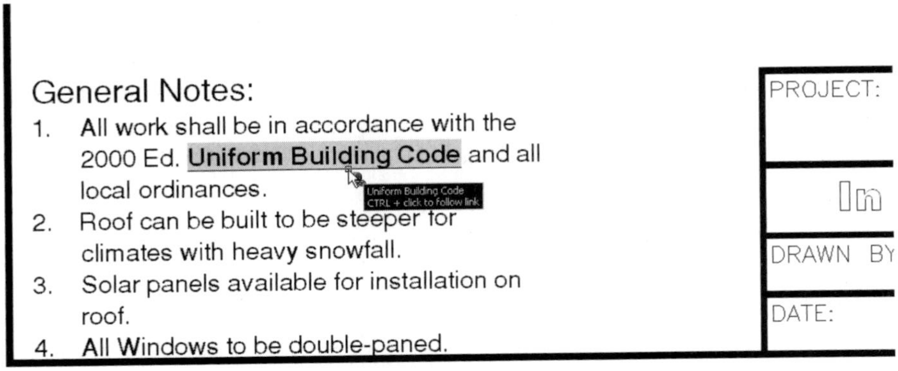

General Notes:

1. All work shall be in accordance with the
    2000 Ed. Uniform Building Code and all
    local ordinances.
    Uniform Building Code
    CTRL + click to follow link
2. Roof can be built to be steeper for
    climates with heavy snowfall.
3. Solar panels available for installation on
    roof.
4. All Windows to be double-paned.

PROJECT:

DRAWN BY

DATE:

FIGURE 8.43: Selecting a hyperlink embedded in Mtext

8. Perform a Zoom Extents, and then save this drawing as
Cabin8e.dwg.

Exploring Other Aspects of Multiline Text

Multiline text has several other features that I can only touch on in this book. I encourage you to experiment with any features that you might find useful to your work.

Using Justification Points

Mtext has justification points similar to those of single-line text, and they behave the same way. The default justification point for Mtext, however, is the upper-left corner of the body of text, and the available options are for nine points distributed around the perimeter of the body of text and at the center (see Figure 8.44).

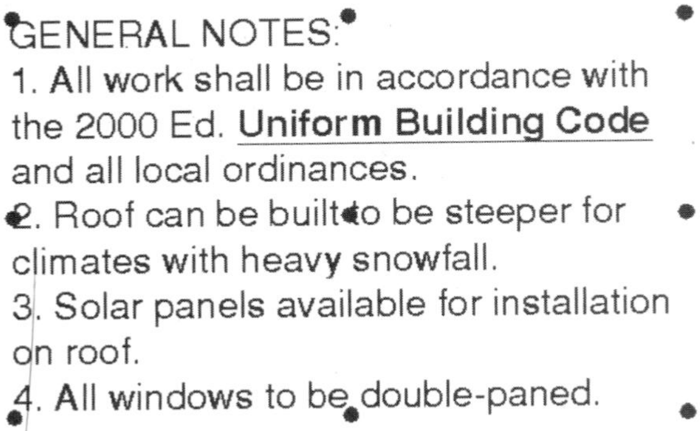

GENERAL NOTES:
1. All work shall be in accordance with
the 2000 Ed. **Uniform Building Code**
and all local ordinances.
2. Roof can be built to be steeper for
climates with heavy snowfall.
3. Solar panels available for installation
on roof.
4. All windows to be double-paned.

FIGURE 8.44: Justification points for Mtext

When you need to modify the justification of Mtext, open the Mtext Editor, place the cursor in the Editing window, and right-click to display a shortcut menu that contains several commands for modifying Mtext, including Justification. I'll describe the other items on this menu in the upcoming "Tools for Modifying Multiline Text" sidebar (see Figure 8.45).

FIGURE 8.45: Justifying the Mtext

Adding Special Characters

With Mtext, you can add special characters—the degree symbol, the diameter symbol, and so on—that aren't included in most font character packages. You'll have a chance to do this in Chapter 12.

If you want to experiment with the Mtext in the cabin drawing, make a copy of it, and place it outside the drawing. Double-click it, and see what you can learn about the Multiline Text Editor, the Text Formatting toolbar, and the Mtext shortcut menu. The "Tools for Modifying Multiline Text" sidebar summarizes the features of the latter two.

TOOLS FOR MODIFYING MULTILINE TEXT

Here's a brief summary of the various features of the Text Formatting toolbar and the Mtext shortcut menu:

The Text Formatting Toolbar

In the first row, the features of the Text Formatting toolbar are as follows:

Style drop-down list   Lists all existing text styles in the drawing file.

Font drop-down list   Sets the font for the selected text or sets the font for subsequently entered text.

Annotative   Toggles the Annotative property for text and dimensions. This property can cause the text to scale automatically as necessary. Chapter 12 covers annotation.

Height drop-down text box   Sets the height for selected text or sets the height for subsequently entered text.

Bold, Italic, Underline and Overline buttons   Changes selected text or sets up for subsequently entered text.

Undo button   Undoes the last editing action.

Redo button   Redoes the last undo.

Stack button   Converts selected text into either of two styles of stacked fractions: horizontal and slanted. Highlight the text, and then click the Stack button to change from one form to the other.

Text Color drop-down list   Changes the color of a selected portion of text or sets a color for subsequently entered text.

Ruler button   Toggles the ruler above the Mtext to be visible or invisible.

OK button   Executes what has been done in the Mtext Editor and returns you to your drawing.

Options button   Opens the Mtext shortcut menu.

In the second row, the features of the Text Formatting toolbar are as follows:

Columns button   Opens a menu for controlling the column options.

Mtext Justification button   Displays a menu with the nine Mtext justification choices.

Paragraph button   Opens the Paragraph dialog box where you can set tab and paragraph spacing, indents, and other paragraph-related parameters.

Left, Center, Right, Justify and Distribute buttons   Justifies the selected text accordingly.

Continues

TOOLS FOR MODIFYING MULTILINE TEXT *(Continued)*

Line Spacing drop-down list   Sets the line spacing for the selected text.

Numbering button   Opens a fly-out menu for controlling numbering and bullets.

Insert Field button   Begins the process of inserting a field in the Mtext in place of selected text or where the cursor rests in the text.

Uppercase and Lowercase buttons   Converts all selected text to uppercase or lowercase, respectively.

Symbol button   Opens a menu of symbols to insert into the Mtext where the cursor rests.

Oblique Angle Spinner buttons   Sets the selected text to an oblique angle off the vertical, from −85° to the left to 85° to the right.

Tracking Spinner buttons   Adjusts the spacing between selected letters from a minimum of 75 percent of the default spacing to a maximum of 4 times the default spacing.

Width Factor Spinner buttons   Adjusts the width of selected letters and the spacing between them from a minimum of 10 percent of the default width and spacing to a maximum of 10 times the defaults.

The Mtext Shortcut Menu

The features of the Mtext shortcut menu are as follows:

Edit   Opens a menu with several common editing commands including Undo, Redo, Cut and Paste.

Learn About MTEXT   Opens the New Features Workshop at the lesson regarding Mtext.

Display Options   Opens a menu where you can select whether certain features, such as the ruler or toolbar, appear.

Insert Field   Opens the Field dialog box, which you use to insert a field into the selected text. If you select text containing a field, this menu item changes to three menu items: Edit Field, Update Field, and Convert Field to Text.

Symbol   Imports symbols (such as diameter, degree, and so on) that aren't available in the font you're using.

Import Text   Imports a word-processing or text file into an AutoCAD drawing. The maximum size allowed is 32KB, so the smallest Microsoft Word document possible is too large; you can, however, use files in text-only or

Continues

TOOLS FOR MODIFYING MULTILINE TEXT *(Continued)*

RTF formats. Clicking the Import Text button opens the Select File dialog box that displays only files with the `.txt` and `.rtf` extensions. You can bring in text files with other extensions if you enter the full filename with its extension and if they aren't larger than 32KB. Text comes in as Mtext and uses the current text style, height setting, and layer. The imported file might not retain complex code fields for such elements as tabs, multiple margin indents, and so on.

Columns   Provides access to the column parameters.

Paragraph   Opens the Paragraph dialog box. It has settings for indenting the first line and subsequent paragraphs of Mtext (similar to what the sliders do on the ruler above the Mtext Editor window) and tab stop positions.

Bullets and Lists   Opens a fly-out menu that offers various options for using the listing features.

Background Mask   Opens the Background Mask dialog box in which you specify color for and activate a background mask to go behind the selected Mtext object.

Mtext Justification   Opens a fly-out menu that contains the nine justification points for Mtext, illustrated earlier, just before this sidebar. Use this to change the justification of selected text or to set up justification for new text.

Find and Replace   Opens the Replace dialog box, in which you search for a word or a series of words (text string) and replace them with text that you specify.

Select All   Highlights all the selected text.

Change Case   Changes the case of all highlighted text to uppercase or lowercase.

AutoCAPS   When checked, capitalizes all text.

Remove Formatting   Removes formatting, such as bold, underline, and so on, from highlighted text.

Combine Paragraphs   Joins highlighted individual paragraphs into one paragraph.

Character Set   Opens a menu of several languages. When applicable, the codes of the selected language are applied to selected text.

Help   Opens a help page on multiline text.

Cancel   Closes the menu.

If You Would Like More Practice…

Trades and other professions other than architecture and construction use text with AutoCAD and LT in the same way as demonstrated in this chapter.

For more practice using single-line text, follow these steps:

1. Close all drawings, and then open Cabin04c-addon.dwg.

2. Using the DesignCenter, bring in the Title and Label text styles from the Cabin8e drawing while it's closed.

3. Place labels on the features that were added:

   ▶ Use the Title text style to identify the addition as GARAGE.

   ▶ Use the Label text style to give the features the following names: WALKWAY, STORAGE, OFFICE, and CAR.

For more practice using Mtext, follow these steps:

1. Open Cabin8e.dwg, and zoom in to the blank space between the structural grid and the top border.

2. Create a new text style called Description that uses the Times New Roman font and a height of 12".

3. Start Mtext, and specify a rectangle for the text that covers the width of the sheet between the borders and occupies the space above the structural grid.

4. Enter the following text exactly as shown here, spelling errors and all:

   This is a design for a small vaction cabin. It contains approximately 380 square feet of living space and includes one bedrooms and one bath. It can be adopted to provide shelter in all climates and can be modified to allow constuction that uses local building materials. Please sund all inquiries to the manufacturer.

5. Double-click the new text, and make these changes:

   a. Correct all spelling errors using the Spell command.

   b. Change *square feet* to sq. ft.

   c. Bold the following: *one bedroom*, *one bath*, *all climates*, and *local building materials*.

   d. Italicize the last sentence.

   e. See whether you can modify the shape of the defining rectangle so that the text fits in the space in the upper-left corner.

Are You Experienced?

Now you can...

- ☑ set up text styles
- ☑ place single-line text in a drawing for titles and room labels
- ☑ create a grid for a drawing
- ☑ modify single-line text
- ☑ construct a title block and place text in it
- ☑ use AutoCAD template files
- ☑ place Mtext in a drawing
- ☑ modify Mtext in several ways
- ☑ add a hyperlink to an Mtext object

CHAPTER 9

Using Dynamic Blocks and Tables

▶ Adding block attributes

▶ Creating dynamic blocks

▶ Creating tables

I n Chapter 7 you explored creating and using blocks to combine separate objects into a single, complex object to aid in selecting objects and editing properties. Chapter 8 covered the addition of text into drawings. In this chapter, you will expand your knowledge of blocks and use text inside tables to display information regarding specific features of the drawing.

The blocks you've worked with have been static collections of objects that you have inserted throughout your drawing as doors or windows. Each instance of the same block was visually identical to the others, and you were able to scale the window blocks, along one axis, without distortion to fit the walls. Blocks can also contain textual information, called *attributes*, specific to an individual block insertion. Blocks do not have to remain static and unchanging. In this chapter, you will learn how to define your blocks so that they can change, as required, without exploding the blocks and modifying the component objects.

After exploring blocks further, you'll learn how to create a table to act as a door schedule, displaying the door manufacturer, unit price, and total cost. A *schedule* is a chart in a drawing that contains logically organized information about a particular component of a project, such as a steel base plate, valve, bolt or screw, door, window, or room finish. Each of these has its own schedule. Information in a door schedule, for example, might include size, material, finish, location, and type of jamb.

Using Attributes for a Grid

The grid lines for a building are usually located at the center lines of structural components, such as walls or columns. You can then identify columns in buildings by letter and number, specifying the intersection of the two grid lines. In the cabin drawing, you used grid lines to indicate the outside edges of exterior walls and the center lines of interior walls. Grids generally have a circle or a hexagon with a number or letter in it at the end of each grid line, with the numbers running in one direction (horizontally or vertically) and letters in the other.

A simple but handy use of attributes is to make the letter or number in the circle an attribute and then make a block out of the attribute and circle. By redoing the grid symbols in the cabin drawing, you'll learn how to set up attributes and create a new block that can be used in any other drawing:

1. Open Cabin8e.dwg. The drawing consists of the floor plan with a structural grid. Freeze the Tblk1 layer, and make sure the Grid layer is current.

2. Zoom in to the floor plan, keeping the grid visible. In this case, the letters run horizontally across the top, and the numbers run vertically along the side.

3. Erase all the circles, letters, and numbers in the grid except those for *A* and *1*. Leave the grid lines intact (see Figure 9.1).

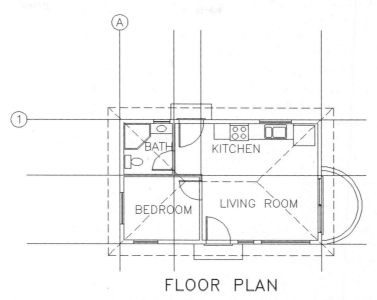

FLOOR PLAN

FIGURE 9.1: The floor plan of **Cabin8e** with all but two grid symbols erased

4. Select the letter *A*, right-click, and then choose Properties from the context menu. The Properties palette displays information about the text (see Figure 9.2). You need to know the text style and height: Label and 1'-0".

5. Close or minimize the Properties palette, and then erase *A* and *1*, but not the circles.

6. Start the Scale command. Select the circle on the top, and press ↵.

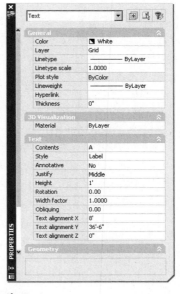

FIGURE 9.2: The Properties palette for the text

7. Use the Endpoint osnap, and pick the endpoint of the grid line where it meets the circle. Enter **1.25**↵. This enlarges the circle.

8. Repeat steps 6 and 7 for the circle on the left side.

9. Choose Draw ➤ Block ➤ Define Attributes to open the Attribute Definition dialog box (see Figure 9.3). In the Attribute area are three text boxes: Tag, Prompt, and Default. The cursor is flashing in the Tag text box. Think of the letter in the grid circle. It's a grid letter, which is a tag that provides the visual textual information.

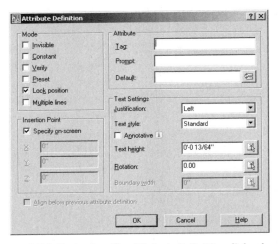

FIGURE 9.3: The Attribute Definition dialog box

10. Enter **grid_letter**. Don't press ↵.

11. Press the Tab key to move to the Prompt text box. Here you enter a prompt, which will ask the future user who will be setting up a grid, for the text to input for the tag.

12. Enter **Enter grid letter**. Press Tab to move to the Default text box. Here you enter a default or sample value that is used if the future user presses ↵ instead of entering a new value. You want it capitalized in this case, so enter A. This sets up the attribute so that the drafter setting up the grid will be prompted to enter the grid letter and will be given a default of *A*. The capital *A* lets the user know that the letter should be uppercase.

13. The lower portion of the dialog box is where you set up parameters for the attribute text: location in the drawing, justification, text style, height, and rotation. Click the Justification drop-down list, and select Middle Center.

14. Choose Label in the Text Style list box. Because the Label text style's height is set to a value other than 0'0", the Text Height text box in the Attribute Definition dialog box is grayed out. Figure 9.4 shows what you should see.

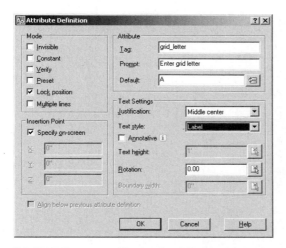

FIGURE 9.4: The Attribute Definition dialog box showing the appropriate values

15. Click OK. Doing so returns you to the drawing to pick an insertion point. Back in the drawing, use the Center osnap, and click the circle at the top of the grid. GRID_LETTER is centered over the circle (see Figure 9.5), and the Attdef command ends.

The text over the circle is called the *attribute definition*. Its function in Auto-CAD is similar to that of a block definition. When you made the win-1 block for the windows, the definition was a 12"-long window with an insertion point. When the win-1 block is inserted, you can use the original block definition to make windows of various sizes. The same is true for the attribute definition. When it becomes part of a block that's inserted, the attribute can be any letter you want. You'll see that happen in a minute.

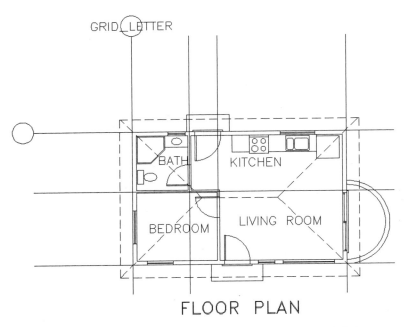

FIGURE 9.5: The first attribute definition placed in the grid circle

First, make a similar attribute definition for the numbered grid symbol:

1. Enter att↵ to start the Attribute Definition command. The Attribute Definition dialog box opens again.

2. Repeat steps 10–15 in the preceding exercise, using the following guidelines:

   a. Enter **grid_number** in the Tag text box.

   b. Enter **Enter grid number** in the Prompt text box.

   c. Enter 1 in the Default text box.

   d. Select Middle Center from the Justification drop-down list.

   e. Click OK, use the Center osnap, and click the grid circle on the left.

The second attribute definition is centered over the circle on the left side (see Figure 9.6).

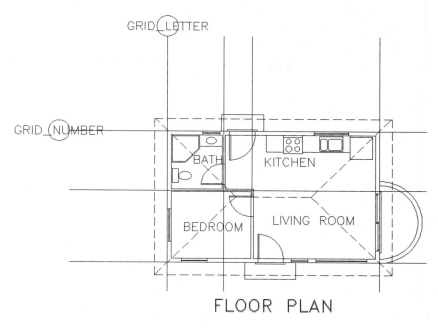

F I G U R E 9 . 6 :   The second attribute definition is placed.

You now have two attribute definitions and are ready to make each of them part of a block that includes the circle over which they're currently centered.

Defining Blocks with Attributes

You have to define two blocks for the grid symbols and their attributes. The insertion point for the block used for the top of the grid should be at the lowest point of the circle. The insertion point for the block used for the left side should be at the point on the circle farthest to the right. Follow these steps:

1. Click the Make Block button on the Draw toolbar to start the Block command, and open the Block Definition dialog box.

2. In the Name drop-down list, enter **grid-v** (for vertical) in the blank space, and then click the Pick Point button in the Base Point area.

3. In the drawing, use the Endpoint osnap, and select the grid line that ends at the circle on top.

4. In the Block Definition dialog box that reopens, click the Select Objects button in the Objects area.

5. In the drawing, select the circle and attribute definition on the top. Press ↵.

6. In the Block Definition dialog box, be sure the Delete button is selected in the Objects area, and click OK. The block is defined and includes the attribute definition. In the drawing, the top circle and attribute definition have been deleted.

7. Start the Block command again. Repeat steps 2–6 to define a second block for the circle and attribute definition on the left side. Use the following guidelines:

   a. Enter **grid-h** in the Name drop-down list.

   b. Click Pick Point. Use the Endpoint osnap, and pick the horizontal grid line that ends at the rightmost point of the grid circle on the left of the floor plan.

   c. When selecting objects, select the circle on the left and its attribute definition.

   When you complete the command, you have a second block definition that includes an attribute definition and no grid circles in the drawing.

Inserting Blocks with Attributes

Let's insert these blocks (which are now grid symbols) at the endpoints of the grid lines. As you insert them, you'll assign them the appropriate letter or number:

1. Be sure the Endpoint osnap is set to be running, and then enter **attdia**↵.

2. If the value in the angle brackets is set to 0, press ↵. Otherwise, enter 0↵.

3. Choose Insert ➢ Block, or enter i↵. In the Insert dialog box, open the Name drop-down list, and select grid-v.

4. Be sure the Specify On-Screen box is checked for Insertion Point but not for Scale and Rotation. Click OK.

5. Click the leftmost vertical grid line in the drawing. Now look at the bottom line in the Command window.

The `attdia` variable defines whether the Insert command opens a dialog box or prompts the user, at the Command prompt, for attribute information. When it is set to 0, no dialog box is used.

```
Enter attribute values
Enter grid letter <A>:
```

This is the text you entered in the Attribute Definition dialog box for the prompt. *A* is the text you entered as the default value. To accept the default value for this grid line, press ↲.

6. This inserts the grid symbol at the endpoint of the leftmost vertical grid line (see Figure 9.7).

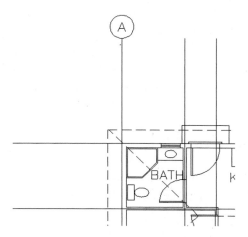

F I G U R E   9 . 7 :   The first grid symbol block is inserted.

7. Press ↲ to restart the Insert command. Click OK to accept grid-v as the current block to be inserted.

8. Click the grid line to the right of the one you just selected.

9. At the Enter grid letter <A>: prompt, enter B↲. The second grid symbol is inserted on a grid line, and the letter *B* is located in the circle. Be sure to use a capital *B* here; the tag will not prevent you from using a lowercase letter, but drawing standards require consistency.

10. Repeat steps 7–9 to insert the other two grid symbols across the top of the floor plan.

11. Continue repeating steps 7–9, but select the grid-h block for the three grid symbols that run down the left side of the floor plan. The results should look like Figure 9.8.

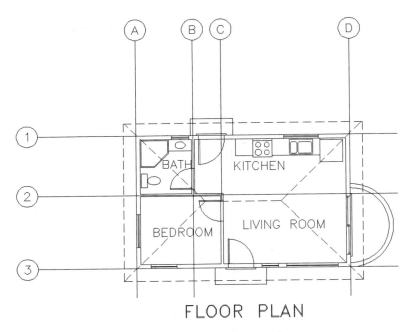

FIGURE 9.8: The grid with all symbols inserted

Editing Attribute Text

To illustrate how you can edit attribute text, let's assume you decide to change the C grid symbol to B1. You must then change the D symbol to C. Here are the steps:

1. Double-click the C grid symbol. Doing so opens the Enhanced Attribute Editor dialog box. You can change several items here, but you want to change only the value.

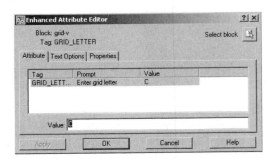

2. Be sure the Attribute tab is selected. Highlight C in the Value text box, enter **B1**, and then click the Apply button. B1 replaces C in the larger window where the tag, prompt, and value appear together. Click OK to close the dialog box.

N O T E Because you set the justification point for the attribute text to Middle Center and located the text at the center of the grid circle, the B1 text is centered in the circle just like the single letters.

3. Double-click the D grid symbol.

4. In the Enhanced Attribute Editor dialog box, repeat step 2 to change D to C. The attributes are updated (see Figure 9.9).

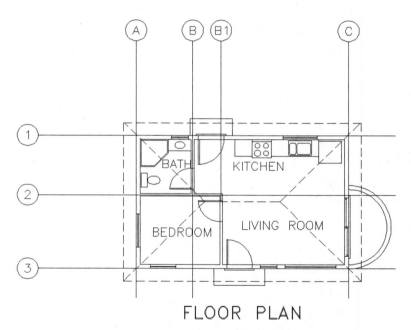

FLOOR PLAN

FIGURE 9.9: The grid symbols after being updated

The exercises have illustrated the basic procedure for defining, inserting, and changing attributes. You can apply these same procedures to the process of setting up a title block in which attributes are used for text that changes from one sheet to the next. You can now move to a more complex application of the attribute feature to see its full power.

Setting Up Multiple Attributes in a Block

The cabin has three rooms and a balcony, with the kitchen and living room sharing the same space. Each room has a different area and floor covering. You can store this information, along with the room name, in the drawing as attributes. You'll set up a block that consists of three attributes (name, area, and covering). You'll then insert the block back into the floor plan. If you remember, the text style for the room labels is LABEL. You'll use that for the attributes.

You have to erase the room labels for now, but it will be handy to mark their justification points. That way, you can insert the attribute exactly where the label text is now. Follow these steps:

1. With the Grid layer current, choose Format ➤ Point Style to open the Point Style dialog box (see Figure 9.10).

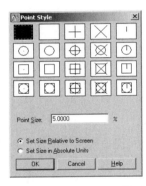

FIGURE 9.10: The Point Style dialog box

A point locates a single location in space, defined by an X, Y, and Z position, with no volume. The Point Style dialog box determines how the marker at the point location appears.

2. Click the fourth point style example in the second row (the one with a circle and an *x*). Then, click OK to close the dialog box.

3. Set the Insertion osnap to be running, and then click the Point button on the Draw toolbar. Place the cursor on the LIVING ROOM text. When the Insertion symbol appears at the lower-left corner, click. Don't end the command yet.

4. Repeat step 3 for the BEDROOM and BATH labels. You don't need an insertion point marker for the KITCHEN label because it will remain as is and have no attributes. The balcony doesn't have text in this drawing, so you can place the attribute anywhere you want. Press Esc to end the Point command.

5. Erase the LIVING ROOM, BEDROOM, and BATH labels. The drawing should look like Figure 9.11.

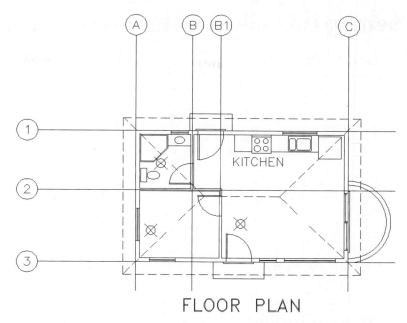

FLOOR PLAN

FIGURE 9.11: The floor plan with markers for insertion points and three room labels erased

6. Make layer 0 current. Choose Draw ➤ Block ➤ Define Attributes to start the Attdef command and open the Attribute Definition dialog box.

7. For Tag, enter **rm_name**. For Prompt, enter **Room name**. For Default, enter **LIVING ROOM**. (This default value will remind the user to use all uppercase letters.)

8. In the bottom half of the dialog box, the settings for the text stay the same; click OK.

9. In the drawing, use the Endpoint osnap, and click the right end of the grid line that has 1 in the circle. This places the first attribute definition in the drawing (see Figure 9.12). Because you're going to make a block out of it and reinsert it into the rooms, you don't have to place the attribute definition where the room labels are; any place on the edge of the drawing is fine.

10. Press ↵ to restart the Attdef command. For this attribute, enter **rm_area** for Tag. For Prompt, enter **Area of room**, and for Default, enter **10.00 Sq. Ft.** This will show the user the proper format for the area.

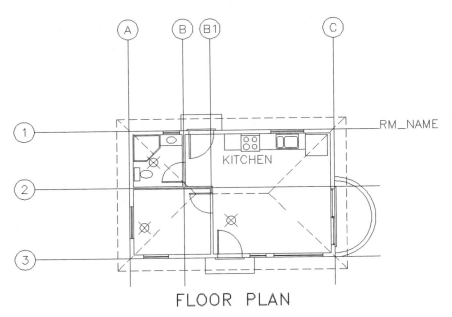

FIGURE 9.12: The room name attribute definition placed in the drawing

11. In the Mode area, click to activate Invisible. The Invisible mode makes the attribute values invisible in the drawing, but they're still stored there.

12. In the lower-left corner of the dialog box, click the Align Below Previous Attribute Definition check box. All the text options fade out (see Figure 9.13). The style is the same as that of the first attribute, and this attribute definition will appear right below the first one.

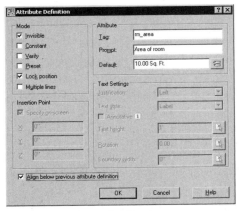

FIGURE 9.13: Setting the proper values in the Attribute Definition dialog box

13. Click OK. The second attribute definition appears in the drawing below the first one.

14. Repeat steps 10–13 to define the third attribute. For Tag, enter **rm_floor**. For Prompt, enter **Floor Material**. For Default, enter **Wood Parquet**. Be sure the Invisible mode is still checked, and select the Align Below Previous Attribute Definition check box, if one isn't already there. Click OK. All three attribute definitions are now in the drawing (see Figure 9.14).

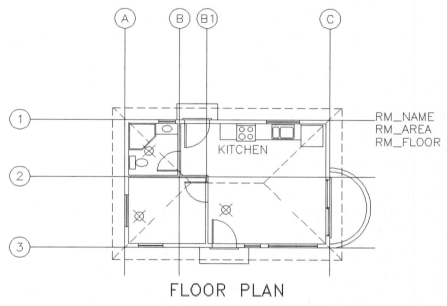

FIGURE 9.14: The floor plan with all three attribute definitions

Now you'll make a block out of the three attributes.

Defining a Block with Multiple Attributes

A block with attributes usually includes lines or other geometrical objects along with the attribute definitions, but it doesn't have to do so. In this case, the three attribute definitions are the sole content of the block, and the block's insertion point is the justification point for the first attribute: the room label text. Follow these steps to define the block:

1. Start the Block command.

2. In the Block Definition dialog box, enter **room_info** for the name.

3. Click the Pick Point button. In the drawing, use the Insertion osnap, and choose the first attribute definition. Doing so aligns the justification point of this attribute with the insertion point of the block.

4. Back in the Block Definition dialog box, click the Select Objects button. In the drawing, pick each attribute definition individually in the order you created them. Selecting them in this order causes them to be listed in the Enter Attributes dialog box in the same order. Press ↵ after selecting them. Then, after being sure Delete is still selected, click OK in the dialog box. The room_info block is defined, and the attribute definitions are deleted from the drawing.

5. Save your drawing as Cabin09a.dwg.

You're almost ready to insert the room_info block in each of the three rooms and near the balcony. But first you need to calculate the area of each room.

Calculating Areas

You can calculate areas in a drawing by using the Hatch command in conjunction with the Properties palette or by using the Area command. Because area calculations are made over and over again in design and construction, the Area command is an important tool. You can calculate an overall area and then subtract subareas from it, or you can add subareas together to make a total. Chapter 11 covers hatches.

For this exercise, you'll use the Area command to calculate the areas of the four floor spaces in the floor plan. Afterward, I'll explain how to find areas using the Hatch command. You need to write down the areas after you make the calculations. Follow these steps:

1. Make a new layer named Area, and make it the current layer.

2. Freeze all the other layers except Balcony and Walls. Your drawing should look like Figure 9.15.

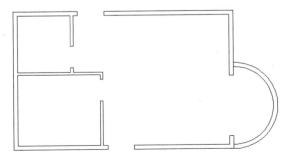

FIGURE 9.15: The floor plan with all layers turned off except Area, Balcony, and Walls

3. Make sure that the Endpoint osnap is running.

4. Draw a closed polyline around the inside of each room.

5. Draw a polyline from the upper-left corner of the balcony to the bottom-left corner (see the left of Figure 9.16).

6. Enter a↵ to activate the Arc feature of the polylines. Until instructed otherwise, the Polyline command will continue to create curved segments.

7. Activate the Midpoint osnap, and then click the inner balcony wall. This creates an arc segment, as shown in the middle of Figure 9.16.

8. Enter cl↵ to close the polylines with an arc segment (see the right of Figure 9.16). You've drawn enough segments to form the polyline around the balcony. Next you'll fit the polyline to the inner walls.

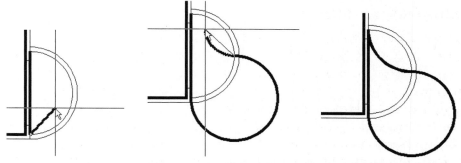

FIGURE 9.16: Draw the first segment of the polyline (left), place the first arc segment (middle), and then close the polyline (right).

9. Select the last polyline. Grips appear at the endpoints of each segment and at the midpoint of the arc segments.

10. Select one of the midpoint grips. Activate the Nearest osnap, and then click anywhere on the inner balcony arc, between the current segment's endpoints.

11. Repeat step 10 with the remaining arc segment.

Now that the perimeter lines are drawn, you need to actually calculate the area bound by them.

1. Right-click any toolbar button and choose ACAD ➤ Inquiry from the shortcut menu to open the Inquiry toolbar. Move it to a blank portion of the drawing area.

2. Click the Area button on the Inquiry toolbar. Be careful—it looks like the Region/Mass Properties button. At the `Specify first corner point or [Object /Add /Subtract]:` prompt, enter o↵ to switch to Object mode, and then select the bathroom polyline.

3. Press the F2 key to open the AutoCAD Text Window, which displays the results of your calculation: `Area = 5616.00 square in. (39.0000 square ft.), Perimeter = 25'-0"`.

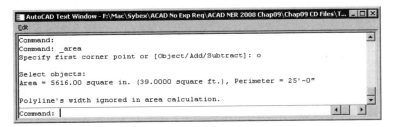

4. Write down the area in square feet. Press ↵ to restart the Area command, enter o↵, and then click the bedroom polyline. The area should be 76.2222 square feet. Write down this number. (You can shorten it to two decimal places.)

5. Repeat this process for the living room, in which you'll have to pick six points. The area should be 236.6667 square feet. Write down 236.67.

6. Repeat this process one last time for the balcony. The area should be 31.8086 square feet. Write down 31.81.

7. Make the Text1 layer current, turn on all the layers except Tblk1, and then freeze the Area layer.

8. Click the X in the corner of the Inquiry toolbar to close it.

N O T E   The Add and Subtract options in the Area command prompt allow you to add together areas you have calculated and to subtract areas from each other. If you're going to add or subtract areas, enter a↵ after you start the Area command. Then, after each calculation, you'll be given the Add and Subtract options. If you don't enter a at the beginning, you can make only one calculation at a time.

To use the Properties palette to calculate an area, select the polyline to be measured, open the Properties palette, and then scroll down to the Area readout in the Geometry rollout. The area appears in square inches and square feet. This also works for hatch patterns, which I'll cover in Chapter 11.

Inserting the Room_Info Block

You have four areas calculated and recorded and are ready to insert the room_info block. When you inserted the grid symbols as blocks with attributes earlier in this chapter, the prompts for the attribute text appeared in the Command window. With multiple attributes in a block, it's more convenient to display all the prompts in a dialog box. Let's change the setting that makes the dialog box replace the Command prompts:

1. Enter attdia↵. At the prompt, enter 1↵. This allows the dialog box containing the prompts to open during the insertion process.

2. Set the Node osnap to be the only one running, and turn on running osnaps. Choose Insert ➢ Block. In the Insert dialog box, select room_info from the Name drop-down list. Click OK. Select the point that marks the justification point for the LIVING ROOM label text to open the Edit Attributes dialog box.

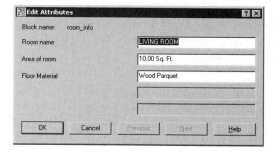

3. The only change you need to make is the value for Area Of Room. The defaults are correct for the other two items.

4. Press the Tab key to highlight the Area Of Room box, and enter 236.67 Sq. Ft. Click OK.

5. This inserts the room_info block into the drawing in the living room. The room label is the only visible attribute (see Figure 9.17). You set the other two to be invisible.

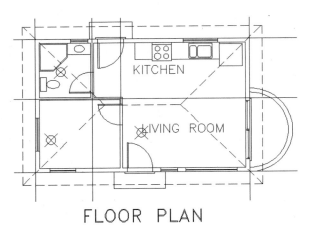

FIGURE 9.17: The first room_info block is inserted.

6. Press ↵ to restart the Insert command. In the Insert dialog box, the room_info block should still be in the Name drop-down list. Click OK.

7. In the drawing, click the point that marks the justification point of the BEDROOM text label. The same three prompts with the same default values appear in the Edit Attributes dialog box.

8. LIVING ROOM is highlighted. Enter **BEDROOM**↵. The highlight bar drops down to the next prompt.

9. For the area, enter **76.22 Sq. Ft.**↵.

10. For the floor material, change Wood Parquet to Linoleum Tile, and then click OK. This inserts the second block in the bedroom. Again, only the room label text is visible.

11. Repeat steps 6–10 for the bathroom, this time replacing the existing text with **BATH**, **39.00 Sq. Ft.**, and **Ceramic Tile**.

12. Repeat steps 6–10 for the balcony. At the Specify insertion point prompt, place the BALCONY label outside the balcony, a little above the midpoint of the arcs. Enter **BALCONY**, **31.81 Sq. Ft.**, and **Wood Plank** for the dialog box values.

13. Erase the points you used to locate the insertion points. Your drawing looks like Figure 9.18.

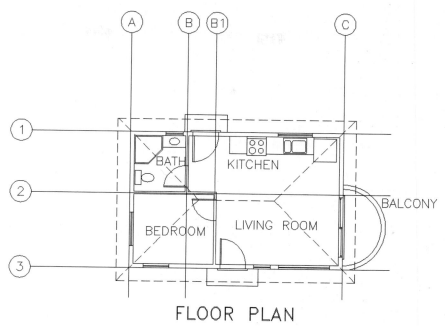

FIGURE 9.18: All room_info blocks inserted

Controlling the Visibility of Attributes

The floor plan looks the same as it did at the beginning of this exercise, except for the addition of the BALCONY label. But it includes more than meets the eye. What was regular text is now an attribute, and your drawing is "smarter" than it was before. The next few steps illustrate the display controls for the visible and invisible attributes:

1. Choose View ➤ Display ➤ Attribute Display ➤ On. All the attributes, including those designated as invisible, appear with the room labels (see Figure 9.19).

2. Press ↵ to restart the Attdisp command, and then enter off↵. All attributes disappear, including the room labels and the letters and numbers in the grid symbols.

3. Press ↵. Enter n↵ to change the setting back to Normal. Along with the room labels, the grid numbers and letters reappear.

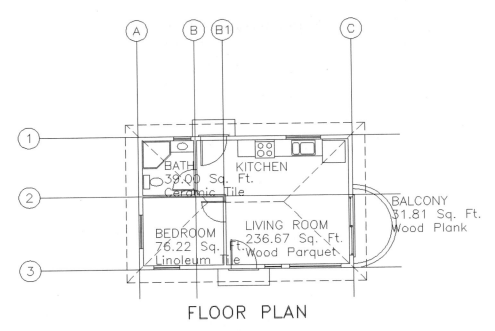

FIGURE 9.19: The floor plan with all attributes displayed

On and Off settings make all attributes visible or invisible, regardless of how you set the Visible/Invisible mode in the attribute definition. The Normal setting allows an attribute to be displayed only if the Visible/Invisible mode was set to Visible in the definition.

Editing Attributes

Once you define attributes and insert them as blocks, you can easily edit any value using the same method you used at the beginning of this chapter to modify a grid number:

1. Choose Modify ➤ Object ➤ Attribute ➤ Single to start the Eattedit command. Select the LIVING ROOM label. The Enhanced Attribute Editor dialog box opens, displaying both the visible and invisible attributes' values for the living room, along with their tags and prompts. You can now change any of the values. When you highlight an attribute, its value appears in the Value text box, where you can edit it.

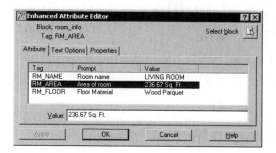

2. You won't make any changes now. Click Cancel to close the dialog box and return to the drawing.

3. Save this drawing in your training folder as Cabin09b.dwg.

EDITING TOOLS FOR ATTRIBUTES

The attribute-editing tools seem complicated because their names are similar, but they are easily distinguishable once you get used to them and know how to use them. Here are descriptions of five attribute-editing tools:

The Edit Attributes Dialog Box

This is the same dialog box displayed in the process of inserting a block that has attributes, if the **attdia** setting is set to 1. It is used to change attribute values only. Enter **attedit↵** to use it to edit values of attributes already in your drawing. You will be prompted to select a block reference in your drawing. When you do that, the Edit Attributes dialog box appears.

The Enhanced Attribute Editor Dialog Box

With this dialog box, you can edit values and the properties of the attribute text—such as color, layer, text style, and so on. When you enter **eattedit↵**—or click Modify ➢ Attribute ➢ Single—and then pick a block that has attributes, the dialog box opens. Double-clicking the block does the same thing.

Using the Properties Palette to Edit Attribute Definitions

Use the Properties palette to edit most properties of attribute definitions before they become part of a block. Select the attribute definition, and then click the Properties button on the Standard toolbar.

Continues

EDITING TOOLS FOR ATTRIBUTES *(Continued)*

The Block Attribute Manager

Click Modify ➤ Object ➤ Attribute ➤ Block Attribute Manager to open the Block Attribute Manager dialog box. There, you can select a block and edit the various parts of each attribute definition that the block contains, such as the tag, prompt, and value.

The –Attedit Command

You can also edit more than one attribute at a time by choosing Modify ➤ Object ➤ Attribute ➤ Global or by typing **atte**↵. The prompt reads Edit attributes one at a time? [Yes/No] <Y>. If you accept the default of Yes, you're taken through a series of options for selecting attributes to edit. Select the attributes to edit, and then press ↵ to end the selection process. A large *x* appears at the insertion point of one of the selected attributes. At this point, you get the following prompt: Enter an option [Value/Position/Height/Angle/Style/Layer/Color/ Next] <N>:, allowing you to modify any of the characteristics listed in the prompt for the attribute with the *x*. Press ↵ to move to the next selected attribute.

If you respond to the first prompt with No, you're taken through a similar set of selection options. You're then asked to enter a current value to be changed and to enter the new value after the change. You can change the values of attributes globally by using the –Attedit command this way.

Exploring Other Uses for Attributes

As well as being used for grid symbols and room, window, and door schedules, attributes are widely used in standardized title blocks. One of the most frequent uses of attributes is in facilities management and interior design. You can specify every piece of office furniture in a building with attributes. You can then extract the data and send it to a furniture specifier that inputs the data into its databases and completes the order. The big office furniture manufacturers sell their own proprietary software that works with AutoCAD and automatically sets up attributes when you insert their blocks of the furniture, which they have predrawn and included in the software package.

Attributes are also being used more and more in maps drawn in AutoCAD, which are then imported into Geographical Information System (GIS) software (a powerful analysis and presentation tool). When map symbols, such as building numbers, are blocks containing an attribute, they're transformed in the GIS program in such a way that you can set up links between the map features (buildings) and database tables that contain information about the map features. In this way, you can perform analyses on the database tables, and the results automatically appear graphically on the map. (For example, you could quickly locate all buildings that have a total usable area greater than a specified square footage.)

In the next section, you'll go through an exercise that demonstrates how you can create dynamic blocks that vary their appearance based on user input.

Creating a Dynamic Block

In Chapter 7, you created blocks for the windows and doors. However, because of its schematic appearance, you were able to scale the window block, but you were not able to do the same with the door block. Performing a scale on the door and swing would have allowed one door block to fit into any size opening, but it would have also scaled the thickness of the door differently for each door width. Dynamic blocks are standard blocks with additional functionality to allow certain features to change without affecting all objects in the block. The door blocks are an excellent opportunity to explore the abilities of AutoCAD's dynamic blocks.

The basic procedure for setting up a dynamic block is as follows:

1. Create the block using the Make Block command.

2. Right-click the block, and choose Block Editor.

3. Click a parameter, and follow the Command window prompts to set up the parameter.

4. Click the Actions tab, and click an action to associate with a parameter; then, follow the Command window prompts to set up the action.

5. Use the Properties palette to rename and specify settings for the parameter and any actions associated with it.

6. Save your work back to the block definition.

7. Close the Block Editor.

You'll work through this process by converting the door3_0 block from Cabin09B into a dynamic block in a new drawing:

1. With Cabin09B as the current drawing, pan up to the floor plan, choose Edit ➤ Copy with Base Point, use the Insertion osnap to select the insertion point of the front door block as the base point,

select the front door block, and press ↵. This copies the door block to the Windows Clipboard.

2. Start a new drawing, and change the linear units to Architectural. Then, choose Edit ➤ Paste, and when prompted to specify the base point, enter 0,0↵.

3. Zoom to extents, and then zoom to .5x. Turn off the UCS icon.

4. Click the door block, right-click, and choose Block Editor from the shortcut menu. The drawing area turns tan, and the Block Authoring palettes open to indicate that you are in the Block Editor.

5. If a dialog box opens asking whether you would like to see how dynamic blocks are created, click the No button. If you want to prevent this dialog box from opening again, check the Do Not Display This Alert Again box.

6. Pan the view, and adjust the Block Authoring palettes so that your screen looks similar to Figure 9.20.

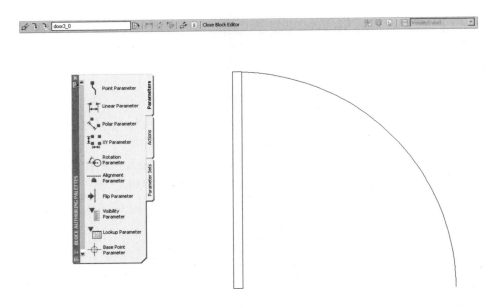

FIGURE 9.20: The door block in the Block Editor

You want to be able to use this door block for openings of the following widths: 2'-0", 2'-6", 3'-0", and 3'-6".

Setting Up Parameters and Actions

You'll use the Linear parameter to set up the 6" increments for the door width. Then, you'll associate a Stretch action with that parameter to allow the door width to change, and you'll associate a Scale action to allow the door swing to change. Follow these steps:

1. Be sure Parameters is the active palette in the Block Authoring palettes, and then click the Linear Parameter icon (Figure 9.21).

2. Make sure the Endpoint osnap is running, click the lower-left corner of the door, and then click the lower endpoint of the door swing.

3. Move the cursor down to position the dimension symbol a little below the door block, and then click to place it (see Figure 9.22).

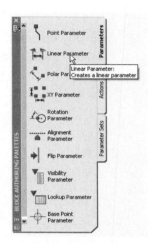

FIGURE 9.21: The Linear Parameter in the Block Authoring palettes

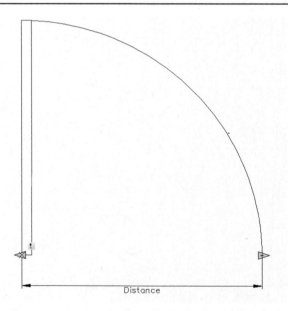

FIGURE 9.22: The Linear parameter is placed.

Note the small exclamation symbol on a square yellow background. This reminds you that no action has been associated with this parameter. You'll set up the Stretch action first:

1. Click the Actions tab on the Block Authoring palettes, and then click the Stretch Action icon.

2. Click the Distance parameter, and then click the right-pointing arrow.

3. Form a crossing window, clicking each of the opposing corners, around the upper half of the door, as shown in Figure 9.23.

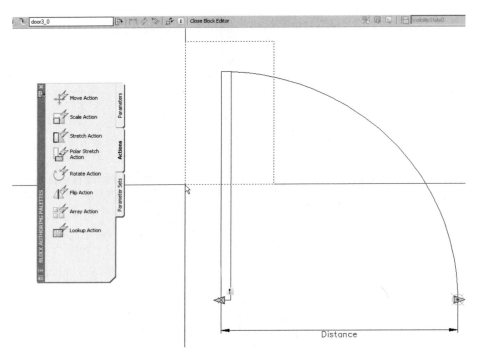

FIGURE 9.23: The crossing window for the Stretch action

4. Select the door, and press ↵.

5. Turn off Polar and Osnap, and then at the `Specify action loca-tion or [Multiplier/Offset]:` prompt, click to place the lightning-bolt action symbol just above the door.

6. Click the Scale Action icon on the Actions palette, select the Distance parameter, select the arc, and then press ↵.

7. At the `Specify action location or [Base type]:` prompt, place the Scale lightning-bolt symbol just outside the arc (see Figure 9.24).

8. Close the Block Authoring palettes.

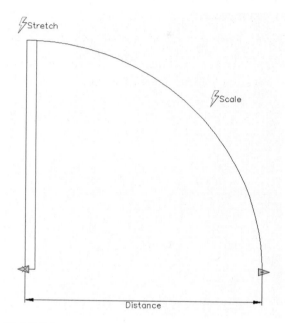

FIGURE 9.24: The two actions have been associated with the parameter.

   This completes your work with the Block Authoring palettes. You'll accomplish the rest of the tasks with the Properties palette.

Fine-Tuning the Dynamic Block with the Properties Palette

The Distance linear parameter shows the width of the opening and is perpendicular to the door's width. You need to set up an offset angle so the door width changes as the opening width changes. Then, you need to set up the incremental widths and rename the parameter and actions. You'll set up the increments first:

1. Open the Properties palette, and select the Distance parameter.

2. In the Property Labels section on the palette, change Distance Label from Distance to Door Opening.

3. Scroll down to the Value Set section, and click the text box for Dist Type, where it says None. Then, open the drop-down list, and select Increment.

4. Moving down, line by line, set Dist Increment to 6", Dist Minimum to 2', and Dist Maximum to 3'6.

5. Deselect the Distance parameter. It now has the increment markers for the door opening widths (see Figure 9.25).

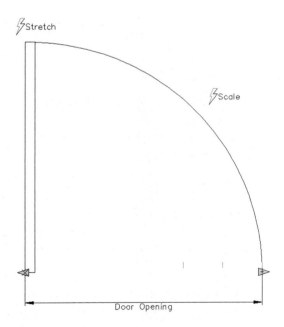

FIGURE 9.25: Dynamic door block with increment markers for the opening widths

Now, the final task is to fine-tune the Stretch and Scale actions that control the door size and swing:

1. Click the Stretch action symbol on the dynamic door block.

2. In the Properties palette, scroll down to the Overrides section; for Angle Offset, enter 90. The Distance multiplier stays at 1.0000 because you don't want the width of the door to change in the same proportion as the width of the opening.

3. In the Misc section, change Action Name from Stretch to **Door Size**.

4. Deselect this action, and select the Scale action.

5. In the Misc section of the Properties palette, change Action Name from Scale to **Door Swing Size**.

6. Close the Properties palette, click the Save Block Definition button on the Block Editor toolbar, and then click the Close Block Editor button to return to the drawing.

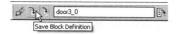

7. Save the drawing as DynDoor.dwg in the same folder as your other Chapter 9 drawings, and then close the drawing.

Inserting a Dynamic Block

When you use this block in your floor plans, insert it just as you would a regular door block. Then, copy it to the various doorway openings in the plan, orient it, and adjust its size to fit the openings. You can easily edit dynamic blocks, which are a versatile feature to have at your disposal.

You'll use the dynamic door block that you just created to replace the doors in your cabin:

1. In the Cabin09b drawing, delete the existing doors, and then freeze the Roof, Headers, Grid, and Fixtures layers. Make the Doors layer current, and then zoom into the cabin. Your drawing should look like Figure 9.26.

The door block that you created in the DynDoor drawing is based on the door3_0 block that already exists in the current drawing. Even if there is no such block inserted in the drawing, the block definition remains part of the drawing file. You will delete the block definition using the Purge command.

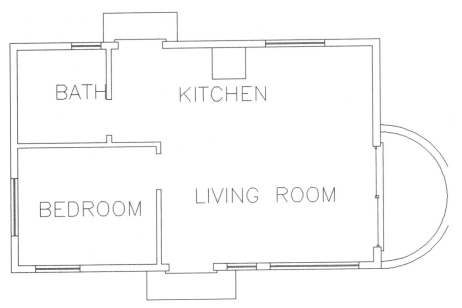

FIGURE 9.26: The cabin drawing with most of the layers frozen and the doors deleted

2. Enter **purge**⏎ to open the Purge dialog box (see Figure 9.27). Expand the Blocks entry to see the two door blocks. Select Blocks, check the Purge Nested Items option, and make sure Confirm Each Object to Be Purged is unchecked. Click the Purge button, and then close the dialog box.

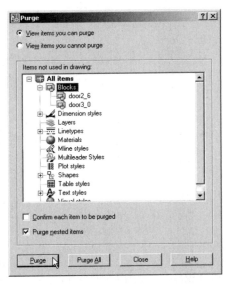

FIGURE 9.27: Deleting the block references with the Purge dialog box

T I P   You can purge only those objects and features that do not exist in the drawing such as deleted blocks, empty layers, or linetypes that are not used. Some items, including layer 0 and the Standard text style, can't be purged.

3. With the Endpoint osnap running, click the Insert Block button in the Draw toolbar.

4. Click the Browse button in the Insert dialog box that opens. Using Browse, you can insert any AutoCAD drawing into another as a block.

5. In the Select Drawing File dialog box, navigate to the folder where you placed the DynDoor drawing (see Figure 9.28). Select it, and then click the Open button.

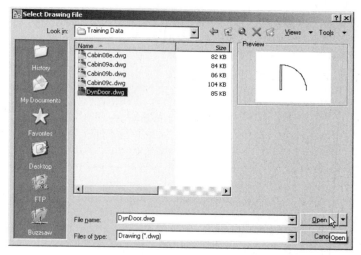

F I G U R E   9 . 2 8 :   Selecting the DynDoor block for insertion

6. Click OK in the Insert dialog box. The dynamic door block appears attached to the cursor. Click the upper-left corner of the front door opening, and press ↵ to accept any of the default values. This is a 3' door, so you don't need to modify the block.

7. Press ↵ to restart the Insert command. In the Insert dialog box, check the Specify On-Screen options under both Scale and Rotation.

8. Click the upper-left corner of the bedroom opening to place the door. Set the X scale to 1 and the Y scale to –1 to flip the door around the y-axis. Enter 270↵ at the rotation prompt. The door is placed properly, but (as shown in Figure 9.29) the default size is too large for the opening.

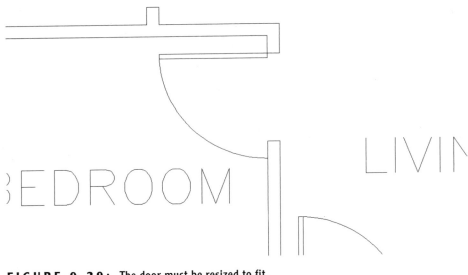

FIGURE 9.29: The door must be resized to fit.

9. Explode the block that you just inserted. In this case, you're not exploding the dynamic door block itself; you're exploding the drawing file that it is nested in so that you can access the block's dynamic properties.

 TIP Checking the Explode option, at the lower-left corner of the Insert dialog box, prior to inserting the block eliminates the need to explode it after the block is inserted. If this option is selected when inserting a nondynamic block, then that block is broken up into its component objects. Checking the Explode option also prevents the block from being inserted with the axes scaled unevenly.

10. Select the door block, and the blue dynamic arrows appear (see Figure 9.30).

11. Select the lower arrow, and drag it up to the corner of the opening. Notice how the length of the door changes as well (see Figure 9.31).

The door block is scaled properly with no distortion to the width of the door itself (see Figure 9.32).

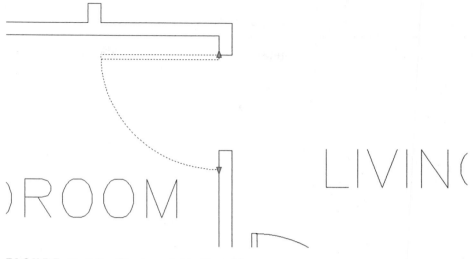

FIGURE 9.30: The dynamic block's resizing arrows

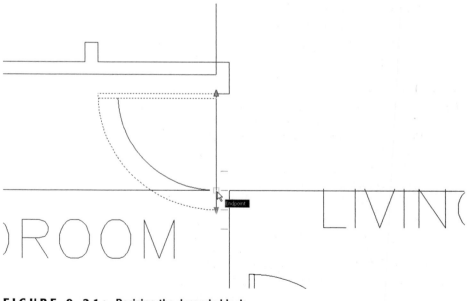

FIGURE 9.31: Resizing the dynamic block

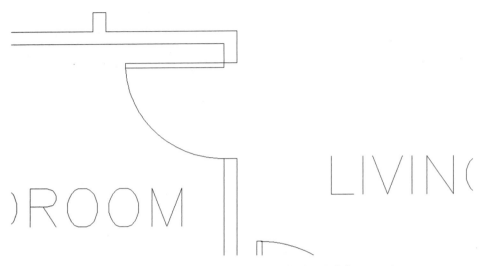

FIGURE 9.32: The dynamic door block scaled to fit the 2'6" door opening.

12. Insert and adjust the remaining doors as necessary. You should explode the two 3'0" doors as well as expose their dynamic grips. Thaw all the layers except Tblk1 and Area, and then zoom out. Your drawing should look like Figure 9.33.

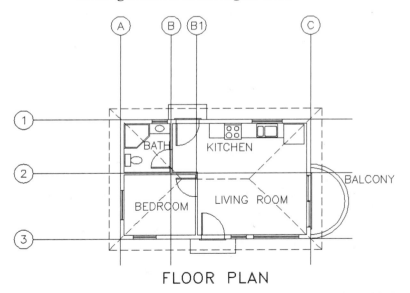

FIGURE 9.33: All the door blocks replaced with the dynamic door blocks and adjusted to fit

13. Save your drawing as Cabin09C.dwg.

This completes the section on dynamic blocks. If you want to experiment with the dynamic block feature, watch the demo in the New Features Workshop, examine the sample dynamic blocks to see how they work and are set up, and try to create one of your own. In the next section, I'll cover the methods for creating a table.

Creating a Table

Most professions that use AutoCAD use tables to consolidate and display data in organized formats. Architectural construction documents usually include at least three basic tables: door, window, and room finish schedules. These are usually drawn in table form, and they display the various construction and material specifications for each door or window type or for each room. To illustrate the AutoCAD tools for creating tables, you'll construct a simple door schedule for the cabin.

You create tables in AutoCAD by first creating a table style and then creating a table using that style—it's a process similar to that of defining a text style and then inserting text in a drawing using that style.

Defining a Table Style

Table styles are more complex than text styles. They include parameters for width and height of rows and columns and, among other elements, at least one text style.

1. Make Cabin9c the current drawing if it isn't already.

2. Create a new layer called Tables, assign it color number 7, and make it the current layer.

3. Choose Format ➤ Table Style to open the Table Style dialog box (see Figure 9.34). On the left is the Styles list box. It displays all the defined table styles. To the right of that is a preview window that displays the current table style—in this case, the Standard style because it's the only one defined so far. Below the Styles list box is a drop-down list called List that gives you options for which table styles to display. To the right of the Preview Of window are four buttons.

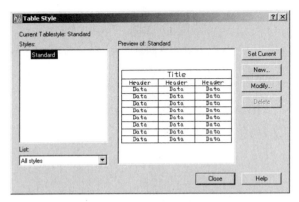

FIGURE 9.34: The Table Style dialog box

4. Click the New button to open the Create New Table Style dialog box. In the New Style Name text box, enter **Door Schedule** to create a new table style name, and click Continue.

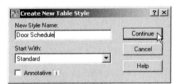

5. The New Table Style dialog box opens with Door Schedule in the title bar (see Figure 9.35). The new style you're defining will be like the Standard style with the changes you make here. The drop-down list in the Cell Styles section contains the three parts of the sample table at the bottom-right corner of the dialog box: Data, Header, and Title. You can specify text and line characteristics for each of the three parts. Be sure the Data option is active.

6. Click the Text tab, and then click the Browse button to the right of the Text Style drop-down list to open the Text Style dialog box. You want a new text style for the door schedule.

7. Define a new style called Table, and use the Arial font and a 0'-0" height. A Height value here allows you to control the height in the New Table Style dialog box. Click Apply, and then click Close. The Table style now appears in the Text Style drop-down list, and the data cells in the two preview windows now show the Arial font.

8. Set Text Height to 6". Leave Text Color and Text Angle at their default settings.

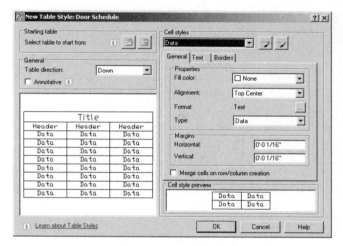

FIGURE 9.35: The New Table Style dialog box

9. Switch to the General tab (see Figure 9.36). Change Alignment to Middle Center.

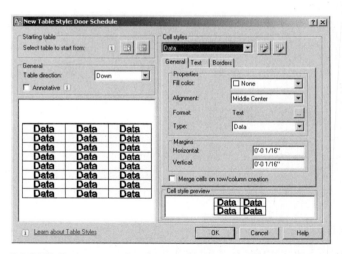

FIGURE 9.36: The General tab of the New Table Style dialog box

10. In the drop-down list at the top of the dialog box, choose Header to expose its parameters. In the Text tab, choose the same text style (Table), and set the height to 9".

11. Choose Title from the drop-down list, select the Table text style again, and set the height to 12". In the General tab, set the Horizontal and Vertical Margins to 4".

You'll leave the Border properties at their default settings. These control the visibility of the horizontal and vertical lines of the table, their lineweights, and their colors. Your profession might have its own standard for these parameters.

12. In the General section, on the left side of the dialog box, make sure Table Direction is set to Down. Click OK to save the new table style.

13. Back in the Table Style dialog box, in the Styles list, click Door Schedule to highlight it, and then click the Set Current button to make it the current table style (see Figure 9.37). Click Close.

Now, let's look at the geometry of the new table.

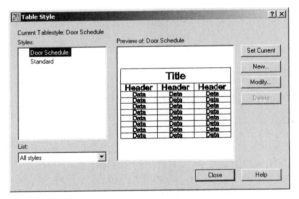

FIGURE 9.37: The Table Style dialog box with Door Schedule as the current table style

Designing a Table

The parameters in the Door Schedule table style have set the height of the rows. You now need to determine the width of the columns and figure out how many columns and rows you need for the door schedule. You do this as you insert a new table. Remember that Door Schedule is the current table style. Follow these steps:

1. Thaw the Tblk1 layer.

 2. Zoom into the upper-left portion of the drawing. Near the bottom of the Draw toolbar, click the Table icon to open the Insert Table dialog

box (see Figure 9.38). In the Table Style Settings area, Door Schedule appears in the Table Style Name drop-down list because it's now the current table style. An abstract version of the table appears below in the Preview area.

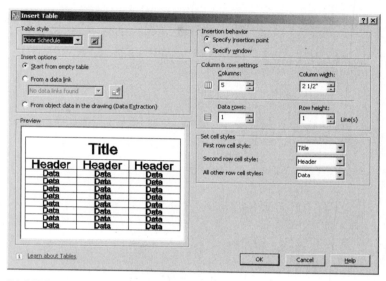

FIGURE 9.38: The Insert Table dialog box

3. On the right side, click the Specify Window radio button if necessary. You'll make a window to define the table. It will fit in the upper-left corner of the drawing. Below, in the Column & Row Settings area, Column Width and Data Rows turn into dashed lines because they are defined by the window that you specify to define the table in the drawing. You need to define only the number of columns. You won't worry about the row height for now; it's determined by the number of lines of text, and you're using only one line of text.

4. You'll have six categories to describe the doors, so set the Columns box to 6. Each column is initially set to the same width. You can adjust it later. Click OK.

5. Back in the drawing, turn off Osnap and Polar on the status bar. Then, click a point near the upper-left corner of the border, just inside it. This establishes the upper-left corner of the new table.

6. Drag the cursor across the drawing and down until the screen displays a table that spans the open area between the border and column line A and has six rows (see Figure 9.39), and then release the mouse button. The new table appears; its title bar has a flashing cursor and a light gray background, it has a dark gray background above and to the left of the table, the columns are lettered, and the rows are numbered. Above the drawing, the Text Formatting toolbar floats.

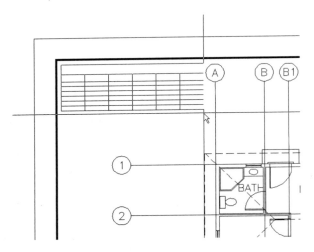

FIGURE 9.39: The new table inserted in the drawing

7. With Caps Lock on, enter **DOOR SCHEDULE**↵. The cursor moves to the upper-left cell on the table. This is the row for the column heads.

8. With Caps Lock on, enter **SYM.**, and press the Tab key. Moving across the header row, enter (in caps) **NAME**, press the Tab key, enter **H&W**, press the Tab key, enter **TYPE**, press the Tab key, enter **MAT'L**, press the Tab key, and then enter **COST**↵. This completes the row of column heads (see the left of Figure 9.40).

9. Partially fill in the data for the door schedule that's shown in the right of Figure 9.40 in the same manner. Pressing the Tab key instead of ↵ moves the activated cell left to right across each row and then down to the next row. Pressing ↵ moves the activated cell down each column and then ends the command. Double-click a cell to activate that cell and display the Text Formatting toolbar again.

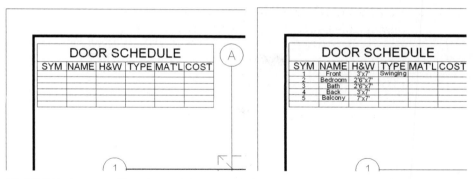

FIGURE 9.40: The table with its title and column heads (left) and the table partially filled in (right)

10. You don't have to enter everything from scratch; it's easy to copy the contents of one cell into other cells. Select the cell with the word SWINGING in it, and then highlight the text. Press Ctrl+C to copy the highlighted text to the Windows Clipboard. Deselect the current cell, and then select the three cells below it by clicking in cell D4, and then, while holding down the Shift key, clicking cell D6. Press Ctrl+V to paste the word SWINGING into each of the selected cells.

11. Complete the Type and Material columns, as shown in Figure 9.41.

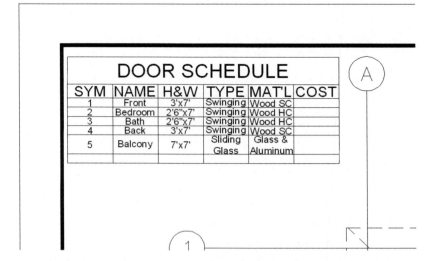

FIGURE 9.41: The table with its text-based cells filled in

Adding a Formula

Currently, all the data cells are configured to hold text information and not numbers. You will now change the Cost column to read the information as numbers and then sum the values in the bottom cell with a formula:

1. Select all the cells below the Cost header in column F. Right-click, and choose Data Format from the context menu that appears, as shown in Figure 9.42.

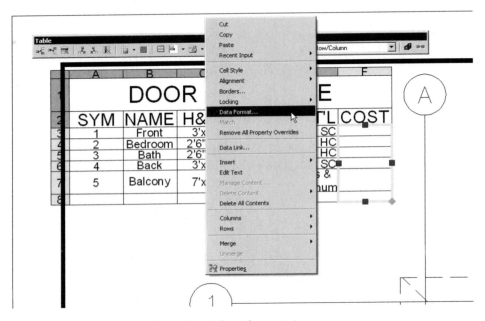

FIGURE 9.42: Select Data Format from the context menu

2. In the Table Cell Format dialog box that opens, choose Decimal Number for Data Type and Decimal for Format. In the Precision drop-down list, choose 0.00.

3. Click the Additional Format button. Then, in the Additional Format dialog box, enter $ in the Prefix text box, as shown in Figure 9.43. Click the OK button in both dialog boxes.

4. In the Cost column, enter 105 for the front and back door, 85 for the bedroom and bathroom doors, and 350 for the balcony door. AutoCAD automatically formats the numbers to two decimal places and adds a dollar sign to each, as in Figure 9.44.

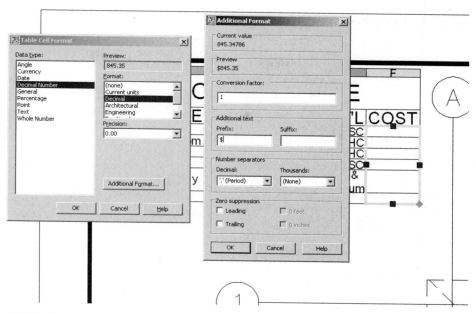

FIGURE 9.43: Formatting the table cells

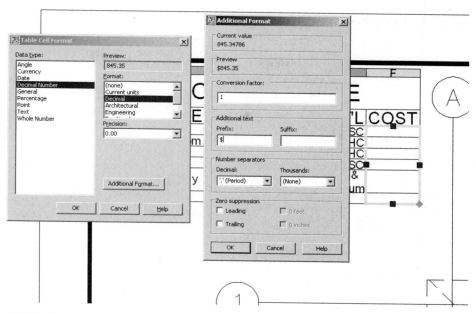

FIGURE 9.44: The Cost column filled in

5. Right-click the empty cell at the bottom of the Cost column, and choose Insert Field from the context menu to open the Field dialog box. The cell must be waiting for input (gray with a flashing cursor) and not selected (yellow border) to insert the field. Double-click the cell if necessary to achieve this state.

6. In the field Names list box, select Formula. The right side of the dialog box changes to display the possible formula parameters.

7. Click the Sum button. The dialog box disappears, and `Select first corner of table cell range:` appears at the command prompt. Click the top cell in the Cost column that corresponds to the front door (F3), move the cursor down to the cell that corresponds to the sliding door (F7), and click. The Field dialog box reappears with the cell's formula in the Formula text box (see Figure 9.45).

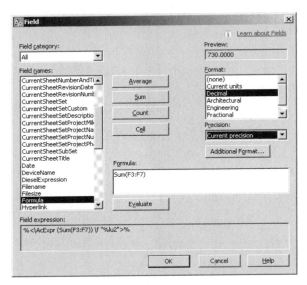

FIGURE 9.45: Adding the formula to the field

8. Set the Precision to 0.00 for the formula; then, in the Additional Format dialog box, add the $ prefix.

WARNING   You would expect that the formatting assigned to the cell previously would carry through to the formula, but it doesn't always. You might need to reformat cells as required.

9. Click OK to close the Field dialog box, and then click OK to close the Text Formatting toolbar. The sum of the door costs resides in the bottom cell, as shown in Figure 9.46. The gray background is just a visual cue that the cell contains a formula and will not print.

DOOR SCHEDULE

SYM	NAME	H&W	TYPE	MAT'L	COST
1	Front	3'x7'	Swinging	Wood SC	$105.00
2	Bedroom	2'6"x7'	Swinging	Wood HC	$85.00
3	Bath	2'6"x7'	Swinging	Wood HC	$85.00
4	Back	3'x7'	Swinging	Wood SC	$105.00
5	Balcony	7'x7'	Sliding Glass	Glass & Aluminum	$350.00
					$730.00

FIGURE 9.46: The completed table with a formula to sum the cost

10. Save this drawing as Cabin09d.dwg.

This concludes the chapter on dynamic blocks and tables. In the next chapter, you'll look at adding the elevations to the drawings.

This has been a quick tour of the features of attributes and the commands used to set them up and modify the data they contain. In the process, you saw several ways you can use them in an AutoCAD drawing. If you continue to work with attributes, you'll find them to be a powerful tool and a way to link information in your AutoCAD drawing to other applications. You also explored the methods for creating dynamic blocks that change as required to match your drawing's needs. Finally, you created a table to display the door schedule information and added a formula to calculate the total cost.

If You Would Like More Practice...

Blocks and attributes are commonly used in title blocks. For more practice using attributes, you can try the following:

▶ Replace the title block text with attributes.

▶ Add attributes to the window blocks.

Try experimenting with the dynamic block functionality by creating window blocks that can be dragged to the appropriate width without resorting to scaling the blocks.

Add a window schedule to calculate the cost of the cabin's windows.

Are You Experienced?

Now you can...

☑ set up blocks with attributes

☑ control the visibility of the attributes

☑ calculate the area of an enclosed space

☑ create dynamic blocks

☑ define a table style

☑ create a table complete with a formula

CHAPTER 10

Generating Elevations

▶ Drawing an exterior elevation from a floor plan

▶ Using grips to copy objects

▶ Setting up, naming, and saving user coordinate systems and views

▶ Transferring lines from one elevation to another

▶ Moving and rotating elevations

Now that you have created all the building components that will be in the floor plan, it's a good time to draw the exterior elevations. *Elevations* are horizontal views of the building, seen as if you were standing facing the building instead of looking down at it, as you do in the floor plan. An elevation view shows you how windows and doors fit into the walls and gives you an idea of how the building will look from the outside. In most architectural design projects, the drawings include at least four exterior elevations: front, back, and one from each side.

I'll go over how to create the front elevation first. Then I'll discuss some of the considerations necessary to complete the other elevations, and you'll have an opportunity to draw these on your own. Finally, you'll look at how to set up interior elevations. They are similar to exterior elevations but are usually of individual walls on the inside of a building to show how objects, such as doors, windows, cabinets, shelves, and finishes, will be placed on the walls.

In mechanical drawing, the item being drawn is often a machine part or a fixture. The drafter uses orthographic projection to illustrate various views of the object and calls them—instead of elevations and plans—*front view*, *top view*, *side view*, and so on. An exercise later in this chapter will give you practice with orthographic projection, but the procedure will be the same, whether you're drawing buildings or mechanical objects.

> *Orthographic projection* is a method for illustrating an object in views set at right angles to each other—front, top, side, back, and so on.

Drawing the Front Elevation

You draw the front elevation using techniques similar to those used on a traditional drafting board. You'll draw the front elevation view of the cabin directly below the floor plan by dropping lines down from key points on the floor plan and intersecting them with horizontal lines representing the heights of the corresponding components in the elevation. Figure 10.1 shows those heights.

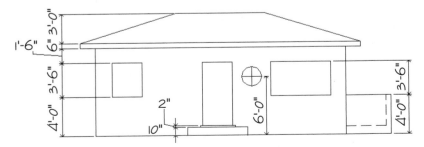

FIGURE 10.1: The front elevation with heights of components

Follow these steps:

1. Open Cabin09D.dwg.

2. Freeze the Grid, Fixtures, Table, and 0 layers. The Area layer should already be frozen, but check it and freeze it too if it is still thawed.

3. Create a new layer called F-elev. Assign it color 42, and make it current. Here's a summary of the steps to do this:

    a. Open the Layer Properties Manager, and then click New Layer.

    b. Enter F-elev, and press ↵.

    c. Click the colored square for the F-elev layer. Enter 42↵.

    d. Click the Set Current icon, or double-click the layer name, and then click OK.

4. Offset the bottom horizontal roofline 24' down. The offset line will be off the screen.

5. Perform a Zoom Extents. Then use Realtime Zoom to zoom out just enough to bring the offset roofline up off the bottom edge of the drawing area.

6. Erase this offset line. Your drawing should look like Figure 10.2.

> **Objects on layers that are frozen are invisible. To make them visible again, "thaw" their layers by clicking the layers' snowflake icons on the Layer Control drop-down list or the Layer Properties Manager.**

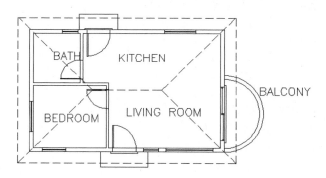

FIGURE 10.2: The floor plan with space below it for the front elevation

Setting Up Lines for the Heights

You need to establish a baseline to represent the ground. Then, you can offset the other height lines from the baseline or from other height lines:

Feel free to activate the Dyn button on the status bar for this chapter.

1. Check the status bar to make sure that Polar, Osnap, and Model are in their on positions while the other buttons are off. The Endpoint osnap should be running. Draw a horizontal ground line across the bottom of the screen using the Line command. Make sure the line extends on the left to a few feet beyond a point directly below the outside edge of the roof and on the right to a few feet beyond a point directly below the right edge of the balcony (see Figure 10.3).

FLOOR PLAN

FIGURE 10.3: The floor plan with the ground line

2. Offset the ground line 10" up to mark the height of the step. Then, offset this new line 2" up to mark the top of the threshold.

3. Move back to the ground line, and offset it 4' up to mark the top of the balcony wall and the bottom of the windows.

4. Offset the bottom line of the windows 3'-6" up to mark the top of the door and windows.

5. Offset the top line of the windows and door 1'-6" up to mark the soffit of the roof.

6. Offset the soffit line 6" up to mark the lower edge of the roof's top surface.

7. Offset this lower edge of the roof's top surface 3' up to mark the roof's ridge (see Figure 10.4).

A *soffit* is the underside of the roof overhang that extends from the outside edge of the roof back to the wall.

FIGURE 10.4: The horizontal height lines for the elevation in place

8. Press ⏎ to end the Offset command.

Each of these lines represents the height of one or more components of the cabin. Now you'll drop lines down from the points in the floor plan that coincide with components that will be visible in the front elevation. The front elevation will consist of the balcony, the front step, the front door and windows, the front corners of the exterior walls, and parts of the roof.

Using Grips to Copy Lines

In the following steps, you'll use grips to copy the dropped lines:

1. Start a line from the lower-left corner of the walls of the building. Select the Perpendicular osnap, and click the ground line. Press ↵ to end the Line command (see the top of Figure 10.5).

2. At the Command: prompt, select the line you just drew. Small squares appear on the line's midpoint and endpoints (see the middle of Figure 10.5). These are *grips*.

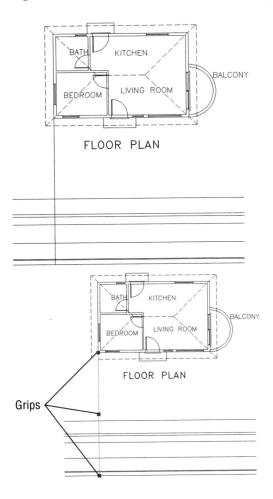

FIGURE 10.5: Dropping a line from the floor plan to the elevation (top), the dropped line with grips (middle), and the copied lines (next page)

Continues

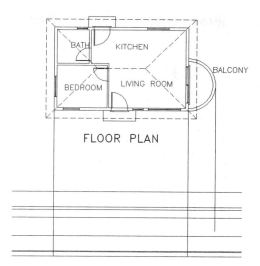

BALCONY

FLOOR PLAN

FIGURE 10.5 *(Continued)*

The Stretch com-
mand is a modifying
tool that you use to
lengthen or shorten
lines and other
objects. You'll have
another chance to
use it in Chapter 11.

3. Click the grip on the upper endpoint. The grip changes color, and the prompt changes to Specify stretch point or [Base point/ Copy/Undo/eXit]:. This is the Stretch command, which is activated by grips. Any time you activate a grip, the Stretch command automatically starts.

4. Right-click, and choose Move from the shortcut menu. Right-click again, and choose Copy from the shortcut menu. This selects the Copy option. You'll use the Move command with its Copy option to copy the line you just selected.

Each of the com-
mands that works
with grips has a Copy
option, which keeps
the original object as
is while you modify
the copy. You can
copy with grips in
several ways that
aren't possible with
the regular Copy
command.

5. With the Endpoint osnap running, select the lower-right corner of the building. The line is copied to this corner.

6. Select the Quadrant osnap, or enter **qua**↵ and click the right extremity of the outside wall line of the balcony. Another line is copied, this time to the balcony. It doesn't extend to the ground line because it was directly copied and therefore is the same length as the other two lines. You'll extend it later.

7. Enter x↵ to end the Move command. Press Esc to deselect the line. Your drawing resembles the bottom of Figure 10.5.

GETTING A GRIP ON GRIPS

In Chapter 7, you saw how to use grips to detect whether an object is a block. Grips actually serve a larger function. The grips feature is a tool for editing objects quickly, using one or more of the following five commands: Stretch, Move, Rotate, Scale, and Mirror. These commands operate a little differently when using grips than when using them regularly.

The commands can also perform a few more tasks with the help of grips. Each command has a Copy option. So, for example, if you rotate an object with grips, you can keep the original object unchanged while you make multiple copies of the object in various angles of rotation. You can't do this by using the Rotate command in the regular way or by using the regular Copy command.

To use grips, follow these steps:

1. When no commands have been started, click an object that you want to modify.

2. Click the grip that will be the base point for the command's execution.

3. Right-click at this point, and choose any of the five commands from the shortcut menu that opens on the drawing area. (You can also cycle through the five commands by pressing the spacebar and watching the Command prompt.)

4. When you see the command you need, execute the necessary option.

5. Enter **x**↵ when you're finished.

6. Press Esc to deselect the object.

The key to being able to use grips efficiently is knowing which grip to select to start the process. This requires a good understanding of the five commands that work with grips.

This book doesn't cover grips in depth, but it introduces you to the basics. You'll get a chance to use the Move command with grips in this chapter, and you'll use grips again when we get to Chapter 12.

Keep the following in mind when working with grips:

▶ Each of the five commands available for use with grips requires a base point. For Mirror, the base point is the first point of the mirror line. By default, the base point is the grip that you select to activate the process, but you can change base points. After selecting a grip, enter **b**↵, and pick a different point to serve as a base point; then, continue the command.

▶ When you use the Copy option with the Move command, you're essentially using the regular Copy command.

Trimming Lines in the Elevation

The next task is to trim the appropriate lines in the elevation, but first you need to extend the line dropped from the balcony down to the ground line:

1. Click the line dropped from the balcony. Grips appear on the line. Click the bottom grip. Select the Perpendicular osnap, and then place the cursor on the ground line. When the Perpendicular symbol appears on the ground line, click. Then, press Esc to deselect the line.

2. Start the Trim command. Select the soffit line, the third line from the top, for a cutting edge for the two building lines, and then press ↲. The two lines to be trimmed are the ones that were dropped from the corners of the building. Pick them anywhere between the soffit line and the floor plan. The lines are trimmed (see Figure 10.6).

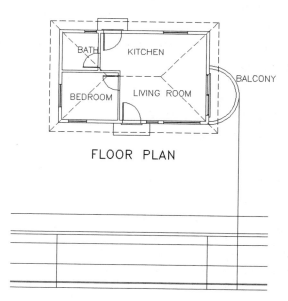

FIGURE 10.6: The building corner lines after being trimmed to the soffit line

3. Press ↲ twice to stop and restart the Trim command. You need to trim a horizontal height line and a vertical dropped line for the balcony. To select cutting edges, pick the line dropped from the balcony and the horizontal height line that represents the top of the balcony wall and the bottom of the windows (see the top of Figure 10.7). Press ↲.

4. To trim the lines properly, click the line dropped from the balcony anywhere above the balcony in the elevation. To trim the horizontal

line representing the top of the balcony wall, pick this line anywhere to the right of the line dropped from the balcony (see the middle of Figure 10.7). The lines are trimmed (see the bottom of Figure 10.7). Press ↵ to end the Trim command.

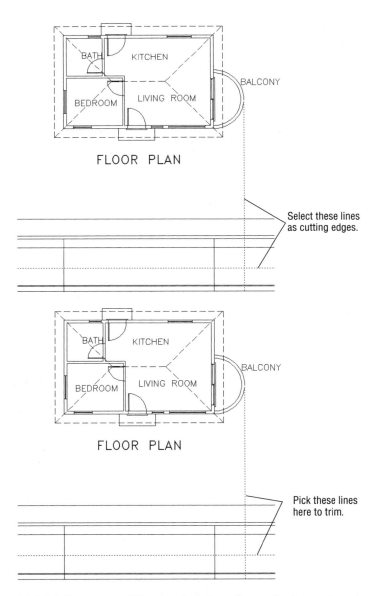

FIGURE 10.7: Trimming the balcony lines: selecting cutting edges (top), picking lines to be trimmed (middle), and the result (next page)

Continues

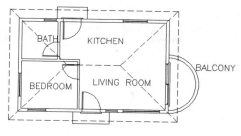

FLOOR PLAN

FIGURE 10.7 *(Continued)*

This is the basic process for generating an elevation: Drop lines down from the floor plan, and trim the lines that need to be trimmed. The trick is to learn to see the picture you want somewhere in all the crossed lines and then to be able to use the Trim command accurately to cut away the appropriate lines.

TIPS FOR USING THE TRIM AND EXTEND COMMANDS

Trim and Extend are sister commands. Here are a few tips on how they work:

Basic operation   Both commands involve two steps: selecting cutting edges (Trim) or boundary edges (Extend) and then selecting the lines to be trimmed or extended. Select the cutting or boundary edges first, and then press ↵. Next, pick lines to trim or extend. Press ↵ to end the commands. You can use the Fence option or a selection window to select several lines to trim or extend at one time.

Trimming and extending in the same command   If you find that a cutting edge for trimming can also serve as a boundary edge for extending, hold down the Shift key, and click a line to extend it to the cutting edge. The opposite is true for the Extend command.

Continues

TIPS FOR USING THE TRIM AND EXTEND COMMANDS *Continued*

Correcting errors   It's easy to make a mistake in selecting cutting or boundary edges or in trimming and extending. You can correct a mistake in two ways:

▶ If you select the wrong cutting or boundary edge, enter **r**↵, and then rechoose the lines that were picked in error. They will unhighlight. If you need to keep selecting cutting or boundary edges, enter **a**↵, and select new lines. When finished, press ↵ to move to the second part of the command.

▶ If you trim or extend a line incorrectly, enter **u**↵, or right-click and choose Undo from the shortcut menu. This undoes the last trim. Click Undo again if you need to untrim or unextend more lines. When you have made all the corrections, continue trimming or extending. Press ↵ to end the command.

If the command ended and you click the Undo button, you will undo all trimming or extending that was done in the preceding command.

Drawing the Roof in Elevation

To draw the roof in elevation, follow these steps:

1. Use the Line command to start a line from the right endpoint of the ridgeline of the roof. Then, click the Snap to None osnap button on the Object Snap toolbar. Draw the line straight down past the soffit line (see the top of Figure 10.8). End the Line command.

2. Click this line to activate grips. Select the grip at its upper endpoint. Press the spacebar once to access the Move command.

3. Enter **c**↵ to start the copy mode, and then click the lower-right and lower-left corners of the roof and the left endpoint of the ridgeline. This copies the dropped line to these three locations (see the bottom of Figure 10.8).

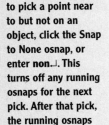

If the osnaps that you have running get in the way of you trying to pick a point near to but not on an object, click the Snap to None osnap, or enter non↵. This turns off any running osnaps for the next pick. After that pick, the running osnaps are reactivated.

N O T E   If you have difficulty picking the left end of the ridgeline, hold the cursor on the lower-left hip line, just above the midpoint. That should produce an endpoint marker where you want it.

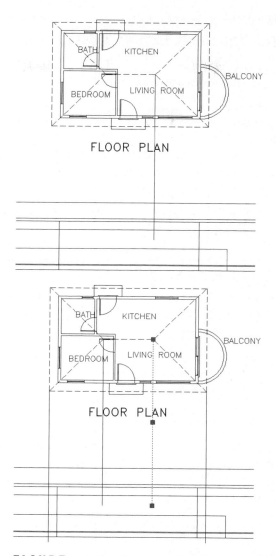

FIGURE 10.8: Dropping a line from the roof (top) and copying this line (bottom)

4. Enter x↵ to end the Move command, and then press Esc to deselect the line.

5. Start the Trim command, and select the two lines dropped from the ridgeline. Press ↵.

6. In the elevation, pick the ridgeline to the left and right of these dropped lines (see the top of Figure 10.9). The ridgeline is trimmed back to its correct length (see the bottom of Figure 10.9). Press ↵.

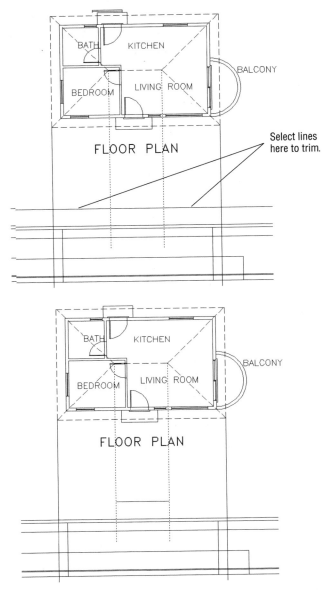

FIGURE 10.9: Selecting the lines to trim (top) and the result (bottom)

7. Erase the two dropped lines that were just used as cutting edges.

8. Restart the Trim command. Select the two lines dropped from the corners of the roof, the horizontal soffit line, and the line 6" above the soffit line to be cutting edges—four lines in all. Press ⏎ (see the top of Figure 10.10).

9. To do the trim, click the dropped lines above and below the two horizontal cutting edges; then, click the two selected horizontal lines to the left and right of the dropped lines—eight picks in all. Press ↵. The roof edge is complete (see the bottom of Figure 10.10).

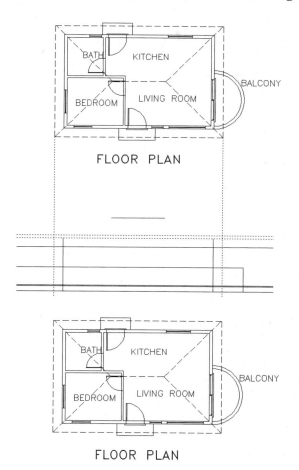

FLOOR PLAN

FLOOR PLAN

FIGURE 10.10: Trimming the lines to form the roof edge (top) and the result (bottom)

10. Use the Line command to draw the two hip lines from the roof edge to the ridgeline. Zoom in to do this if you need to do so; use Zoom Previous when you're finished to view the completed front elevation of the roof (see Figure 10.11).

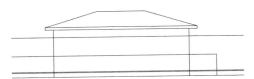

FIGURE 10.11: The completed roof in elevation

Putting in the Door, the Step, and the Windows

To finish the front elevation, all you need to add is the front door, the windows, the front step, the threshold, and a few finishing touches. You'll do the door and all the windows, except the round one, in a single cycle. You'll save the step and threshold for later. Here is the procedure:

1. Use Zoom Window to zoom in to as close a view as possible that still displays as much of the drawing as you need. You'll need to see the entire elevation, the front wall of the floor plan, and the lower half of the balcony, so make your zoom window large enough to enclose just those elements (see the top of Figure 10.12). I call this process *strategic zooming*.

2. Draw a line from the left end of the leftmost window in the front wall of the floor plan to the ground line, using the Perpendicular osnap for the second point. End the Line command.

3. Select the line to display its grips, and then click the upper grip on this line at the Command: prompt to activate it. Follow the same process as you did in steps 2 and 3 of the "Drawing the Roof in Elevation" section to copy this line to the following:

▶ Each endpoint of the jamb line of each window in the front wall, except the 2' circular one just to the right of the front door

▶ Each edge of the front door opening

Watch your Endpoint osnap symbol carefully.

4. Enter x↵ to end the Move command. Press Esc to deselect the line (see the bottom of Figure 10.12).

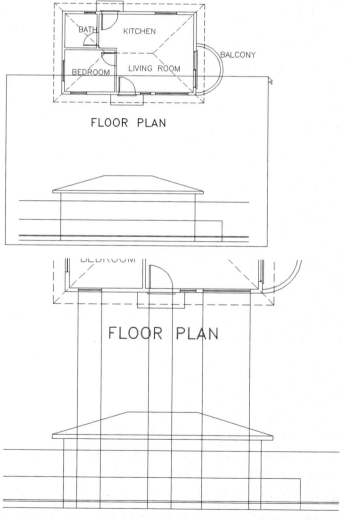

FIGURE 10.12: The window for zooming in closer (top) and dropping a line from a window and copying it to the edges of the windows and the front door (bottom)

Before you begin trimming all these lines, study the floor plan and elevation for a minute, and try to visualize the two rectangular windows and the door in the middle of all the crossing lines. You'll trim a few at a time, working from the top down.

5. Start the Trim command. For cutting edges, select the horizontal line representing the top of the windows and doors, and select the six lines you just dropped from the floor plan. Press ↵.

6. To trim, pick the horizontal line at each segment between the windows and the door and near the endpoints of the line (four places). Then, pick each selected dropped line above the tops of the windows and door (six places). This makes 10 places to pick. Press ↵. Figure 10.13 shows the results of the trim.

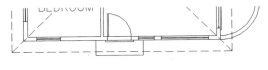

FLOOR PLAN

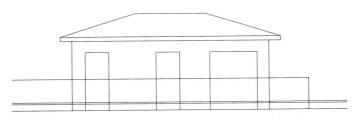

FIGURE 10.13: Trimming the top of the door and windows

Moving down, trim the lines that form the bottom of the windows.

7. Start the Trim command. Select the following as cutting edges:

   ▶ The horizontal line representing the bottom of the window and the top of the balcony wall

   ▶ The four vertical lines forming the sides of the windows

   ▶ The vertical line representing the right edge of the front wall, between the rightmost window and the balcony

   Once you have the selection, press ↵.

N O T E It will be helpful if you zoom in to a closer view of the front elevation when you're picking lines to trim. After step 8, use Zoom Previous.

8. To trim, pick the horizontal line at the following places:

▶ Between the windows (one pick)

▶ Between the right edge of the 6' window and the right edge of the building (one pick)

▶ Where it extends to the left of the leftmost window (one pick)

Then, pick the vertical lines that extend below the bottoms of the windows (four picks). This will be a total of seven picks. Press ↵. Figure 10.14 shows the results of the trim.

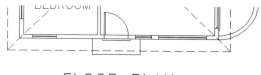

FLOOR PLAN

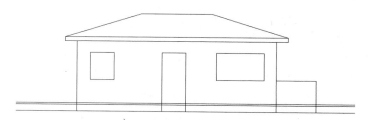

FIGURE 10.14: Trimming the bottom of the windows

Now, you'll draw the step and threshold and the bottom of the door:

1. Drop a line down from the left corner of the threshold to a point past the ground line. Use grips to copy this line to the other corner of the threshold and to the two corners of the step. End the grips (see the top of Figure 10.15).

2. Zoom in to a close view of the step and threshold. Use the Trim command to trim away the lines so that the result looks like the bottom of Figure 10.15. You'll probably have to stop and restart the command a couple of times in order to make all the trims you need. Figure 10.15 shows one way to do it, in summary form.

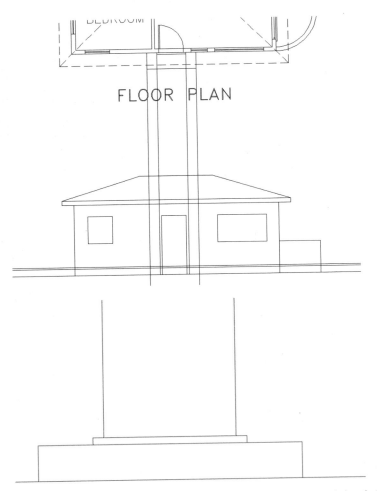

FIGURE 10.15: Dropped and copied lines for the step and threshold (top) and the finished step and threshold (bottom)

a. Create the step first. For cutting edges, select the two lower horizontal lines and the two outer vertical lines. To trim, pick each of these lines (except the ground line) in two places above and below or to the left and right of the step (six picks).

b. Create the threshold. For cutting edges, select the four lines that form the outside edges of the threshold. To trim, pick each of these lines (except the line that forms the top of the step) in two places above and below or to the left and right of the threshold (six picks).

   c. Trim the left and right edges of the door up to the top of the threshold (as in the bottom of Figure 10.15).

3. When you're finished, use Zoom Previous to see a view of the front elevation and the bottom of the floor plan.

The results show a nearly complete front elevation. To finish it, you need to put in the round window and complete the balcony. You'll then add some final touches. Take another look at Figure 10.1 (shown earlier), and note that the center of the round window is 6' above the ground line. Follow these steps:

1. Offset the ground line 6' up.

2. Start the Line command; then, click the Snap to Insert button on the Object Snap toolbar, or enter **ins.**⏎. Click the 2' window in the floor plan to start a line at the insertion point of this block reference. Draw the line down through the newly offset line. Next, draw a circle, using the intersection of these two lines as the center, and give it a 12" radius.

3. Start the Trim command, and select the circle as a cutting edge; press ⏎.

4. Pick the intersecting lines passing through the circle in four places outside the circle. This finishes the round window (see Figure 10.16).

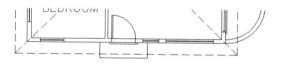

FLOOR PLAN

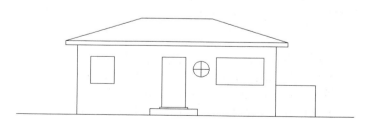

FIGURE 10.16: The completed round window

5. Make a zoom window around only the front elevation.

6. Offset the vertical line representing the balcony's right edge 6" to the left. Then, offset the ground line up 10". These lines will serve to indicate the balcony's floor and inside wall.

7. Fillet these two lines at their intersection with a radius of zero. Then, trim the balcony floor line back to the right wall line of the cabin.

8. Select these two new lines. Right-click and choose Properties from the context menu to open the Properties palette.

9. Click Linetype. Then, open the Linetype list, and click Dashed. Close the Properties palette, and press the Esc key. The lines are changed to dashed lines to indicate that they are hidden in the elevation (see Figure 10.17).

10. Use Zoom Previous twice to a view of the completed front elevation with the entire floor plan.

> This is a rare case in which you are assigning a linetype to an object rather than to a layer. (See "Assigning a Color or a Linetype to an Object Instead of a Layer" in Chapter 6.)

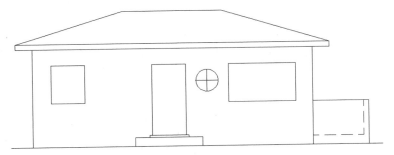

FIGURE 10.17: The completed balcony

Adding the Finishing Touches

You have gleaned all the information you can from the floor plan to help you with the front elevation. You may, however, want to add some detail to enhance the appearance of the elevation:

1. Try zooming in and adding detail to the windows and door, and place an extra step leading to the front step. Figure 10.18 shows an example. Yours can be different.

2. Use Zoom Previous to a full view of your drawing when you're finished.

3. Save this drawing as Cabin10a.dwg.

FIGURE 10.18: The front elevation with detail added

Generating the Other Elevations

The full set of drawings that contractors use to construct a building includes an elevation for each side of the building. In traditional drafting, the elevations are usually drawn on separate sheets. This requires transferring measurements from one drawing to another by taping drawings next to each other, turning the floor plan around to orient it to each elevation, and using several other cumbersome techniques. You do about the same on the computer, but it's much easier to move the drawing around. You'll be more accurate, and you can quickly borrow parts from one elevation to use in another.

Making the Rear Elevation

Because the rear elevation shares components and sizes with the front elevation, you can mirror the front elevation to the rear of the building and then make the necessary changes:

1. Open Cabin10a.dwg if it's not already open. You need to change the view to include space above the floor plan for the rear elevation.

2. Use Pan Realtime to move the view of the floor plan to the middle of the screen. Then, use Zoom Realtime to zoom out the view enough to include the front elevation.

3. Start the Mirror command. Use a window to select the front elevation, and press ↵.

4. For the mirror line, select the Midpoint osnap, and pick the left edge
line of the roof in the floor plan.

5. With polar tracking on, hold the crosshair cursor directly to the right
of the point you just picked (see the left of Figure 10.19), and pick
another point. At the `Erase source objects?[Yes/No]<N>:`
prompt, press ↵ to accept the default of No. The front elevation is
mirrored to the rear of the cabin (see the right of Figure 10.19).

You can now make the necessary changes to the rear elevation so that
it correctly describes the rear of the cabin. But you might find it easier to work if the view is right side up.

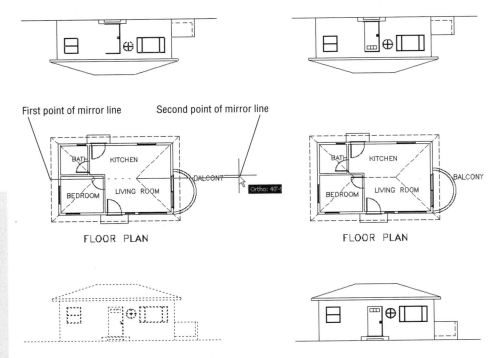

The *user coordinate system* (UCS) defines the positive X and Y directions relative to your drawing. A drawing can have several UCSs but can use only one at a time. The *world coordinate system* (WCS) is the default UCS for all new drawings and remains available in all drawings.

FIGURE 10.19: Specifying a mirror line (left) and the result (right)

6. Choose View ➤ Display ➤ UCS Icon ➤ On to display the UCS icon.
(You turned it off in Chapter 9.) Take a look at the icon for a moment.

The two arrows in the icon show the positive X and Y directions of the current UCS, the WCS, which is the default system for all Auto-CAD drawings. You'll change the orientation of the icon to the drawing and then change the orientation of the drawing to the screen.

7. If your UCS icon is in the lower-left corner of the screen, go to step 8. Otherwise, choose View ➤ Display ➤ UCS Icon ➤ Origin. This should move the icon to the lower-left corner of the screen.

8. Enter ucs↵ z↵ 180↵. This rotates the icon 180° around the z-axis to an upside-down position. The square box disappears, meaning that you're no longer using the default WCS.

9. Choose View ➤ 3D Views ➤ Plan View ➤ Current UCS. The entire drawing is rotated 180°, and the mirrored front elevation, which will eventually be the back elevation, is now right side up. Note that the UCS icon is now oriented the way it used to be, but the square in the icon is still missing. This signals that the current UCS is no longer the WCS.

10. Use Zoom Realtime to zoom out enough to bring the outermost lines of the drawing slightly in from the edge of the drawing area. Don't exit Realtime Zoom yet. Right-click, and choose Zoom Window from the shortcut menu.

Move the cursor above and to the left of the floor plan; then, click and hold down the mouse button. Drag open a window that encloses the floor plan and mirrored elevation. Release the mouse button. Press Esc to end Realtime Zoom (see Figure 10.20). Now you can work on the rear elevation.

When a check mark is next to Origin in the menu, the UCS icon sits at the origin (or the 0,0 point) of the drawing. When Origin is unchecked, the icon sits in the lower-left corner of the screen.

You used the UCS command to reorient the UCS icon relative to the drawing. You then used the Current option of the Plan command to reorient the drawing on the screen so that the positive X and Y directions of the current UCS are directed to the right and upward, respectively. This process is a little bit like turning your monitor upside down to get the correct orientation, but it's easier.

When you access Zoom Window from the Zoom Realtime shortcut menu, it behaves differently from the regular Zoom Window command. It requires a click-and-drag technique.

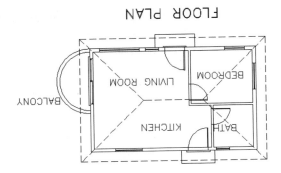

FIGURE 10.20: The cabin drawing rotated 180° and zoomed in

Revising the Rear Elevation

A brief inspection will tell you that the roof, balcony, and building wall lines don't need any changes. The windows and door need revisions, as do the step and threshold:

▶ The round window needs to be deleted.

▶ The two remaining windows need resizing and repositioning.

▶ The door, threshold, and step need repositioning.

▶ The step needs resizing.

You can accomplish these tasks quickly by using commands with which you're now familiar:

1. Erase the round window.

2. Erase the vertical lines from the remaining windows (see the top of Figure 10.21).

3. Drop lines down from the jambs of the two windows in the back wall of the floor plan, past the bottoms of the windows in elevation (see the middle of Figure 10.21).

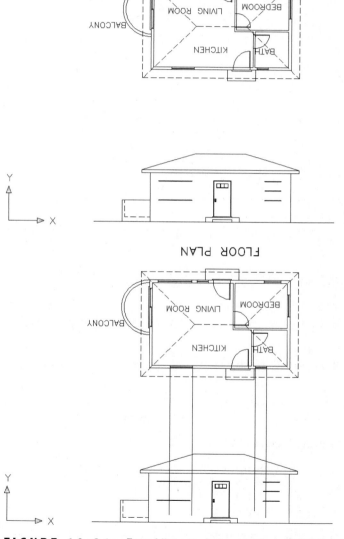

FIGURE 10.21: Erased lines (top), dropped lines (middle), and the revised rear elevation (next page)

Continues

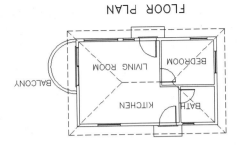

FIGURE 10.21 *(Continued)*

4. Extend the horizontal window lines that need to meet the dropped lines, and trim all lines that need to be trimmed. (You can use the Fillet command here instead of the Trim and Extend commands, but pick lines carefully.) Add any detail that you added to the Front elevation earlier in this chapter.

5. Use a similar strategy to relocate and resize the step. You can move the door and threshold into position by using any of several procedures, including dropping a guideline or using the Temporary Tracking Point osnap—or for LT users, using the Tracking tool—with polar tracking. Use Zoom Window and Zoom Previous as needed. The finished rear elevation looks like the bottom of Figure 10.21.

6. You need to save the UCS you used to work on this elevation so that you can quickly return to it in the future, from the WCS or from any other UCS you might be in. Enter **ucs**↵ **s**↵. For the UCS name, enter **rear_elev**↵. This will allow you to recall it if you need to work on this elevation again.

You can save any UCS in this way. The WCS is a permanent part of all drawings, so you never need to save it.

7. You can also save the view to be able to quickly recall it. Choose View ➤ Named Views to open the View Manager dialog box. You can also start the View command by typing v↵.

8. Click New to open the New View dialog box.

9. In the View Name text box, enter **rear_elev**. Click the Current Display radio button, and click OK. Back in the View dialog box, rear_elev appears in the list of views (see Figure 10.22). Click OK again. Now you can restore the drawing to its original orientation with the front elevation below the floor plan and right side up. Click OK to close both dialog boxes.

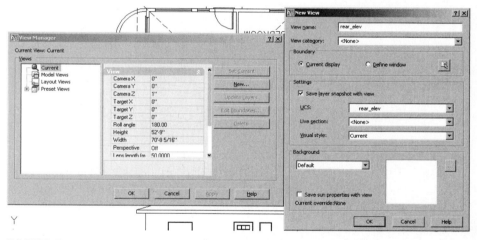

FIGURE 10.22: Saving a view in the View Manager and New View dialog boxes

You can name and save any view of your drawing and then restore it later.

10. Enter ucs↵↵ to restore the WCS as the current coordinate system.

11. Choose View ➤ 3D Views ➤ Plan View ➤ Current UCS. This zooms to Extents view and displays a plan view of the drawing with the X and Y positive directions in their default orientation. You can also enter plan↵ ↵ to restore the plan view of the WCS.

You created a new UCS as a tool to flip the drawing upside down without changing its orientation with respect to the WCS. Now, you'll use it again to create the left and right elevations.

Making the Left and Right Elevations

You can generate the left and right elevations using techniques similar to those you have been using for the front and back elevations. You need to be able to transfer the heights of building components from the front elevation to one of the side elevations. To do this, you'll make a copy of the front elevation, rotate it 90°, and then line it up so you can transfer the heights to the right elevation. It's quite easy:

1. Use Zoom Realtime to zoom out slightly; then, zoom in to a view of the floor plan and front elevation. Pan the drawing so that the floor plan and front elevation are on the left part of the drawing area. You need to transfer the height data from the front elevation to the right elevation. To ensure that the right elevation is the same distance from the floor plan as the front elevation, you'll use a 45° line that extends down and to the right from the rightmost and lowermost lines in the floor plan.

2. Turn on polar tracking, and be sure the Increment Angle is set to 45°. Also, make sure that the Otrack button on the status bar is toggled on. Then, set the Quadrant and Endpoint osnaps to running, and be sure the Midpoint osnap isn't running.

3. Start the Line command. Move the crosshair cursor to the right edge of the outside arc of the balcony in the floor plan. Hold it there for a moment. A cross appears at the Quadrant point. Don't click yet.

4. Move the crosshair cursor to the lower-right corner of the step in the floor plan, and hold it there until a cross appears at that point. Don't click yet.

5. Move the crosshair cursor to a point directly to the right of the corner of the step and directly under the right quadrant point of the balcony (see the top of Figure 10.23). Vertical and horizontal tracking lines appear and intersect where the crosshair cursor is positioned, and a small x appears at the intersection. A tracking tooltip also appears.

6. Click to start a line at this point.

7. Move the crosshair cursor down, away from this point and to the right at a negative 45° angle (or a positive 315° angle). When the 45° polar tracking path appears, enter 40'↵. Press ↵ again. This completes the diagonal reference line (see the bottom of Figure 10.23).

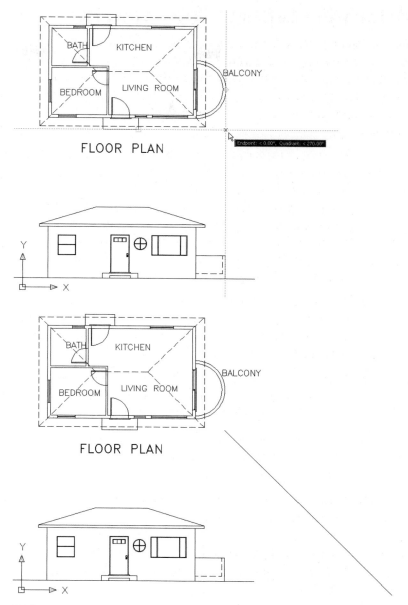

FIGURE 10.23: Starting a diagonal reference line with tracking points (top) and the completed diagonal line (bottom)

8. Turn off Quadrant as a running osnap.

9. Start the Copy command, and select the entire front elevation and nothing else. Then, press ↵.

10. For the base point, select the left endpoint of the ground line.

11. For the second point, pick the Intersection osnap, and place the cursor on the diagonal line. When the x symbol with three dots appears, click. Then, move the cursor to any point on the ground line of the front elevation. An x appears on the diagonal line where the ground line would intersect it if it were longer (see the top of Figure 10.24).

12. When the x appears, click to locate the copy. Press Esc to end the Copy command. Zoom out to include the copy; then, use Zoom Window to include the floor plan and front elevations (see the bottom of Figure 10.24). Press Esc to terminate the Copy command.

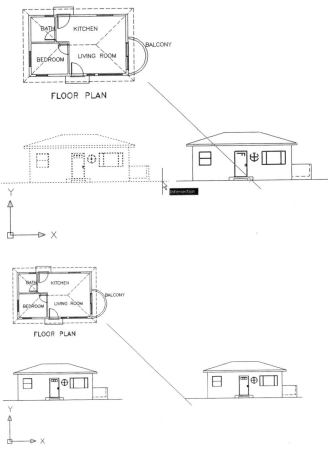

FIGURE 10.24: Making a copy of the front elevation (top) and adjusting the view (bottom)

13. Start the Rotate command, and select this copy of the front elevation; then, press ⏎. Pick the Intersection osnap, and click the intersection of the diagonal line with the ground line. For the angle of rotation, enter 90⏎ (see the top of Figure 10.25).

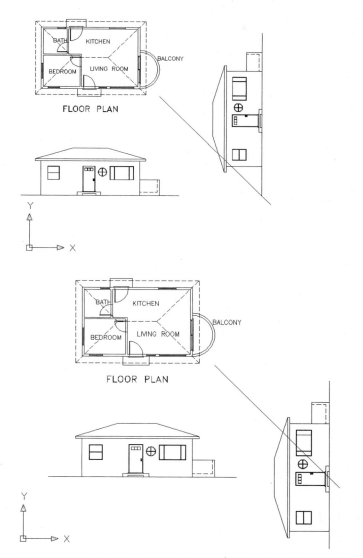

F I G U R E   1 0 . 2 5 : Rotating the copy of the front elevation (top) and the moved copy with the view adjusted (bottom)

14. Start the Move command, and when prompted to select objects, enter
    p↵↵. The rotated front elevation is selected. For the base point, click a
    point in a blank space to the right of the upper endpoint of the ground
    line of the rotated elevation. For the second point, move the cursor
    down using polar tracking until the top of the ground line is lower
    than the bottom line of the front step in the plan view. Then, click.

15. Zoom out and use Zoom Window to adjust the view (see the bottom
    of Figure 10.25).

If you're working on a smaller monitor than I am, you might have to do some
extra zooming in and out that isn't mentioned in these steps.

The rest of the process for creating the right elevation is straightforward and
uses routines you have just learned. Here's a summary of the steps:

1. Set up a new UCS for the right elevation. (Enter **ucs**↵ **z**↵ **90**↵.) Use
   the Plan command to rotate the drawing to the current UCS.

2. Drop lines from the floor plan across the height lines, which you'll
   produce from the copied elevation.

3. Trim these lines as required, and add any necessary lines.

4. Erase the copy of the front elevation and the diagonal transfer line.

5. Use grips to adjust the length and placement of the ground line.
   (Click one of the grips on the endpoint, move the cursor left or right,
   and click again.)

6. Name and save the UCS and view.

> You won't be able to get the height line for the sliding-glass doorframe from the front elevation. It's 2" below the top window line.

T I P   When creating elevations, you might accidentally draw a line over
an existing line. To catch this error, start the Erase command, and use a crossing window to select the suspect line. In the command window, the number of
objects selected appears. If more than one line has been selected, cancel,
restart the Erase command, and pick the line again. This time, only the extra
line is selected, and you can erase it. If more than two lines are on top of each
other, repeat the process.

You can create the left elevation from a mirrored image of the right elevation.
Here are the steps:

1. Mirror the right elevation to the opposite side.

2. Set up a UCS for the left elevation (**ucs**↵ **z**↵ **-90**↵). Use the Plan command to rotate the drawing to the current UCS.

3. Revise the elevation to match the left side of the cabin.

4. Name and save the UCS and view.

When you have completed all the elevations, follow these steps:

1. Return to the WCS.

2. Display the Plan view.

3. Erase any remaining construction lines and the rotated front elevation.

4. Copy and rotate the FLOOR PLAN label under each of the plans, and edit their content appropriately.

5. Zoom out slightly for a full view of all elevations. The drawing looks like Figure 10.26.

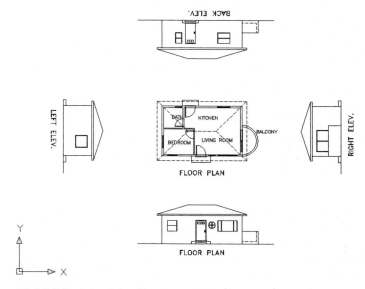

FIGURE 10.26: The finished elevations

6. Create three more layers named B-elev, L-elev, and R-elev, all using color 42.

7. Change the layer for each elevation's line work and label to the associated layer that you just made.

8. Save the drawing as Cabin10b.dwg.

Once an elevation is drawn, you can rotate it to the same orientation as the front elevation and move it to another area of the drawing.

Considering Drawing Scale Issues

This last view raises several questions: How will these drawings best fit on a page? How many pages will it take to illustrate these drawings? What size sheet should you use? At what scale will the drawing be printed? In traditional hand drafting, you wouldn't be able to draw the first line without answers to some of these questions. You have completed a great deal of the drawing on the computer without having to make decisions about scale and sheet size because, in AutoCAD, you draw in real-world scale or full-scale. This means that when you tell AutoCAD to draw a 10' line, it draws it 10' long. If you inquire how long the line is, AutoCAD will tell you that it's 10' long. Your current view of the line might be to a certain scale, but that changes every time you zoom in or out. The line is stored in the computer as 10' long.

You need to make decisions about scale when you're choosing the sheet size, putting text and dimensions on the drawing, or using hatch patterns and noncontinuous linetypes. (Chapter 11 covers hatch patterns.) Because you have a dashed linetype in the drawing, you had to make a choice about scale in Chapter 6, when you assigned a linetype scale factor of 24 to the drawing. You chose that number because when the drawing consisted of only the floor plan and the view was zoomed as large as possible while still having all objects visible, the scale of the drawing was about ½" = 1'-0". That scale has a true ratio of 1:24, or a scale factor of 24. You'll get further into scale factors and true ratios of scales in the next chapter.

If you look at your Cabin10b drawing with all elevations visible on the screen, the dashes in the dashed lines look like they might be too small, so you might need to increase the linetype scale factor. If you were to thaw the title block's layer now, you would see that your drawings won't all fit. Don't worry about that now. Beginning with the next chapter, and right on through the end of this book, you'll need to make decisions about scale each step of the way.

Drawing Interior Elevations

You construct interior elevations using the techniques you learned for constructing exterior elevations. You drop lines from a floor plan through offset height lines and then trim them away. Interior elevations usually include fixtures, built-in cabinets, and built-in shelves, and they show finishes. Each elevation consists of one wall and can include a side view of items on an adjacent wall if the item extends into the corner. Not all walls appear in an elevation—usually only those that require special treatment or illustrate special building components. You might use one elevation to show a wall that has a window and to describe how the window is treated or finished and then assume that all other windows in the building will be treated in the same way unless noted otherwise. Figure 10.27 shows a few examples of interior wall elevations. Try to identify which walls of the cabin each one represents.

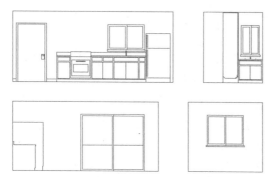

FIGURE 10.27: Samples of interior elevations of the cabin

In the next chapter, you'll learn how to use hatch patterns and fills to enhance floor plans and elevations.

If You Would Like More Practice...

Here are three exercises for practicing the techniques you learned in this chapter. The last one will give you practice in basic orthogonal projection.

Exterior elevations   Open Cabin10b.dwg, and move the right, left, and rear elevations around so they fit in a line.

Interior elevations   For some practice with interior elevations, try drawing one or two elevations, using Figure 10.27 (shown earlier) as a guide. You can measure the heights and sizes of various fixtures in your own home or office as a guide. Save what you draw as Cabin10c.dwg.

Orthogonal projection   Draw the three views of the block shown in Figure 10.28 following the procedures you used for the cabin elevations, except that, in this case, use the procedure that mechanical drafters employ; that is, draw the front view first, and then develop the top and right side views from the front view.

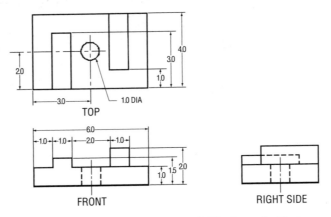

FIGURE 10.28: Front, top, and side views of a block

Are You Experienced?

Now you can...

- ☑ draw an exterior elevation from a floor plan
- ☑ use grips to copy objects
- ☑ add detail to an elevation
- ☑ set up, name, and save a UCS and a new view
- ☑ transfer height lines from one elevation to another
- ☑ copy, move, and rotate elevations

CHAPTER 11

Working with Hatches and Gradients

- ▶ Selecting a predefined hatch pattern and applying it to a drawing
- ▶ Setting up and applying user-defined hatch patterns
- ▶ Modifying the scale and shape of a hatch pattern
- ▶ Specifying the origin of a hatch pattern
- ▶ Filling an enclosed area with a solid color
- ▶ Filling up an enclosed area with a gradient
- ▶ Setting up and using palettes and palette tools

Hatches can be abstract patterns of lines, they can be solid *fills*, or they can resemble the surfaces of various building materials. Gradients are visual features that shift from one solid color to another over a specified distance. To give the appearance of texture to a drawing, an AutoCAD user will hatch in areas or fill them in with a solid color or gradient. Solid fills in a drawing can give a shaded effect when printed using *screening*, plotting an object using less than 100 percent ink density, which results in a look quite different from the solid appearance in the AutoCAD drawing on the screen. Chapter 15 covers screening.

In an architectural floor plan, the inside of full-height walls are often hatched or filled to distinguish them from low walls. Wood or tile floors can be hatched to a parquet or tile pattern. In a site plan, hatches distinguish between areas with different ground covers, such as grass, gravel, or concrete. When you're working with elevations, you can hatch almost any surface to show shading and shadows, and realistic hatch patterns can illustrate the surfaces of concrete, stucco, or shingles. Hatches and fills are widely used in mechanical, landscaping, civil, structural, and architectural details as a tool to aid in clear communication. Be sure that your hatch patterns add to the readability of your drawings and do not hinder it by making the drawings appear cluttered.

To learn how to hatch and fill areas, you'll start with some of the visible surfaces in the front elevation of the cabin. You'll then move to the floor plan and then hatch the floors and put hatch patterns and fills in the walls and a gradient on the balcony. You'll use the Hatch and Gradient dialog box for all hatches and gradients. It's a tool with many options that you can use to create a sense of depth or texture to your drawings.

A key part of a hatch pattern is the boundary of the pattern. You define the area being hatched through a procedure called *ray casting* in which AutoCAD searches the drawing for lines or objects to serve as the hatch boundary.

Hatching the Front Elevation

Hatches and fills should be on their own layers so they can be turned off or frozen without also making other objects invisible. You'll begin the exercise by creating new layers for the hatches and assigning colors to them:

1. Open the Cabin10b.dwg drawing. It should contain the floor plan, elevations, and the door schedule. Freeze the layers for the right, left, and back elevations and, if necessary, the table, title block, and grid.

T I P   To see the best visual effect from putting hatch patterns on the front elevation, change the background color for the drawing area to white. Choose Tools ➣ Options to open the Options dialog box, and then click the Display tab. Click the Colors button, and make the change.

2. Set up three new layers as follows:

Layer Name	Color
Hatch-elev-brown	42
Hatch-elev-gray	Gray (8)
Hatch-elev-black	Black (White) (7)

3. Make the Hatch-elev-gray layer current. Now any new objects you create will be assigned to this layer.

4. Click the Hatch icon on the Draw toolbar to open the Hatch And Gradient dialog box (see Figure 11.1). Be sure the expansion arrow in the lower-right corner is pointing to the left. If it isn't, click it to expand the dialog box to its full size. You'll use this dialog box to choose a pattern, set up the pattern's properties, and determine the method for specifying the boundary of the area to be hatched. The Hatch tab should be active. If it's not, click the tab. Predefined and ANSI31 should appear in the Type and Pattern drop-down lists, respectively. If not, open the lists, and select those options.

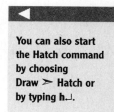

You can also start the Hatch command by choosing Draw ➢ Hatch or by typing h↵.

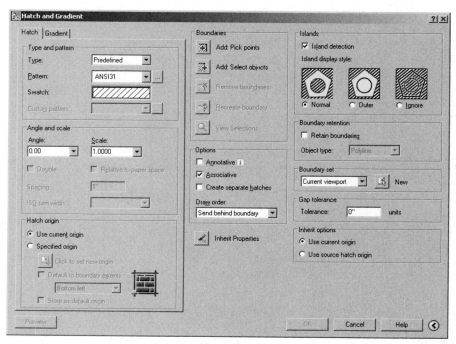

FIGURE 11.1: The Hatch And Gradient dialog box

5. Move to the right of the Pattern drop-down list, and click the Browse button to open the Hatch Pattern Palette dialog box (see Figure 11.2). This palette is where you select the actual hatch pattern that you'll use. Of the four tabs, ANSI is active, and the ANSI31 pattern is highlighted.

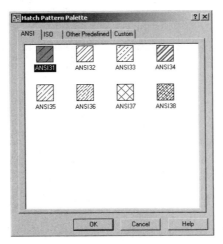

FIGURE 11.2: The Hatch Pattern Palette dialog box

6. Click the Other Predefined tab. Find the AR-RROOF pattern, click it, and then click OK. Back in the Hatch And Gradient dialog box, note that AR-RROOF has replaced ANSI31 in the Pattern drop-down list. A new pattern appears in the Swatch preview box, which is below the Pattern list (see Figure 11.3).

You can change the Scale and Angle settings in their drop-down lists, which are below the Swatch preview box. In the Angle drop-down list, the preset angle of 0.00 is fine, but you need to adjust the Scale setting.

7. The Scale drop-down list contains preset scale factors that range from 0.2500 to 2.0000. To set the scale to 6, you have to enter it manually. In the Scale drop-down list, delete 1.0000, and enter 6, but do not press ↵; just proceed to step 8, and continue the procedure. (That is, create the hatch, and then press ↵. The next time you open the dialog box in the current drawing, you'll see that 6 has been added to the drop-down list and is displayed as 6.0000.)

8. In the Options section in the middle of the dialog box, check the Associative option. Associative hatches automatically update the areas they cover whenever their boundaries change. If you delete any component of the boundary, however, the hatch becomes nonassociative.

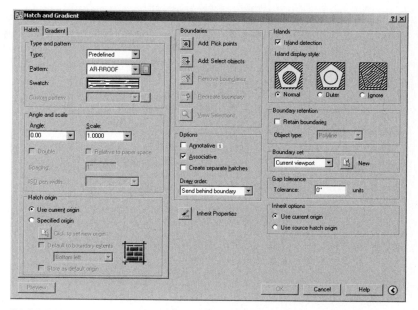

FIGURE 11.3: The Hatch And Gradient dialog box with the AR-RROOF pattern chosen

9. Move to the upper middle of the dialog box, and click the Add: Pick Points button. This returns you to the drawing.

10. In the elevation view, click the middle of the roof area. The lines that form the boundary of the roof area become dashed, displaying an outline of the area to be hatched (see Figure 11.4).

FLOOR PLAN

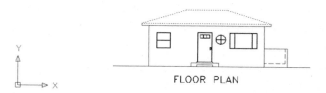

FLOOR PLAN

FIGURE 11.4: The roof's boundary is selected.

11. Right-click, and choose Preview from the shortcut menu. In the preview drawing, look at how the hatch will appear. This hatch looks fine for now.

12. Press ↵ or right-click to accept this hatch. The hatch is now placed in the roof area (see Figure 11.5).

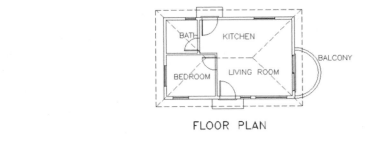

FLOOR PLAN

FLOOR PLAN

FIGURE 11.5: The finished hatch pattern in the roof area

13. Zoom in to a view of just the front elevation. Notice how the appearance of the hatch pattern changes as the roof gets larger on the screen.

Looking at Hatch Patterns

Let's take a short tour through the available patterns:

1. Start the Hatch command.

2. In the Hatch And Gradient dialog box, be sure that the Hatch tab is active. Then, click the Browse button next to the Pattern drop-down list to open the Hatch Pattern Palette dialog box.

3. Make the Other Predefined tab active if it isn't already. Look at the display of hatch patterns. Eleven pattern names begin with *AR-*, including the one just used. These patterns have been designed to look like architectural and building materials, which is why you see

the AR prefix. In addition to the roof pattern you just used, you'll see several masonry wall patterns, a couple of floor patterns, and one pattern each for concrete, wood shakes, and sand.

4. Scroll down the display, and observe the other non-AR patterns. They're geometrical patterns, some of which use common conventions to represent various materials.

5. Click the ANSI tab, and look at a few of the ANSI patterns. These are abstract line patterns developed by the American National Standards Institute and are widely used by public and private design offices in the United States.

6. Click the ISO tab. These are also abstract line patterns developed by another organization, the International Organization for Standardization. The Custom tab is empty unless custom hatch patterns have been loaded into your copy of AutoCAD.

7. Click Cancel in the Hatch Pattern Palette dialog box. Click Cancel again to close the Hatch And Gradient dialog box.

As you work with hatch patterns, you'll need to adjust the scale factor for each pattern so the patterns will look right when the drawing is printed. The AR patterns are drawn to be used with the scale factor set approximately to the default of one to one (displayed as 1.0000) and should need only minor adjustment. However, even though the treatment you just chose for the roof is an AR pattern, it is something of an anomaly. Instead of using it as is, you had to change its scale factor to 6.0000 to make it look right in the drawing.

T I P   When you're using one of the AR patterns, leave the scale factor at 1.0000 until you preview the hatch; then you can make changes. This rule also applies to the 14 ISO patterns displayed on the ISO tab of the Hatch Pattern Palette dialog box.

For the rest of the non-AR patterns, you'll need to assign a scale factor that imitates the true ratio of the scale at which you expect to print the drawing. Table 11.1 gives the true ratios of some of the standard scales used in architecture and construction.

TABLE 11.1: Standard Scales and Their Corresponding Ratios

Scale	True Scale Factor
1" = 1'-0"	12
½" = 1'-0"	24
¼" = 1'-0"	48
⅛" = 1'-0"	96
1/16" = 1'-0"	192

The scale is traditionally written by mixing inches with feet in the expression, which causes some confusion. For example, the third scale in the table, commonly called *quarter-inch scale*, shows that a quarter inch equals one foot. A true ratio of this scale must express the relationship using the same units, as in ¼" = 1'-0". Simplifying this expression to have no fractions, you can translate it to, say, 1" = 48". This is how you arrive at the true scale factor of 48, or the true ratio of 1:48.

As you continue through this chapter, take special note of the various scale factors used for different hatch patterns.

Hatching the Rest of the Front Elevation

You'll apply hatches to the foundation, front door, and front wall. You'll then work with some special effects.

Using a Concrete Hatch on the Foundation

For the foundation hatch, keep the Hatch-elev-gray layer current. Follow these steps:

1. To represent the top of the foundation, draw lines from the upper-left and upper-right corners of the step to the edges of the building (see the top of Figure 11.6). Activate osnaps as needed.

2. Start the Hatch command. Then, click the Browse button next to the Pattern drop-down list in the Hatch And Gradient dialog box.

3. Activate the Other Predefined tab. Find and select the AR-CONC pattern, and click OK.

4. Open the Scale drop-down list, and select 1.0000.

5. Click Add: Pick Points. Then, in the drawing, click once in each rectangle representing the foundation. The borders of these areas dash.

6. Right-click, and choose Preview. Then, right-click again to accept the hatch. The concrete hatch pattern is applied to the foundation surfaces (see the bottom of Figure 11.6).

FIGURE 11.6: The front elevation with foundation lines drawn (top) and the resulting hatches in place (bottom)

Hatching the Front Door and Wall

For the front door, you'll use a standard hatch pattern, ANSI31. This is the default pattern when you first use the Hatch command, but now the default pattern is the last one used. Here are the steps:

1. Start the Hatch command, and click the Browse button.

2. Activate the ANSI tab. Select ANSI31, and click OK.

3. In the Scale text box, highlight 1.0000, and enter 18. Then, click Add: Pick Points.

4. Click the middle of the door. The edges of the door and door still become dashed.

5. Right-click, and choose Preview. If you stopped with a simple rectangular door, right-click again. The door is hatched (see Figure 11.7). If not, then go on to step 6.

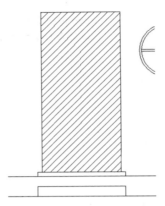

FIGURE 11.7: Hatching the simple door

If you created a more complex door, notice how the inner, closed areas are also dashed. AutoCAD refers to these nested, closed areas as *islands*, and you must instruct the program how to hatch these areas. For example, should the hatch pattern stop at the first island it encounters and discontinue filling in the areas altogether? Should it ignore any islands and fill the boundary completely? Should it stop at the perimeter of the first island, skip the area between that island and the perimeter of the next, and then restart the hatch pattern inside the next nested boundary? The third option is the default solution; unless you direct otherwise, AutoCAD will alternate hatching in every other closed island area.

6. Click the spacebar to return to the Hatch And Gradient dialog box. In the Islands area, click the Outer radio button or graphic. This instructs AutoCAD to stop the hatch at the first island and disregard any nested islands.

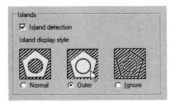

7. Click the Preview button at the lower-left corner of the dialog box, and then right-click to accept the hatch. The hatch stops at the first island, as shown in Figure 11.8.

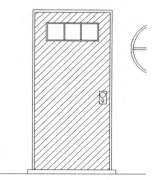

FIGURE 11.8: Hatching the complex door

8. Change the current layer to Hatch-elev-brown.

9. Start the Hatch command, and go through the same process to apply a hatch to the wall. This time, you'll use the AR-RSHKE pattern, which looks like wood shingles (often called *shakes*). Here is a summary of the steps:

   a. Click the Browse button.

   b. Activate the Other Predefined tab, select the AR-RSHKE pattern, and click OK.

   c. Set Scale to 1, and click Add: Pick Points.

   d. Pick any place on the front wall that's not inside a window or a window frame.

   e. Right-click, choose Preview, and then right-click again.

The wall is hatched (see Figure 11.9).

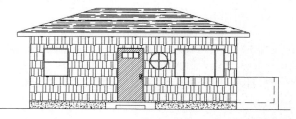

FIGURE 11.9: The hatching of the front wall is complete.

> **T I P**   Using the Preview option is not required each time you create a hatch, but it's a useful tool. It can prevent you from having to erase or undo and then re-create a hatch.

Using a Solid Fill Hatch

The windows will be hatched with a solid fill. You apply this hatch in the same way as the other hatches you've been using, except that you don't have a choice of scale or angle:

1. Make Hatch-elev-black the current layer.

2. Start the Hatch command, and then click the Swatch sample box. This is another method of opening the Hatch Pattern Palette dialog box. Make sure the Other Predefined tab is active, and select the first pattern, SOLID. Click OK. Back in the Hatch And Gradient dialog box, note that the text boxes for Scale and Angle aren't available. These don't apply to solid fills.

3. Click Add: Pick Points. In the drawing, select a point in the middle of each of the glass panes. You'll have to click the round window four times because of the mullions (the separators between the panes).

4. Right-click, choose Preview, and then right-click again. The windows have a solid black (or white) fill (see Figure 11.10).

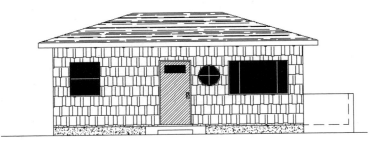

FIGURE 11.10: The windows with a solid fill hatch

> **T I P**   Depending on the quality and resolution of your monitor, solid fills can appear to flow over thin, nonhatched areas. This is only an illusion; the hatch actually stops at the border, as you can see if you zoom into an area in question.

Adding Special Effects

To finish the front elevation, you need to show shading and work a little with a curved surface.

Implying Shading with a Gradient

When shaded surfaces are illustrated on an exterior elevation, they give a three-dimensional quality to the surface. You'll put some additional hatching at the top portion of the wall to illustrate the shading caused by the roof overhang.

You need to hatch the top 2'-6" of the wall with a gradient. To determine the boundary line of the hatch, you'll turn off the layer that has the shake pattern. You'll then create a guideline to serve as the lower boundary of the hatch:

1. Make a new layer named Hatch-hidden, and make it current. Then, turn off the Hatch-elev-brown layer.

2. Use the Rectangle command and the Endpoint osnap to start a rectangle at the top of the left wall, just beneath the soffit.

3. At the `Specify other corner point or [Area/Dimensions/ Rotation]:` prompt, enter `@25',-2'6↵` to make a rectangle that extends the width of the cabin and down 2'-6" from the soffit. In Figure 11.11, the rectangle is in bold for clarity.

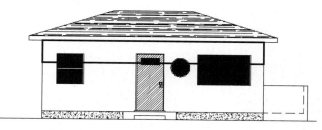

FIGURE 11.11: Creating the boundary for the forthcoming gradient

4. Make the Hatch-elev-black layer current, and then start the Hatch command. In the Hatch And Gradient dialog box, click the Gradient tab. This is similar in layout to the Hatch tab (see Figure 11.12).

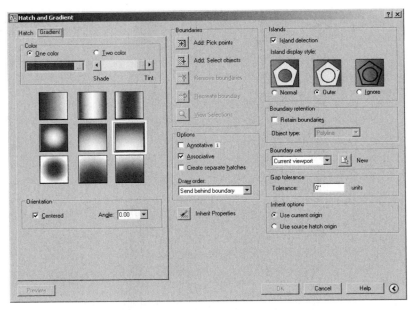

FIGURE 11.12: The Gradient tab of the Hatch And Gradient dialog box

5. In the Color area, make sure One Color is selected, and then click the Browse button next to the color swatch to open the Select Color dialog box. Unlike hatches, gradients do not get their color from the layer they are on; you must explicitly select the color. Select color 250 in the bottom row of swatches (see Figure 11.13), and then click OK.

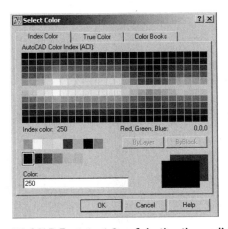

FIGURE 11.13: Selecting the gradient color

6. Click the middle sample pattern in the column on the right. This causes the gradient to shift from opaque to clear, in a linear fashion, from top to bottom.

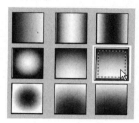

7. Click the Add: Pick Points button, and then click a point just below the soffit. Preview the hatch, and then accept it. You hatch should look like Figure 11.14.

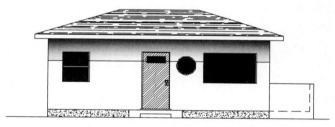

FIGURE 11.14: The gradient shaded effect

8. Freeze the Hatch-hidden layer, and thaw the Hatch-elev-brown layer. The rectangle disappears and the shakes return, but the gradient hides a portion of them. You need to move the shading behind the hatch pattern.

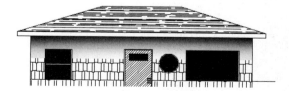

9. Select the gradient. At the command prompt, enter **draworder↵ b↵**. The gradient moves behind the shakes.

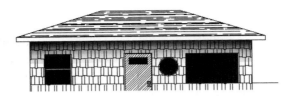

Start the Hatch command, and go through the same process to apply a hatch to the balcony wall. Here is a summary of the steps:

a. Access the Gradient tab.

b. Select the upper-left gradient sample, the pattern that gets lighter as it flows to the right. This is the opposite of the pattern you want, but it's the closest available.

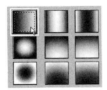

c. Set the Angle to 180, and uncheck and then recheck the Centered option. This is required to force AutoCAD to reevaluate the Angle value. The gradient pattern reverses direction.

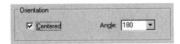

d. Click Add: Pick Points, and then click twice in the balcony, once in the large white area and again between the hidden lines and the solid lines. All the balcony lines should appear dashed.

e. Preview, and then accept the hatch. Your elevation should look like Figure 11.15.

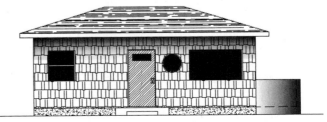

FIGURE 11.15: The gradient applied to the balcony area

Modifying a Hatch Pattern

You won't know for sure whether the hatch patterns will look right until you print the drawing, but you can at least see how they look together now that you've finished hatching the elevation:

1. Use Pan Realtime to display both the floor plan and the elevation on the screen (see the left of Figure 11.16). The roof hatch could be a little denser. You can use the Modify Hatch command to change the hatch scale.

2. Double-click the roof's hatch pattern or select it, right-click, and choose Hatch Edit from the context menu.

3. In the Hatch Edit dialog box, change the scale from 6.000 to 4.

4. Click OK. The roof hatch pattern is denser now (see the right of Figure 11.16).

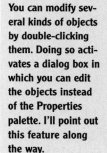

You can modify several kinds of objects by double-clicking them. Doing so activates a dialog box in which you can edit the objects instead of the Properties palette. I'll point out this feature along the way.

FLOOR PLAN

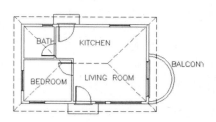

FLOOR PLAN

FLOOR PLAN

FLOOR PLAN

FIGURE 11.16: Full view of the drawing with the hatching completed for the front elevation (left) and the same view with the roof hatch modified (right)

5. Save this drawing as Cabin11a.dwg.

You can use the Hatch Edit command to change the pattern, scale, or angle of an existing hatch.

Using Hatches in the Floor Plan

In the floor plan, you can use hatches to fill in the walls or to indicate various kinds of floor surfaces. You'll start with the floors.

Hatching the Floors

So far, you've used only predefined hatch patterns—the 69 patterns that come with AutoCAD. You can also use a *user-defined pattern*, which is a series of parallel lines that you can set at any spacing and angle. If you want to illustrate square floor tile, select the Double option of the user-defined pattern, which uses two sets of parallel lines—one perpendicular to the other, resulting in a tiled effect.

Creating the User-Defined Hatch Pattern

You'll use the user-defined pattern for a couple of rooms and then return to the predefined patterns. Follow these steps:

1. With Cabin11a open, zoom in to the floor plan. Make the Headers and Doors layers visible if necessary, and thaw the Fixtures layer. You can use the header lines to help form a boundary line across an entryway to a room and to keep the hatch pattern from extending to another room.

2. With the floor plan in full view, zoom in to the bathroom, and freeze the Roof layer. Even if the rooflines are dashed, they will still form a boundary to a hatch.

3. Create a new layer called Hatch-plan-floor. Assign it color 142, and make it current.

4. Start the Hatch command. Be sure the Hatch tab is active.

5. Open the Type drop-down list, and select User-Defined. The list closes, and User Defined replaces Predefined as the current pattern type. The Pattern and Scale drop-down lists aren't available, but the Spacing text box is.

6. In the Spacing text box, change 1" to 9". Slightly above and to the left of that, click the Double check box to activate it. Then, click Add: Pick Points.

7. Back in the drawing, be sure no osnaps are running. Then, click a point in the bathroom floor, not touching the fixture lines or the door. Click the floor between the door swing and the door, being careful to not touch the door.

8. Right-click, and choose Preview from the shortcut menu. The tiled hatch pattern should fill the bathroom floor and stop at the header while not going onto the door or fixtures (see Figure 11.17). If the tile pattern looks OK, right-click again.

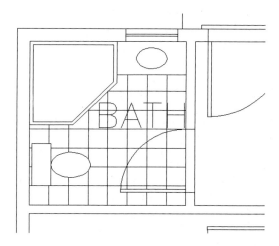

FIGURE 11.17: The tiled hatch pattern in place

Note that the user-defined pattern has no scale factor to worry about. You simply set the distance between lines in the Spacing text box.

 W A R N I N G If you can't get the Hatch command to hatch the desired area, you might have left a gap between some of the lines serving as the hatch boundary. This can prevent AutoCAD from being able to find the boundary you intend to use. Zoom in to the areas where objects meet, and check to see that they really do meet or increase the Gap Tolerance value on the right side of the dialog box.

Controlling the Origin of the Hatch Pattern

Often, a designer wants to lay out the tile pattern such that the pattern is centered in the room or starts along one particular edge. For this project, the tiles are set to start in the center of the room and move out to the edges, where they're cut to fit. You'll use the HPORIGIN setting to set this up in the bedroom:

1. Use Pan Realtime to slide the drawing up until the bedroom occupies the screen. Use Zoom Realtime to zoom out if you need to do so.

2. Turn Otrack on (on the status bar), and set the Midpoint osnap to be running.

3. Start the Hatch command. In the Hatch Origin area in the lower-left corner, select the Specified Origin radio button, and then click the Click To Set New Origin button.

4. Back in the drawing, place the cursor at the midpoint of the inside wall line on the left. A cross (called a *tracking point*) appears inside the triangular Midpoint osnap symbol. Don't click.

5. Move to the wall line at the upper part of the room, and do the same thing. Then, move the cursor straight down until it's positioned directly to the right of the first acquired tracking point. When the cursor is positioned properly, two tracking lines and a tooltip appear (see the top of Figure 11.18). Click. This sets the origin of any subsequently created hatch patterns at the center of this room.

6. The user-defined pattern type is still current, and the spacing is set to 9". Change the spacing to 12". Be sure Double is still checked, and then click Add: Pick Points.

7. In the drawing, pick a point anywhere in the middle of the bedroom and between the door swing and the door, similar to what you did in the bathroom. Right-click, and choose Preview.

8. Inspect the drawing to see whether the hatch looks right, and then right-click again. This places the hatch of 12" tiles in the bedroom (see the bottom of Figure 11.18). Note how the pattern is centered left to right and top to bottom.

The default setting for HPORIGIN is 0,0, or the origin of the drawing. Each time you change this setting, all subsequent hatch patterns will use the new setting as their origin. For most hatches, the origin isn't important; but if you need to control the location of tiles or specific points of other hatch patterns, you can reset the hatch origin before you create the hatch.

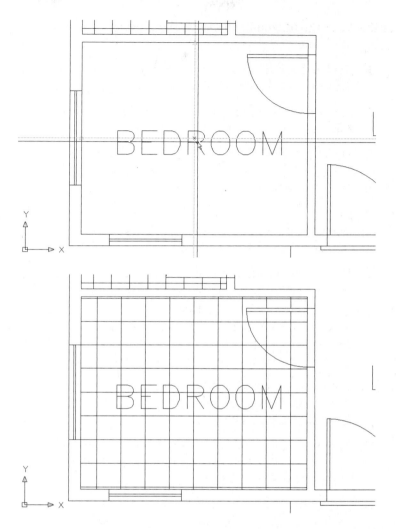

FIGURE 11.18: Hatching the bedroom: the two tracking lines (top) and the finished, centered hatch (bottom)

Finishing the Hatches for the Floors

To finish hatching the floors, you'll use a parquet pattern from the set of predefined patterns in the living room and kitchen and another user-defined pattern on the balcony:

1. Use Pan Realtime and Zoom Realtime to adjust the view so it includes the living room, kitchen, and balcony.

2. Start the Hatch command, and set the current pattern type to Predefined.

3. Click the Browse button, and activate the Other Predefined tab. Select the AR-PARQ1 pattern. Set the scale to 1, and be sure the angle is set to zero. Then, click Add: Pick Points.

4. Click anywhere in the living room. Then, click between each of the door swings and doors for the front and back doors. Check the dashed boundary line to be sure that it follows the outline of the floor.

5. If any of the text appears dashed as well, choose Ignore in the Islands section of the Hatch And Gradient dialog box.

6. Right-click, and choose Preview from the menu. The squares look a little small.

7. Press Esc to return to the Hatch And Gradient dialog box. Reset the scale to 1.33.

8. Click the Preview button. This looks better. Right-click to accept the hatch. The parquet pattern is placed in the living room and kitchen (see Figure 11.19).

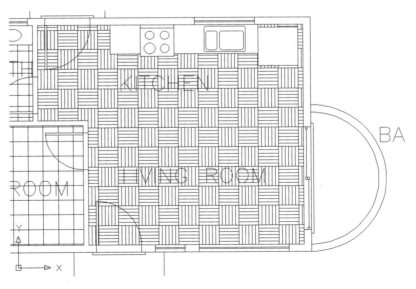

FIGURE 11.19: The parquet hatch in the living room and kitchen

T I P   If you find the text difficult to read with the dense hatch pattern, you have a few options. You can place a rectangle, on the Hatch-hidden layer, around the text and then instruct AutoCAD to respect the islands they create. You can change the text to a filled-in, TrueType font that stands out better, or you can instruct AutoCAD to plot the text denser than the hatches.

9. Start the Hatch command. In the Hatch Origin area, be sure Specified Origin is selected, and then click the Click To Set New Origin button. The Midpoint osnap should still be running. Pick the threshold line that extends across the sliding-glass door opening near its midpoint.

10. Back in the Hatch And Gradient dialog box, set User-Defined to be the pattern type.

11. Clear the Double check box. Set the spacing to 0'6". Click Add: Pick Points.

12. Click anywhere on the balcony floor.

13. Right-click, and then choose Preview. Right-click again. The balcony floor is hatched with parallel lines that are 6" apart (see Figure 11.20).

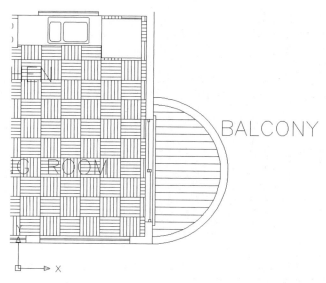

F I G U R E   1 1 . 2 0 :   The user-defined hatch on the balcony floor

Modifying the Shape of Hatch Patterns

The next exercise will demonstrate how hatches are associative. An *associative* hatch pattern automatically updates when you modify the part of a drawing that is serving as the boundary for the pattern. You'll be changing the current drawing, so before you begin making those changes, save the drawing as it is. Follow these steps:

1. Zoom out and pan to get the floor plan and front elevation in the view.

2. Save this drawing as Cabin11b. You'll use the Stretch command to modify it.

3. Zoom in to the front elevation. Turn on polar tracking.

4. Click the Stretch button on the Modify toolbar.

5. Pick a point above and to the right of the ridge of the roof in elevation. Drag a window down and to the left until a crossing selection window encloses the ridgeline of the roof (see the top of Figure 11.21). Click to complete the window. Then, press ↵ to finish the selection process.

6. For the base point, choose a point in the blank area to the right of the elevation.

7. Hold the cursor directly above the point you picked so that the polar tracking line and tooltip appear; then, enter 3'↵.

8. The roof is now steeper and the hatch pattern has expanded to fill the new roof area (see the bottom of Figure 11.21).

9. Use Zoom Previous. Save this drawing as Cabin11c.dwg.

Hatches are a necessary part of many drawings. You've seen a few of the possibilities AutoCAD offers for using them in plans and elevations.

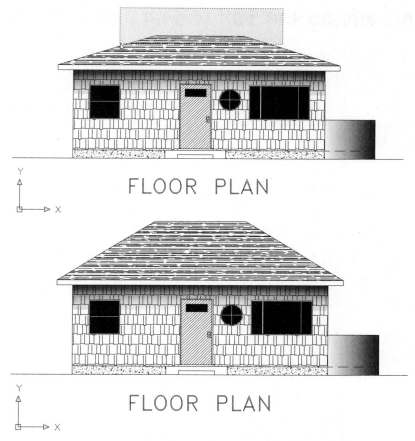

FLOOR   PLAN

FLOOR   PLAN

FIGURE   11 . 21 :   The crossing selection window (top) and the modified roof with the adjusted hatch pattern (bottom)

Creating and Managing Tool Palettes

If you find yourself using particular hatch patterns over and over in various drawings, make them available at a moment's notice instead of setting them up each time. AutoCAD's tool palettes let you do just that. Now you'll go through the process of setting up a couple of palettes and customizing them to contain specific hatch patterns, blocks, and commands that are used with the cabin drawings. From these exercises, you'll get the information you need to set up your own custom palettes.

Creating a New Tool Palette

You'll create a new tool palette and then populate it with the blocks you've used so far in the cabin drawing:

1. Click the Tool Palettes icon on the Standard toolbar to display the palettes on the screen. Then, place the cursor on a blank space on the palettes, right-click, and choose New Palette. A new blank palette displays with a small text box on it.

2. Enter **Cabin Blocks**↵ to name the new palette.

3. Open the DesignCenter by clicking the DesignCenter button on the Standard toolbar or by entering **adc**↵.

4. On the left side of the DesignCenter, navigate to the Cabin11b drawing. When you find it, click the + sign to its left. The list of types of drawing content in it opens below the drawing.

5. Select Blocks from this list. Now the right side of the DesignCenter displays the three blocks in Cabin11b, either as small images or by name only. Click the arrow on the Views button in the upper-right corner of the DesignCenter, and choose List as the view option (see Figure 11.22).

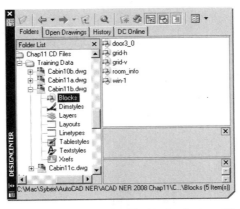

FIGURE 11.22: The DesignCenter with the List view option

6. Select door3_0, and then hold down the Shift key and click win-1 to select all five blocks. Click and drag the five blocks over to the new palette. Small images of the blocks appear on the Cabin Blocks palette (see Figure 11.23), and they're now available for any drawing. Simply drag a block off the palette onto the drawing. You can then fine-tune its location, rotate it, and so forth. Any layers used by the block are also brought into the drawing.

7. Place the cursor on door3_0 on the new palette, right-click, and then select Properties to open the Tool Properties dialog box. It displays information about door3_0 (see Figure 11.24).

8. Close the Tool Properties dialog box.

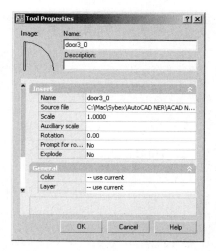

FIGURE 11.23:
The new Cabin Blocks tool palette

FIGURE 11.24:
The Tool Properties dialog box

Setting Up a Palette for Hatches

To create a palette for hatches, you'll create and name a new palette using the same procedure as in the preceding section, but the hatches get onto the palette in a different way:

1. Right-click a blank space on the Cabin Blocks palette, choose New Palette, and then enter **Cabin Hatches.**⏎ in the text box.

2. Zoom in on the front elevation of the cabin, and click the roof hatch to display a grip.

3. Move the cursor to a portion of the roof hatch that isn't close to the grip, and then click and drag the hatch pattern over to the new palette (see Figure 11.25).

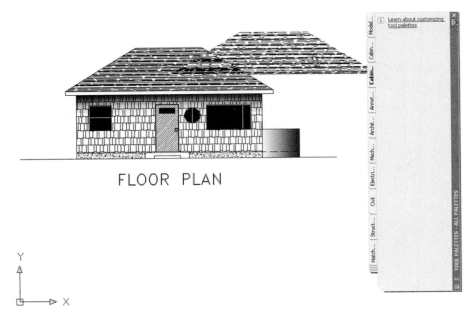

FIGURE 11.25: Copying the roof hatch to the new palette

4. When the cursor is over the palette and a horizontal line appears there, release the mouse button. The roof hatch is now positioned on the palette and available for use in any drawing. Simply drag it off the palette and into the enclosed area in the drawing that you want to hatch with the pattern.

5. Place the cursor on the new swatch of AR-RROOF, right-click, and choose Properties. The Tool Properties dialog box opens (see Figure 11.26).

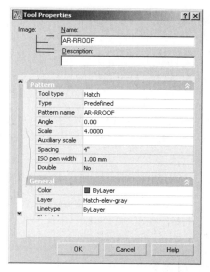

FIGURE 11.26: The Tool Properties dialog box for the hatch pattern

6. Change the name from AR-RROOF to **Cabin Roof**. Enter a description of what the hatch represents, such as **Composition Roofing**. Notice that the hatch has the angle and scale used on the roof and that it's also on the Hatch-elev-gray layer. Use the slider at the left to view all the properties. Click OK to close the dialog box and update the palette (see Figure 11.27).

FIGURE 11.27: The Cabin Hatches palette after the first hatch is renamed

By using the Tool Properties dialog box, you can also give hatches color. You can place all the hatches that you've used for the cabin so far on the palette in the same manner. They retain the properties they had in the original drawing, but by using the Tool Properties dialog box, you can change those properties.

Creating a Palette for Commands

Take a moment to look at a few of the sample palettes that come with AutoCAD, and check the properties of some of the items that you see. In addition to blocks and hatches, there are also command icons. These are placed on the palette in a slightly different way from blocks and hatches:

1. Right-click the Cabin Hatches palette in a blank area, and choose New Palette from the shortcut menu.

2. Name the new palette **Commands**.

3. Be sure that any objects created by the commands you want to place on the Commands palette are visible on your screen. If they aren't in the drawing area, pan or zoom to display them, or create new ones.

4. Click an object such as a line that you want to be able to reproduce with a single command, and then drag it to the palette just as you dragged the hatches in the previous section. This adds the object's creation command to the palette.

5. Drag several additional objects of various kinds onto the Commands palette (see Figure 11.28).

FIGURE 11.28: The Commands palette with four command icons

When you need to use one of these commands, click the icon on the palette.

If you set the palettes to Auto-hide, they fold under the palette title bar. When you put your cursor on the bar, the palettes display and then hide a moment after your cursor moves off the palettes. To activate Auto-hide, right-click the palette title bar, and choose Auto-hide from the shortcut menu.

This has been a brief introduction to the palette feature. I encourage you to experiment with the various options to become familiar with them, so you can use them as you find the need. Try right-clicking a blank portion of a palette and investigating the commands available on the resulting shortcut menu. From this menu, you can delete any palette, and you can copy and paste tools from one palette to another.

If You Would Like More Practice...

If you would like to practice what you've learned in this chapter, here are a couple of extra exercises.

Creating a Hatch Pattern for the Roof in Plan View

To create your hatch pattern for the roof, make these changes and additions to Cabin09c:

1. Thaw the Roof layer, make it current, and change its linetype from Dashed to Continuous. Turn off all other layers.

2. Put a chimney in the roof approximately as shown on the top of Figure 11.29. Close the gaps in the rooflines using the Line command.

3. Create a new layer called Hatch-plan-roof. Assign it the same color you're using for the Roof layer. Make this new layer current.

4. Apply the AR-RSHKE pattern to each quadrant of the roof, changing the rotation angle by 90° for each adjacent area. Use a scale of 1.0000. When you pick the quadrant with the chimney, select the Outer island option, and then pick a point in the quadrant that is outside the chimney rectangle. The result should look like the middle of Figure 11.29.

5. Move the chimney rectangle and circle to a different location in the quadrant, and see the results (see the bottom of Figure 11.29). The hatch adjusts. What happens if you move the circle and rectangle that make up the chimney to a different quadrant or to a location completely off the roof? Try it.

6. Don't save these changes.

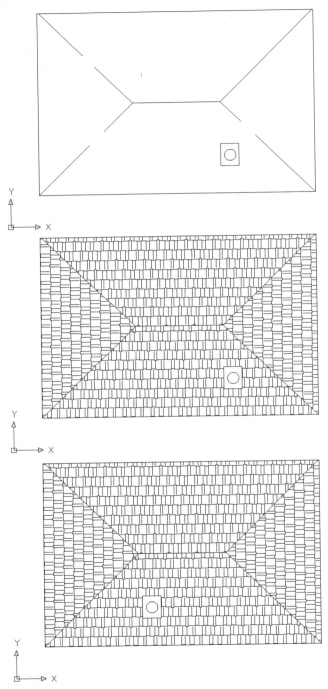

FIGURE 11.29: The roof with continuous lines and with a chimney (top), the new hatch for the roof (middle), and the roof hatch with the chimney moved (bottom)

Creating Your Hatch Palette

It's true that you can use any hatch pattern to represent anything you want, but most professions follow some sort of standard, even if loosely. The ANSI31 pattern of parallel lines is probably the most widely used pattern. Although according to the ANSI standard it "officially" represents Iron, Brick, and Stone Masonry, it's universally accepted as any cross-section view of any material—that is, the part of the object that was sliced through to make the view.

Create a new palette of hatches that you might use in your work. Use the same method demonstrated in the previous section of this chapter:

1. Open the DesignCenter, and find `acad.pat`. If you performed a typical installation of AutoCAD, the file should be in the `C:\Program Files\AutoCAD 2008\UserDataCache\Support` folder. LT users should substitute `AutoCAD LT 2008` for `AutoCAD 2008` in the path. Open that file.

2. Use the Large Icon view to view the patterns on the right side of the DesignCenter.

3. On the right side of your screen, create a new tool palette, and name it **Hatches**.

4. Back in the DesignCenter, scroll through and drag any patterns you might use over to the new Hatches palette.

5. Close the DesignCenter.

6. Hold the cursor briefly over the name of each hatch to display a tooltip that describes the purpose of the hatch.

7. If you've brought any patterns to the palette that you don't want there after all, right-click each of them, and choose Delete from the shortcut menu. Don't worry about changing any of the properties, such as Scale or Rotation. That will come later, as you begin to use these hatches in your own work.

8. Check out the tools on the Hatches sample palette that comes with AutoCAD. To access a list of all the available sample palettes, move the cursor over to the tabs that identify each palette. Then, move it down just below the lowest tab where you see the edges of the tabs that are hidden. Click the edges of the hidden tabs, and choose a palette from the list to be brought forward and displayed as the top tab. Right-click some of the hatches or fills, and note how the rotation and scale vary for hatches that look the same on the palette. One

hatch, such as ANSI31, might be repeated several times on the same palette, with each occurrence having a different scale or rotation. Note that the names of the hatches and fills have been removed from the sample hatch palette. Can you figure out how to do this or how to store the names?

Are You Experienced?

Now you can...

☑ **create a predefined hatch pattern and apply it to a drawing**

☑ **set up and apply user-defined hatch patterns**

☑ **create a polar array of a line**

☑ **use lines to indicate a curved surface**

☑ **modify the scale of a hatch pattern**

☑ **modify the shape of a hatch pattern**

☑ **control the origin of a hatch pattern**

☑ **create and populate a tool palette for blocks, hatches, or commands**

CHAPTER 12

Dimensioning a Drawing

- ▶ Setting up a dimension style
- ▶ Dimensioning the floor plan of the cabin
- ▶ Modifying existing dimensions
- ▶ Modifying existing dimension styles

Dimensions are the final ingredient to add to your cabin drawing. To introduce you to dimensioning, I'll follow a pattern similar to the one I used in Chapter 8 on text.

Introducing Dimension Styles

Dimension styles are similar to text styles but give you more options to control. You set them up in the same way, but many parameters control the various parts of dimensions, including the dimension text.

Before you start setting up a dimension style, you need to make a few changes to your drawing to prepare it for dimensioning:

1. Open Cabin11b.dwg, the cabin without the extended roof, and zoom in to the upper half of the drawing.

2. Create a new layer called Dim1. Assign white as its color, and make it current.

3. Freeze all the remaining layers except Balcony, Doors, Steps, Text1, Roof, Walls, and Windows.

4. Set the Endpoint osnap to be running.

5. Set the status bar so that only the Osnap and Model buttons are in their on positions.

6. Right-click any button on any toolbar on the screen to display the toolbar menu. Click Dimension to open the Dimension toolbar on the drawing area in the form of a floating toolbar.

7. Move the Dimension toolbar to the top of the drawing area, being careful to avoid docking it. (You learned about moving toolbars around on the screen in Chapter 1.) Your drawing will look like Figure 12.1.

Making a New Dimension Style

Each dimension has several components: the dimension line, arrows or tick marks, extension lines, and the dimension text (see Figure 12.2). An extensive set of variables that is stored with each drawing file controls the appearance and location of these components. You work with these variables through a series of dialog boxes designed to make setting up a dimension style as easy and trouble free as possible. Remember that AutoCAD is designed to be used by drafters from many trades and professions, each of which has its own standards for drafting. To satisfy these folks' widely varied needs, AutoCAD dimensioning features have many options and settings for controlling the appearance and placement of dimensions in drawings.

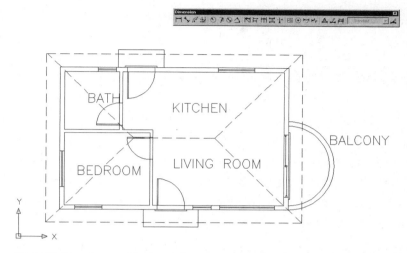

FIGURE 12.1: The floor plan of the cabin with the Dimension toolbar at the top of the drawing area

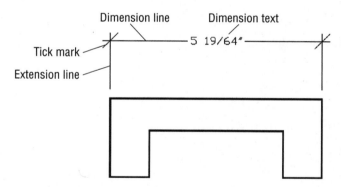

FIGURE 12.2: The parts of a dimension

Naming a Dimension Style

Every dimension variable has a default setting, and these variables as a group constitute the default Standard dimension style. As in defining text styles, the procedure is to copy the Standard dimension style and rename the copy—in effect, making a new style that is a copy of the default style. You then make changes to this new style so it has the settings you need to dimension your drawing. Follow these steps:

 1. Click the Dimension Style button on the right end of the Dimension toolbar to open the Dimension Style Manager dialog box (see

Figure 12.3). On the top left in the Styles list box, you'll see Standard highlighted.

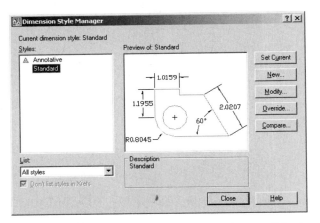

FIGURE 12.3: The Dimension Style Manager dialog box

2. Click the New button on the right side of the Dimension Style Manager dialog box to open the Create New Dimension Style dialog box.

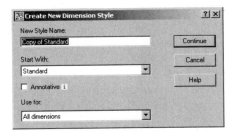

3. In the New Style Name text box, Copy of Standard is highlighted. Enter **DimPlan**, but don't press ↵ yet. Notice that Standard is in the Start With drop-down list just below. Because it's the current and only dimension style in this drawing, the new dimension style you're about to define will begin as a copy of the Standard style. This is similar to the way in which new text styles are defined (as you saw in Chapter 8). The Use For drop-down list allows you to choose the kinds of dimensions to which the new style will be applied. In this case, it's all dimensions, so you don't need to change this setting.

4. Click the Continue button. The Create New Dimension Style dialog box is replaced by the New Dimension Style: DimPlan dialog box (see Figure 12.4). It has seven tabs containing parameters that define the dimension style. You have created a new dimension style that is a copy of the Standard style, and now you'll make the changes necessary to set up DimPlan to work as the main dimension style for the floor plan of the cabin.

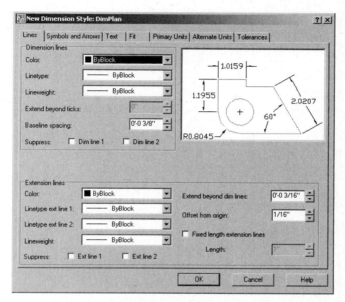

FIGURE 12.4: The New Dimension Style dialog box with DimPlan as the current style and Lines as the active tab

5. Be sure the Lines tab is active (on top). If it's not, click it.

Using the Lines Tab

You'll use the Lines tab to control the appearance of the dimension and extension lines:

1. In the Dimension Lines area, you need to change the Extend Beyond Ticks setting from 0" to 3/32", but this setting is inaccessible right now because the default arrowheads don't allow extensions of the dimension line.

2. In the Extension Lines area, highlight the Extend Beyond Dim Lines setting, change it to 1/8", and then press ↵. This setting controls how far the extension line will extend beyond the dimension line.

You'll return to both of these after you work on the settings in the next tab.

Setting Up the Symbols And Arrows Tab

The Symbols And Arrows tab has settings that control the appearance of arrowheads and other symbols related to dimensioning:

1. Click the Symbols And Arrows tab, and then, in the Arrowheads area, click the down arrow in the first drop-down list to open the list of arrowheads.

2. Click Architectural Tick. The drop-down list closes with Architectural Tick displayed in the first and second drop-down lists. In the preview window above the Arc Length Symbol area, a graphic displays the new arrowhead type. It doesn't display the actual thickness that the tick mark line will have in your drawing.

3. In the Arrow Size spin box, highlight the default setting, and change it to 1/8".

4. Click the Lines tab. In the Dimension Lines area, the Extend Beyond Tick setting is available. Highlight the 0, and change it to 3/32". Then, click the Symbols And Arrows tab. After the changes, the tab should look like Figure 12.5.

> **Tick marks are used almost exclusively by the architecture profession. This list contains options for several kinds of arrowheads, dots, and so on.**

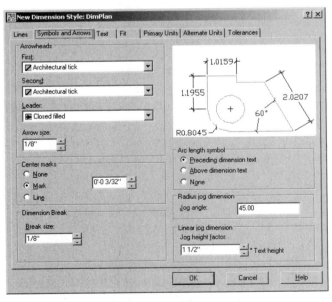

FIGURE 12.5: The Symbols And Arrows tab with the settings for the Dim-Plan style

Making Changes in the Text Tab

The settings in the Text tab control the appearance of dimension text and how it's located relative to the dimension and extension lines:

1. Click the Text tab in the New Dimension Style dialog box. Settings in three areas affect the appearance and location of dimension text. Look ahead to Figure 12.6 to see the Text tab. The preview window appears in all tabs and is updated automatically as you modify settings. Move to the Text Appearance area in the upper-left corner of the dialog box, where six settings control how the text looks. You're concerned with only two of them.

2. Click the Browse button that sits at the right end of the Text Style drop-down list to open the Text Style dialog box. Set up a new text style called Dim that has the following parameters:

   ▶ romand.shx font

   ▶ 0'-0" height

   ▶ 0.8000 width factor

   ▶ All other settings at their default

   If you need a reminder about creating text styles, refer to Chapter 8. Apply this text style, click the Set Current button, and then close the Text Style dialog box.

3. Back in the Text tab, open the Text Style drop-down list, and select the new Dim style from the list.

4. Change the Text Height setting to 3/32".

 T I P Setting the text height to 0' 0" in the Text Style dialog box allows the Text Height parameter of the dimension style to dictate the actual height of the text in the drawing. This allows many different dimension styles to use the same text style, each producing text with different heights. If you give the text a nonzero height in the Text Style dialog box, then that height is always used, and the Text Height parameter of the dimension style is disregarded.

5. Move down to the Text Placement area. These settings determine where the text is located, vertically and horizontally, relative to the dimension line. You need to change two settings here.

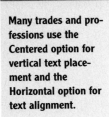

Many trades and professions use the Centered option for vertical text placement and the Horizontal option for text alignment.

6. Open the Vertical drop-down list, and select Above. At this setting, the text will sit above the dimension line and not break the line into two segments. Set Offset From Dim Line to 1/32".

7. Move to the Text Alignment area. The radio buttons control whether dimension text is aligned horizontally or with the direction of the dimension line. The ISO Standard option aligns text depending on whether the text can fit between the extension lines. Only one of the buttons can be active at a time. Horizontal should already be active. Click the Aligned With Dimension Line button. Notice how the appearance and location of the text changes in the preview window. This finishes your work in this tab; the settings should look like those in Figure 12.6.

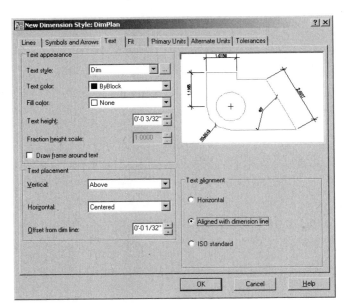

FIGURE 12.6: The Text tab with settings for the DimPlan style

This dialog box has four more tabs with settings, but you'll be making changes in only two of them: Fit and Primary Units.

Working with Settings in the Fit Tab

The settings in the Fit tab control the overall scale factor of the dimension style and how the text and arrowheads are placed when the extension lines are too close together for both text and arrows to fit:

1. Click the Fit tab in the New Dimension Style dialog box. Look ahead to Figure 12.7 to see the Fit tab.

2. In the upper-left corner, in the Fit Options area, click the Text radio button. This causes the text to be moved from between the extension lines when it won't fit properly.

3. In the Text Placement area, click the Over Dimension Line, Without Leader radio button.

4. Make no changes in the Fine Tuning area for now. Move to the Scale For Dimension Features area. Be sure the Use Overall Scale Of radio button is active. Set the scale to 96. The settings in the Fit tab should look like those in Figure 12.7.

For your own work, you might have to experiment with the settings in this tab.

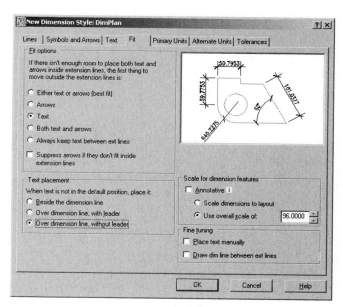

FIGURE 12.7: The new settings in the Fit tab

Setting Up the Primary Units Tab

In the preview window, you might have noticed that the numbers in the dimension text maintain a decimal format with four decimal places, rather than the feet and inches format of the current architectural units. Dimensions have their own units setting, independent of the basic units for the drawing as a whole. In the Primary Units tab, you'll set the dimension units:

1. Click the Primary Units tab, and take a peek ahead at Figure 12.8 to see how it's organized. It has two areas: Linear Dimensions and Angular Dimensions, each of which has several types of settings.

2. In the Linear Dimensions area, starting at the top, make the following changes:

    a. Change the Unit Format setting from Decimal to Architectural.

    b. Change the Fraction Format setting to Diagonal.

    c. In the Zero Suppression area, uncheck 0 Inches.

> **N O T E**   Zero Suppression controls whether the zero is shown for feet when the dimensioned distance is less than one foot and whether the zero is shown for inches when the distance is a whole number of feet. For the cabin drawing, you'll suppress the zero for feet, but you'll show the zero for inches. So, 9" will appear as 9", and 3' will appear as 3'-0".

3. In the Angular Dimensions area, leave Decimal Degrees as the Units Format setting, and change Precision to two decimal places, as you did for the basic drawing units in Chapter 3. For now, leave the Zero Suppression area as it is. After these changes, the Primary Units tab looks like Figure 12.8.

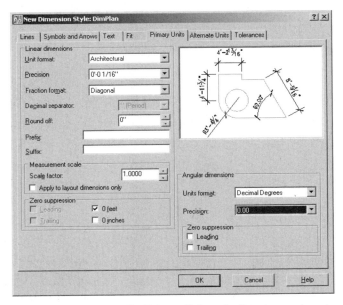

FIGURE 12.8: The Primary Units tab after changes have been made

Of the last two tabs, any industry involved in global projects can use the Alternate Units tab, and the mechanical engineering trades and professions use the

Tolerances tab. You won't need to make any changes to these tabs for this tutorial, but you'll take a brief look at them in the following sections.

It's time to save these setting changes to the new DimPlan dimension style and begin dimensioning the cabin:

1. Click the OK button at the bottom of the New Dimension Style dialog box. You're returned to the Dimension Style Manager dialog box (see Figure 12.9).

DimPlan appears with a gray background in the Styles list box, along with Standard and Annotative. In the lower-right corner of the dialog box, in the Description area, you'll see the following information about the new style: the name of the original style that the new style is based on and the changes that were made to the original style to create the new style. Unfortunately, the area is much too small to display all the changes you've made, so use Table 12.1 later in this section as a reference.

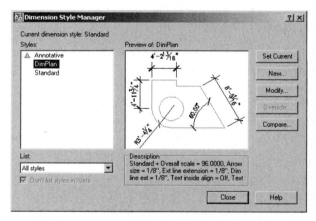

FIGURE 12.9: The Dimension Style Manager dialog box with DimPlan listed

2. Click DimPlan to highlight it in a dark blue; then, click the Set Current button. Finally, click the Close button. You're returned to your drawing, and the Dimension toolbar displays DimPlan in the Dim Style Control drop-down list. This indicates that DimPlan is now the current dimension style.

You have made changes to 16 settings that control dimensions. This isn't too many, considering that there are more than 50 dimension settings. Table 12.1 summarizes the changes you've made to make the dimensions work with the cabin drawing.

TABLE 12.1: Changes Made So Far

Tab	Setting	Default Setting	DimPlan
Lines	Arrowheads	Closed Filled	Architectural Tick
	Arrow Size	3/16"	1/8"
	Dim Line – Extend Beyond Ticks	0"	3/32"
	Ext. Line – Extend Beyond Ticks	3/16"	1/8"
Text	Text Style	Standard	Dim
	Text Height	3/16"	3/32"
	Text Vertical Justification	Centered	Above
	Offset From Dim Line	3/16"	1/32"
	Text Alignment	Horizontal	Aligned With Dimension Line
Fit	Fit Options	Either Text or Arrow (Best Fit)	Text
	Text Placement	Beside The Dimension Line	Over Dimension Line, Without Leader
	Overall Scale	1.0000	96.0000
Primary Units	Unit Format	Decimal	Architectural
	Fraction Format	Horizontal	Diagonal
	Zero Suppression	Feet, Inches	Feet only
	Angular Precision	No decimal places	Two decimal places

The next two sections describe dimensioning features that you won't use in the cabin project. If you would rather begin dimensioning the cabin and look at this material later, skip to the "Placing Dimensions on the Drawing" section.

You'll change a few more settings throughout the rest of this chapter as you begin to dimension the cabin in the next set of exercises. You'll now look briefly at the Alternate Units and Tolerances tabs.

Exploring the Alternate Units Tab

If your work requires your dimensions to display both metric and architectural units, use the Alternate Units tab in the New Dimension Style dialog box. In the example shown here, the primary units setting is Architectural, which you set in the previous section. Now you'll set up the alternate units:

1. Click the Dimension Style button on the Dimension toolbar.

2. Highlight DimPlan if it's not already highlighted.

3. Click the Modify button.

4. Click the Alternate Units tab. (Look ahead to Figure 12.10 to see what the style will look like when you're finished here.) You'll make only three or four changes on this tab.

5. In the upper-left corner of the tab, select the Display Alternate Units check box. This makes the rest of the settings on the tab available to you for making changes.

6. If Decimal isn't displayed in the Unit Format drop-down list, select it.

7. If Precision isn't set to 0, open that drop-down list, and select that level of precision.

8. Set Multiplier For Alt Units to 25.4. This makes millimeters the alternate units.

9. In the lower-right quarter of the tab, in the Placement area, select Below Primary Value. This has the effect of placing the alternate units below the primary units and on the opposite side of the dimension line. The tab should look like the top of Figure 12.10, and if the cabin were dimensioned using alternate units, the resulting dimensions for the upper portion of the floor plan would look like the bottom of Figure 12.10.

10. Click the Cancel button; you don't need to save these settings. You won't be using alternate units when you dimension the cabin.

If you want centimeters to be the alternate units, change the Multiplier For Alt Units setting to 2.54, and set Precision to 0.00.

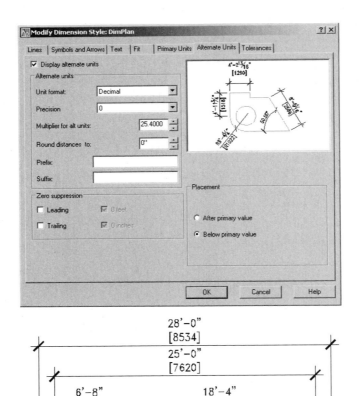

FIGURE 12.10: The Alternate Units tab after being set up for millimeters (top) and the resulting horizontal dimensions (bottom)

Exploring the Tolerances Tab

AutoCAD offers features whose options help you create several kinds of *tolerances* (allowable variances from the stated dimension). In the Tolerances tab, you have four methods for doing what is called *lateral tolerances*, the traditional kind of tolerance that most draftspeople use. This is the *plus or minus* kind of tolerance. Open the Modify Dimension Style dialog box, and look at the choices in the Method drop-down list shown in Figure 12.11.

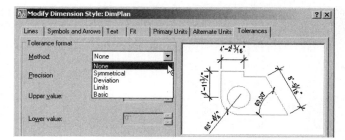

FIGURE 12.11: The top of the Tolerances tab, showing the Method drop-down list options

Each of these is a method for displaying a plus or minus type of tolerance:

Symmetrical   This method is for a single plus or minus expression after the base dimension. It's used when the upper allowable limit of deviation is identical to that for the lower limit, as in 1.0625 ± 0.0025.

Deviation   This method is for the instance in which the upper allowable deviation is different from that of the lower deviation. For example, the upper limit of the deviation can be +0.0025, and the lower limit can be −0.0005. The two deviation limits are stacked and follow the base dimension.

Limits   In this method, the tolerances are added or subtracted to the base dimension, resulting in maximum and minimum total values. The maximum is placed over the minimum. In the example for the Symmetrical method, 1.0650 is the maximum and on top of 1.0600, the minimum.

Basic   The base dimension is left by itself, and a box is drawn around it, indicating that the tolerances are general, apply to several or all dimensions in boxes, and are noted somewhere else in the drawing. Often, basic dimensions appear when a dimension is theoretical or not exact.

When you select one of these options, the settings in the tab become available. If you select Deviation, all settings become available:

Precision   Controls the overall precision of the tolerances.

Upper Value and Lower Value   The actual values of the tolerances.

Scaling For Height   The height of the tolerance text. A value of 1 here sets the tolerance text to match that of the base dimension. A value of greater than 1 makes the tolerance text greater than the base dimension text, and a value of less than 1 makes it smaller than the base dimension text.

Vertical Position   Where the base dimension is placed vertically relative to the tolerances. It can be in line with the upper or lower tolerance or in the middle.

The Zero Suppression options at the bottom, when checked, suppress extra zeros that occur before or after the decimal point. If you set up the Tolerances tab as shown in the top of Figure 12.12, a dimension looks like the one shown in the bottom of Figure 12.12.

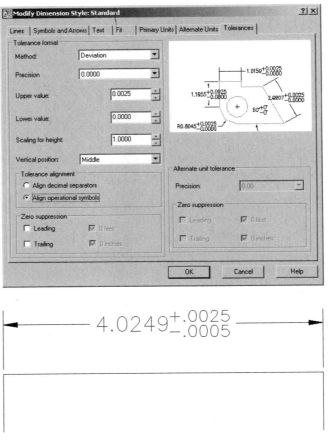

FIGURE 12.12: The Tolerances tab with some settings changed (top) and a dimension with deviation tolerances (bottom)

A more complex family of tolerances is available through the Dimension tool-bar. It's called *geometric tolerancing* and involves setting up a series of boxes that contain symbols and numbers that describe tolerance parameters for form, position, and other geometric features. Usually two to six boxes appear in a row, with the possibility of multiple rows. These all constitute the *feature control frame*, which eventually is inserted in the drawing and attached in some way to the relevant dimension. Follow these steps:

1. Click the Tolerance button on the Dimension toolbar to open the Geometric Tolerance dialog box, in which you set up the feature control frame. The black squares will contain symbols, and the white rectangles are for tolerance or datum values or for reference numbers.

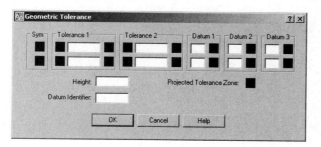

2. Click in the top SYM box on the left to open the Symbol window, which contains 14 standard symbols that describe the characteristic form or position that the tolerance is being used for. When you select one of the symbols, the window closes, and the symbol is inserted into the SYM box. Click the icon in the top row that consists of two concentric circles.

3. Click the first black square of Tolerance 1. This inserts a diameter symbol.

4. Click the last black square of Tolerance 1. The Material Condition window opens and displays the three material condition options. When you click one, it's inserted.

You can insert any of these three symbols in Tolerance 2 and Datum 1, 2, or 3, if you need them.

5. Fill in the actual tolerance value(s) and datum references in the text boxes.

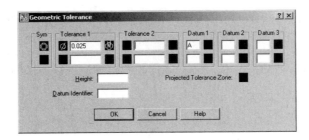

6. When you're finished, click OK. You can insert the feature control frame into your drawing like a block and reference it to a part or a dimension, as shown in Figure 12.13.

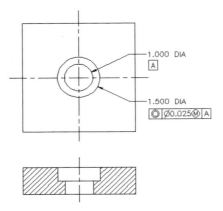

FIGURE 12.13: Geometric dimensioning on a machined part

This exercise was intended solely to show you the tools that AutoCAD provides for setting up the most commonly used lateral and geometric tolerances when you use the Tolerances tab in the Dimension Style dialog box and the Tolerance button on the Dimension toolbar. My intention here isn't to explain the methodology of geometric tolerances or the meanings of the various symbols, numbers, and letters used in them. That is a subject beyond the scope of this book.

Placing Dimensions on the Drawing

Upon returning to your drawing, it should still look almost exactly like Figure 12.1 (shown earlier), and it should have the following:

▶ A new layer called Dim1, which is current

▶ A new dimension style called DimPlan, which is current and is now displayed in the drop-down list on the Dimension toolbar

▶ Most of the layers frozen

▶ The Endpoint osnap running

▶ On the status bar: Ortho, Polar, and (for AutoCAD) Otrack off

▶ A new text style called Dim, which is current

Placing Horizontal Dimensions

First, you'll dimension across the top of the plan, from the corner of the building to the center of the interior wall, and then to the other corner. Then, you'll dimension the roof.

1. Click the Linear button at the left end of the Dimension toolbar to activate the Dimlinear command. The prompt says Specify first extension line origin or <select object>:.

2. Pick the upper-left corner of the cabin walls. The prompt changes to Specify second extension line origin:. At this point, zoom in to the bathroom area until you can see the wall between the bathroom and kitchen, as well as the back wall, close up.

3. Activate the Midpoint osnap, and click the upper jamb line of the bathroom door opening when the triangle appears at the jamb's midpoint (see Figure 12.14).

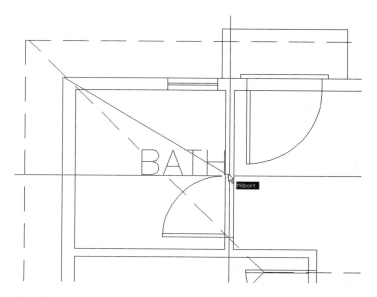

FIGURE 12.14: Selecting the jamb with the Midpoint osnap

4. Use Pan Realtime, hold down the scroll wheel of your mouse or the middle mouse button to pan the drawing down until there's room above the roofline to place the dimension. Notice how the dimension appears in a dashed form attached to, and moving with, the cursor (see the top of Figure 12.15). Also notice that the right extension line starts just above the midpoint of the jamb you picked.

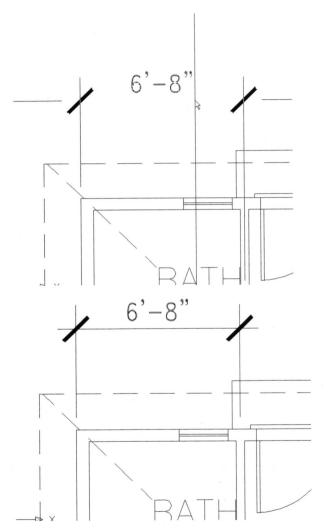

FIGURE 12.15: The dimension attached to the cursor (top) and adjusted after placement (bottom)

5. Move the cursor until the dimension line is about 3' above the back step. Click to place it.

   6. Click anywhere on the new dimension. Five grips appear. Click the
   grip at the bottom of the right extension line. Select the Perpendicular osnap, and move the cursor up to the exterior wall line. When the
   osnap marker appears, click. The right extension line is adjusted.
   Press Esc to remove the grips (see the bottom of Figure 12.15).

Your first dimension is completed.

When dimensioning walls, you usually dimension to the outside of the exterior
ones and to the center of the interior ones. The next dimension will run from the
right side of the first dimension to the right corner.

> **N O T E**   Studs are the vertical 2" × 4" or 2" × 6" members in the framing
> of a wall. When dimensioning buildings that have stud walls, architects usu-
> ally dimension to the face of the stud for the outside walls, but I won't go into
> that level of detail in this book.

Using the Continue Command

AutoCAD has an automatic way of placing adjacent dimensions in line with one
another—the Continue command. You use it as follows:

   1. Zoom out, and pan until you have a view of the upper wall and
   roofline, with space above them for dimensions (see Figure 12.16).

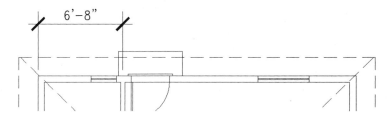

FIGURE 12.16: The result of zooming and panning for a view of the top
of the floor plan

   2. Click the Continue button on the Dimension toolbar. The prompt says
   `Specify a second extension line origin or [Undo/Select]`
   `<Select>:`. All you need to do here is pick a point for the right end of
   the dimension—in this case, the upper-right corner of the walls.

   3. Click the upper-right corner of the cabin. This draws the second dimension in line with the first (see Figure 12.17). Note that the same prompt
   has returned to the Command window. You could keep picking points
   to place the next adjacent dimension in line, if you needed one. Press
   Esc to cancel the Continue command.

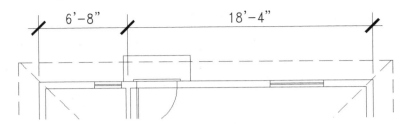

FIGURE 12.17: The completion of the Continue command

With the Continue command, you can dimension along a wall of a building quickly just by picking points. AutoCAD assumes that the last extension line specified for the previous dimension will coincide with the first extension line of the next dimension. If the extension line you need to continue from isn't the last one specified, press ↵ at the prompt, pick the extension line you want to continue from, and resume the command.

Another automatic routine that you can use with linear dimensions is called Baseline.

Using the Baseline Command

The Baseline command gets its name from a style of dimensioning called *baseline*, in which all dimensions begin at the same point (see Figure 12.18). Each dimension is stacked above the previous one. Because of the automatic stacking, you can use the Baseline command for overall dimensions. AutoCAD will stack the overall dimension a set height above the incremental dimensions.

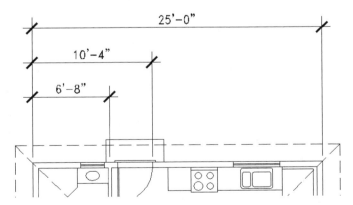

FIGURE 12.18: An example of baseline dimensions

1. Click the Baseline button on the Dimension toolbar. The prompt says Specify a second extension line origin or [Undo/Select] <Select>:, just like the first prompt for the Continue command.

2. Press ↵ to choose the Select option.

3. Pick the extension line that extends from the upper-left corner—the first extension line of the first dimension.

4. Pick the upper-right corner of the walls, and then press Esc to cancel the Baseline command. The overall dimension is drawn above the first two dimensions (see Figure 12.19). (The Baseline command will keep running until you cancel it, just like the Continue command.)

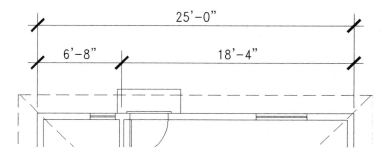

FIGURE 12.19: The completion of the overall dimension with the Baseline command

The Baseline command assumes the baseline is the first extension line of the last dimension. For the cabin, that would be the extension line that extends from the far-left wall. You want the baseline to be the extension line above the upper-left corner of the walls, so press ↵ to select that extension line.

It would be nice to have a dimension for the roof spaced the same distance above the overall dimension as the overall dimension is spaced above the incremental dimensions. The Baseline command can help you do this:

1. Start the Baseline command again. This time, don't press ↵. You'll use the first extension line of the last dimension for your baseline.

2. Pick the upper-right corner of the roof. This places a dimension above the overall dimension (see the top of Figure 12.20). Press Esc to cancel the Baseline command. To finish placing the roof dimension, you need to move the left extension line of this last dimension to the upper-left corner of the roof.

3. Click the text of the roof dimension. Grips appear in five places on the dimension, and the dimension ghosts (see the middle of Figure 12.20).

4. Click the grip at the bottom of the left extension line to activate it.

5. Click the upper-left corner of the roof, and then press Esc. The extension line moves, and the dimension text updates to display the full length of the roof (see the bottom of Figure 12.20).

This completes the horizontal dimensions for the back wall.

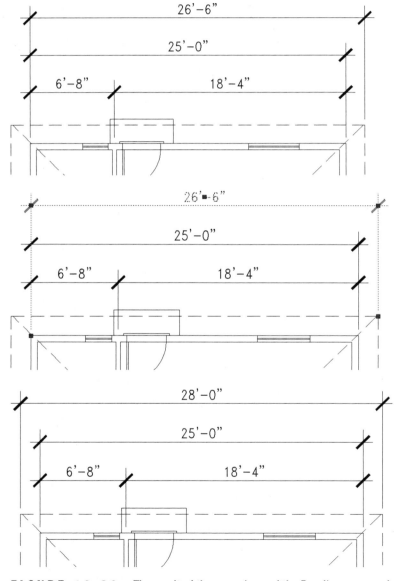

FIGURE 12.20: The result of the second use of the Baseline command (top), starting grips to modify the dimension (middle), and the result (bottom)

Setting Up Vertical Dimensions

Because you can use the Linear command for vertical and horizontal dimensions, you can follow the steps in the previous exercise to do the vertical dimensions on the left side of the floor plan. The only difference from the horizontal dimensioning is that there is no jamb line whose midpoint can be used to establish the center of the interior wall between the bedroom and bathroom. The following steps will take you through the process of placing the first vertical dimension. You'll then be able to finish the rest of them by yourself.

1. Pan and zoom to get a good view of the left side of the floor plan, including the space between the roof and the border (see Figure 12.21).

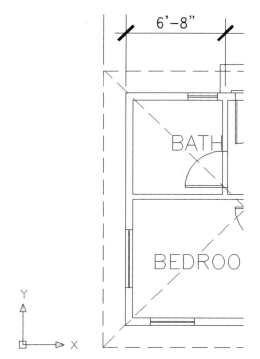

FIGURE 12.21: The result of zooming and panning for a view of the left side of the floor plan

2. Start a vertical dimension from the top of the left exterior wall.

3. Activate the Perpendicular osnap, and place the second point perpendicular to the inside of the bathroom wall (see the left of Figure 12.22).

4. Select the dimension, and then click the grip at the lower-right end of the extension line. The Stretch function of the grip-editing tools is active by default.

5. The interior walls are 4" thick, so you need to move the extension line down 2" (see the right of Figure 12.22). Enter @2<270↵ or @0,-2↵, depending on which method you prefer.

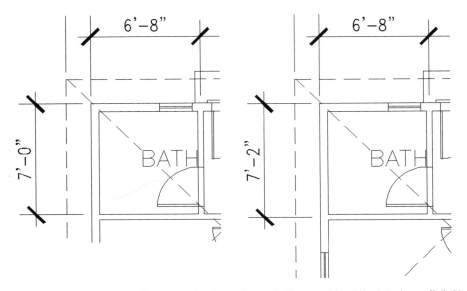

FIGURE 12.22: The dimension drawn to the bathroom side of the interior wall (left), and the extension line moved to the center of the wall (right)

Finishing the Vertical Dimensions

You place the rest of the vertical dimensions using a procedure similar to the one you used to complete the horizontal dimensions. Here is a summary of the steps:

1. Use the Continue command to dimension the bedroom.

2. Use the Baseline command to place an overall dimension.

3. Click the Linear button, and then press ↵ at the command prompt to indicate that you want to select the object to dimension.

4. Click the left vertical roofline, and then place the dimension to the left of the existing vertical dimensions.

The completed vertical dimensions will look like Figure 12.23.

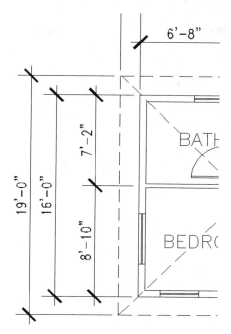

FIGURE 12.23: The completed vertical dimensions

The next area to dimension is the balcony:

1. Pan to a view of the balcony. Include some space below and to the right of it.

T I P   When you have a floating toolbar on the screen, using the Zoom Window command doesn't take into account the area that the floating toolbar takes up. When you can, it's better to use Pan Realtime and Zoom Realtime tools to adjust your view in this situation.

2. Start the Linear tool, and pick the lower-right corner of the building walls.

3. Use the Quadrant osnap, and pick near the rightmost edge of the outside balcony wall.

4. When the dimension appears, move it a couple of feet below the bottom roofline, and place it there (see Figure 12.24).

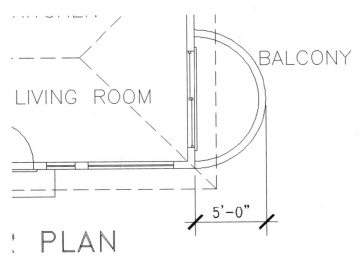

FIGURE 12.24: The horizontal balcony dimension

This is enough on vertical and horizontal linear dimensions for now. You'll now look at some other kinds of dimensions.

Using Other Types of Dimensions

AutoCAD provides tools for placing radial and angular dimensions on the drawing and for placing linear dimensions that are neither vertical nor horizontal. You'll use the Radial tool to dimension the inside radius of the balcony.

Using Radial Dimensions

On the Dimension toolbar are icons for radial, jogged, and diameter dimensions. They all operate the same way and are controlled by the same settings.

Follow these steps to place a radial dimension at the balcony:

1. Click the Osnap button on the status bar to temporarily disable any running osnaps.

2. Click the Radius button to start the Dimradius command.

N O T E Most of the commands used for dimensioning are prefaced with a *dim* when you enter them at the command line; that is the name of the command. For example, when you click the Radius button on the Dimension toolbar or choose Dimension ➤ Radius from the menu bar, you see _dimradius in the Command window to let you know that you have started the Dimradius command. You can also start this command by entering **dimradius**⏎ or **dra**⏎ (the command alias).

3. Click the inside arc of the balcony a slight distance above the midpoint. The radial dimension appears in dashed form. Where you pick the arc determines its angle of orientation. The dimension text then stays attached to the cursor (see Figure 12.25).

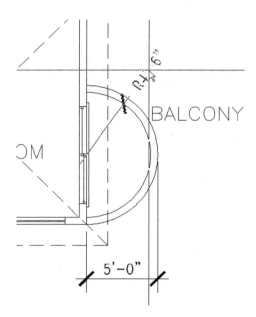

F I G U R E   1 2 . 2 5 : The radial dimension initially positioned in the arc

4. Notice that the tick mark used for linear dimensions is used here also. You should have an arrowhead for the radial dimension. Press Esc to cancel the command.

You'll have to alter the dimension style to specify an arrowhead for radial dimensions.

Setting Up Parent and Child Dimensioning Styles

The DimPlan dimension style that you set up at the beginning of this chapter applies to all dimensions and is called the *parent* dimension style. But you can change settings in this dimension style for particular types of dimensions, such as the radial type, for example. This makes a *child* dimension style. The child version is based on the parent version, but it has a few settings that are different. In this way, all your dimensions will be made using the DimPlan dimension style, but radial dimensions will use a child version of the style. Once you create a child dimension style from the parent style, you refer to both styles by the same name, and you call them a dimension style *family*. Follow these steps to set up a child dimension for radial dimensions:

1. Click the Dimension Style button on the Dimension toolbar to open the Dimension Style Manager dialog box. It looks like Figure 12.26.

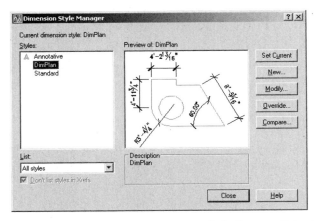

FIGURE 12.26: The Dimension Style Manager dialog box with DimPlan current

T I P   When the Dimension toolbar is docked to either side of the drawing area, the Dim Style Control drop-down list does not display. You can, however, change the current dimension style from the Styles toolbar.

2. Be sure DimPlan is highlighted in the Styles list, and then click the New button to open the Create New Dimension Style dialog box.

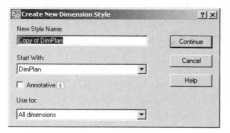

3. Open the Use For drop-down list, and select Radius Dimensions. Then, click the Continue button. The New Dimension Style dialog box opens and has the seven tabs you worked with earlier. Its title bar now includes Radial, and the preview window shows a radial dimension.

4. Activate the Symbols And Arrows tab. Then, move to the Arrowheads area, and open the second Arrowhead drop-down list.

5. Select Right Angle. Notice how the preview window now illustrates a radial dimension with a right-angle arrowhead.

6. Click the Text tab.

7. In the Text Placement area, open the Vertical drop-down list, and select Centered.

8. Click OK to close the New Dimension Style: DimPlan: Radial dialog box.

9. In the Dimension Style Manager dialog box, notice the Styles list. Radial is now a child style of the parent style DimPlan (see Figure 12.27). Click Close to close the Dimension Style Manager dialog box.

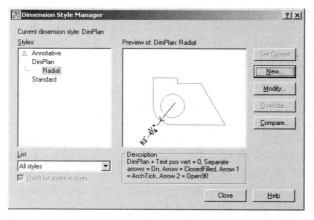

F I G U R E   1 2 . 2 7 : Radial child dimension style in the DimPlan family

10. Click the Radius button on the Dimension toolbar.

11. Click the inside arc of the balcony at a point about 30° above the right quadrant point. The radius dimension appears in dashed form, and it now has an arrow instead of a tick mark.

12. Move the cursor to the outside of the balcony, and place the dimension text so that it looks similar to Figure 12.28.

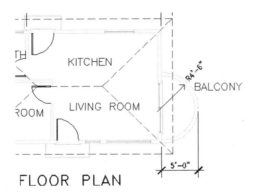

FIGURE 12.28: The radius dimension for the balcony

When placing the radial dimension, you have control over the angle of the dimension line (by where you pick the arc) and the location of the dimension text (by where you pick the second point).

Using Leader Lines

You will use the Multileader command to draw an arrow to features in the drawing to add descriptive information. As of AutoCAD 2008, leaders are no longer part of the dimension family, and you can find them on the Multileader toolbar. Before you create a leader, you need to create a multileader style:

1. Right-click a blank area of any toolbar, and choose Multileader from the menu that appears.

2. Click the Multileader Style button at the right end of the Multileader toolbar.

3. Click the New button in the Multileader Style Manager. In the Create New Mulitleader Style dialog box that opens, enter **DimPlan Leader** in the New Style Name box, and then click Continue (see Figure 12.29).

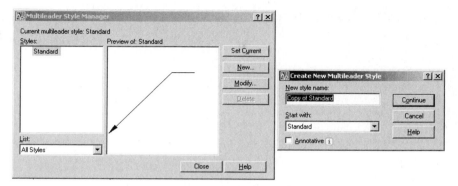

FIGURE 12.29: Creating a new multileader style

4. The Modify Multileader Style dialog opens (see Figure 12.30). This is where you define the leader properties. In the Leader format tab, expand the Symbol drop-down list, in the Arrowhead section, and choose Right Angle. Set Size to 1'.

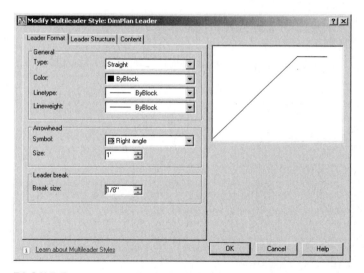

FIGURE 12.30: The Modify Multileader Style dialog box

5. Click the Leader Structure tab. The landing is the horizontal line at the end of the leader, just before the text. Make sure the Set Landing Distance option is checked, and then enter 10" in the text box.

6. Switch to the Content tab. Expand the Text Style drop-down list, choose Dim, and set the text height to 9".

7. In the Leader Connection area, set both the Left Attachment and Right Attachment options to Middle of Top Line. This places the middle of the top line of the leader text even with the landing.

8. Set the Landing Gap value to 6".

9. Click the OK button.

10. In the Multileader Style Manager, the DimPlans Leaders style appears at the top of the Styles list box (see Figure 12.31). Select it, click Set Current, and then click the Close button.

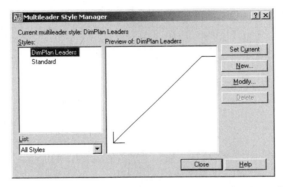

FIGURE 12.31: The DimPlan Leaders multileader style

Adding the Leader

To add the leader, follow these steps:

1. Click the Multileader button on the Multileader toolbar.

2. Start the Nearest osnap, and then pick a point between the balcony radius's dimension text and the roofline.

3. At the Specify leader landing location: prompt, click a point above and to the right of the balcony. The Text Formatting toolbar opens, and a text prompt appears near the landing.

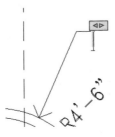

4. Enter **Cover balcony w/⏎ beige stucco**, and then click the OK button in the Text Formatting toolbar.

> **T I P** To reposition a leader without moving the arrow, click it, and then click the grip at the middle of the landing. Move the cursor, and then the text, landing, and one end of the leader line all will move with it.

5. Pan down so that you can see the two windows to the right of the front door.

6. Add a leader that starts at the 6' window and then extends below and to the left. Enter **All windows to be double paned** at the text prompt.

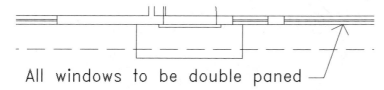

All windows to be double paned

7. Several leader lines can extend from a single landing. Click the Add Leader button, and then at the `Select a multileader:` prompt, click the last leader you made. An arrowhead with a leader appears attached to the cursor. Use the Nearest osnap to select a point on the surface of the 2' window, and then press ⏎.

8. Reposition the text as necessary. Your drawing should look similar to Figure 12.32.

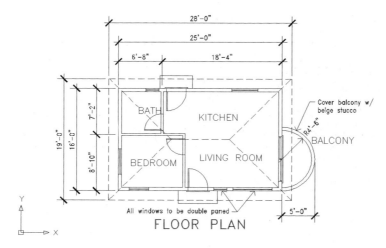

FIGURE 12.32: The cabin drawing with leaders

9. Save this drawing as `Cabin12a.dwg`.

Using Aligned and Angular Dimensions

To get familiar with the aligned and angular dimension types, play around with the two commands, using the rooflines to experiment. Here's how to set up Cabin12a to work with aligned and angular dimensions:

1. Make the Roof layer current.

2. Turn off all other layers by following these steps:

   a. Click the Layer Properties Manager button.

   b. In the Layer Properties Manager dialog box, place the cursor anywhere on the list of layer names, and right-click to open a menu.

   c. Choose Select All but Current on the menu. Then, click one of the lightbulbs for any highlighted layer in the On column.

   d. The lightbulbs for all selected layers turn off, indicating that those layers have been turned off. The Frozen or Thawed status of each layer is unchanged.

   e. Highlight the Dim1 layer, click the New Layer button, and name the new layer Dim2. By Selecting Dim1 first, Dim2 is created using the same properties including color, linetype, and status. Make Dim2 current.

   f. Click OK to close the dialog box and return to the drawing. Everything has disappeared except the rooflines.

3. Pan and zoom to get a closer view of the roof.

4. Set the Endpoint osnap to be running. Now you're ready to dimension.

Using Aligned Dimensions

Aligned dimensions are linear dimensions that aren't horizontal or vertical. You place them in the same way that you place horizontal or vertical dimensions with the Linear command. You can also use the Baseline and Continue commands with aligned dimensions.

Use the Aligned command to dimension a hipline of the roof. Try it on your own. Follow the prompts. It works just like the Linear dimension command.

 Start the Aligned command by clicking the Align button on the Dimension toolbar. Look ahead to Figure 12.33 to see the results you should get.

Using Angular Dimensions

The angular dimension is the only basic dimension type that uses angles in the dimension text instead of linear measurements. Generally, tick marks aren't used with angular dimensions, so you need to create another child dimension style for this type of dimension. Follow the steps given earlier in this chapter in the "Setting Up Parent and Child Dimensioning Styles" section for setting up the Radial child style. The only change you need to make is on the Symbols And Arrows tab: replace the Architectural tick with the Right Angle arrowhead.

Try making an angular dimension on your own. Turn off running osnaps. You can start the Angular command by clicking the Angular button on the Dimension toolbar. Follow the prompts, and pick two of the hiplines to dimension the angle between them.

Figure 12.33 illustrates angular and aligned dimensions on the roof.

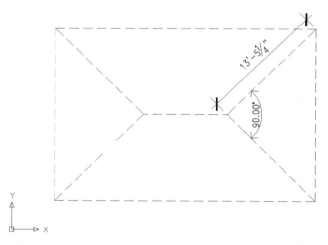

FIGURE 12.33: The roof with angular and aligned dimensions

When you change settings for a dimension style, dimensions created when that style was current automatically update to reflect the changes. You'll modify more dimensions in the next section.

You have been introduced to the basic types of dimensions—linear, radial, leader, and angular—and some auxiliary dimensions—baseline, continue, and aligned—that are special cases of the linear type. You can also use the baseline and continuous dimensions with angular dimensions.

Turn all the layers on, but leave their Frozen/Thawed states as is. Make the Dim1 layer current, and then freeze the Dim2 layer.

Using Ordinate Dimensions

Ordinate dimensions are widely used by the mechanical and civil engineering professions and related trades. They differ from the kind of dimensioning you have been doing so far in this chapter in that ordinate dimensioning specifies X and Y coordinate values for specific points in a drawing based on an absolute or relative Cartesian coordinate system, rather than on a distance between two points. This method is used to dimension centers of holes in sheet metal or machine parts and to locate surveying points on an area map.

You don't need ordinate dimensions in the cabin project, so you'll now go through a quick exercise in setting them up to dimension the holes in a steel plate. Doing so will give you a glimpse of the tools that AutoCAD provides for this type of work. If you aren't interested in ordinate dimensioning, move on to the next section, "Modifying Dimensions," to modify the dimensions you've already created for the cabin.

1. Open a new drawing, and leave the units at the default of Decimal with a precision of four decimal places. Turn polar tracking on.

2. Set up a new text style, and set 0.125 as the height. Click Apply and then Close to make it the current text style.

3. Draw a rectangle using 0,0 as the first point and 6,–4 as the second.

4. Use Zoom to Extents, and then zoom to .5x. Turn off the UCS icon.

5. Draw a circle somewhere in the upper-left quadrant of the rectangle with a radius of 0.35 units; then, using Polar Tracking mode or Ortho mode, copy that circle once directly to the right and once directly below the original and to two other locations not aligned with any other circle so the configuration looks something like the left of Figure 12.34.

6. Set the Endpoint and Center osnaps to be running, and turn on Ortho mode.

   What you care about with ordinate dimensioning isn't how far the holes are from each other but how far the X and Y coordinates of the centers of the holes are from a reference point on the plate. You'll use the upper-left corner of the plate as a reference point, or *datum point*, because it's positioned at the origin of the drawing, or at the 0,0 point.

7. Click the Ordinate button on the Dimension toolbar.

8. Click the upper-left corner of the rectangular plate, and then move the cursor straight up above the point you picked. When you're about

an inch above the plate, click again. This sets the first ordinate dimension (see the left of Figure 12.34).

9. Press the spacebar to repeat the Dimordinate command, and then repeat step 8 for the four circles near the middle or upper portions of the plate, using their centers as points to snap to and aligning the ordinate dimensions by eye. The lower circle is in vertical alignment with the one above it, so it needs no horizontal dimension. Place an ordinate dimension on the upper-right corner of the plate to finish. Press the F8 key to toggle Ortho mode off if you need to jog an extension line. The result should look like the right of Figure 12.34.

10. Repeat this procedure for the Y ordinate dimensions. Once again, ignore any circles that are in vertical alignment, but include the upper-left and lower-left corners of the plate (see the bottom of Figure 12.34).

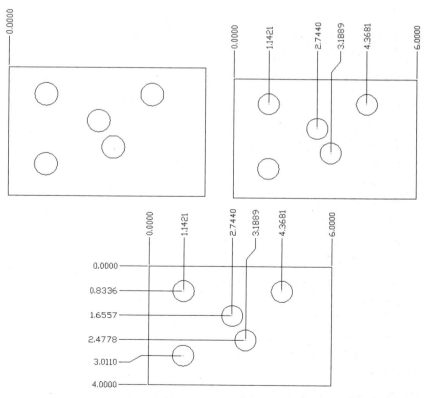

F I G U R E   1 2 . 3 4 : Placing the first ordinate dimension (left), finishing up the X coordinate dimensions (right), and placing the Y coordinate dimensions (bottom)

In civil engineering, ordinate dimensions are used almost the same way but displayed differently. A datum reference point is used, but the dimensions are displayed at each point. This is because the points are a set of surveying points spread randomly over a large area, and the datum or reference point might be miles away (see Figure 12.35).

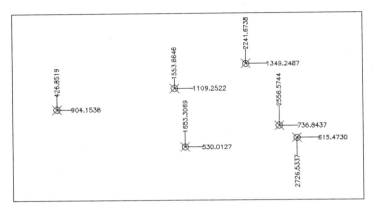

FIGURE 12.35: A sample surveyor's datum points with ordinate dimensions

The final part of this chapter will be devoted to teaching you a few techniques for modifying dimensions.

Modifying Dimensions

You can use several commands and grips to modify dimensions, depending on the desired change. Specifically, you can do the following:

- ▶ You can change the dimension text content.
- ▶ You can move the dimension text relative to the dimension line.
- ▶ You can move the dimension or extension lines.
- ▶ You can change the dimension style settings for a dimension or a group of dimensions.
- ▶ You can revise a dimension style.

The best way to understand how to modify dimensions is to try a few.

Modifying Dimension Text

You can modify any aspect of the dimension text. You'll look at how to change the content first.

Editing Dimension Text Content

To change the content of text for one dimension, or to add text before or after the dimension, use the Properties palette. You'll change the text in the horizontal dimensions for the roof and walls:

1. Zoom and pan until your view of the floor plan is similar to Figure 12.36.

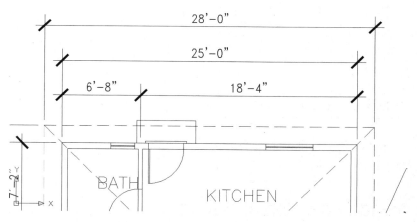

FIGURE 12.36: A modified view of the floor plan

2. Select the horizontal roof dimension at the top of the drawing. Right-click, and choose Properties.

3. In the Properties palette, scroll down to the Text rollout, and expand it if necessary.

4. Highlight the Text Override field, and enter <> **verify in field**↵. The phrase is appended to the dimension (see the top of Figure 12.37). The <> instructs AutoCAD to add the phrase to the dimension text; if you had not prefixed the override with <>, then the phrase would have replaced the dimension text entirely.

4. Press the Esc key, and then click the dimension just below the roof dimension.

5. In the Text Override box, enter <> %%P↵. The ± symbol is now appended to the text (see the bottom of Figure 12.37).

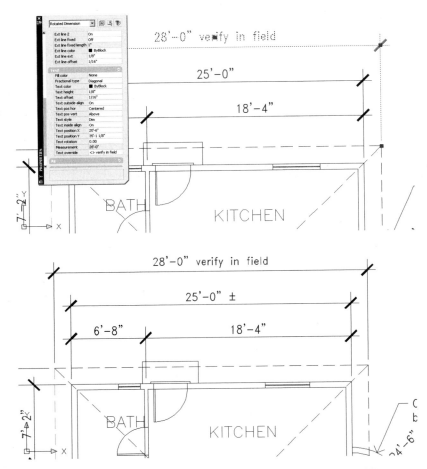

FIGURE 12.37: Adding a phrase to dimension text (top) and adding a special character (bottom)

@ ▾   Unless you have all the ASCII symbol codes memorized, it might be easier to insert symbols into dimension text using the Ddedit command. To
do this, enter ddedit↵, select the dimension text, place the cursor where you want
the symbol to appear, and then click the Symbol button to see a list of available
symbols to choose from and their related ASCII codes. Click the symbol name to
be added.

Next, you'll learn about moving a dimension.

Moving Dimensions

You can use grips to move dimensions. You used grips to move the extension
line of the roof dimension when you were putting on the vertical and horizontal
dimensions. This time, you'll move the dimension line and the text:

1. Zoom in to a view of the right side of the floor plan until you have a
   view that includes the entire balcony and its dimensions, as well as
   the entire right cabin wall.

2. Select the 5'-0" dimension. Its grips appear.

3. Click the grip on the right tick mark to activate it.

4. Move the cursor up until the dimension text is above the balcony.
   Click again to fix it there. Click the grip that's on the text, and with
   polar tracking on, move the text slightly to the right to clear it from
   the roofline. Then, press Esc (see the top of Figure 12.38). The
   dimension, line, and text move to a new position, and the extension
   lines are redrawn to the new position.

5. Mirror the leader horizontally, and then, using the text grip, move it
   below the balcony and left of its current location. Select the grip at
   the tip of the arrow, and move it to the lower portion of the balcony.
   Use the Nearest osnap to place the arrowhead precisely on the arc
   (see the middle of Figure 12.38).

6. Select the radial dimension text, move it below and outside the balcony, and then move the BALCONY text so that it doesn't overlap the
   dimension (see the bottom of Figure 12.38).

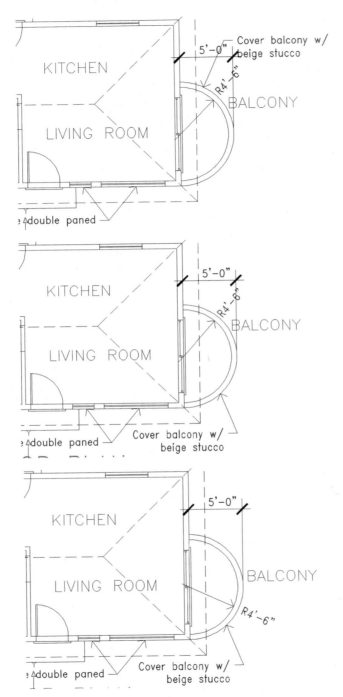

FIGURE 12.38: Moving the balcony dimensions with grips: the linear dimension (top), the leader (middle), and the radial dimension (bottom)

To finish the changes to the balcony, you need to suppress the left extension line of the 5'-0" dimension because it overlaps the wall and header lines.

Using Dimension Overrides

You suppress the left extension line with the Properties palette, which allows you to change a setting in the dimension style for one dimension without altering the style settings. Follow these steps:

1. Double-click the 5'-0" dimension to open the Properties palette.

2. Scroll down to the Lines And Arrows rollout. If this section isn't open, click the double arrows to the right.

3. Scroll down the list of settings in this section, and click Ext Line 1. Then, click the down arrow in the right column to open the drop-down list. Click Off. This suppresses the left extension line on the linear balcony dimension (see Figure 12.39).

4. Close the Properties palette. Press Esc to deselect the dimension.

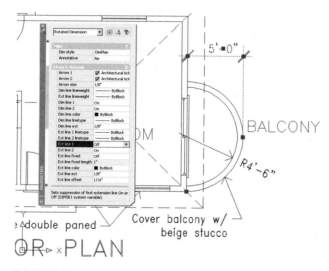

FIGURE 12.39: The 5'-0" dimension with the left extension line suppressed

To illustrate how dimension overrides work, you suppressed an extension line without having to alter the dimension style. Extension lines are usually the thinnest lines in a drawing. It's usually not critical that they be suppressed if they coincide with other lines, because the other lines will overwrite them in a print.

However, in this example, the left extension line of the 5'-0" dimension for the balcony coincides with the line representing the header of the sliding door. If the Headers layer is turned off, you will have to suppress or move the extension line of this dimension so it won't be visible spanning the sliding door opening. Also, if you dimension to a noncontinuous line, such as a centerline, use the Dimension style override features to assign special linetypes to extension lines. In the practice exercises at the end of this chapter, you'll get a chance to learn how to incorporate centerlines into your dimensions.

Dimensioning Short Distances

When you have to dimension distances so short that both the text and the arrows (or tick marks) can't fit between the extension lines, a dimension style setting determines where they are placed. To see how this works, you'll redo the horizontal dimensions above the floor plan, this time dimensioning the distance between the roofline and wall line, as well as the thickness of the interior wall. The setting changes that you made in the Fit tab when you set up the DimPlan dimension style will help you now:

1. Zoom and pan to a view of the upper portion of the floor plan so that the horizontal dimensions above the floor plan are visible (see Figure 12.40).

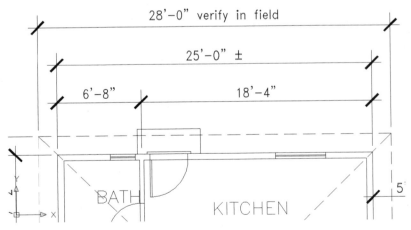

FIGURE 12.40: The new view of the upper floor plan and its dimensions

2. Use the Erase command to erase the three dimensions that are below the roof dimension. Each dimension is a single object, so you can select the three dimensions with three picks or one crossing window.

3. Activate the running osnaps, click the Linear button, and pick the upper-left corner of the roof. Then, pick the upper-left corner of the wall lines. Place the dimension line about 3' above the upper roofline (see the top of Figure 12.41).

4. Click the Continue button. Click the upper end of each interior wall line, click the upper-right corner of the wall lines, and finally click the upper-right corner of the roof (see the bottom of Figure 12.41). Press Esc to cancel the Continue command.

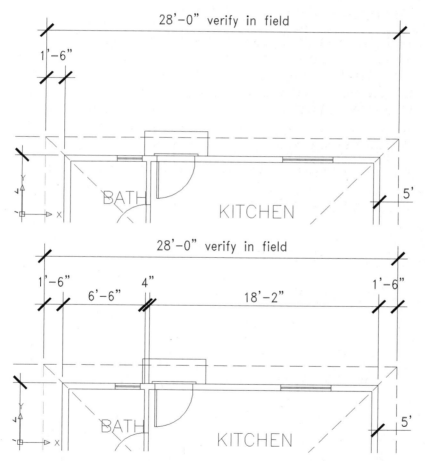

FIGURE 12.41: The first dimension is placed (top) and the other dimensions (bottom)

5. Save the drawing as Cabin12b.dwg.

This concludes the exercises for dimensions in this chapter. Working successfully with dimensions in your drawing requires an investment of time to become familiar with the commands and settings that control how dimensions appear, how they are placed in the drawing, and how they are modified. The exercises in this chapter have led you through the basics of the dimensioning process. For a more in-depth discussion of dimensions, refer to *Mastering AutoCAD 2008 and AutoCAD LT 2008* by George Omura (Wiley, 2007).

The next chapter will introduce you to external references, a tool for viewing a drawing from within another drawing.

If You Would Like More Practice...

In the first practice exercise, you'll get a chance to use the dimensioning tools that you just learned. After that is a short exercise that shows a technique for incorporating centerlines into dimensions.

Dimensioning the Garage Addition

Try dimensioning the garage addition to the cabin that was shown at the end of Chapter 4 (Cabin04c-addon). Use the same techniques and standards of dimensioning that you used in this chapter to dimension the cabin:

1. Dimension to the outside edges of exterior walls and to the centerlines of interior walls.

2. Use the DimPlan dimension style you set up and used in this chapter. Close all files that you used in this chapter, and open Cabin04c-addon.dwg. Then, use the DesignCenter to bring over the DimPlan dimension style, the Dim text style, and the Dim1 layer.

3. Add text to this drawing as shown in Figure 12.42.

4. When you're finished, save this drawing as Cabin12b-addon.dwg.

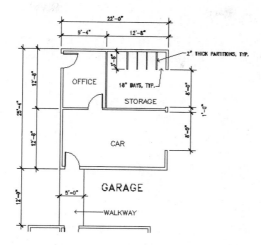

FIGURE 12.42: The walkway and garage dimensioned

Dimensioning to a Centerline

This exercise will take you through a series of steps to show you how to use centerlines as replacements for extension lines in dimensions. I'll use as many of the default settings for AutoCAD as I can to give you a look at what *out-of-the-box*, or *vanilla*, AutoCAD looks like—that is, how drawings look if you use the default settings for text styles, dimension styles, units, and so forth. The drawing you'll make is similar to the one you made in Chapter 2, but you know much more now:

1. Choose File ➤ New; then, in the Create New Drawing dialog box, select the acad.dwt template.

2. Start the Rectangle command, and click a point in the lower-left quadrant of the drawing area. For the second point, enter @6,2↵.

3. Turn off the UCS icon, use Zoom to Extents, and then zoom to .5x. Pan to move the new rectangle down a little (see Figure 12.43).

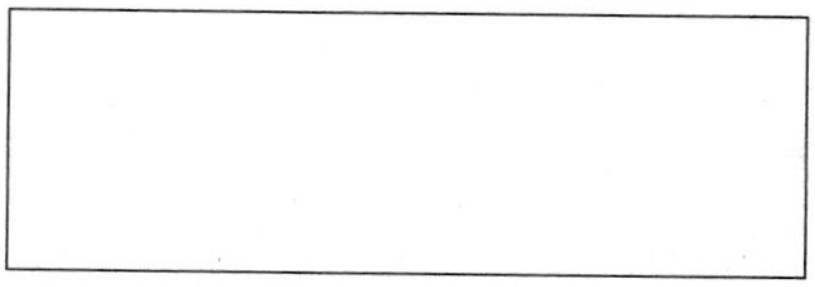

FIGURE 12.43: The rectangle after panning down

You want to dimension from the upper-left corner of the rectangle to the center of the upper horizontal line and then to the upper-right corner. You'll select the Dimension command from the menu bar and use the default dimension settings:

1. Create a new layer called Dim, accept the White color, and make Dim current. Set the Endpoint and Midpoint osnaps to be running, and then choose Dimension ➢ Linear. Click the upper-left corner of the rectangle, and then click the midpoint of the upper horizontal line of the rectangle. Drag the dimension line up to a point about one unit above the upper line of the rectangle, and click. This places the first dimension.

2. Click the dimension to make grips appear. Click the grip that is at the midpoint of the upper horizontal line of the rectangle, and with Polar on, drag it down to a point below the rectangle. Press Esc to deselect the dimension.

3. Choose Dimension ➢ Continue, and select the upper-right corner of the rectangle. Doing so places the second dimension. Press Esc to end the command.

4. On the Properties toolbar, open the Linetype Control drop-down list, and select Other. In the Linetype Manager dialog box, click the Load button.

5. In the Load Or Reload Linetypes dialog box, scroll down, find and click Center2, and then click OK. The Center2 linetype now appears in the Linetype Manager dialog box. Click OK.

6. Double-click the left dimension to open the Properties palette. In the Lines And Arrows area, click Ext Line 2 Linetype. Open the drop-down list, and select Center2. Press Esc to deselect the dimension.

7. Select the right dimension. On the Properties palette, return to the Lines And Arrows area, and click Ext Line 1 Linetype. Open the drop-down list, and select Center 2. Press Esc to close the Properties palette.

Now there is a centerline through the rectangle that's part of the dimensions. As a final touch, you'll put a centerline symbol at the top of the center line by using the MText command:

1. Start the MText command, and make a small defining window somewhere in a blank portion of the drawing area.

2. Right-click the drawing area, and select Symbol. In the fly-out menu that displays, select Center Line. A centerline symbol now appears in the MText Editor. Highlight it, and change its height from 0.2000 to 0.4000.

3. With the text still highlighted, click the MText Justification button in the Text Formatting toolbar. From the fly-out menu that appears, click Bottom Center. Click OK in the Text Formatting toolbar to execute the changes.

4. Click the centerline symbol to activate the grips. Click the lower middle grip, and then click the upper end of the centerline. This locates the symbol.

5. Turn off osnaps, be sure Polar is on, and click the same grip you did in the previous step. Move the symbol up slightly to create a space between it and the centerline (see Figure 12.44).

This completes the exercise.

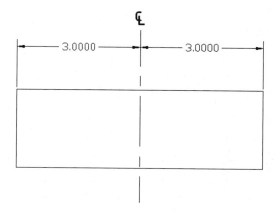

FIGURE 12.44: The centerline symbol and a centerline used as part of two dimensions

Doing Other Exercises

Use the skills you've learned in this chapter to do the following:

▶ Set up a dimension style for your own use.

▶ Dimension a drawing as you would in your own profession or trade.

▶ Dimension any of the other drawings offered in previous chapters, such as the block, the gasket, or the parking lot.

Are You Experienced?

Now you can...

- ☑ create a new dimension style and child style
- ☑ place vertical and horizontal dimensions in a drawing
- ☑ use radial, aligned, and angular dimensions
- ☑ create multileader lines for notes
- ☑ modify dimension text
- ☑ override a dimension style
- ☑ modify a dimension style

CHAPTER 13

Managing External References

- ▶ Understanding external references
- ▶ Creating external references
- ▶ Modifying external references
- ▶ Converting external references into blocks

The floor plan of a complex building project might actually be a composite of several AutoCAD files that are linked together as external references to the current drawing. This enables parts of a drawing to be worked on at different workstations (or in different offices) while remaining linked to a central host file. In mechanical engineering, a drawing might similarly be a composite of the various subparts that make up an assembly.

External references are .dwg files that have been temporarily connected to the current drawing and are used as reference information. The externally referenced drawing is visible in the current drawing. You can manipulate its layers, colors, linetypes, and visibility, and you can modify its objects, but it isn't a permanent part of the current drawing. Changes made to the xref's appearance, such as color or linetype, in the current drawing do not apply to the xref source drawing.

External references are similar to blocks in that they behave as single objects and are inserted into a drawing in the same way. But blocks are part of the current drawing file, and external references aren't.

Blocks can be exploded back to their component parts, but external references can't; however, external references can be converted into blocks and become a permanent part of the current drawing. In Chapter 7, you were able to modify the window block and, in so doing, update all instances of the window block in the drawing without having to explode the block. With an external reference—usually called an *xref*—you can apply the same updating mechanism. To manage external references, you need to learn how to set up an xref, manipulate its appearance in the host drawing, and update it.

Before you set up the xref, you'll create a site plan for the cabin. You'll then externally reference the site plan drawing into the cabin drawing. In Figure 13.1, the lines of the site plan constitute the xref, and the rest of the objects are part of the host drawing. After these exercises, you'll look at a few ways that design offices use external references.

Drawing a Site Plan

The site plan you'll use has been simplified so that you can draw it with a minimum of steps and get on with the external referencing. The following are essential elements:

- ▶ Property lines
- ▶ Access road to the site
- ▶ North arrow
- ▶ Indication of where the building is located on the site

The first step is to draw the property lines.

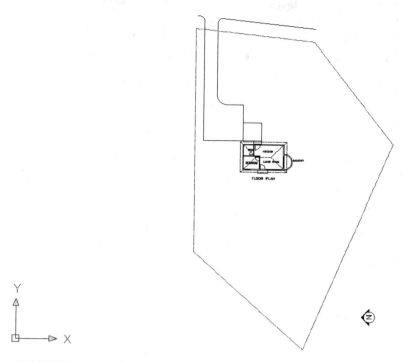

FIGURE 13.1: The site plan with the cabin as an external reference

Using Surveyor's Units

You draw property lines using surveyor's units for angles and decimal feet for linear units. In laying out the property lines, you'll use relative polar coordinates: you'll enter coordinates in the format @*distance<angle*, in which the distance is in feet and hundredths of a foot, and the angle is in surveyor's units to the nearest minute.

Introducing Surveyor's Units

Surveyor's units, called *bearings* in civil engineering, describe the direction of a line from its beginning point. The direction (bearing), described as a deviation from the north or south toward the east or west, is given as an angular measurement in degrees, minutes, and seconds. The angles used in a bearing can never be greater than 90°, so bearing lines must be headed in one of the four directional quadrants: northeasterly, northwesterly, southeasterly, or southwesterly. If north is set to be at the top of a plot plan, south is down, east is to the right, and west is to the left. Thus, when a line from its beginning goes up and to the right, it's headed in a northeasterly direction. And when a line from its beginning goes down and to the left, it's headed in a southwesterly direction, and so on. A line that is headed in a northeasterly direction with a deviation from true north of 30° and 30 minutes is shown as N30d30'E in AutoCAD notation.

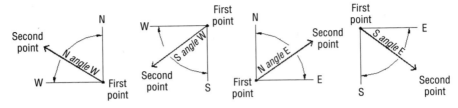

With the surveyor's unit system, a sloping line that has an up-and-to-the-left direction has a down-and-to-the-right direction if you start from the opposite end. So, in laying out property lines, it's important to move in the same direction (clockwise or counterclockwise) as you progress from one segment to the next.

Laying Out the Property Lines

You'll set up a new drawing and then start at the upper-right corner of the property lines and work your way around counterclockwise:

1. Open Cabin12b.dwg from your Training Data folder (or the folder in which your training files are stored). Choose File ➤ Save As, and save the drawing as Cabin13a.dwg.

2. Click the QNew button on the Standard toolbar, and open a new file using the acad.dwt template.

3. From the menu bar, choose Format ➤ Units to open the Drawing Units dialog box, and change the Precision value, in the Length area, to two decimal places (0.00).

> **You're using decimal linear units in such a way that 1 decimal unit represents 1 foot. In AutoCAD and LT, the foot symbol (') is used only with architectural and engineering units.** ▶

4. In the Angle area, open the Type drop-down list, and select Surveyor's Units. Then, change the Precision value to the nearest minute (N0d00' E). Click OK. You'll need an area of about 250' × 150' for the site plan.

5. Open the Format menu again, and choose Drawing Limits. Press ⏎ to accept the default of 0.00,0.00 for the lower-left corner. Enter 250,150⏎. Don't use the foot sign.

6. Right-click the Snap button on the status bar, and choose Settings. Change Snap Spacing to 10.00, and change Grid to 0.00. Then, select the Grid check box to turn on the grid, but leave Snap off. Click OK.

7. In the drawing, enter z⏎ a⏎. Then, zoom to .85x to see a blank space around the grid (see Figure 13.2).

FIGURE 13.2: The site drawing with the grid on

8. Create a new layer called Prop_line. Assign it the color number 172, and make it current.

9. Start the Line command. For the first point, enter **220,130**↵. This starts a line near the upper-right corner of the grid.

10. Be sure Snap is turned off. Then, enter the following:

> @140<n90dw↵
>
> @90<s42d30'w↵
>
> @140<s67d30'e↵
>
> @80<n52d49'e↵
>
> c↵

The property lines are completed (see Figure 13.3).

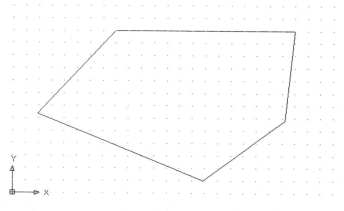

FIGURE 13.3: The property lines on the site drawing

Drawing the Driveway

The driveway is 8' wide and set in 5' from the horizontal property line. The access road is 8' from the parallel property line. The intersection of the access road line and the driveway lines forms corners, each with a 3' radius. The driveway extends 70' in from the upper-right corner of the property.

Let's lay this now:

1. Choose Format ➤ Units from the menu bar. Change the Length units to Architectural and the Angle units to Decimal Degrees. Then, set the Length Precision to $\frac{1}{16}$" and the angular precision to 0.00. Click OK. Because of the way AutoCAD translates decimal units to inches, your drawing is now only $\frac{1}{12}$th the size it needs to be. (Use the Distance command to check it.) You'll have to scale it up.

2. Click the Scale button on the Modify toolbar.

3. Enter all↵↵. For the base point, enter 0,0↵.

> You can also start the Scale command by choosing Modify ➤ Scale from the menu bar or by entering sc↵.

4. At the Specify scale factor or [Copy/Reference]: prompt, enter 12↵. Then, click Grid on the status bar to turn off the grid.

5. Use Zoom to Extents, and then zoom out a little. The drawing looks the same, but now it's the correct size. Check it with the Dist command, which you encountered in Chapter 7, or dimension some of the lines. Delete any dimensions that you make (the value will appear in the Command window).

6. Offset the upper, horizontal property line 5' down. Offset this new line 8' down.

7. Offset the rightmost property line 8' to the right (see the top of Figure 13.4).

8. Create a new layer called Road. Assign it the color White, and make the Road layer current.

9. Select the new lines, open the Layer Control drop-down list, and click the Road layer to move the selected lines to the Road layer. Press Esc to deselect the lines.

10. Extend the driveway lines to the access road line. Trim the access road line between the driveway lines.

11. Fillet the two corners where the driveway meets the road, using a 3' radius (see the bottom of Figure 13.4).

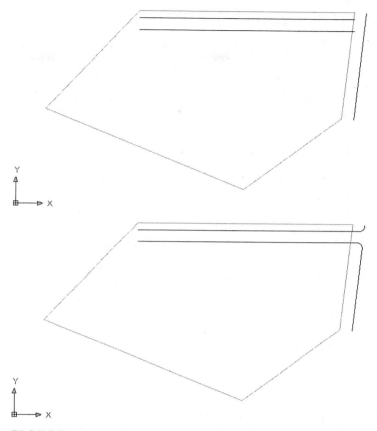

FIGURE 13.4: Offset property lines (top) and the completed intersection of the driveway and access road (bottom)

Finishing the Driveway

A key element of any site plan is information that shows how the building is positioned on the site relative to the property lines. Surveyors stake out property lines. The building contractor then takes measurements off the stakes to locate one or two corners of the building. In this site, you need only one corner because you're assuming the cabin is facing due west. A close look at Figure 13.1, shown earlier in this chapter, shows that the end of the driveway lines up with the outer edge of the back step of the cabin. Below the driveway is a square patio, and its bottom edge lines up with the bottom edge of the back step. So, the bottom corner of the back step coincides with the lower-left corner of the patio. This locates the cabin on the site (see Figure 13.5).

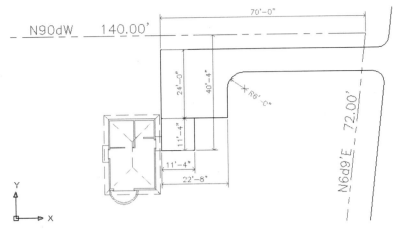

FIGURE 13.5: The driveway and patio lined up with the cabin

Imagine the site being on a bluff of a hill overlooking land that falls away to the south and west, providing a spectacular view in that direction. To accommodate this view, you'll want to change the orientation of the cabin when you externally reference it into the site drawing:

1. On the status bar, turn on Polar, and be sure the Endpoint osnap is running. Then, draw a line from the upper-right corner of the property lines straight up to a point near the top of the screen.

2. Offset this line 70' to the left. This will mark the end of the driveway.

3. Draw a line from the lower endpoint of this offset line down a distance of 40'-4". Then, using polar tracking, continue this line 11'-4" to the right.

4. Offset the 40'-4" line 11'-4" to the right. Offset the newly created line 11'-4" to the right as well.

5. Offset the upper driveway line 24' down. These are all the lines you need to finish the site plan (see the top of Figure 13.6).

6. Finish the driveway and patio by using the Trim, Fillet, and Erase commands as you have in previous chapters. The radius of the corner to fillet is 6' (see the bottom of Figure 13.6). Erase the two guidelines you drew in steps 1 and 2.

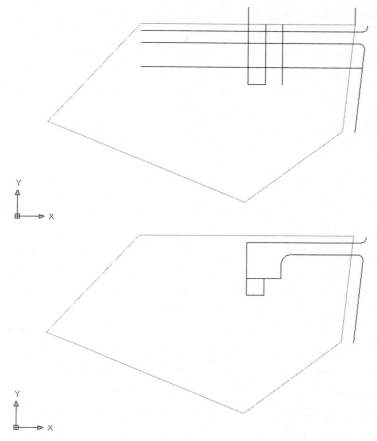

FIGURE 13.6: The offset lines (top) and the finished driveway and patio (bottom)

7. Make layer 0 current, draw a north arrow, and place it in the lower-left corner.

8. Open the Layer Properties Manager dialog box, and change the linetype for the Prop_line layer to Phantom. (You'll have to load it; see Chapter 6.)

9. Enter **ltscale**⏎, and then enter **100**⏎. You'll see the Phantom linetype for the property lines.

10. Save this drawing in your training folder as Site13a.dwg.

This completes the site plan. The next step is to attach the site plan as an external reference into the cabin drawing.

Setting Up an External Reference

When you set up an external reference, you go through a process similar to that of inserting a block into a drawing, as you did in Chapter 7. You select the drawing to be referenced and specify the location of its insertion point. There are options for the X scale factor, Y scale factor, and rotation angle, as there are for inserting blocks. And here, as with blocks, you can set up the command so that it uses the defaults for these options without prompting you for your approval.

Using the External References Palette

You can run all external reference operations through the External References palette, which you can open by choosing Insert ≻ External References from the menu bar or by entering xr↵. To set up a new external reference, choose Insert ≻ DWG Reference. The External References palette references image files and DWF or DGN underlay files as well as other AutoCAD drawings. DWF files are image files produced by several Autodesk products and are similar to Adobe PDF files. Files that have the .dgn extension are drawings created with the MicroStation software.

Also, the Reference toolbar has five command buttons related to externally referenced files. You open it the same way you opened the Dimension toolbar in the preceding chapter: right-click any toolbar on the screen, and then choose Reference from the shortcut menu. But unless you're an advanced user, I don't recommend using the Reference toolbar while working through this chapter, for two reasons. First, six other buttons on the toolbar used for Image commands allow you to import raster drawings into AutoCAD and adjust them, operations not covered in this book. Second, the toolbar doesn't include all the xref commands I'll be covering. If you have already opened this toolbar, click the X in the upper-right corner to close it. The following two series of steps will guide you through the process of attaching Site13a to Cabin13a as an xref:

1. With Cabin13a as the current drawing, zoom out, and then create a new layer called Site. Use the default color of White/Black, and make the Site layer current.

2. Choose Insert ≻ DWG Reference to open the Select Reference File dialog box.

3. Locate the Training Data folder (or the folder in which your training files are stored), and select Sitea. Then, click Open to open the External Reference dialog box (Figure 13.7).

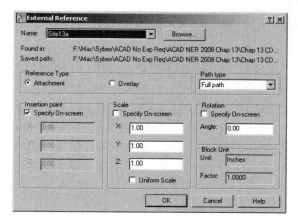

FIGURE 13.7: The External Reference dialog box with Site13a as the named reference

The file being referenced, Site13a, appears in the Name drop-down list at the top of the dialog box, with the full path of the file's location just below. The bottom half contains three options for the insertion process, which are like those in the Insert dialog box that you used for inserting blocks in Chapter 7. Note that only the insertion point is specified on the screen. The Scale and Rotation options should be set to use their default settings. If they aren't, click the appropriate check boxes so that this dialog box matches that in the previous graphic. Continue as follows:

1. Be sure Attachment is selected in the Reference Type area, and then click OK. You return to your drawing, and the site plan drawing appears and moves with the crosshair cursor.

2. Pick any point to the lower left of the cabin to be the insertion point, and then zoom to the drawing's extents. The xref drawing is attached and appears in the site plan (see Figure 13.8).

The attached xref appears exactly as it did when it was the current drawing. When you use this file as part of a site plan, or part of the cabin drawing, you don't want all the information be visible. In fact, you want most of the information invisible. You'll accomplish this by freezing many of the layers in the xref drawing, as explained in the next chapter.

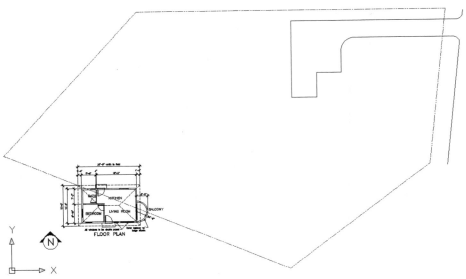

FIGURE 13.8: The Site13a drawing attached to the Cabin 13a drawing

Moving and Rotating an Xref

Now you need to move the site plan and rotate it to its position next to the patio:

1. Freeze the Dim1 layer.

2. Start the Rotate command, click the site plan, and then press ↵.

3. To specify a location for the base point, click anywhere near the middle of the drawing area, and then enter 90↵. The site lines are rotated to the correct orientation (see the top of Figure 13.9).

4. Be sure the Endpoint osnap is running. Then use the Move command to move the lower-right corner of the patio to the lower-left corner of the back step (see the bottom of Figure 13.9).

5. Use Zoom Previous to a view of the whole site. The cabin is oriented correctly on the site (see Figure 13.10). This is the same view as in Figure 13.1 (shown earlier).

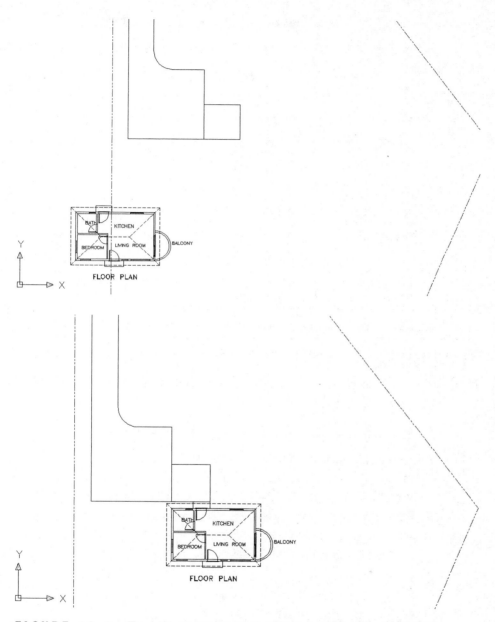

FIGURE 13.9: The cabin rotated (top) and positioned next to the patio (bottom)

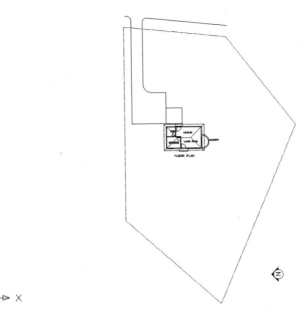

FIGURE 13.10: The cabin xref is located on the site drawing.

You have established Site13a as an external reference in this drawing. The next step is to make revisions to Site13a and see how they affect the xref.

USING THE LAYER STATES MANAGER

You use the Layer States Manager to save the current setup of various *properties* and *states* of layers in the current drawing. You can activate it by clicking the Layer States Manager button in the Layer Properties Manager dialog box. You can perform all the operations for controlling the Layer States Manager through this dialog box.

To set up a new layer state, follow these steps:

1. In the Layer Properties Manager dialog box, set up the layer properties and states as you want them to be saved, and then click the Layer States Manager button.

2. In the Layer States Manager dialog box, enter a name for the new layer state.

Continues

USING THE LAYER STATES MANAGER *(Continued)*

3. In the Layer Settings to Restore area, check the layer settings you want to save as part of the new layer state. (You'll learn about Plot/No Plot, Current VP Frozen/Thawed, Lineweight, Plot Style, and New VP Frozen/Thawed in Chapters 14 and 15.)

4. Click Close to save the new layer state.

You also use the Layer States Manager dialog box to manage existing layer states. Here are its features:

Layer States list box   Displays a list of previously set up layer states.

Restore button   Restores the layer state that is highlighted in the Layer States list box.

Delete button   Deletes a layer state. This doesn't affect the current layer setup.

Import button   Imports a .las file as a new layer state in the current drawing.

Export button   Exports the chosen saved layer state to be saved as a .las file.

To modify a layer state, restore it to be the current layer state, and then change it. To rename a layer state, highlight it, click its name, and type the new name.

Modifying an Xref Drawing

You can modify an xref drawing by making it the current drawing, making the modification, saving the changes, making the host drawing current, and reloading the xref. AutoCAD users can also modify an xref by using a special modification command while the host drawing is current. You'll start by opening Site13a.dwg and adjusting the width of the road. Then you'll make Cabin13a current again and use AutoCAD to modify the site plan, as an xref, adding a walkway around two sides of the cabin.

Modifying an Xref by Making It the Current Drawing

Because you found such a spectacular site for the cabin, you want to add a deck around what was originally the front door and is now the west-facing entrance:

1. With Site13a as the current drawing, zoom in to the area that includes the road and patio.

2. Offset the lower road line 2' downward.

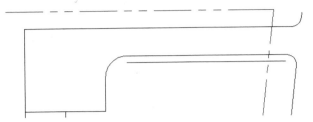

3. Fillet the right side with a radius of 3' and the left at 6'.

4. Delete the original line and radii. Your access road is now 10' wide.

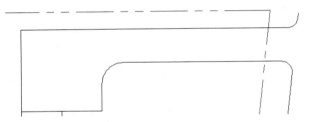

5. Save the Site13a drawing.

   This concludes the modifications you'll make to the site plan in this exercise, although you'll make more later. Now you can return to the cabin drawing.

6. Switch to the Cabin13a file. A balloon message appears at the bottom of the AutoCAD window, pointing to the Manage Xrefs icon in the tool tray. This is indicating that an externally referenced drawing has been saved after it was attached to the current drawing. You could click the blue link text to reload the file, but for this exercise, you will take a look at the External References palette and reload it from there.

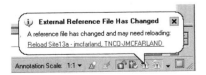

7. Open the External References palette, as shown in Figure 13.11, and stretch it to make it wider. The palette shows most of the pertinent information regarding the externally referenced files in the scene

including the status. In this case, the palette indicates that Site13a needs reloading.

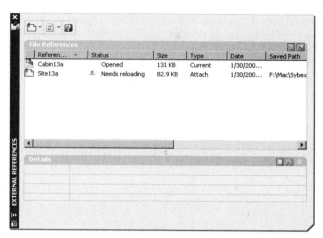

FIGURE 13.11: The External References palette showing the status of the xrefs

8. Select the Site13a xref in the palette, right-click, and choose Reload. This causes AutoCAD to reevaluate the external reference and update the current drawing. The cabin drawing now shows the 10'-wide access road from the site plan drawing (see Figure 13.12).

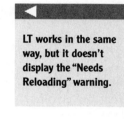

LT works in the same way, but it doesn't display the "Needs Reloading" warning.

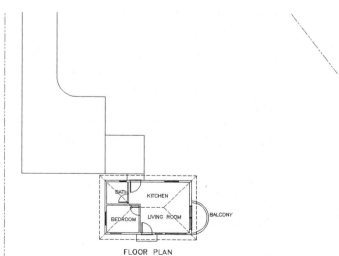

FLOOR PLAN

FIGURE 13.12: The cabin drawing with the updated site plan xref

9. Close the Site13a file, but leave the Cabin13a file open.

10. Save the cabin drawing as Cabin13b.dwg.

In this exercise, you saw how a host drawing is updated when the drawing that is externally referenced is made current, modified, saved, and then reloaded as an xref. This is a good example of the power of layers. You can set them up one way in the actual drawing and another way in the xref of that drawing in a host file. In fact, you can externally reference the same drawing into any number of host files; have the layer characteristics of visibility, color, and linetype be different in each host file; and save them as such with each host file. Xref is a powerful feature of AutoCAD, and you'll learn more about the possible applications of this tool toward the end of this chapter.

Modifying an Xref from Within the Host Drawing

In Chapter 7, you used the Xref And Block In-Place Editing tool to update the window block. You can use the same tool here for editing an xref while the host drawing is the current drawing. You can't create a new layer with this tool, but many of the regular editing commands are available when you use it. You'll make a few modifications to the site plan xref to illustrate this feature.

AutoCAD LT 2008 doesn't have the In-Place Xref And Block Edit feature. To keep your drawing current with the book, read through the following section to see what changes you're making, and then use the technique for modifying Site13a that you used in the previous section. That is, make Site13a current, make the modifications described in the following exercise, save the changes, make Cabin13b current, and use the External References palette or the balloon warning link to reload Site13a. Then continue with step 9 in the following exercise.

> **The Edit Reference In-Place command edits both blocks and xrefs. So, in AutoCAD's technical vocabulary for this command and its prompts, both blocks and xrefs are referred to as *references*.**

1. In the Cabin13b file, make layer 0 current.

2. Zoom in to the cabin floor plan, but leave enough room to see the patio and about 5' in front to the house (see Figure 13.13).

3. Choose Tools ➢ Xref And Block In-Place Editing ➢ Edit Reference In-Place. You're prompted to select the reference to edit. Click any object from the site plan xref. Alternately, you can double-click the xref directly instead of accessing the tool from the menu system.

4. The Reference Edit dialog box opens (see Figure 13.14). On the Identify Reference tab, Site13a is listed as the selected xref, and a preview window illustrates the xref drawing.

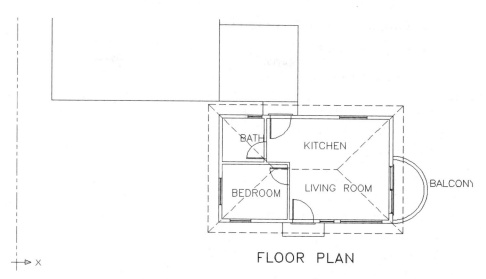

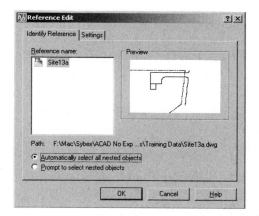

FIGURE 13.13: The cabin drawing with the updated site plan xref

FIGURE 13.14: The Reference Edit dialog box

5. Click OK. The Refedit toolbar appears, and the cabin objects turn gray to indicate that they are not editable while the drawing is in referenced edit mode.

W A R N I N G   If you have the AutoSave tool set to automatically save
your drawing periodically (Tools ≻ Options ≻ Open and Save ≻ File Safety
Precautions or savetime↵), this feature is disabled during reference editing.

You're now free to use many of the Draw and Modify commands on
the site plan drawing that you just selected.

6. Open the Layer Properties Manager, and notice that several new layers now appear.

At the top are 0Prop_line and 0Road, and lower in the list are
Site13|Prop_line and Site13a|Road. The layer names separated by the
pipe (|) symbol indicate that these are layers from the externally ref-
erenced Site13 drawing and are referred to as *xref-dependent*. One
restriction in the layer tools is that you can't make an xref-dependent
layer current in the host drawing. The layers at the top of dialog box,
the ones with the $ symbols, will hold any objects created on them
and then shift those objects to the proper xref layer at the conclusion
of the editing session.

7. Make the 0Road layer current, and then draw a 3'-0" sidewalk along
the west and north sides of the cabin. The sidewalk will be narrower
between the cabin and the patio (see Figure 13.15).

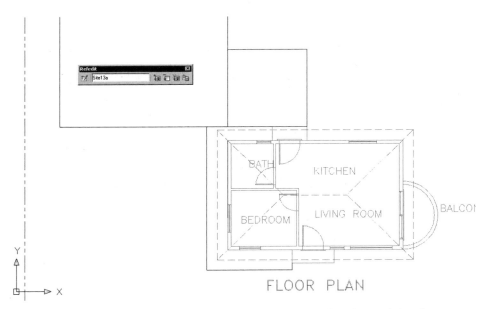

F I G U R E   1 3 . 1 5 :   The new sidewalk created in the externally referenced site plan

8. Move to the Refedit toolbar. On the far right end, click the Save Reference Edits button. When the warning dialog box opens, click OK. Your changes to the site plan are now saved back to the Site13a file.

9. Use Zoom to Extents, and then zoom out a little to a view of the whole site (see Figure 13.16). Save this drawing. It's still named Cabin13b.dwg.

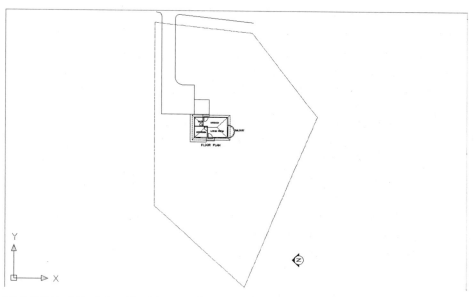

FIGURE 13.16: The Site13c drawing with the revised xref of the cabin

In this exercise, you saw how a host drawing is updated when its external reference is changed and how you can control the appearance of objects in the xref drawing from the host drawing by working with the xref-dependent layers. You also saw how you can modify objects in the xref from the host drawing by using the in-place xref editing tool. A drawing can serve as an external reference in several host drawings at the same time and have a different appearance in each one, including location, rotation, and scale. The results of in-place xref editing, however, must be saved back to the original drawing in order to be viewed in the xref. In-place xref editing is usually done only when the results are meant to be permanent changes in the original source drawing.

Adding an Image to a Drawing

Not only can you externally reference other drawing files into the current drawing, but you can also reference image files. Using this feature, you can add digital photographs or scanned images such as artist renderings and construction forms to a drawing. The procedure is similar to adding an externally referenced drawing; just follow these steps:

1. Create a new layer named Image, make it current, and then open the External References palette.

2. Right-click a blank area below the existing filenames, and choose Attach Image from the context menu to open the Select Image File dialog box.

3. Most of the common image file formats are compatible with AutoCAD 2008. Navigate to the file that you want to attach, and then click the Open button (see Figure 13.17).

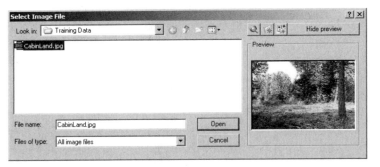

F I G U R E   1 3 . 1 7 : The image to be referenced in the Select Image File dialog box

T I P   When you select an image file, a preview appears in the Select Image File dialog box. You can use the arrow buttons on the keyboard to quickly change the selection and associated preview image.

4. The Image dialog box that opens is similar to the External Reference dialog box that you saw earlier in this chapter. Click OK.

5. In the drawing area, click once, move the cursor, and then click again to create the rectangular frame for the image. The image appears

inside the frame. The exact size of the frame is unimportant for this exercise, so ignore it for now. In the next chapter, you will decide how to view the image in the context of the rest of the drawing.

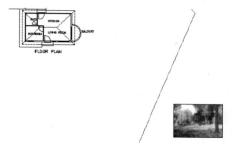

The imageframe variable determines the visibility of the image frame and how it reacts when clicked. Setting the variable to 0 (zero) causes the frame to be invisible and also prevents the image from being selected. Setting the variable to 1 displays the frame, allows it to be selected, and also shows the frame when the drawing is plotted (plotting is covered in Chapter 15). Setting imageframe to 2 displays the frame in the viewport, allows it to be selected, but does not show the frame when the drawing is plotted. This variable affects all the images in the drawing.

6. Enter imageframe↵ 2↵ to set the variable to 2.

That's all there is to adding images to AutoCAD drawings. You can move and rotate the image using the same tools as with any other object. You can resize the image by selecting the frame and adjusting the grips. You get access to some rudimentary image-editing tools when you double-click the image frame. Feel free to experiment with them, but do not be concerned about altering the image file; these adjustments affect only the image's display inside AutoCAD.

Putting Xrefs to Use

External references have many different uses. I'll describe two common applications to illustrate their range.

Suppose you're working on a project as an interior designer and a subcontractor to the lead architect. The architect gives you a drawing of a floor plan that is still undergoing changes. You load this file onto your hard disk, in a specially designated folder, and then externally reference it into your drawing as a background—a drawing to be used as a reference to draw over. You can now proceed to lay out furniture, partitions, and so on, while the architect is still refining the floor plan.

At an agreed-on time, the architect gives you a revised version of the floor plan. You overwrite the one that you have on your computer with the latest version. You can then reload the xref into your furniture layout drawing, and the newer version of the floor plan will be the background. In this example, the lead architect might also send the same versions of the floor plan to the structural and mechanical engineers and the landscape architect, all of whom are working on the project and using the architect's floor plan as an xref in their respective host drawings (see Figure 13.18).

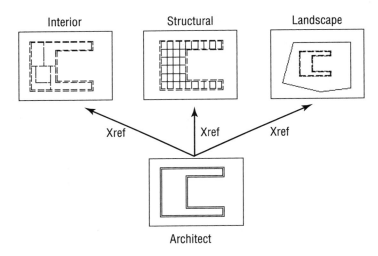

FIGURE 13.18: A single floor plan as an xref to three subcontractors

Xrefs are often used when parts of a job are being done in an office where a network is in place. Suppose a project involves work on several buildings that are all on the same site. By using xrefs, each building can be externally referenced to the site plan. This keeps the site plan drawing file from getting too large and allows the project work to be divided among different workstations; in addition, the project manager can open the host site plan and keep track of progress on the whole project (see Figure 13.19).

These two applications for setting up xrefs in relation to a host file are applicable to almost any profession or trade using AutoCAD.

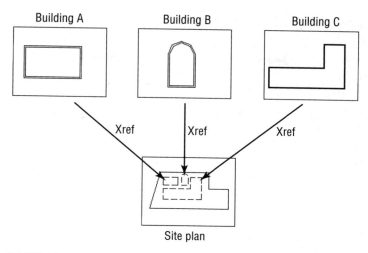

FIGURE 13.19: Three buildings as xrefs to a single site plan

Exploring Additional Xref Features

You have seen how you can modify an xref in the host or the original drawing and how to bring in images. A few other features of external references deserve mention.

Setting the Xref Path

When you attach an xref to the host drawing, AutoCAD stores the name of the xref and its path.

 N O T E   The path of a drawing file is the name of the drive, folder, and subfolder where a file is stored, followed by the name of the drawing.

Each time you open the host drawing, AutoCAD searches for any xrefs saved with the host file and displays them in the host drawing. If the xref drawing is moved to a new folder after the xref has been attached, AutoCAD won't be able to find the xref and can't display it. To avoid that situation, you must update the host drawing with the new path to the xref file. Let's go through a quick exercise to illustrate how this works:

1. Save and close the Cabin13c.dwg drawing.

2. Use Windows Explorer to create a new subfolder called Xref within the training folder you previously set up. Move Site13a to this folder.

3. Return to AutoCAD, and open `Cabin13c.dwg` again. The xref doesn't show up, but a little line of information appears in the host drawing where the insertion point of the xref was located. If you zoom in, you can read the information: it's the original path and filename of the xref.

4. Press F2 to switch to the AutoCAD text screen for a moment, and note the line that says `Resolve Xref "Site13a":` followed by the path and then `cannot be found`. AutoCAD is unable to find the xref because the path has changed. Press F2 again.

5. Open the External References palette (choose Insert ➤ External References). In the File References area where xrefs are listed, the path appears for each xref under the heading Saved Path (see Figure 13.20). You can slide the scroll bar to the right—or widen the palette—to see the full path. Notice also that the Status column for this xref reads "Not Found."

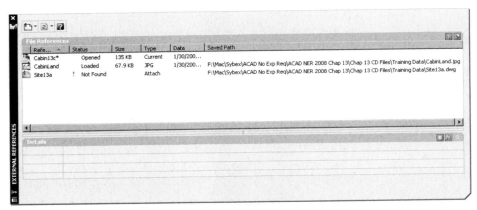

FIGURE 13.20: The missing xref is identified in the External References palette.

6. Click the `Site13a` xref to highlight it. Move down to the Details area, and click the blank space to the right of Found At. A button with three dots appears at the right end of the blank space.

7. Click the three dots. This opens the Select New Path dialog box. Find the `Site13a` drawing in the new `Xref` folder. Highlight it, and click Open.

8. Back in the External References palette, the path has been updated for `Site13a`. Click the X at the top of the palette title bar. Use Zoom Previous one or two times. The xref is restored in your drawing.

W A R N I N G   When you're working with xrefs, be careful where you store files that are acting as xrefs to other files.

Binding Xrefs

On occasion, you'll want to permanently attach an xref to the host drawing. If you send your drawing files to a printing service to be plotted, including a set of xref files can complicate things. Also, for archiving finished work, it might be better to reduce the number of files. There might also be occasions when the xref has been revised for the last time and no longer needs to be a separate file. In all these situations, you'll use the Bind command to convert an external reference into a block that is stored permanently in the host drawing:

1. Open the External References palette, and right-click Site13a in the File References list.

2. Choose Bind from the shortcut menu to open the Bind Xrefs dialog box.

The two options in the Bind Type area have to do with how layers are treated when an xref is bound to the host drawing. The default is Bind. It sets the xref layers to be maintained as unique layers in the host drawing. With the Insert option, layers that have the same name in the two drawings are combined into one layer. None of the layers in Site13a has the same name as any layers in Cabin13c. Let's use the Insert option.

3. Change the Bind Type to Insert, and click OK. The xref disappears from the list of xrefs.

4. Close the External References palette. Your drawing looks unchanged.

5. Click the site plan, and then enter list↵. The AutoCAD Text Window shows that the cabin is now a block reference.

6. Press F2, and then open the Layer Properties Manager. The site plan's layers all become layers in the Cabin13c drawing and no longer have the Site13a| prefix.

7. Click OK, and then choose Insert ➤ Block. In the Insert dialog box, open the Name drop-down list. Site13a is listed here as a block, along with the window and door blocks that you created in Chapter 7. A few additional blocks might be on the list. These blocks are used by the dimensions in the drawing.

8. Close the drop-down list by clicking a blank portion of the dialog box. Then, click Cancel to return to your drawing. The site plan is now a permanent part of the Cabin13c drawing. If you need to make changes to the site plan part of the drawing, you can explode it and use the Modify commands. Or, if you're running AutoCAD, you can use the In-Place Xref and Block Edit tool that you used previously in Chapter 7 to modify the window block and, again in this chapter, to modify the rooflines and erase the front step.

9. You do not want to save the changes in this drawing. Click File ➤ Close, and then click No in the dialog box that opens.

10. Move the Site13a file back into the Training Data folder where it was prior to starting the exercises in the "Exploring Additional Xref Features" section.

This has been a quick tour of the basic operations used to set up and control external references. There are more features and commands for working with xrefs than I've covered here, but you now know enough to start working with them.

Exploring the Other Features of Xrefs

What follows are a few additional operations and features that you might find useful when you delve more deeply into external references. Play around a little, and see what you can do:

▶ Externally referenced drawings can have drawings externally referenced to them. These are called *nested* xrefs. There is no practical limit to the number of levels of nested xrefs that a drawing can have.

▶ You can't explode an xref, but you can detach it from the host. The Detach command is on the shortcut menu that appears when you right-click an xref in the External References palette.

▶ Large, complex drawings that are externally referenced often have their insertion points coordinated in such a way that all xrefs are attached at the 0,0 point of the host drawing. This helps keep drawings aligned properly. By default, any drawing that is externally referenced into a host drawing uses 0,0 as its insertion point. But you can change the coordinates of the insertion point with the Base command. With the drawing you want to change current, enter base↵, and enter the coordinates for the new insertion point.

▶ You can limit which layers and, to some degree, which objects in a drawing are externally referenced in the host drawing by using indexing and demand loading.

▶ A host drawing can be externally referenced into the drawing that has been externally referenced into the host, causing a circular reference. This is called an *overlay* and is an option in the Attach Xref dialog box. Overlays ignore circular xrefs.

▶ If you freeze the layer that was current when an xref was attached, the entire xref is frozen. Turning off this same layer has no effect on the visibility of the xref.

▶ The Unload button in the External Reference dialog box lets you deactivate xrefs without detaching them from the host file. They stay on the list of xrefs and can be reloaded at any time with the Reload button. This option can be useful when you're working with complex drawings that have many xrefs.

If You Would Like More Practice...

In this chapter, you externally referenced the site plan drawing into the cabin drawing, as an architect who was designing the project might have done. If you were the architect, you might want to have several additional drawings. Try doing this:

1. Create several new drawings of furniture and a shed. Each object is to have its own layer. Make more than one drawing for some of the objects, such as two beds or tables.

2. Add digital images, on their own layers, that show real-world examples of the furniture.

3. Externally reference all the furniture and shed drawings into the cabin drawing.

4. Use the Layer States Manager, as covered in Chapter 6, to create layer states for each combination of furniture.

Are You Experienced?

Now you can...

- ☑ draw a basic site plan
- ☑ use surveyor's units to lay out a property line
- ☑ attach an external reference
- ☑ revise a drawing that is externally referenced
- ☑ modify an xref from the host drawing
- ☑ update an xref path
- ☑ bind an xref to a host file
- ☑ insert image files into an AutoCAD drawing

Using Layouts to Set Up a Print

▶ Putting a title block in a layout

▶ Setting up viewports in a layout

▶ Aligning viewports

▶ Controlling visibility in viewports

▶ Adding text in a layout

In Chapter 13, I introduced external references, which are useful and powerful tools for viewing one drawing from within the current drawing. This chapter builds on the material I introduced in Chapter 13. Here you'll learn to use external references in Layout display mode, which will allow you to get even more mileage out of them. External references help you combine several drawings into a composite; layouts allow you to set up and print several views of the same file. The layout is a view of your drawing as it will sit on a sheet of paper when printed.

Each layout has a designated printer and paper size for the print. You adjust the positioning of the drawing and the scale of the print. The part that is difficult to understand is the way two scales are juxtaposed in the same file: the scale of the drawing on the printed paper (usually a standard scale used by architects, such as ¼" = 1'-0") and the scale of the layout, which is almost always 1:1, or the actual size of the paper. Other professions, such as mechanical or civil engineering, set up their drawings the same way. They may use a different set of standard scales for the drawing on the printed paper, but the layout almost always remains 1:1.

One way to visualize how a layout works is to think of it as a second drawing, or a specialized layer, that has been laid over the top of your current drawing. Each layout that you create will have one or more *viewports*—special windows through which you will view your project at a scale to be printed. The layouts are usually at a scale of 1:1 (actual size) and contain some of the information that you originally included with the building lines, such as the border and title block, notes, the scale, north arrow, and so on.

Think for a moment about drawing the floor plan of a building on a traditional drafting table. You draw the building to a scale such as ⅛" = 1'-0". Then, on the same sheet of paper, you print a note using letters that are, say, ⅛" high. If you look at those letters as being on the same scale as the building, they would measure 1' high, and that's what we've been doing on the cabin drawing so far. But in traditional drafting, you don't think that way; instead, you work with two scales in the drawing without thinking about it. So, a letter is ⅛" high (actual size), and a part of the building that measures ⅛" on the paper is thought of as being 1' long (at a scale of ⅛" = 1'-0"). Layouts are designed to let you juggle two or more scales in a drawing in the same way in order to set up the drawing to be printed.

Setting Up Layouts

You will begin working with Cabin13c, the complete cabin drawing so far. All the layers will be turned on and thawed, and you will use the layouts to control the layer visibility (see Figure 14.1). This drawing is essentially complete and ready to print. For now, you will modify this drawing and create layouts for it to get a basic understanding of what layouts are and how they are activated and set up. Then, in the next chapter, you'll print this drawing, both with and without a layout.

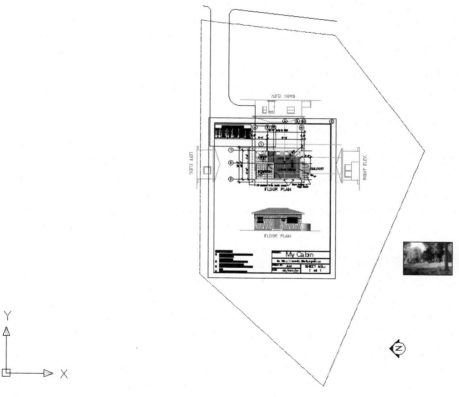

FIGURE 14.1: Cabin13c with all layers visible

In setting up a new layout, you will use an 8.5" × 11" sheet:

1. Open Cabin13c.dwg, and thaw the Tblk1 layer. Notice the border of the drawing and the rectangle just outside the border that represents the edge of the sheet of paper on which the print will be made. You will recall from Chapter 8 that when you constructed the border and title block for this drawing, you had to calculate the size of the border for a scale of ⅛" = 1'-0". This was based on a rectangle 68' wide by 88' high, which you then offset 3' to make the border. With layouts, you don't have to make this kind of calculation; you draw the border actual size.

2. Before creating a new layout, choose Tools ➤ Options to open the Options dialog box, and click the Display tab. In the Layout Elements area (lower-left corner), be sure all the check boxes are selected, and then click OK.

   Each layout has settings that spell out which plotting device is to be used to print the layout and how that print will appear. You specify these settings through a *page setup* that becomes associated with the layout.

3. Look at the lower-left corner of the drawing area. Next to the Model tab, you will see two layout tabs.

   Click the Layout1 tab. After a moment, the Page Setup Manager dialog box opens (see the top of Figure 14.2). This is where you create a new page setup—or assign an existing one—to be associated with the new layout.

4. Click New to open the New Page Setup dialog box. In the New Page Setup Name text box, enter **Cabin FPlan**, and click OK. This opens the Page Setup dialog box, which has Layout1 added to the title bar (see the bottom of Figure 14.2). The dialog box has 10 areas containing settings that control how the drawing will fit on the printed page and what part of the drawing is printed.

▶

This chapter is designed so that you can follow along even if you don't have a printer hooked up to your computer or if your printer isn't the one referred to in the text.

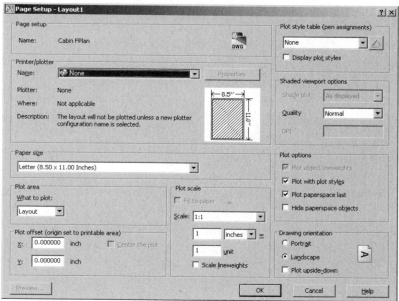

FIGURE 14.2: The Page Setup Manager dialog box (top) and the Page Setup dialog box with Layout1 added to the title (bottom)

5. In the Paper Size area, be sure the drop-down list is set to Letter. In the Printer/Plotter area, HP 5000 GN PS is the selected printer here, but yours may be different. If your computer is linked to more than one printer, make sure you choose a printer that takes 8.5" × 11" paper.

Click the Properties button next to the Name drop-down list to open
the Plotter Configuration Editor dialog box. Click the Device And
Document Settings tab. In the upper area, highlight Modify Standard
Paper Sizes (Printable Area). In the Modify Standard Paper Sizes area
below, scroll down to Letter size and highlight it. At the bottom of
this area are displays of data about the Letter sheet size, including, in
the example, Printable Area: 8.08" × 10.58". This shows the maximum
area that your printer can print on an 8.5" × 11" sheet of paper and
thus gives you an idea of how close to the edge of the paper the
printer will print. Jot down the printable area. In this example, it's
8.08 × 10.58 inches. Yours may be different.

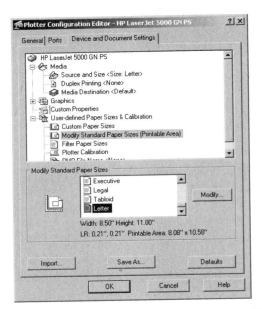

FIGURE 14.3: The Plotter Configuration Editor dialog box

Click Cancel to close this dialog box.

N O T E   I use the terms *print* and *plot* interchangeably in this book, as I
do *printer* and *plotter*. In the past, *plot* and *plotter* referred to large-format
devices and media, but that's not necessarily true today. *Print* and *printing*
are more widely used now because of changes in the technology of the large-
format devices.

6. Back in the Page Setup dialog box, move to the Drawing Orientation (lower-right corner) area, and select Portrait.

7. The Plot Area area contains a drop-down list with three options for selecting what portion of the drawing area is to be plotted. Be sure that Layout is selected.

8. In the Plot Scale area, the scale to be used is 1:1. If it's not already selected, open the Scale drop-down list, and select 1:1 from the list of preset scale choices.

9. In the Page Setup area (upper-left corner), Cabin FPlan appears as the current page setup. You'll ignore the other areas of this dialog box for now.

10. Click OK. You are returned to the Page Setup Manager dialog box. Cabin FPlan is now on the Page Setups list.

11. Highlight Cabin Fplan, and click Set Current. The layout area behind the dialog box changes to match the parameters you set in the Page Setup dialog box. Click Close to close the Page Setup Manager dialog box. You are returned to your drawing, and Layout1 appears (see Figure 14.4).

The Scale drop-down list contains by default 33 preset scales and a custom option. To delete unnecessary scales, add new ones, edit existing ones, or rearrange the order of the listing, enter scalelistedit.⏎ to open the Edit Scale List dialog box.

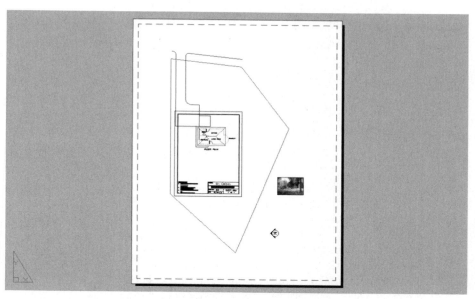

FIGURE 14.4: Layout1 for the cabin

12. You don't want the current *viewport*, the window that lets you see your drawing from the layout. You will make your own shortly. Enter e↵ all↵↵ to erase all the objects in the layout tab. Everything disappears, but don't worry—your cabin drawing is intact.

13. Save your drawing as Cabin14a.dwg.

With the way I have set up AutoCAD for this book, the drawing area now displays a white sheet of paper resting on a gray background. You'll be changing two elements in the layout: you'll cut a new viewport and move the title block into the layout. The viewport creates a hole, or a window, in the layout so that you can see through the layout to the drawing of the building. You can think of the building as residing "underneath" the layout. Near the outer edge of the white rectangle is a rectangle of dashed lines. This represents the 8.20" × 10.27" printable area of your printer—everything within the dashed border will be printed.

UNDERSTANDING MODEL SPACE AND PAPER SPACE

So far in this book, you have been drawing in the Model tab, also called *model space*. You have put all the drawing's information—lines, dimensions, text, the title block, and so on—into model space. Everything that must be drawn to scale is placed in model space and other items, such as notes and the title block, are usually placed in *paper space*, or the space that resides in the layout tabs. Think of model space as the real world where everything is drawn at full scale.

Paper space is located outside of the model space world and is the size of the paper that you intend to plot the drawing on. While in paper space, you can look into model space through a window called a *viewport*. The appearance of the objects seen through the viewport is determined by the viewport scale. At a ⅛"=1' viewport scale, all model space objects seen through the view appear at ⅟₉₆th their drawn size. Each viewport can be set to its own scale.

To work on the cabin itself, you need to move the cursor to model space. You can do this in two ways. One is to click the Model tab. This temporarily removes the layout and leaves you with just the drawing, or *model*. The other way is to switch to model space while a layout is active. You'll try that method now.

Moving the Border to the Layout

You have already created the title block in model space, so you just need to move it to the layout. As in any other Windows program, you can use the cut/copy/paste tools to move objects between model and paper space. You will select and then cut the title block from model space, paste it to a layout tab, and then adjust it to fit. Here is the procedure:

1. Click the Model tab. The paper space view disappears, and the cabin view returns.

2. Select all the title block objects including the two borders, but leave the notes unselected. You can do this quickly using a crossing selection window around the lower-right corner of the title block.

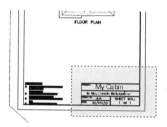

3. Choose Edit ➤ Cut, or hold the Ctrl button down and then press the X key. The title block disappears as it is cut to the Windows Clipboard.

4. Click the Layout1 tab, and then choose Edit ➤ Paste As Block, or hold down the Shift and Ctrl keys and then press the V key.

5. At the Specify insertion point: prompt, click a point near the lower-left corner of the dashed border. The exact location is not important because you will be adjusting the border location shortly.

6. The title block is inserted, but it is much too large for the available layout area. Select it and then press the Scale button in the Modify toolbar, or enter sc↵.

7. Turn off running osnaps, and then pick a point in the lower-left corner as the base point for the scale operation. At the Specify scale factor or [Copy/Reference] <0'-1">: prompt, enter 1/96↵. The title block is scaled to ¹⁄₉₆th its original size, or the ratio of ⅛" to 1' (see the top of Figure 14.5).

As the term *model space* implies, the lines and other AutoCAD objects that make up the components of the cabin are often referred to as a *model*. This distinguishes them from other AutoCAD objects, such as the title block and border, that often reside on a layout.

8. Move the title block so that the inner border line is centered inside the dashed border of the layout. Your layout tab should look like the bottom of Figure 14.5.

FIGURE 14.5: The title block pasted into the Layout1 tab and scaled (top) and then moved within the dashed boundary (bottom)

9. You inserted the title block as a block only to make it easier to select and scale; in other words, you don't need to retain it as a block. Select the title block, and explode it.

10. Select the thin outer border, outside of the dashed line, and delete it. Your title block is ready to use.

Creating the Paper Space Viewport

Now that the title block is copied into the layout, you need to be able to view the model hidden behind it. You will do this by creating a viewport with the Mview command:

1. Open the Layer Properties Manager, create a new layer named VP, assign it the color red, and make VP the current layer. Click the printer icon in the Plot column to set this as a nonplotting layer—you want to be able to see the viewport objects on the screen, but you don't want to see them in prints of the drawings.

T I P   It's useful to assign a color to the layer that you place your viewport on that will stand out in your drawing so you are reminded that the viewports, while an essential part of the drawing, are usually designed to be invisible.

2. Enter mview↵. Then, at the Specify corner of viewport or [ON/OFF/Fit/Shadeplot/Lock/Object/Polygonal/Restore/ LAyer/2/3/4] <Fit>: prompt, click a point even with the top of the text boxes and near the left edge of the title block border.

3. Click a point near the upper-right corner of the title block border as the opposite corner of the viewport (Figure 14.6).

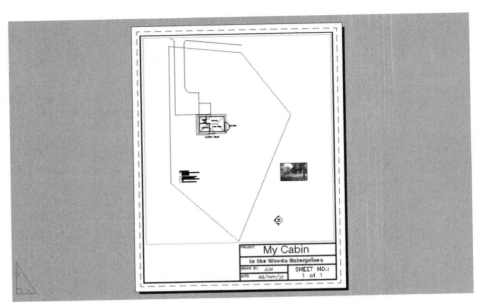

FIGURE 14.6: The title block and viewport showing the cabin scene

4. Place your cursor over an object inside the cabin, click just one time, and then move the cursor. Rather than selecting the object, you began a selection window. Drag the window around some of the objects near the cabin, and then click again. Nothing is selected.

5. Notice how the horizontal and vertical lines that emit from the cursor extend all the way to the edges of the drawing window. This informs you that you are currently working in paper space and can select only paper space objects such as the title block border and text. To work on the cabin itself, you need to move the cursor to model space. You can do this in two ways. One is to click the Model tab. This temporarily removes the layout and leaves you with just the drawing, or *model*. The other way is to switch to model space while a layout is active.

N O T E   If the lines of your crosshair cursor don't ordinarily extend to the edges of the drawing area, choose Tools ➢ Options to open the Options dialog box, and click the Display tab. In the lower-left corner, where it says Crosshair Size, move the slider all the way to the right, and click Apply. The new setting will be 100, and the crosshairs extend to the drawing area edges.

6. Place your cursor within the title block area, and this time double-click. The viewport border becomes bolder, and the cursor lines extend only to that border. You are now in model space and are able to select the model space objects, but not any objects that reside in paper space.

7. Notice the familiar L-shaped UCS icon in the lower-left corner of the viewport. It wasn't there a moment ago; it appears only in the current viewport. When the cursor is in paper space, the UCS icon changes to a triangular shape, in the lower-left corner of the Auto-CAD window, with an X and Y on its axis lines.

When you activate model space while a layout is active, it is like opening a window and reaching through the opening to touch the drawing of the building behind the window.

 N O T E You can control the visibility of the UCS icon in each viewport and in paper space by choosing View > Display > UCS Icon and then clicking On. When the check mark next to On is visible, the UCS icon appears. When the layout is active, the icon is a triangle and sits outside the layout.

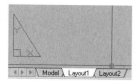

8. Move the cursor outside of the viewport area, and watch as it changes from a crosshair cursor to an arrow. This is another visual cue that the focus of the program is in model space even though the cursor is beyond the limits of the viewport boundary.

9. Double-click the cursor to the side of the title block area. The crosshair cursor returns, and you are back in model space.

 T I P You can also click the Model button at the right end of the status bar to move from model space to paper space. When in paper space, the button label is Paper, and you can click it to switch to model space.

Setting the Viewport Scale

The layout is set to print to an 8½" × 11" paper, and you want the contents of the viewport to plot to a specific scale. In this section, you will adjust the viewport scale to display the model space objects at ⅛"=1' by assigning a viewport scale.

1. Double-click inside the viewport to enter model space.

2. Right-click any toolbar, and choose Viewports from the context menu to open the Viewports toolbar.

3. Expand the Viewport Scale Control drop-down list, and choose 1/8" = 1'-0". The viewport zooms into the model space to the proper scale.

4. Use the Pan Realtime tool inside the viewport to adjust the position of the cabin so that the floor plan and front elevation occupy most of the viewport (see Figure 14.7).

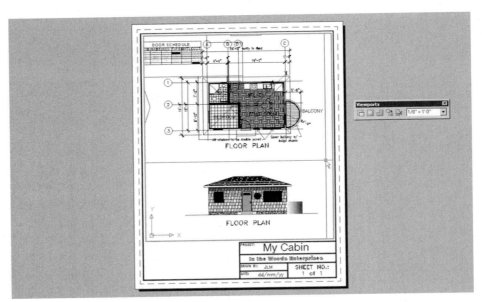

FIGURE 14.7:   The cabin drawing zoomed into the floor plan and front elevation

5. The scene is a bit cluttered, but that will be rectified in the next section. Double-click the gray area outside the title block to switch back to paper space.

6. Click the Single Viewport button in the viewport toolbar or use the Mview command to make a second viewport in the bottom-left corner of the title block. It's perfectly acceptable if the two viewports overlap each other. Another instance of the entire cabin drawing's model space appears in the new viewport.

7. Double-click inside the new viewport to make it active, then zoom and pan until the notes are visible, and then switch back to paper space. Your drawing should look similar to Figure 14.8.

T I P   Items such as tables and notes can go in either model space, as shown in this exercise, or in paper space. When in paper space, it's easy to develop and maintain a consistent text or table style that appears the same in all drawings. When notes and tables are in model space, you have the flexibility to change their sizes simply by zooming in or out in the viewport. Model space objects can also be shown in any number of layouts in the same drawing. You'll develop your own standard or adhere to your company's standard for note and table placement.

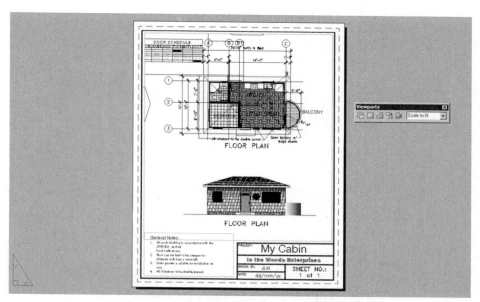

F I G U R E   1 4 . 8 : The cabin drawing zoomed into the floor plan and front elevation

Copying the Layouts

The layout that you made is an excellent starting point. You will adjust the title block information and then duplicate the layouts several times to accommodate the different views of your cabin. Each time a layout is copied, all of its contents, including the viewports and their settings, are copied with it. These copies are not interdependent, and any changes made to one are not reflected in the others.

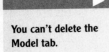

You can't delete the Model tab.

1. Right-click the Layout2 tab, choose Delete from the context menu, and then click OK in the warning dialog box that opens. You'll be copying Layout1 and don't need this one.

2. Double-click the Layout1 tab to highlight the name. Enter **Cabin FPlan and F Elev**↵ to rename the layout. Always give your layouts short, descriptive name to help identify them when you are searching for a particular content.

3. Right-click the layout tab, and choose Move or Copy from the context menu.

4. In the Move Or Copy dialog box that opens, select the (Move To End) item in the Before Layout list box. You can use this dialog box to copy a layout or to rearrange the order of the existing layouts. Click the Create a Copy option in the lower-left corner, and then click OK.

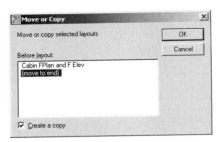

5. A copy of the layout appears to the right of the original with "(2)" appended to its title.

6. Copy the layout three more times for a total of five layout tabs and one Model tab. All the layout tabs are identical at this point.

7. Rename the five new tabs to Cabin FPlan Dims, Cabin LElev RElev, Cabin BElev, and Cabin Site (see Figure 14.9).

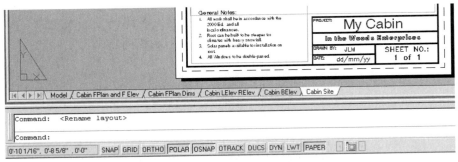

FIGURE 14.9: There are now five layout tabs for the cabin drawing.

Adjusting a Viewport's Contents

The model space for the drawing is too cluttered to be useful. A drawing that looks like this would not be acceptable in most work environments, and one of the strengths of AutoCAD is its ability to easily adjust existing objects in the drawing. In this section, you will spread out the objects in model space and then specify which viewports display which layers.

1. Click the Model tab to view the drawing in model space.

2. Open the Layer Properties Manager. Select all the layers, and then thaw and turn them all on.

3. Zoom in to see all the cabin views, notes, image, and the table. Your drawing should look similar to Figure 14.10.

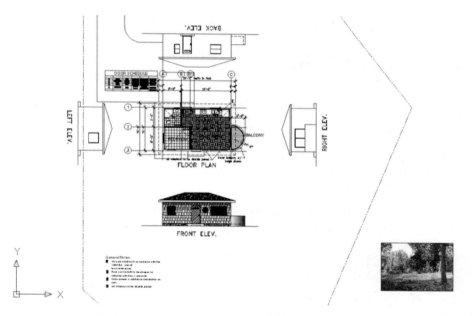

FIGURE 14.10: The cabin drawing with all layers thawed

4. Click the Ortho button, and then select and move the Back elevation toward the top of the screen and away from the grid bubbles.

5. Turn Ortho off. Select the table, and move it to the right of the general notes at the bottom of the screen. Its exact location is unimportant because, like the notes, the table will be zoomed to fit a viewport.

N O T E The viewports in layouts are called *floating* viewports because they can be moved around. They always reside in the layout portion of the drawing. There is another kind of viewport in AutoCAD called a *tiled* viewport, which is fixed and exists only in model space. For brevity, in this chapter, I will refer to floating viewports as *viewports*.

6. Click the Cabin FPlan and F Elev tab. Double-click the "1 of 1" text in the Sheet No. section of the title block, and edit it to read 1 of 5.

7. Double-click inside the viewport area. The goal here is to not display any objects that do not pertain to the current layout. This is where a well-thought-out and carefully followed layering scheme really pays some dividends.

8. Right-click any toolbar, and choose Layers II from the context menu. The Layers II toolbar contains some handy tools for maintaining the layers in your drawing.

9. In the Layers II toolbar, click the Layer Freeze button, and then place your cursor back into the viewport area. The cursor is now a pickbox.

10. Click a dimension; all the dimensions disappear. You did not freeze the Dim1 layer in the drawing by picking the dimension; you froze the Dim1 layer only in that particular viewport. Open the Layer Properties Manager, and locate the Dim1 layer. As you can see in Figure 14.11, the Freeze column shows the layer as thawed, but the VP Freeze column shows Dim1 as frozen. All columns that start with VP relate only to the active viewport. When the Model tab is selected, these columns do not appear in the Layer Properties Manager. If you switch to the Model tab, you would see the Dim1 layer is still visible.

11. Click the Layer Freeze button again, and then click the dimension that measures the hipline, the roofline from the left elevation, a polyline used to calculate the floor plan areas, and the patio that is part of the externally referenced site plan.

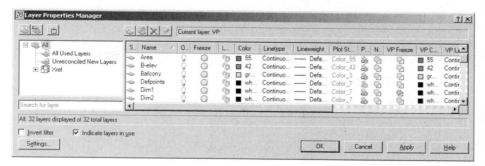

FIGURE 14.11: The Layer Properties Manager showing the status of the Dim1 layer

12. With the two variables ltscale (linetype scale) and psltscale (paper space linetype scale) both set to 1, the noncontinuous linetypes will appear the same in both model space and paper space. To change the scale of the dashed rooflines, enter **ltscale⏎ 0.4⏎**. The roofline dashes are smaller.

13. Click the Esc key to terminate the command, and then double-click outside the title block to enter paper space. Your drawing should look similar to Figure 14.12.

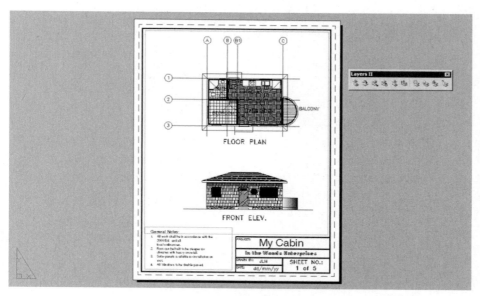

FIGURE 14.12: The Cabin FPlan and F Elev layout after freezing layers in the viewport

Adjusting the Other Viewports' Contents

Each of the remaining layouts has a specific purpose, and each requires a different set of layer conditions. You will use the same tools in the other viewports as you did for the viewport in the Cabin FPlan and F Elev tab:

1. Click the Cabin FPlan Dims tab. This looks like the preceding tab before you made adjustments to the content that it displayed.

2. Double-click in the larger viewport, and then click the Layer Freeze button.

3. Click a grid bubble and a grid line to freeze these components' layers in the viewport. Click the patio, the roofline of the left elevation, an area polyline, one of the hatch patterns, and each one of the components of the front elevation.

4. Press Esc, and then double-click outside the viewport. Select the larger viewport border, and then click one of the lower grips that appear at the corners. Move one lower grip of the viewport upward, and the other lower grip moves as well to maintain the constant shape of the viewport.

5. Press Esc to deselect the larger viewport, and then select and move the smaller VP until it is centered below the larger.

6. Double-click inside the smaller viewport, and then zoom and pan until the door schedule fits the viewport nicely. If you don't see the schedule, open the Layer Properties Manager, and make sure the VP Freeze column shows the layer as thawed in the viewport. If you like, you can adjust the viewport's grips to make it larger.

7. Switch back to paper space, and then change Sheet No. to read "2 of 5." When you are done, the layout should look like Figure 14.13.

8. Click the Cabin LElev RElev tab, and then delete the smaller viewport.

9. Adjust the size of the larger viewport so that it takes up the upper half of the title block border. Copy it downward so that you have two identical viewports stacked one on top of the other (see Figure 14.14).

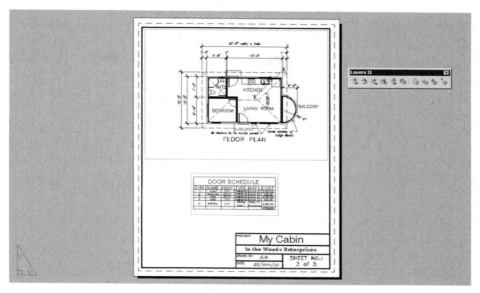

FIGURE 14.13: The Cabin FPlan Dims layout after freezing layers in the viewport

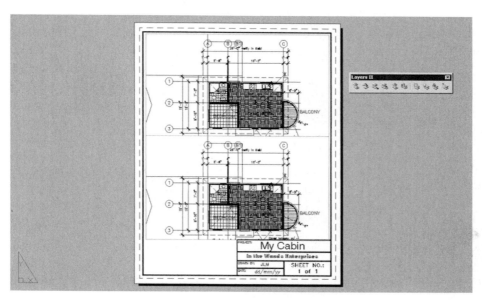

FIGURE 14.14: Two identical viewports before adjusting their content

10. Double-click the upper viewport, and then pan until you see the left elevation. This elevation needs to be rotated to be viewed properly in the viewport. You don't want to rotate the structure itself, because that would affect the drawing should you need to revise it. Instead, you will rotate the UCS.

11. Choose Tools ➤ New UCS ➤ Z, and then enter -90↵ at the Specify rotation angle about Z axis <90.00>: prompt.

12. Enter plan↵ ↵ The viewport contents rotate negative 90°, and the viewport is zoomed outward to show the extents of the model space.

13. Scale the viewport to ⅛" = 1' using the Viewports toolbar, or enter zoom↵ 1/96XP↵ at the command prompt. The XP in the Zoom command identifies the zoom factor in relationship to the scale factor of the paper space, usually 1 = 1.

14. Pan the viewport until the left elevation is centered, and then VP Freeze any layers that you don't want displayed.

15. Repeat the process with the lower viewport to display the right elevation. In this case, the UCS should be rotated around the z-axis positive 90°.

16. Exit model space, and then change the Sheet No. designation to 3 of 5. This layout should look like Figure 14.15.

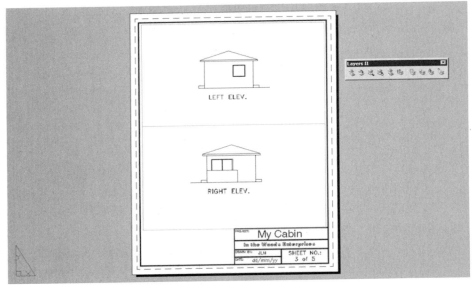

FIGURE 14.15: The Cabin RElev layout after rotating the UCSs and adjusting the viewports' content

17. Switch to the Cabin BElev layout tab, and delete the smaller viewport. Follow the procedure from the second layout tab with the goal of showing the back elevation in the viewport. The UCS should be rotated 180° around the z-axis.

18. In paper space, change Sheet No. to 4 of 5. This layout should look like Figure 14.16.

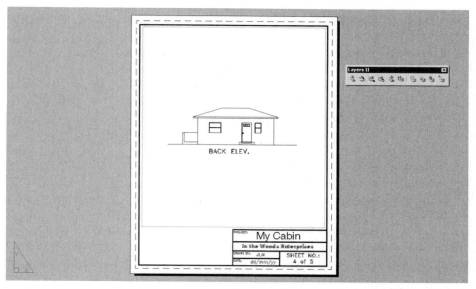

FIGURE 14.16: The Cabin BElev layout after rotating the UCS and adjusting the viewport's content

19. Switch to the Cabin Site tab, and enter the larger viewport. Enter zoom↵ 1/360xp↵ to scale the viewport to 1" = 30'.

20. Freeze everything in the viewport except the walls, doors, windows, roof, site plan, and north arrow. If you zoom in to select any of the smaller objects, be sure to use Zoom Previous to revert to the required zoom factor.

21. Double-click the smaller viewport, and then zoom into the image that was referenced into the drawing.

22. Change Sheet No. to 5 of 5. This layout should look like Figure 14.17.

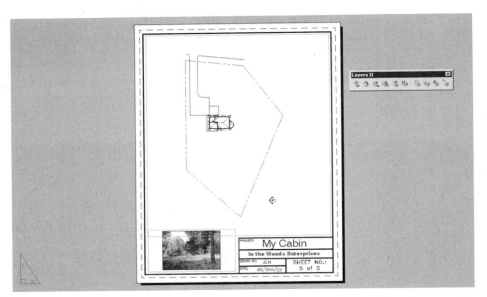

FIGURE 14.17: The Cabin Site layout after scaling the viewport and freezing unwanted layers

23. Save your drawing as Cabin14b.dwg.

You've made a set of five drawings complete with scaled viewports and designated content. In the next section, you will look at a couple of ways to protect the drawing from accidental errors.

Aligning Viewports

You want to display the two opposite elevations with one building directly below the other. To accomplish this, you will need to perform some steps in model space and some on the layout, so you'll be switching back and forth while keeping the Cabin LElev RElev layout visible:

1. Click the Cabin LElev RElev layout tab. Click Paper on the status bar to switch to model space. Then move the cursor onto the viewports. The one that is active is the one where the crosshair cursor is visible.

 T I P   When model space is active, only one viewport can be active at a time. This is the one with the crosshair cursor. The active viewport's border also appears thicker. You can manipulate objects in the active viewport. To make a viewport active, place the arrow cursor in it, and double-click.

2. The UCS of both viewports must match to use the align function correctly. Enter **ucs↵ w↵** to change the current viewport UCS to the WCS. Repeat the process in the other viewport.

3. Turn on Endpoint as a running osnap.

4. Enter **mvsetup↵**. Then enter **a↵** to select the Align option.

5. Enter **v↵** to select the Vertical option.

5. At the Specify basepoint: prompt, click the top of the outside right wall where it meets the roofline.

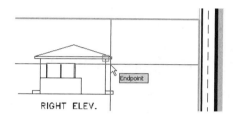

6. At the next prompt, click the other viewport, and then click the top of the right wall. The elevation in the second viewport is panned laterally so that it is aligned with the elevation in the first viewport (see Figure 14.18). Press Esc to end the Mvsetup command.

LT users can skip to the "Aligning Viewports for LT" section (following step 6) for an alternate series of steps.

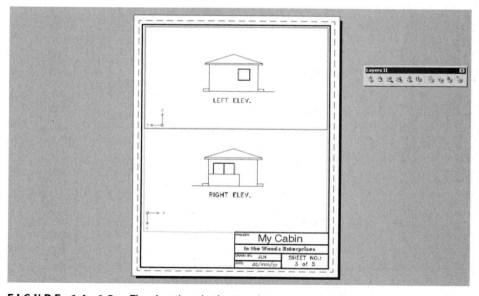

F I G U R E   1 4 . 1 8 : The elevations in the two viewports are aligned.

Aligning Viewports for LT

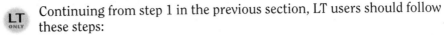

Continuing from step 1 in the previous section, LT users should follow these steps:

2. Click Polar to turn it on, and then click in the top viewport to make it active. Use Pan Realtime to pan the drawing so that the front elevation is positioned halfway between the top and bottom of the 8½" × 11" sheet.

3. Turn on polar tracking. Click the Model button on the status bar to switch to paper space.

4. Use the Endpoint osnap to draw a line from the top of one of the right walls of the upper elevation down over the lower viewport.

5. Switch back to model space, and make the lower viewport active.

6. Enter -p↵. Click the Endpoint osnap, and click the top of the right wall.

7. Move the cursor to the right or left until the horizontal crosshair of the cursor lines up with the horizontal line you just drew, as best you can eyeball it, and then click.

8. End the Pan command, switch to paper space, and erase the vertical line.

Now you have the result as in Figure 14.18 (shown earlier). You have one or two more things to do to finish the layout.

Locking and Turning Viewports Off

One of the common errors that you will make when working with viewports is zooming or panning while in a viewport and then failing to return the viewport to its proper appearance. You can prevent yourself, or anyone else, from editing the viewport view by locking the viewport. This feature doesn't prevent you from editing the content of the viewport—just how you access and view it. When you execute a pan or zoom while inside a locked viewport, AutoCAD temporarily exits the viewport, pans or zooms the equivalent amount in paper space, and then returns to model space. There is a slight lag in time when panning or zooming with this feature on, but it is much less than the time you may spend correcting or reissuing a set of drawings that have viewports at the wrong scale factor. Follow this procedure to lock a viewport:

1. Click the Cabin FPlan and F Elev tab.

2. Select the larger viewport, right-click, and then choose Display Locked ➤ Yes from the context menu. The viewport is now locked.

WHAT YOU DO IN MODEL SPACE AND PAPER SPACE (LAYOUTS)

Here's a partial list of some of the tasks you do in the two environments.

Model Space

You can do the following tasks in model space:

▶ Zoom to a scale in a viewport (1/*scale factor* xp).

▶ Work on the building (or the project you are drawing).

▶ Make a viewport current.

▶ Control layer visibility in the current viewport.

Paper Space (Layouts)

You can do the following tasks in paper space:

▶ Create viewports.

▶ Modify the size and location of viewports.

▶ Use the Viewports toolbar to set a viewport's scale.

▶ Lock/unlock the scale of the display in a viewport.

▶ Turn viewports on or off.

▶ Add a title block and border.

Turning Off Viewports

Beyond controlling the visibility of layers in each viewport, you can also turn off a viewport so that all model space objects within it are invisible:

1. Select the small viewport, and then click the Properties button.

2. In the Properties palette, be sure the Misc section is open, and then open the drop-down list next to On, and click No. Close the Properties palette. Then press Esc to deselect the viewport. The small viewport goes blank, and all that is visible is its border (see Figure 14.19).

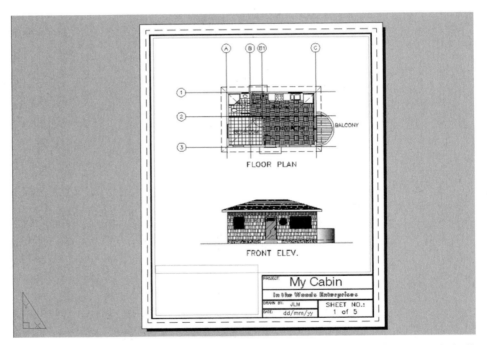

FIGURE 14.19: The Cabin FPlan and F Elev layout with the smaller viewport turned off

4. Reselect the small viewport, and click Properties to turn it back on.

5. Save this drawing as Cabin14C.dwg.

Being able to turn off viewports can be an advantage for a complex drawing with many viewports or for one with a lot of information in each viewport. Remember that even though all the layouts in this drawing are based on one drawing, AutoCAD is drawing at least part of that drawing in each viewport. In a complex drawing, this can slow down the computer, so it's handy to be able to temporarily turn off any viewports on which you aren't working. It's also an easy way to check which objects are in model space and which are on the layout (or in paper space).

You will work with the viewports and layouts again in the next chapter, where you will round out your knowledge of AutoCAD by learning the principles of plotting and printing AutoCAD drawings.

If You Would Like More Practice...

Create another layout for Cabin14C that is has a landscape orientation and is sized to fit a 30" × 42" paper. Create four or more layouts: one for the site plan and the others for various views of the drawing. Your new layout may look something like Figure 14.20.

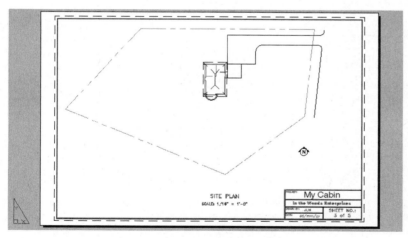

FIGURE 14.20: An additional layout for Cabin14c

Save this drawing as Site13-extra.dwg.

Are You Experienced?

Now you can...

- ☑ create a layout and associate it with a page setup
- ☑ copy a border and title block to a layout
- ☑ set up viewports on layouts
- ☑ cut and paste in AutoCAD
- ☑ zoom to a scale in a viewport
- ☑ lock the display of a viewport
- ☑ align viewports
- ☑ control layer visibility in individual viewports
- ☑ control the visibility of viewport boundaries
- ☑ edit the text in a layout
- ☑ turn viewports off and on

CHAPTER 15

Printing an AutoCAD Drawing

- ▶ Setting up a drawing to be printed
- ▶ Using the Plot dialog box
- ▶ Assigning lineweights to layers in your drawing
- ▶ Selecting the part of your drawing to print
- ▶ Previewing a print
- ▶ Printing a layout
- ▶ Publishing multiple layouts
- ▶ Looking at plot styles

With today's equipment, there is no difference between printing and plotting. *Printing* used to refer to smaller-format printers, and *plotting* used to refer to pen plotters, most of which were for plotting large sheets. But the terms are now used almost interchangeably. Pen plotters have almost universally been replaced by large-format ink-jet plotters with a few extra settings that other printing devices don't have. Otherwise, as far as AutoCAD is concerned, the differences between plotters and laser, ink-jet, and electrostatic printers are minimal. In this book, printing and plotting have the same meanings.

Getting your drawing onto paper can be easy, if your computer is connected to a printer that has been set up to print AutoCAD drawings and AutoCAD has been configured to work with your printer. If these initial conditions are met, you can handily manage printing with the tools you'll learn in this chapter. If you don't have the initial setup, you'll need to get some help either to set up your system to make AutoCAD work properly with your printer or to find out how your system is already set up to print AutoCAD drawings.

You'll be using a couple of standard setup configurations between AutoCAD and printers to move through the exercises. You might or might not be able to follow each step to completion, depending on whether you have access to an 8.5" × 11" laser or ink-jet printer, a larger-format printer, or both.

You will print the Cabin14a drawing from the layout tabs at its default 8½" × 11" sheet and at 30" × 42" sheet size.

Even if your printer won't let you print in all these formats, we suggest you follow along with the text. You'll at least get to preview how your drawing would look if printed in these formats, and you'll be taking large strides toward learning how to set up and run a print for your drawing. The purpose of this chapter is to give you the basic principles for printing, regardless of whether you have access to a printer.

Using the Plot Dialog Box

The job of getting your AutoCAD file onto hard copy can be broken into five tasks. You'll need to tell AutoCAD the following:

- ► The printing device you'll use
- ► The lineweight assigned to each object in your drawing
- ► The portion of your drawing you're printing
- ► The sheet size you're printing
- ► The scale, orientation, and placement of the print on the sheet

You handle most of these tasks in the Plot dialog box:

1. Open Cabin14c (see Figure 15.1). Click the Cabin FPlan and F Elev tab to make it active. Ensure that you are in paper space.

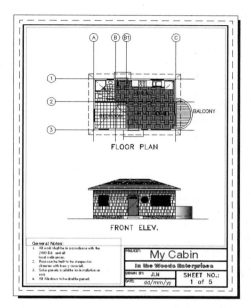

F I G U R E   1 5 . 1 : The Cabin14a drawing showing the floor plan and front elevation

2. Click the Plot button on the Standard toolbar to open the Plot dialog box. The title bar includes the name of the layout tab because, in this case, you're printing a drawing from paper space. If you print from model space, the title bar displays the word *Model*. This dialog box is similar to the Page Setup dialog box that you worked with in Chapter 14 when you were setting up layouts (see Figure 15.2).

This dialog box does have some differences, however:

▶ The dialog box is smaller, but you can expand it to include four more areas of information and settings on the right side. (Yours might open in this expanded form.)

▶ It has an additional area called Number of Copies.

You can also open the Plot dialog box by choosing File ➢ Plot, by pressing Ctrl+P, or by entering plot↵ or print↵.

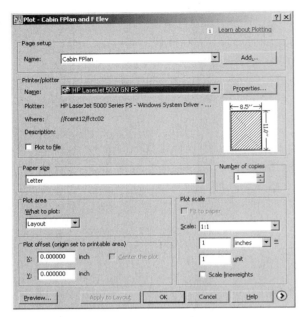

FIGURE 15.2: The Plot dialog box

UNRECONCILED LAYERS

If you receive a Layer Notification Warning dialog box or a notification bubble stating that you have unreconciled layers, you must address the situation before plotting the drawing. *Unreconciled layers* are new layers that have been added since the last time the drawing was saved, the Plot command was used, or a layer state was saved. The purpose of the warning or notification is to cause you to look at these new layers and determine whether any action is required. Open the Layer Properties Manager, and click Unreconciled New Layers in the left pane to display the list in the right pane. Select all the layers shown, right-click, choose Reconcile Layer from the context menu, and then click OK to close the Layer Properties Manager. All layers are now reconciled, and the warnings should discontinue until you add any new layers.

First, you'll take a quick tour of this dialog box. Then, you'll start setting up to print.

You'll see seven areas of settings on this unexpanded version of the dialog box. Some of the buttons and boxes won't be activated. We'll mention others only in passing, because their functions are for more advanced techniques than those covered in this book. These functions are available when in the Model tab as well.

Printer/Plotter

In this area, the Name drop-down list contains the various printing devices to which AutoCAD has been configured, with the current one, the HP LaserJet 5000GN PS, displayed in Figure 15.2. Yours might say None or display a different printer. Just below the list, the name of the driver and the assigned port or network path and asset name are displayed for the selected printer. Clicking the Properties button to the right opens the Plotter Configuration Editor dialog box, which has three tabs of data specific to the current printer. Most of this will already be set up by your Windows operating system. Back in the Plot dialog box, the Plot to File check box, when selected, directs AutoCAD to make and save the print as a .plt file, rather than sending it to a printer. Many reproduction service bureaus prefer to receive .plt files to print, rather than AutoCAD .dwg files with all their required support and externally referenced files (fonts, images, external references, and so on).

Paper Size and Number of Copies

In the Paper Size area, the drop-down list contains paper sizes that the current plot device can handle. To the right is the Number of Copies area, which is self-explanatory. When you have a large run of pages to print, it's prudent to print a single copy of each, check for errors or omissions, and then print multiple copies of each page.

Plot Area

In the Plot Area area, a drop-down list contains the options for specifying what to print in your drawing. You have already decided which layers will be visible when the print is made by freezing the layers in each viewport whose objects you don't want to print. Now you must decide how to designate the area of the drawing to be printed. As you go through the options, it's useful to think about the choices with regard to two printing possibilities: printing the whole drawing and printing just the floor plan. Using layouts removes much of the guesswork from the plotting process.

To illustrate how these options work, we'll make a couple of assumptions. First, the 1:1 Scale option is selected in the Plot Scale area, so AutoCAD will try to print the drawing at full scale. Second, the drawing will be in portrait orientation. Click the right-pointing expansion arrow in the lower-right corner to expand the dialog box. Be sure Portrait is selected in the Drawing Orientation section, and then click the left-pointing arrow again to close the expansion.

The Display Option

The Display option, on the What to Plot drop-down list, prints what's currently on the screen, including the blank area around the drawing. With the sheet in portrait orientation and with the origin in the lower-left corner of the paper space area, choose this option. Click the Preview button in the lower-left corner of the Plot dialog box. The plot preview will look like Figure 15.3. The drawing doesn't fit well on the sheet with this option. It's oriented and sized correctly, but with the beginning of the plot area in the lower-right corner of the paper space area, it's printed above and to the right of where it should be. A considerable amount of clipping has also occurred, and much of the drawing is not displayed. Printing to Display is a quick method of plotting everything that is shown in the layout tab but is rarely the best solution when plotting in model space. Click Esc to exit the preview mode.

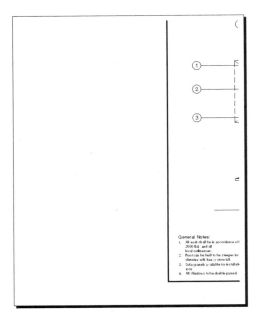

FIGURE 15.3: The cabin drawing printed to Display

The Extents Option

When you select the Extents option, AutoCAD tries to fill the sheet with all visible objects in the drawing. Choose the Extents option, and then click the Preview button; the results will look like Figure 15.4. This is closer to acceptable than the Display option, but it's not quite right. The border is off center because the extents of the drawing begin at the lower-left corner white area in paper space that represents the actual paper. This is a good method to use if the border is not plotted or if there is no border at all. Be aware that if any objects exist in paper space to the left or below the drawing area, these will shift the beginning of the extents and reduce the amount of the actual drawing area that is visible. Click Esc to return to the Plot dialog box.

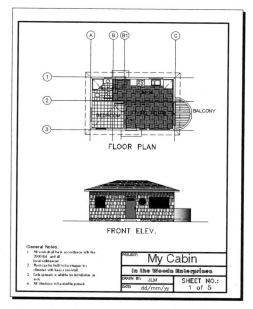

FIGURE 15.4: The drawing printed to Extents

The Limits Option

Do you remember the drawing limits for the cabin drawing that you set in Chapter 3? As a refresher, perform the following steps:

1. Click Cancel to cancel the plot, and then click the Model tab. Plotting to Limits is not available in a layout.

2. Start the Plot command again. If necessary, assign the same plotter, and then choose Limits from the What to Plot drop-down list. In the Plot Scale section, click the Fit to Paper option—plotting at 1:1 in the Model tab would result in only a miniscule portion of the vast drawing area actually getting plotted. When you print to Limits, AutoCAD prints only what lies within the limits, and it pushes what's within the limits to the corner that is the origin of the print.

3. Click the expansion arrow in the lower-right corner, and be sure Portrait is selected in the Drawing Orientation area. Then, click the Preview button in the lower-left corner (see Figure 15.5). This print won't work here because the limits don't cover the entire drawing, and the title block has already been moved into paper space. Also, the limits are in landscape orientation, so the portion of the drawing to be printed doesn't fit properly on the paper. Printing to Limits can be a good tool for setting up a print, but you'll usually reset the limits from their original defining coordinates to new ones for the actual print.

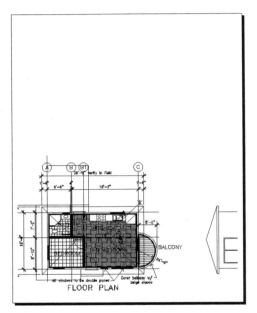

FIGURE 15.5: The grid showing the cabin, with a preview of the drawing printed to Limits

4. Right-click, and choose Exit from the shortcut menu to exit the preview.

If you are in a layout tab of a .dwg file, the Limits option is replaced by Layout in the What to Plot drop-down list in the Plot Area area.

The View Option

When printing to View, you tell AutoCAD to print a previously defined view that was saved with the drawing. When plotting from model space, the View option isn't displayed in the What to Plot drop-down list if you haven't defined and saved any views yet. The View option is never available when plotting from paper space.

1. Switch to the Cabin FPlan and Elev tab, and then restart the Plot command.

2. Expand the What to Plot drop-down list, and click View. A new drop-down list appears to the right.

3. Expand the new drop-down list, and choose right_elev.

4. Click the Preview button, and the preview should look similar to Figure 15.6. A view is always taken from the same fixed location. In the preceding chapter, you moved several components of the cabin drawing and might need to update the named views to reflect this. The View option for What to Plot is a valuable tool for setting up partial prints of a drawing.

5. Press Esc to exit the preview, and then click Cancel to close the Plot dialog box.

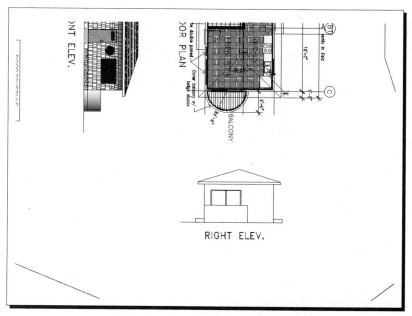

FIGURE 15.6: Plotting model space to a named view

The Window Option

Using a window to define the area of a plot is the most flexible of the five methods described so far. It's like using a zoom window in the drawing. When you select this option, you're returned to your drawing. In your drawing, make a window around the area you want to print. When you return to the Plot dialog box, a Window button appears in the right side of the Plot Area area (see Figure 15.7), in case you need to redefine the window.

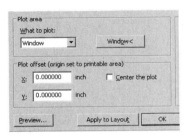

FIGURE 15.7: The Plot Area area in the Plot dialog box with its drop-down list open and the Window button displayed next to it

AutoCAD will print only what is in the window you made, regardless of how it fits on the sheet. This method is similar to the View method just discussed. The difference is that the View method prints a previously defined view (one that was possibly defined by a window, but could also be defined in other ways), and the Window method prints what is included in a window that you define as you're setting up the plot. The window used by the Window method can't be saved and recalled at a later time.

These are five ways to specify what to print in paper or model space. You'll use the Window option in the exercise that follows to print a portion of the drawing from model space. Later in this chapter, you will revisit and plot from the layout tabs.

Plot Scale

On the right edge of the plot dialog box is the Plot Scale area, where you control the scale of the plot. When the Fit to Paper check box is selected, AutoCAD takes whatever area you have chosen to print and automatically scales it so that it will fit on the selected page size. When this option is unchecked, the Scale drop-down list becomes available. This list contains 33 preset scales to choose from, plus a Custom option. Some of the scales in the list are displayed as pure ratios, such as 1:50. Others are shown in their standard format, such as ¼" = 1'-0". Below the drop-down list is a pair of text boxes for setting up a custom scale. When you choose a preset scale, these text boxes display the true ratio of the current scale.

To set up a custom scale, you choose the units you're using in your drawing (inches or millimeters), and enter a plotted distance in the text box just below the Scale drop-down list. Then, in the Units text box below that, enter the number of units in your drawing that will be represented by the distance you entered in the text box above. The inches (or millimeters) distance is an actual distance on the plotted drawing, and the units distance is the distance the plotted units represent. For ¼" scale (¼" = 1'-0"), you can enter several combinations:

= Text Box	Units Text Box
¼ inches	1'
1 inches	4'
1 inches	48 inches

Layouts are plotted at a scale of 1:1. I'll come back to this and other scale issues as you prepare a drawing for printing.

Plot Offset and Plot Options

Below the Plot Area area is the Plot Offset (Origin Set to Printable Area) area, which contains two text boxes and a check box. Select the Center the Plot check box to center the plot on the printed sheet. If this check box isn't selected, by default AutoCAD places the lower-left corner (or the origin) of the area you have specified to plot at the lower-left corner (or origin) of the printable area of the current paper size. By changing the settings in the X and Y text boxes, you can move the drawing horizontally or vertically to fit on the page as you want. When the Center the Plot check box is selected, the X and Y text boxes are disabled for input but display the offset distance from the lower-left corner of the sheet that was necessary to center the drawing.

Just as each drawing has an origin (0,0 point), each plotter creates an origin for the plot. Usually it's in the lower-left or upper-left corner, but not always. When the plot is being made, the printer first locates the origin and starts the print there, moving laterally from the origin in the opposite direction of the paper feed. If the origin is in the lower-left corner, the print might come out looking like the left of Figure 15.8. If the origin is the upper-left corner, the print will look like the right of Figure 15.8. The origin point has less of an impact as plotter technology develops. Many machines already have a self-centering capability.

By using the X and Y settings in the Plot Offset area, you can make one margin wider for a binding. To center your drawing on the page, select the Center the Plot check box (see the bottom of Figure 15.8). If layouts are set up and being used for printing, they determine this setting, and the Center the Plot check box is unavailable.

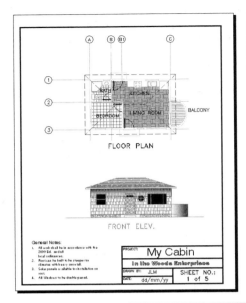

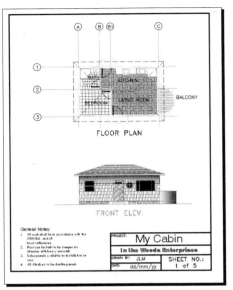

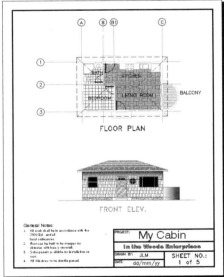

FIGURE 15.8: A print with its origin in the lower-left corner (left), in the upper-left corner (right), and with the drawing centered (bottom)

TIP Usually, 8.5" × 11"–format printers are configured to the portrait orientation. If your drawing is also set to that orientation, the origin of the plot will be in the lower-left corner. If your drawing is in the landscape orientation, the plot origin will move to the upper-left corner of the page because the plot has been rotated to fit on the page.

Setting the material to be printed accurately on the page will be a result of trial and error and getting to know your printer. We'll return to this topic shortly, when we show how to get ready to print.

The Expanded Plot Dialog Box

If the Plot dialog box hasn't already been expanded, click the right-pointing arrow in the lower-right corner to expand it to include four additional areas in a stack on the right. For now, we're primarily concerned about the one on the bottom (see Figure 15.9).

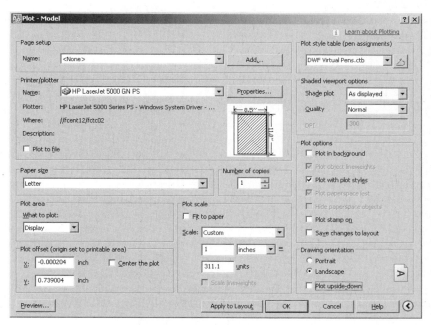

FIGURE 15.9: The expanded Plot dialog box

Drawing Orientation   The settings in this area are self-explanatory. The radio buttons serve as a toggle between the portrait and landscape orientation, and the Plot Upside-Down check box serves as an on/off toggle.

Plot Options   This area has seven check boxes that don't concern you now.

Shaded Viewport Options   This area has settings to control the plot for renderings and shaded views, which will be covered in the later chapters.

Plot Style Table (Pen Assignments)   We'll discuss plot styles and pen assignments later in this chapter.

You have taken a quick tour of the Plot dialog box, and you still have a drawing, Cabin14c, to print. Let's print it. As you set up the print, refer to this section for an explanation of the steps, if necessary.

Printing a Drawing

Your task is to print Cabin14c from model space at a scale of $\frac{1}{8}$" = 1'-0" on an 8.5" × 11"–format laser printer. In this exercise, you'll use the default system printer, which is set up for an 8.5" × 11"–format printer. If you have an 8.5" × 11"–format printer, you should be able to follow the steps. If you don't have a printer, you can still get familiar with printing by following along with the steps.

The first step is to freeze some layers and assign lineweights to the remaining visible layers.

Determining Lineweights for a Drawing

Click Cancel to close the Plot dialog box, and look at the Cabin14c drawing as a whole. You need to decide on weights for the various lines. The floor plan is drawn as if a cut were made horizontally through the building just below the tops of the window and door openings. Everything that was cut will be given a heavy line. Objects above and below the cut will be given progressively lighter lines, depending on how far above or below the cut the objects are located.

In this system, the walls, windows, and doors will be heaviest. The roof, headers, fixtures, and steps will be lighter. For emphasis, you'll make the walls a little heavier than the windows and doors. In the front elevation, the hatch pattern will be very light, and the outline of the various components will be heavier, for emphasis. Text and the title block information will use the default lineweight. These are general guidelines; weights will vary with each drawing.

N O T E Lineweight standards vary for each trade and profession that uses AutoCAD. Details usually follow a system that is independent from the one used by other drawings in the same set. Section lines, hidden lines, center lines, cutting plane lines, break lines, and so on, all will be assigned specific lineweights.

You'll use four lineweights for this drawing:

Weight	Thickness in Inches
Very light	0.005
Light	0.008
Medium	0.010
Heavy	0.014

In Cabin14c, 15 layers are visible in the Cabin FPlan and F Elev layout as it's currently set up. Their lineweights will be assigned as follows:

Layer	Lineweight
Balcony	Light
Dim1	Very light
Doors	Medium
F-elev	Medium
Fixtures	Light
Hatch-elev-black	Very light
Hatch-elev-brown	Very light
Hatch-elev-gray	Very light
Headers	Light
Roof	Very light
Steps	Light
Tblk1 (the notes)	Medium
Text1	Medium
Walls	Heavy
Windows	Medium

When you look at the lineweights currently assigned to these layers and at the thickness you need these lineweights to be, you can generate a third chart that shows what lineweight needs to be assigned to each group of layers:

Thickness	Layers
0.005	Dim1, all visible Hatch layers, Roof
0.008	Balcony, Fixtures, Headers, Steps
0.010 (default)	Doors, F-elev, Tblk1, Text, Windows
0.014	Walls

Now it's time to freeze the unwanted layers and assign the lineweights to the remaining layers in the drawing:

1. Open the Layer Properties Manager, and make the VP layer current.

2. Freeze the following layers: 0, Area, B-elev, Dim2, Grid, Hatch-hidden, Hatch-plan-floor, Image, L-elev, R-elev, all four Site layers, and Tables. The VP and Defpoints layers do not plot anyway, so you don't need to be concerned with them at this time.

3. Click the Dim1 layer to highlight it. Hold down the Ctrl key, and click the three Hatch-elev layers and the Roof layer to select them. Then, release the Ctrl key.

4. In the Lineweight column of the Layer Properties Manager dialog box, click one of the highlighted Default words to open the Lineweight dialog box (see Figure 15.10).

FIGURE 15.10: Assigning a lineweight in the Lineweight dialog box

5. Click 0.005". Then, click OK. The Lineweight dialog box closes. In the Layer Properties Manager dialog box, the five highlighted layers now have a lineweight of 0.005" assigned to them.

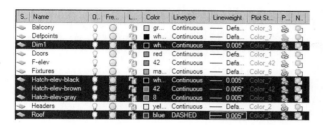

6. Click the Balcony layer near the layer's name.

7. Hold down the Ctrl key, and click Fixtures, Headers, and Steps.

8. Click one of the highlighted Default words. The Lineweight dialog box opens.

9. Click 0.008". Then, click OK. The newly highlighted layers now have a lineweight of 0.008" assigned to them.

10. You can leave Default as the linetype for the Doors, Windows, and Text1 layers because the thickness they need is the default thickness of 0.010". Click the Walls layer, and use the same procedure to assign it the thickness of 0.014".

11. Click OK to close the Layer Properties Manager dialog box.

12. Enter lw↵ to open the Lineweight Settings dialog box.

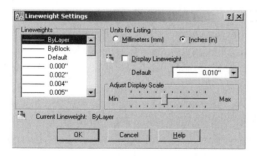

N O T E   Notice the Default drop-down list on the right, in which 0.010" is displayed. This tells you that the default lineweight thickness is 0.010", which is what you assumed in step 9.

13. Click Cancel to close the dialog box.

14. Set the linetype scale to 24 (ltscale↵ 24↵)

You have assigned the lineweights. When the print is complete, you can judge whether these lineweight assignments are acceptable or need to be adjusted. In an office, a lot of time is invested in developing a lineweight standard that can be used in most drawings.

Setting Other Properties of Layers

Two other properties of layers deserve mention: Plot and Description. Both appear in the Layer List window of the Layer Properties Manager dialog box.

The Plot feature is a two-way toggle that controls whether the objects on a layer are printed. By default, the control is off. When this feature is activated for a particular layer, objects on that layer aren't printed but remain visible on the screen. You used this feature to render the VP layer unplottable, and in the future you might designate a layer for in-house notes and data that you don't intend to be seen by those who will eventually view your printed drawings and then set the layer to not be printed.

A Description column appears at the far right of the Layer List window. Clicking in this column on the blue bar of a highlighted layer opens a text box in which you can enter a description of the layer. Layer names are often in code or use abbreviations that don't fully describe what objects are on that layer. Here's a place to remedy that.

Setting Up the Other Parameters for the Print

Now that you have set the lineweights, it's time to move to the Plot dialog box and complete the setting changes you need to make in order to print this drawing. You'll use the Window option to select what you'll print.

1. Start the Plot command.

2. In the Plot dialog box, check the Printer/Plotter area to be sure you have the correct printer displayed in the drop-down list. Also check the Paper Size area to be sure you have Letter (8.5 × 11) as the selected paper size. Then, move down to the Plot Area area, open the What to Plot drop-down list, and select Window.

3. In the drawing, disable any running osnaps. To start the window, pick a point just above the dimensions and to the right of the word BALCONY.

4. To complete the window, click a point just below the FRONT ELEV. text and to the left of the dimensions. Back in the Plot dialog box, Window

is displayed in the What to Plot drop-down list, and a new Window button appears on the right side of the Plot Area area. Click this button if you need to redo the window after viewing a preview of the plot.

5. If you have not already done so, click the right-pointing arrow in the lower-right corner of the Plot dialog box to display another column of areas. In the Drawing Orientation area in the lower-right corner, be sure Portrait is selected.

6. In the Plot Scale area, uncheck Fit to Paper, open the Scale drop-down list, and select 1/8" = 1'0". Notice that the text boxes below now read .125 and 12, a form of the true ratio for ⅛" scale.

7. In the Plot Offset area, click the Center the Plot check box.

This completes the setup for the first plot. Before you waste paper, it's a good idea to preview how it will look as a result of the setup changes.

Previewing a Print

The Preview feature gives you the opportunity to view your drawing exactly as it will print.

1. Click the Preview button. The computer takes a moment to calculate the plot and then displays a full view of your drawing as it will fit on the page (see Figure 15.11). If a Plot Scale Confirm dialog box opens, click OK.

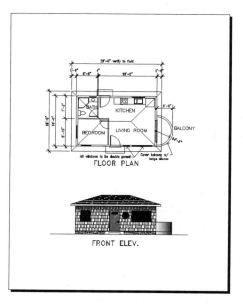

FIGURE 15.11: The preview of the cabin drawing, ready to print

On the right side of the Printer/Plotter area of the Plot dialog box, AutoCAD displays a partial preview of the plot, in diagram form, as you set it up. If there is problem with the setup, it displays red lines to warn you, but sometimes it isn't accurate. It's better to use the Preview feature where you see a WYSIWYG view of the plot.

2. Right-click, and choose Zoom Window from the shortcut menu.

3. Make a window that encloses the bathroom and a couple of the dimensions. You have to click and hold down the mouse button, drag open the window, and then release. The new view displays the lineweights you have set up (see Figure 15.12).

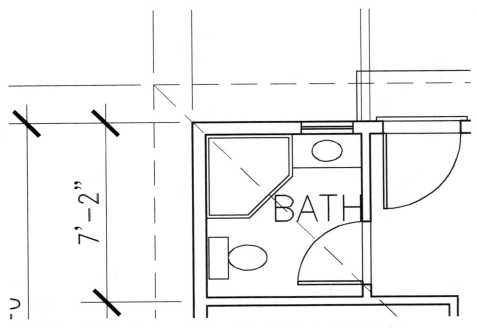

FIGURE 15.12: The zoomed-in view of the cabin showing the lineweights

4. Right-click, and choose Zoom Original from the shortcut menu to return to the first preview view.

5. Right-click again, and choose Exit to return to the Plot dialog box. If your print was oriented correctly on the sheet, you're ready to print. If not, recheck the setup steps for errors.

6. At the bottom of the Plot dialog box, click the Apply to Layout button, and then click OK. The computer begins calculating the print and eventually sends it to the printer.

 7. After the print is done, a notification button appears at the lower-right corner of the AutoCAD window to inform you. You can turn

notifications on and off by right-clicking the Plot/Publish Detail icon in the AutoCAD tray and choosing the appropriate option.

8. Save this drawing as Cabin15a.dwg.

N O T E   You can change a setting in the Lineweight Settings dialog box to be able to see lineweights in your drawing before you preview a plot, but they aren't very accurate unless you're using layouts. When you print from model space, you have to preview the drawing from the Plot dialog box to see how the lineweights look.

When your print comes out, it should look like Figure 15.11 (shown earlier). Check the lineweights of the various components on the print. You might have to make adjustments for your particular printer.

Next you'll plot the drawing using the layouts you created in Chapter 14.

Printing a Drawing Using Layouts

As a comparison to the preceding exercise, you'll print the drawing from the layout tabs. When a layout tab has been set up properly and is active, you print at a scale of 1:1. The elements of the drawing on the layout are then printed actual size, and the model space portion of the drawing is printed at the scale to which the viewport has been set. Follow these steps:

1. Click the Cabin FPlan and F Elev layout tab. For a review of layouts and viewports, see Chapter 14. Your layout should look like Figure 15.13.

2. Open the Layer Properties Manager dialog box, and thaw all the frozen layers. You can do this quickly by right-clicking any layer, choosing Select All from the context menu, and then clicking any frozen layer's snowflake icon. Click OK to close the dialog box.

3. Start the Plot command.

4. You're using the same printer, paper size, and orientation as before, so make sure those parameters are the same.

5. Make sure that, in the Plot Area area, the current choice displayed in the What to Plot drop-down list is Layout instead of Limits.

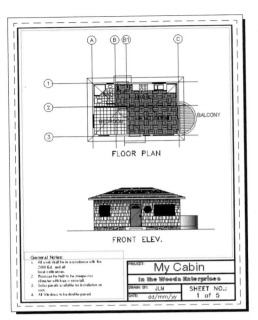

FIGURE 15.13: The cabin drawing ready for printing from a layout tab

6. In the Plot Scale area, the scale has been set to 1:1. This is what you want.

7. In the Plot Offset area, the Center the Plot check box is grayed out; it isn't needed when using a layout to plot.

8. There are no changes to make. Because this layout was set up for printing when it was created, all the settings in the Plot dialog box are automatically set correctly.

9. In the lower-left corner, select Preview. Your preview should look like Figure 15.14. Notice how the title block is centered in the preview just as it is in the layout.

10. Right-click, and choose Exit to close the preview window. Click OK to start the print. If you don't have a printer or if you're just following along, click Cancel to cancel the print at this point.

This exercise was intended to show you that once a layout has been created, most of the setup work for printing is already done for you. This greatly simplifies the printing process because the parameters of the print are determined before the Plot command begins.

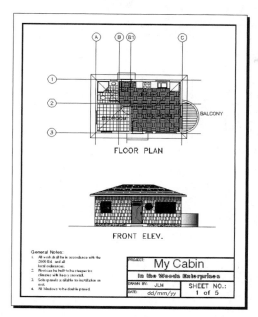

FIGURE 15.14: The preview of the current layout

Printing a Drawing with Multiple Viewports

Multiple viewports in a layout don't require special handling. The print is made with the layout active at a scale of 1:1. For the next print, you'll use a different printer—one that can handle larger sheet sizes. If you don't have access to a large-format printer, you can still configure AutoCAD for one and preview how the print would look.

Printing with a Large-Format Printer

The procedure here varies little from the one you just followed to print the layout at 1:1 scale. Here you will scale the viewport up to fit on a larger sheet for presentation purposes:

1. Save the current drawing to your training folder as Cabin15b, but don't close it yet.

2. This drawing has several layout tabs. In this exercise you'll print the site plan, so be sure the Cabin Site layout is active (see Figure 15.15).

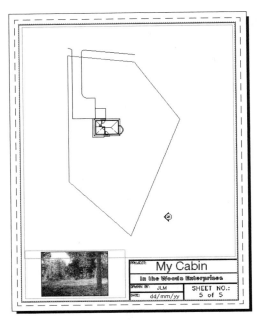

FIGURE 15.15: The cabin drawing with the Cabin Site layout active

 N O T E   In a true production environment, it might be a better choice to create a large-format layout to accommodate large-format plots.

3. Start the Plot command.

4. In the Plot dialog box, expand the Plotter Name drop-down list and, if you have one, select a wide format plotter. In the Paper Size area, choose any large size paper that is used by the plotter.

5. In the Plot Area area, choose Extents, and then click the Center the Plot option.

6. In the Plot Scale area, check the Fit to Paper option, and then check Scale Lineweights. Scale Lineweights causes AutoCAD to scale the lineweights relative to the amount the layout is scaled to fit to the paper.

7. Click the Preview button. The white area around the border isn't even (see Figure 15.16). This is because the aspect ratio of the layout is different from that of the 30" × 42" paper.

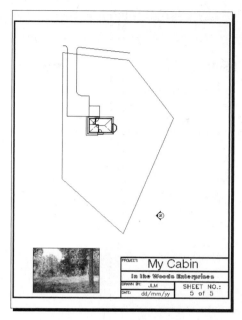

FIGURE 15.16: Preview of the Cabin Site tab

8. Right-click, and choose Exit from the shortcut menu to cancel the preview. If you have a large-format printer configured and can plot this drawing at full size, click OK to start the print. Otherwise, click Cancel.

9. Save this drawing as Cabin15b.dwg.

For the last exercise in this chapter, you'll set up AutoCAD to print all the paper space layouts at one time.

Publishing Multiple Layouts

In AutoCAD terminology you plot a single layout or view one or more times. The term *publishing* refers to assigning several layouts or views to plot in sequence one or more times. In this exercise, you will publish all your layout tabs at one time.

1. Choose File ➤ Publish to open the Publish dialog box (see Figure 15.17). This shows all the tabs including the Model tab.

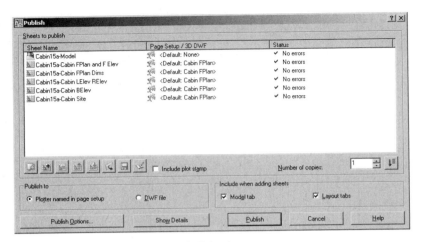

FIGURE 15.17: The Publish dialog box

2. You don't want to plot the Model tab, so select it, and then click the Delete Sheet button below the Sheets to Publish list box.

3. To prevent the Model tab from automatically being added in the future, uncheck the Model Tab option in the Include When Adding Sheets section in the bottom-right corner of the dialog box.

    In the Page Setup/3D DWF column, you can see that all the layouts are set to <Default:Cabin FPlan>. This indicates that all the layouts will use the original page setup designated when the first layout, Cabin FPlan and F Elev, was created. Remember, the other four layouts were copied from this original layout.

4. Click the Publish button. In the Save Sheet List dialog box, click Yes. This provides you with the opportunity to save this publish job as a Drawing Set Description (.dsd) file so that it can be reloaded with the Load Sheet List button. Not in all instances will all the layouts in a drawing be plotted at one time. By creating .dsd files for frequently published layout combinations, you can reduce the amount of time required to produce hard-copy prints.

5. In the Save List As dialog box that opens, name the .dsd file, and navigate to your current working directory to place it.

6. Click the Publish button. The Publish dialog box closes, and the plots begin. An extensive number of plots can take a while to finish,

depending on the size and complexity of the drawings and speed of the printer. The publish operation takes place in the background so you can continue to work on your drawings as the publishing occurs.

Only one publish operation can occur at one time. If you start one operation before the previous one is completed, you will see a Job Already in Progress dialog box indicating that you must wait before starting the next one.

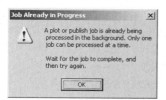

A Few Words About Plot Styles

So far in this chapter, you have assigned lineweights to layers. We have assumed that any printer is monochromatic and converts all colors in the AutoCAD drawing to black. Laser printers usually are monochromatic, but they might print the lighter colors in your drawing as screened. If you have access to a large-format ink-jet plotter, you might have the option to print in monochrome or color. In that case, you might have objects in your drawing that are one color, but you want them printed in another color. Plot styles offer a means to handle these kinds of situations. You don't have to use plot styles in AutoCAD, but you might need to work on a drawing that uses them. We'll finish this chapter with a tour of the various dialog boxes and procedures for setting up and assigning plot styles.

Introducing Plot-Style Table Files

A *plot style* is a group of settings that is assigned to a layer, a color, or an object. It determines how that layer, color, or object is printed. Plot styles are grouped into plot-style tables that are saved as files on your hard drive. Two kinds of plot styles exist:

▶ Color-dependent, which are assigned to colors in your drawing

▶ Named, which are assigned to layers or objects

For LT the path is similar but uses an AutoCAD LT 2008 **folder and one called** R13 **instead of** R18.0.

Leave AutoCAD for a moment, and use Windows Explorer to navigate to the following folder: C:\Documents and Settings*your name*\Application Data\Autodesk\AutoCAD 2008\R18.0\enu\Plot Styles. Open the subfolder called Plot Styles. Figure 15.18 shows the contents of the Plot Styles folder. Thirteen plot-style table files are already set up. Nine of them are color-dependent plot-style table files, with the extension .ctb, and four are named plot-style table files, with the extension .stb. (If you can't see the .ctb and .stb extensions, choose Tools ➤ Folder Options ➤ View, and uncheck Hide Extensions for Known Filetypes.) Finally, you'll see a shortcut to the Add-A-Plot Style Table Wizard, which you use to set up custom plot-style tables. Close Windows Explorer, and return to AutoCAD.

Name ▲	Size	Type
acad.ctb	5 KB	AutoCAD Color-dependent Plot Style Table File
acad.stb	1 KB	AutoCAD Plot Style Table File
Add-A-Plot Style Table Wizard	1 KB	Shortcut
Autodesk-Color.stb	1 KB	AutoCAD Plot Style Table File
Autodesk-MONO.stb	1 KB	AutoCAD Plot Style Table File
DWF Virtual Pens.ctb	6 KB	AutoCAD Color-dependent Plot Style Table File
Fill Patterns.ctb	5 KB	AutoCAD Color-dependent Plot Style Table File
Grayscale.ctb	5 KB	AutoCAD Color-dependent Plot Style Table File
monochrome.ctb	5 KB	AutoCAD Color-dependent Plot Style Table File
monochrome.stb	1 KB	AutoCAD Plot Style Table File
Screening 25%.ctb	5 KB	AutoCAD Color-dependent Plot Style Table File
Screening 50%.ctb	5 KB	AutoCAD Color-dependent Plot Style Table File
Screening 75%.ctb	5 KB	AutoCAD Color-dependent Plot Style Table File
Screening 100%.ctb	5 KB	AutoCAD Color-dependent Plot Style Table File

FIGURE 15.18: The contents of the Plot Styles folder

Understanding How Plot-Style Table Files Are Organized

Plot-style table files are assigned to a drawing and contain all the plot styles needed to control how that drawing is printed. Color-dependent plot styles control printing parameters through color. There are 255 of them in each color-dependent plot-style table, one for each color. Named plot-style tables, on the other hand, have only as many plot styles as are necessary, possibly only two or three. You'll now look at a plot-style table and see how it's organized:

1. In AutoCAD, choose File ➤ Plot Style Manager to open the Plot Styles dialog box. It's much like the Windows Explorer view of Auto-CAD's Plot Styles subfolder. In fact, it's another view of the same folder. Your view might have large icons and might not display all the details.

2. Double-click the first acad file in the list. It's the one that says Auto-CAD Color-Dependent Plot Style Table File in the right column of Figure 15.18. This opens the Plot Style Table Editor dialog box with acad.ctb in its title bar (see Figure 15.19). This dialog box has three tabs. The General tab displays information and a Description text box for input.

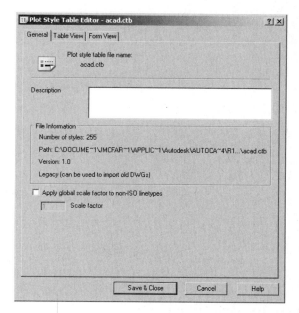

FIGURE 15.19: The General tab of the Plot Style Table Editor dialog box for the acad.ctb file

3. Click the Table View tab (see Figure 15.20). Now you see the plot styles across the top and the plot style properties listed down the left side. This tab organizes the information like a spreadsheet. Use the scroll bar to assure yourself that there are 255 plot styles. Notice that each plot style has 12 properties, plus a text box for a description. This tab displays the plot-style information in a way that gives you an overview of the table as a whole.

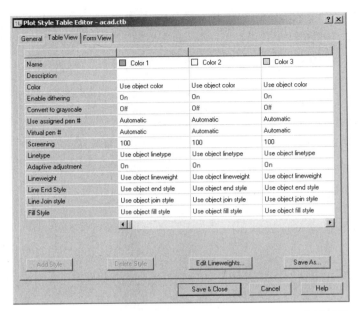

FIGURE 15.20: The Table View tab of the Plot Style Table Editor dialog box for the acad.ctb file

4. Click the Form View tab (see Figure 15.21). The same information is organized in a slightly different way. Here the plot styles are listed in the box on the left. You can highlight one or more plot styles at a time. The properties of the highlighted styles appear on the right. This view is set up to modify the properties of chosen plot styles. Notice that the first property, Color, has Use Object Color assigned for all plot styles. This means that red objects are plotted in red, blue in blue, and so on. You can override this by expanding the drop-down list and selecting another color.

5. Close the Plot Style Table Editor, and open the color-dependent mono-chrome file by double-clicking it. Click the Table View tab. Now, look at the Color property. All plot styles have the color Black assigned (see Figure 15.22).

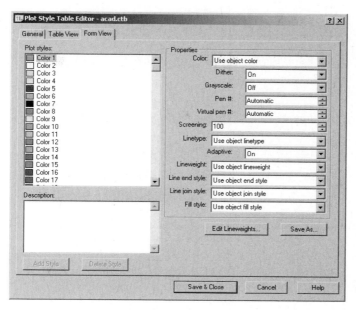

FIGURE 15.21: The Form View tab of the Plot Style Table Editor dialog box for the acad.ctb file

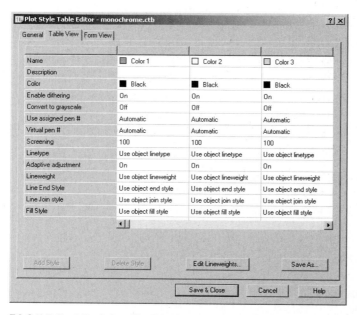

FIGURE 15.22: The Table View tab of the Plot Style Table Editor dialog box for the monochrome.ctb file

6. Close that plot-style table file, and open `acad.stb` and `monochrome
.stb` to see how few plot styles they contain.

7. Close the Plot Style Table Editor dialog box, and close the Plot Styles
dialog box.

The `monochrome.ctb` and `.ctb` files will print all colors in your drawing as
black, but they won't change the colors in the AutoCAD file.

Assigning Plot-Style Tables to Drawings

Each drawing can be assigned only one kind of plot-style table file: color-dependent
or named. This is determined when the drawing is first created.

 N O T E Even though the type of plot style for a new drawing is fixed in
the Plot Style Table Settings dialog box, two utility commands let you
switch the type of plot style that a drawing can have and assign a different
one. They are the Convertpstyles and Convertctb commands.

Follow these steps:

1. Choose Tools ➢ Options to open the Options dialog box, and click the
Plot and Publish tab. Then, click the Plot Style Table Settings button
near the lower-right corner of the dialog box. Doing so opens the Plot
Style Table Settings dialog box. In the uppermost area are the two radio
buttons that control which type of plot style a drawing will accept,
color-dependent or named (see Figure 15.23). New drawings will accept
only the type of plot style that is selected here.

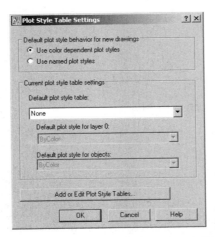

FIGURE 15.23: The Plot Style Table Settings dialog box

2. Below the radio buttons is the Default Plot Style Table drop-down list. Here you can select a plot-style table file (of the type selected by the radio buttons) to be automatically assigned to new drawings. One of the options is None.

3. Close the Plot Style Table Settings dialog box. Then, close the Options dialog box.

Throughout this book, all the drawings that you created (or downloaded) were set up to use color-dependent plot styles, so you can assign this type of plot style to the drawing. Usually you do this by assigning a particular plot-style table file to a layout or to model space. To finish our tour, and this chapter, you'll assign one of the available plot-style table files to the Cabin15b drawing and use the Preview option to see the results:

1. Make Cabin15b the current drawing, if it isn't already.

2. Click the Cabin FPlan and F Elev layout tab to make it current, if it isn't already.

3. Start the Plot command, and make sure the extension of the dialog box at the right is open. If it's not, click the right-pointing arrow in the lower-right corner to open it. In the upper-right corner, make sure None is displayed in the Plot Style Table drop-down list, and then click the Preview button. AutoCAD displays the preview in the same colors used in the drawing (see Figure 15.24).

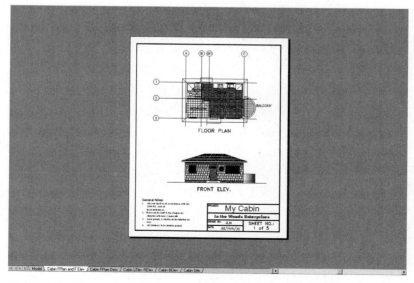

FIGURE 15.24: Preview of Layout1 without a plot-style table assigned to it

4. Exit the Preview display, and then click the Cancel button to cancel the plot.

5. Right-click the current layout tab, and choose Page Setup Manager. In the Page Setup Manager dialog box, highlight Cabin FPlan in the Page Setups list, and click Modify. Doing so opens the Page Setup dialog box.

6. Notice that in the Plot Style Table (Pen Assignments) area, None is selected. No plot-style table file has been assigned to this layout.

7. Open the drop-down list.

   All the available .ctb (color-dependent plot-style table) files are listed. You can choose one or click New at the bottom of the list and create your own. Once one is chosen, you can click the Edit button to modify it and make a new plot style out of it.

8. Select monochrome.ctb.

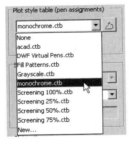

9. Click Preview in the lower-left corner. All lines and filled areas in the drawing are solid black (see Figure 15.25).

10. Exit Preview.

11. Repeat steps 5–10, and select a different .ctb file from the Plot Style Table drop-down list. (I recommend trying Screening 50%.ctb and Grayscale.ctb.) When you get back to the preview, you'll see the difference.

12. Exit the Plot dialog box, and save the drawing as Cabin15c.dwg.

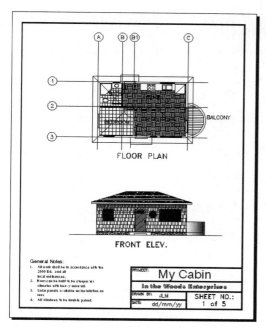

FIGURE 15.25: Preview with the `monochrome.ctb` plot-style table assigned to Layout1

Summing Up

This has been a quick tour of and introduction to the plot-style feature, which helps control how your drawing will plot. Getting consistently good output from your AutoCAD drawings involves an investment of time by you or the office CAD manager/information technologist to set up the best configuration of your printers and AutoCAD. As you have seen, layouts provide a good tool for setting up plots, once the configuration is right.

The next two chapters that follow contain tutorials and discussions about drawing in 3D (for AutoCAD users only). You'll also find a glossary of terms related to AutoCAD, LT, building construction, and design that have been mentioned in the book. The Sybex website (`www.sybex.com`) offers a collection of all AutoCAD drawing files and adjunct files that you use or generate through the course of this book. Advanced readers can download these files and begin reading anywhere in the book.

For readers who do not wish to continue learning the 3D aspects of AutoCAD, I hope you have found the book useful in helping you learn AutoCAD 2008 and AutoCAD LT 2008. Good luck in your future with AutoCAD. Please contact Sybex with any questions that arise while you work your way through the book (`www.sybex.com`).

Are You Experienced?

Now you can...

- ☑ set up a drawing to be printed
- ☑ assign lineweights to layers in your drawing
- ☑ select the area of your drawing to print
- ☑ choose a sheet size to print your drawing on
- ☑ control the orientation and origin of the print
- ☑ set the scale of the print
- ☑ preview a print
- ☑ print a layout
- ☑ publish multiple layouts
- ☑ navigate through the plot-style features

CHAPTER 16

Creating 3D Geometry

▶ Setting up a 3D workspace

▶ Using the Polysolid tool

▶ Using the Boolean functions

▶ Extruding 2D objects

▶ Creating 3D surfaces

▶ Changing the 3D viewpoint

LT has a few 3D
viewing tools but
none of the 3D
solids modeling
tools that AutoCAD
supports. Therefore,
this chapter doesn't
apply to users of LT.

Nothing in AutoCAD is quite as fascinating as drawing in 3D. Compared with a traditional 3D rendering of a building on a drafting board that uses vanishing points and projection planes, a true 3D computerized model of a building that can be rotated and viewed from any angle, as well as from the inside, offers a world of difference. Many architectural firms still use the drafting board to create 3D presentation drawings, even though they use AutoCAD for their construction drawings. But more and more of them are using AutoCAD's 3D features to create either perspective drawings or simple 3D models that are then traced over by hand in the process of creating the final presentation drawing. It's useful to acquire some skills in working in 3D, and it's also a lot of fun.

Constructing a 3D model of a building requires many of the tools that you've been using throughout this book and some new ones that you'll be introduced to in this chapter. Your competence in using the basic drawing, editing, and display commands is critical to your successful study of 3D for two reasons. First, drawing in 3D can be more complex and difficult than drawing in 2D, and it can be frustrating until you get used to it. If you aren't familiar with the basic commands, you'll become that much more frustrated. Second, accuracy is critical in 3D drawing. The effect of errors is compounded, so you must be in the habit of using tools, such as the osnap modes, to maximize your precision.

Don't be discouraged; just be warned. Drawing in 3D is a fascinating and enjoyable process, and the results you get can be astounding. I sincerely encourage you to make the effort to learn some of the basic 3D skills presented here.

Many 3D software packages are on the market today, and some are better for drawing buildings than others. Often, because of the precision that AutoCAD provides, a 3D .dwg file is exported to one of these specialized 3D packages for further work, after being laid out in AutoCAD. Two other Autodesk products, 3ds Max and Autodesk VIZ, are designed to work with AutoCAD .dwg files and maintain a constant link with AutoCAD-produced files. Sometimes drawings are created in 2D, converted to 3D, and then refined into a shaded, colored, and textured rendering with specific lights and shadows. In this chapter, you'll look at the basic techniques of *solid modeling*, and we'll touch on a couple of tools used in *surface modeling*. In the process, you'll learn some techniques for viewing a 3D model.

Modeling in 3D

You'll begin by building a 3D model of the cabin, using several techniques for creating 3D *solids* and *surfaces*. When you use solid modeling tools, the objects you create are solid, like lumps of clay. They can be added together or subtracted from one another to form more complex shapes. By contrast, 3D surfaces are composites of two-dimensional planes that stretch over a frame of lines the way a tent surface stretches over the frame inside.

As you construct these 3D objects, you'll get more familiar with the UCS, learn how it's used with 3D, and begin using the basic methods of viewing a 3D model.

Setting Up a 3D Workspace

By this time, you've learned how to set up the toolbars and palettes in such a way that they work well for drawing in 2D. Your first task in transitioning into 3D begins by setting up a new workspace for working in 3D.

Let's start with Cabin07c. This version of the cabin has all the basic components of the floor plan on their respective layers, with no hatch patterns, no text, and no elevations or title block. If you haven't been following through the whole book and saving your work progressively, you can download this file from this book's page on the Sybex website, www.sybex.com. You can also follow along if you have another floor plan to use for the exercise that isn't much more complex than that of the cabin. Follow these steps:

1. Open Cabin07c.dwg. When the floor plan displays, make the Walls layer current, and turn off all other layers. Your drawing will look like Figure 16.1. Try to start thinking of it in three dimensions. The entire drawing is on a flat plane parallel to the monitor screen. When you add elements in the third dimension, they project straight out of the screen toward you if they have a positive dimension and straight through the screen if they have a negative dimension. The line of direction is perpendicular to the plane of the screen and is called the *z-axis*. You're familiar with the x- and y-axes, which run left and right and up and down, respectively, think of the z-axis as running into and out of the screen.

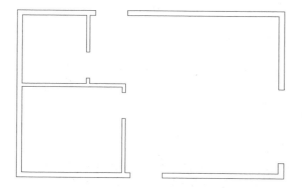

FIGURE 16.1: Cabin07c with all layers turned off except Walls

2. Choose Tools ➤ Workspaces ➤ Save Current As. In the Save Work-space window, enter **2D Drawing** (or any name you prefer), and click Save. This saves your current workspace so that you can return to it whenever you want.

3. If the UCS icon isn't visible on your screen, choose View ➤ Display ➤ UCS Icon ➤ On to place a check mark next to On. The UCS icon appears again. You turned it off in Chapter 5 and then used it in Chapter 10, to help construct some of the elevations, and you'll use it again in a moment. For now, keep an eye on it as the drawing changes. Remember that the icon's arrows indicate the positive direction for the x-, y-, and (in 3D) z-axes.

4. Now you'll change the view from a plan view of the drawing—looking straight down at it—to one in which you're looking down at it from an angle. Choose View ➤ 3D Views ➤ SW Isometric. (SW means from the southwest.) The view changes to look like Figure 16.2. Notice how the UCS icon has altered with the change of view. The X and Y arrows still run parallel to the left side and front of the cabin, but the icon and the floor plan are now at an angle to the screen, and the z-axis is visible. The crosshair cursor now has a third crosshair, and each one is a different color.

N O T E   A common convention in 3D graphics is to color vectors or other axes to indicate elements; red indicates the x-axis, green indicates the y-axis, and blue indicates the z-axis. The phrase used to remember this is: RGB = XYZ. You'll see this convention used several times while working on this and the next chapter.

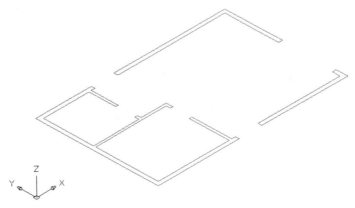

FIGURE 16.2:   The walls as seen from the SW Isometric view

5. Choose Tools ➤ Workspaces ➤ 3D Modeling. The toolbars, drawing area, and command window are reorganized. Two palettes are docked to the right of the drawing area. The top one is called the *Dashboard*; it contains several control panels. Each panel holds commands for accomplishing specific tasks associated with working with 3D models, such as making the objects, editing them, navigating through 3D space, setting up lights and cameras, rendering, and so on. You can identify each control panel by the tooltip that appears when you place the cursor in the icon in the panel's upper-left corner. When you select a command from one of the control panels, the window on the right displays palettes containing tools, objects, and materials useful to the selected tool. Below the Dashboard are the Tool palettes with the Modeling tab selected (see Figure 16.3).

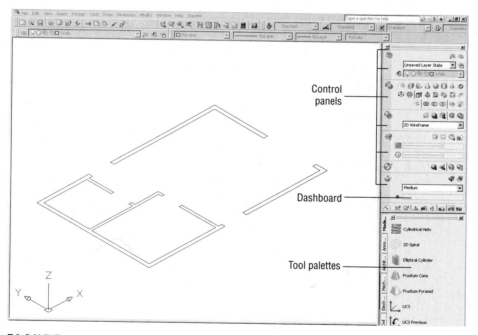

FIGURE 16.3: The 3D Modeling workspace showing the Dashboard and Tool palettes

Just as you fine-tuned and customized your 2D workspace as you worked your way through the earlier chapters, you'll do the same with the 3D workspace. Make a few changes now:

1. Click the X in the upper-right corner of the Tool palettes to turn them off for now. You won't use the palettes much in the next few pages, and when you need them, you can easily open them again. Leave the Dashboard exposed.

2. In the drawing area, zoom to extents; then, zoom out a little, and pan down to create some space above the floor plan for the 3D walls.

3. Drag the Workspaces toolbar (the short one to the left of the Standard toolbar) into the drawing area, and click the X in its title bar to turn it off. Then, drag the Standard and Layers toolbars to the left to fill the space left by the Workspace toolbar. Display the Styles and Layers toolbars if necessary, and then adjust the Command window so three lines of text are displayed.

4. Open the Visual Styles drop-down list on the Dashboard's Visual Styles control panel, and select 3D Wireframe.

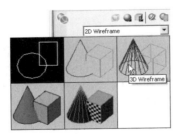

The drawing area takes on a grey background, and the UCS icon changes (Figure 16.4).

5. Choose Tools ➤ Options ➤ Display. At the lower-left corner of the Display tab, drag the Crosshair Size slider to the left to a value of approximately 5. This reduces the size of the crosshair cursor's lines in the drawing area.

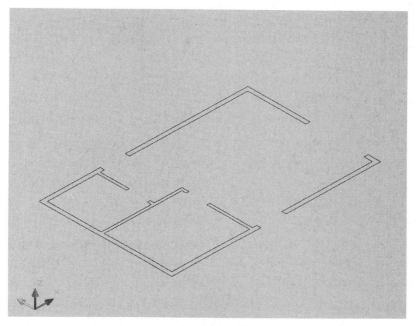

FIGURE 16.4: The drawing using the 3D Wireframe visual style

Making the Walls

The main task ahead is to create a *3D model* of the cabin. You'll use solid elements for the cabin's walls, doors, windows, floor, and steps. You'll learn several ways of viewing your work as you progress. To make the walls, you'll start with the polysolid object and then, like a sculptor, remove from the polysolid everything that isn't an interior or exterior wall. The elements to be removed are the void spaces for the doors and windows. Follow these steps:

1. Set the Endpoint osnap to be running, and be sure Ortho, Polar, and Otrack are turned off. Create a new layer called 3D-Walls-Ext, assign it color 22, and make it current.

2. Click the Polysolid tool on the Dashboard's 3D Make control panel (the control panel at the top of the Dashboard).

3. At the Command: _Polysolid 0'-4", Width = 0'-0¼", Justification = Center Specify start point or [Object/ Height/Width/Justify] <Object>: prompt, type h↲ 9'↲ to set the object height to 9'-0".

When you assign colors for 3D layers in the following pages, avoid using grays or other colors that are similar to the 3D gray background color.

4. The exterior walls are 6" thick, so the polysolid object should be 6" thick as well. Enter w↵ and then 6↵ at the Specify width < 0'-0¼">: prompt.

5. The Justification option determines the side of the polysolid for which you will pick the endpoints. You will be picking the outside lines of the cabin in a counterclockwise order, so the justification must be set to Right. Enter j↵ r↵.

6. You're now ready to begin creating the walls. Click the corner of the cabin nearest to the bottom of the screen, and then move the cursor. The first wall appears and is tied to the cursor, as shown in Figure 16.5.

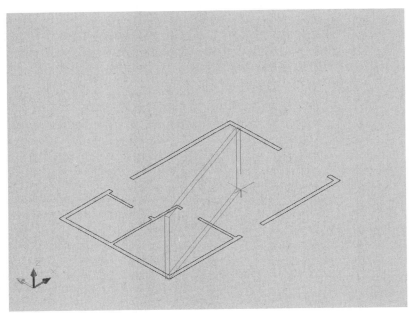

FIGURE 16.5: Starting the first polysolid wall

7. Click the next three outside wall endpoints, starting with the one to the current location's upper right. When only one segment separates the last segment from the first, enter c↵ to close the polysolid.

Adding the Interior Walls

The interior cabin walls are thinner than the exterior walls and will probably have a different material assigned to them. You will make a new layer for these walls and change the polysolid parameters.

1. Create a new layer called 3D-Walls-Int, assign it color 44, and make it the current layer.

2. Zoom into the lower-left corner of the cabin so that you can see the bedroom and bathroom walls.

3. Start the polysolid command from the Dashboard or by typing **psolid**↵ at the command prompt.

4. Enter **w**↵ **4**↵ to change the width to 4".

5. Starting with the endpoint nearest to the front door, draw the two walls that enclose the bedroom, right-click, and choose Enter to terminate the command.

6. Press the spacebar to restart the command, and then draw the remaining bathroom wall. Make sure that it is justified properly, and then zoom to extents. Your drawing should look similar to Figure 16.6.

You can also start the Polysolid command by choosing Draw ➢ Modeling ➢ Polysolid.

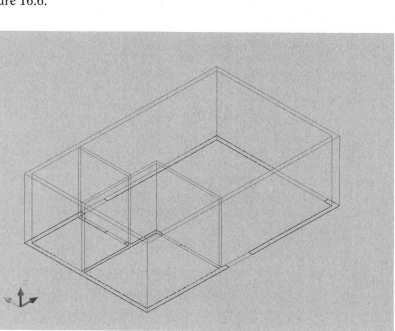

FIGURE 16.6: The cabin with the walls drawn as polysolids

Creating the Door and Window Block-Outs

Before you add the geometry for the doors and windows, you must make the openings in the walls. You accomplish this using the Boolean tools, the features used to create a single object from the volumes of two overlapping objects, called *operands*. There are three Boolean functions: union, subtraction, and intersection. Union combines the two volumes, subtraction deletes one object and the overlapping volume shared with the other, and intersection deletes both objects, leaving only the shared volume behind. For the doors and windows, you will make *block-outs*; that is, you'll make solid boxes the size of the openings and then use the Subtract command to create the voids by removing the boxes as well as the volume they share with the walls. The boxes act as block-outs, volumes that are to be deleted, and their only function is to help delete part of the polysolid wall.

1. Make a new layer named Door_win_bool, and set it as the current layer. Freeze the two 3D-Wall layers, and thaw the Windows and Headers layers.

2. In the Visual Styles panel of the Dashboard, set the style to Conceptual. This is a flat-shaded style with bold lines.

> See Figure 10.1 in Chapter 10 for the door and window heights above the floor.

3. Zoom in to the cabin so that you can see the front door and the bedroom window.

4. Click the Box button in the 3D Make panel of the Dashboard, or enter box↵ at the Command prompt. You will be making a block-out that will act as the operand that is removed from the polysolid.

5. The box object requires three items of information to be constructed: two points that define the opposing corners and a height value. At the prompts, click two opposite corners of the front door.

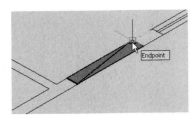

6. At the Specify height or [2Point]: prompt, enter 7'6↵. The box appears in place (see Figure 16.7).

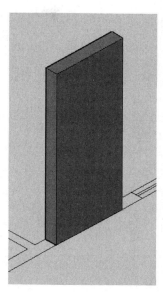

FIGURE 16.7: The first door operand created in place

7. Copy the front door object to the back door location using the End-point osnap for precision.

8. Repeat steps 4 through 7 to create the two internal doors and the sliding-glass door.

9. When using the Boolean functions, it's best not to have a situation where the two operands have coplanar faces. Select one box, and if a Selecting Subobjects On Solids dialog box opens, check the Don't Show Me This Again option and then close it. The boxes grips appear all around the base and a single grip at the top.

   Dragging the triangular grips changes the lengths of the sides of the box but doesn't change the angles between the sides. The square grips move the corners of the box or the box itself, and the single top grip changes the box's height.

10. Click the triangular grip on the front of the box, and drag it forward to pull the front of the box out from the front of the cabin. It doesn't have to be a great distance, just enough so that the box and the frozen polysolid don't share the same plane.

◄

When we instruct you to *pick* an object when working in 3D, you need to click an edge of the object or a line that helps define the object.

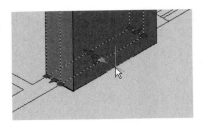

11. Drag the rear triangular grip backward, and position it off the inside of the exterior wall.

12. Repeat the process for the other four door block-outs so that each is thicker than their associated opening.

13. The doors do not rest on the ground plane but are 1'-0" above it to accommodate the step and threshold. Start the Move command, and then select all the doors. At the Specify base point or [Displacement] <Displacement>: prompt, pick a point anywhere on the screen. At the Specify second point or <use first point as displacement>: prompt, enter @0,0,12↵. The third number in the sequence is the distance in the z-axis the boxes are moved. Your screen should look similar to Figure 16.8.

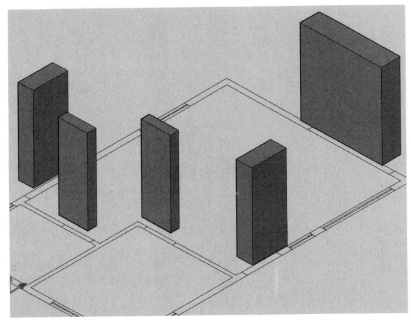

FIGURE 16.8: The thick door block-outs elevated above the ground plane

Creating the Window Block-Outs

As you might expect, making the window block-outs will be just like the doorway openings. The only difference is that the bottoms of the window openings sit at a different height above the 2D floor plan. Here are the steps:

1. Create the boxes for all the window block-outs except the round window at the front of the cabin. All the windows are 3'-6" tall.

T I P   After you make the first window box, the default height for the Box command is the correct height for the remaining windows. When prompted for the height, just press the spacebar or ↵.

2. Change the thicknesses of the boxes so they overlap the thickness of the outside wall.

3. Move the windows 4'-0" in the Z direction.

4. Zoom in to the circular window area.

   You need to use a cylinder to make the circular window opening, but cylinders are always created with the height extending in the Z direction. You'll need to change the UCS icon to make the cylinder.

5. Enter ucs↵ x↵ 90↵. The UCS icon rotates such that the plane defined by the x- and y-axes is parallel to the front wall and the z-axis points toward the front of the cabin.

6. Click the Cylinder icon on the 3D Make control panel. Then, follow the prompts in the Command window.

7. Use the Insertion osnap to locate the center point for the base of the cylinder at the insertion point of the 2' window.

8. Specify the radius for the base of the cylinder by using the Endpoint osnap and clicking the point where one of the window jamb lines meets the front wall.

If you don't have the Osnap toolbar on your screen, Shift+ right-click, and select Insert from the Osnap menu.

9. Specify the height of the cylinder by typing -12↵. The cylinder is placed and extends into the cabin. It has an abbreviated, almost abstract form.

10. Select the cylinder, and then, using the triangular grip at the center of the circular face, extend the cylinder's height toward the front of the cabin.

11. Use Zoom Previous. Use the Move command, polar tracking, and the direct distance entry to move the cylinder up 6'.

12. Enter ucs↵↵ to return the UCS icon to the WCS orientation.

13. Thaw the 3D-Walls-Ext and 3D-Walls-Int layers. Your drawing should look like Figure 16.9.

14. Save your drawing as Cabin16a.dwg.

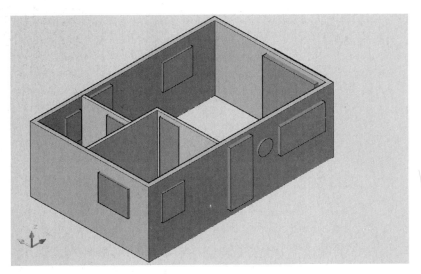

F I G U R E   1 6 . 9 : The drawing with the block-outs in place

Cutting the Openings

You are ready to start the Boolean processes. When prompted to select an object, be sure to click on the edge of the 3D objects and not a face, or the selection will not be successful.

1. Click the Subtract button in the 3D Make panel of the Dashboard, or enter subtract↵.

2. At the Select solids and regions to subtract from … prompt, select the exterior wall, and then press ↵ to end the selection process. You can perform the Boolean functions on several objects at one time, but first, you will do it to only one.

3. At the Select solids and regions to subtract … prompt, select the front door, and then press ↵. The door is subtracted from the wall (see Figure 16.10).

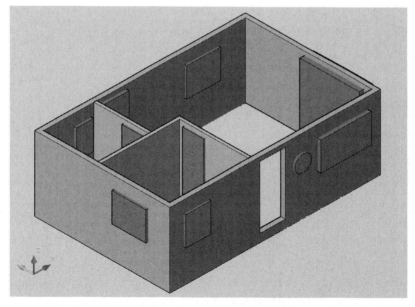

FIGURE 16.10: The front door subtracted from the front wall of the cabin

4. Start the Subtract command again, and select the exterior wall only.

5. When prompted for the objects to subtract, select all the remaining exterior doors and windows. All the openings appear on the cabin's exterior walls, as shown in Figure 16.11.

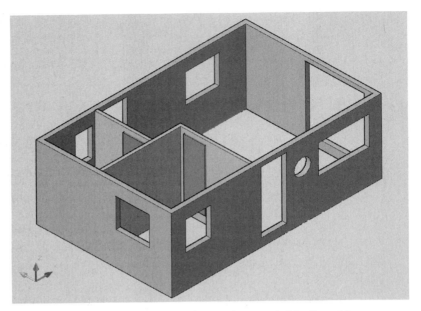

FIGURE 16.11: All the exterior openings created for the cabin

6. Repeat the subtraction process on the two interior walls to remove the bathroom and bedroom door areas.

Creating the Floor, Steps, and Thresholds

In designing the cabin, you didn't draw a floor, but one was implied. The three exterior doorway openings have thresholds that indicate a change in level from the cabin floor down to the steps and the balcony. You'll now create additional line work to make the thresholds and steps:

1. Continuing from the previous set of steps, click the Layer Properties Manager icon on the Layers toolbar, and do the following:

   a. Create new layers called 3D-Floor, 3D-Step, and 3D-Thresh, and make 3D-Thresh current.

   b. Freeze the two 3D-Walls layers and the Windows layer.

   c. Thaw the Steps layer.

To see where you're going, look ahead to Figure 16.12. You'll use the Extrude command to create a series of solids that represent the thresholds and boxes for the steps and the floor.

2. Use the Zoom Window tool to set up a view of the front door opening and its threshold.

3. Draw a polyline around the perimeter of the threshold using the Close option to make the last segment.

4. The Extrude command extends a 2D object in the Z direction, creating surfaces on the newly formed sides and end caps. Click the Extrude tool in the 3D Make panel, select the threshold polyline, and then press ↵. At the Specify height of extrusion or [Direction/Path/Taper angle] <-1'-0">: prompt, enter 2.05↵. The first threshold is completed.

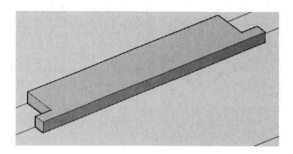

5. Make similar extruded thresholds for the back door and the sliding-glass door.

6. Select all three thresholds, and move them 10" up in the Z direction.

7. Make the 3D-Step layer current. Using the existing step lines as a guide, create boxes for the front and rear steps, and give them heights of 10". The tops of the steps are aligned with the bottoms of the thresholds. Your drawing should look like Figure 16.12.

8. Make the 3D-Floor layer current. To make the floor, first draw a polyline around the inside perimeter of the cabin, making sure that you include the gap between the inside face of the exterior wall and the steps.

T I P   You can use the Orbit command transparently, without leaving the current command, by typing **orbit**, executing the change, and then pressing Esc to resume the current command.

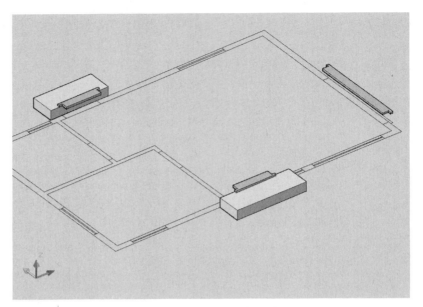

FIGURE 16.12: The steps and thresholds in place

9. Start the Extrude command, select the floor polyline, and then extrude it 10" (see Figure 16.13).

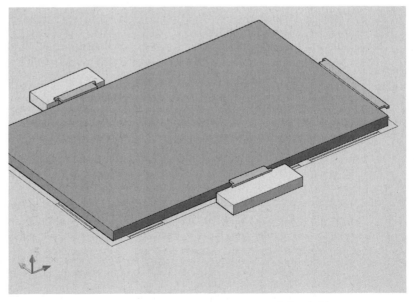

FIGURE 16.13: The 3D floor with the steps and thresholds

Completing the Doors and Windows

Now that the openings are in place, you just need to build the geometry for the doors and windows. These can be as compete as you like them with sills, drip grooves, tapered panels, kick plates, and so on. For the exercise in this book, you'll create fairly simple frames, door panels, and glazing.

1. Make a new layer named 3D-Win-Frame, and set it as the current layer. Freeze the 3D-Wall-Ext layer, and zoom into the bedroom window.

2. Click the Ducs button in the status bar to turn on Dynamic UCS mode. When you are in a command, Ducs causes the current UCS to adapt to the orientation of whichever face the cursor is over.

3. Start the Box command, click the lower-left outside corner of the bedroom window, and then move the cursor away from that corner. The box starts to form with the orientation parallel to the outside wall and the UCS icon temporarily relocated to the endpoint (see the top of Figure 16.14). Click the opposite outside corner of the window for the base of the new box (see the bottom of Figure 16.14).

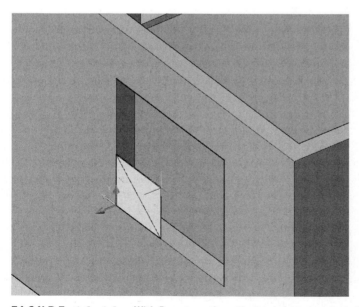

FIGURE 16.14: With Ducs turned on, the box's base is oriented parallel to the wall (above); the box's base completed (next page).

Continues

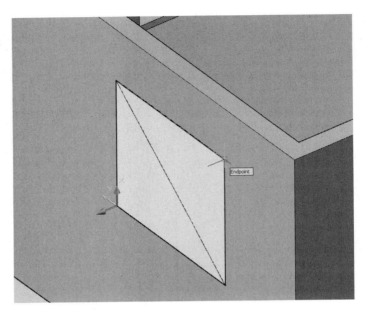

FIGURE 16.14   *Continued*

4. At the Specify height or [2Point] <3'-6">: prompt, enter -4↵.

5. Turn off Ducs, select the box, and move it 1" in the positive X direction to center it in the wall.

6. The box that you just made will be the frame for the bedroom window. Now you need to make a block-out to subtract to form the opening and the glazing. Copy the window frame in front of the bedroom wall, and then select the copy to expose its grips.

7. Turn on polar tracking, and then select each of the four outward-pointing triangular grips along the perimeter and move them 1" toward the inside of the box (see the left of Figure 16.15). Click the triangular grip on the front of the box, and drag it forward to make the box significantly thicker (see the right of Figure 16.15).

8. Move the block-out box until it overlaps the window frame box. Make sure you use polar tracking or Ortho mode to constrain the movement to the x-axis.

9. Switch to the 3D Wireframe visual style, and then, using the Subtract Boolean function, subtract the block-out from the frame. Switch back to the Conceptual visual style, and your window should look similar to Figure 16.16.

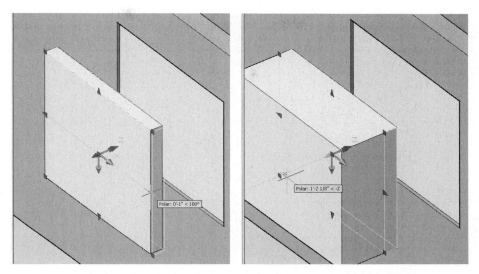

FIGURE 16.15: Moving the block-out's perimeter grips to shrink it slightly (left) and increasing the box's depth (right)

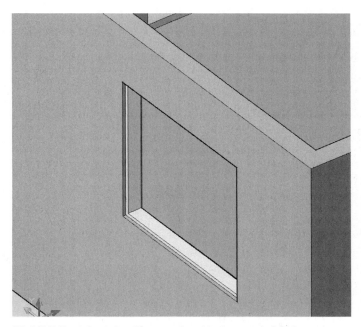

FIGURE 16.16: The completed bedroom window frame

10. Create a new layer named 3D-Glazing, give it a light blue color, and make it current.

11. A polyline can be drawn only in the XY plane, but a 3D polyline can be drawn along any axis. Enter **3dpoly**⏎ at the command line, or choose Draw ➣ 3D Polyline.

12. Turn on the Midpoint running osnap, and then draw the 3D polyline using the midpoints of the frame's four, 4" wide inner corners. Switch to the 3D Wireframe visual style if you have trouble locating the midpoints, and then switch back to Conceptual when you are done.

13. Use the Extrude tool to extrude the glazing 0.25". If you have trouble selecting the 3D Polyline, use the Last option at the Select Objects: prompt. Your bedroom window should look like Figure 16.17.

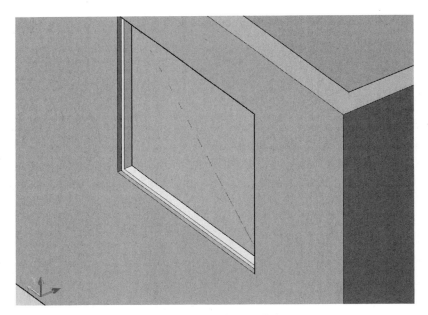

FIGURE 16.17: The completed bedroom window

14. Repeat the process in this section to make the other four rectangular windows in the cabin. When you're done, your drawing should look similar to Figure 16.18.

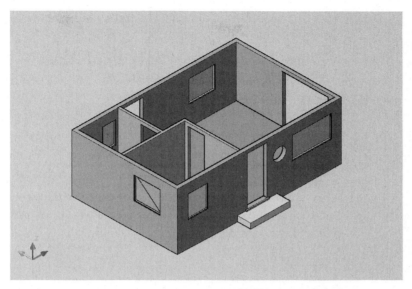

FIGURE 16.18: The cabin after the four rectangular windows and frames are finished

Making the Circular Window

So far, you've used only the box object as the block-out and window frame. For the circular window, you'll use the cylinder:

1. Zoom in close to a view of the circular window opening on the front wall. Use the Visual Style drop-down list to change to the 3D Wireframe visual style. You'll need to change the UCS icon to make the cylinder.

2. To make sure you are the correct starting point, reset the UCS to the WCS by typing **ucs↵ w↵**. To rotate the UCS properly for this exercise, enter **ucs↵ x↵ -90↵**. The UCS icon rotates such that the plane defined by the x- and y-axes is parallel to the front wall and the z-axis points away from you.

3. Make the 3D-Win-Frame layer current. Click the Cylinder icon on the 3D Make control panel, and then follow the prompts in the Command window.

4. Use the Insertion osnap to locate the center point for the base of the cylinder at the insertion point of the 2' window.

5. Specify the radius for the base of the cylinder by using the Endpoint osnap and clicking the point where one of the window jamb lines meets the front wall.

6. Specify the height of the cylinder by typing 4↵. Move the cylinder 1" in the Z direction by starting the Move command, selecting the cylinder, picking a base point, and then typing @0,0,1↵.

7. Create another cylinder with the same base point, but assign it a radius of 11" and a height of 12". You can temporarily freeze the layers containing the walls, floor, steps, and thresholds if necessary, but be sure to thaw them when you are done.

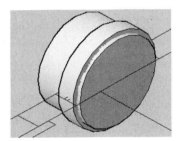

8. Subtract the smaller cylinder from the larger cylinder.

9. Make the 3D-glazing layer current, and then create one more cylinder at the insertion point of the circular window. Give this new window a radius of 11" and a height of 0.25", and then move it 3" in the Z direction to center it in the frame.

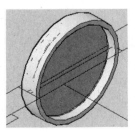

10. Use the Move command, polar tracking, and the direct distance entry to move the frame and glazing up 6'.

11. Enter ucs↵↵ to return the UCS icon to the WCS orientation.

Adding the Pivot Doors

For this exercise, you will represent the four pivot doors with simple boxes. Later, if you choose, you can add knobs and glass panes if you like.

1. Add a new layer named 3D-Pivot-Doors, and make it current.

2. Zoom into the front door and start the Box command. Rather than moving the primitives as you have been, here you'll use object tracking to place the start point.

3. Switch to the 3D Wireframe visual style, click the Otrack button in the status bar, and make sure Polar is on as well.

4. Start the Box command, and then, at the Specify first corner or [Center]: prompt, place you cursor near the bottom-left outside corner of the front door until a small cross and the endpoint appear. Move the cursor in the Y direction until the tracking vector appears, and then enter 2↵ to set the first corner of the door 2" from the corner of the opening.

5. Enter @36,2↵ to place the second point of the 3'-0" door. Give the door a height of 7'-6", and then copy it, using the Endpoint snaps, to the back door location. Using the Conceptual visual style, you cabin should look like Figure 16.19.

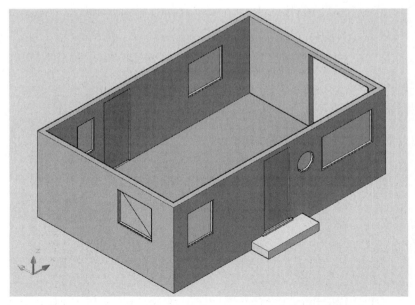

FIGURE 16.19: The cabin after the two external doors are in place

6. Thaw the 3D-Walls-Int layer, and then repeat the process to create the two interior walls. Because the interior walls are only 4" thick, you must start the box just 1" from the face of the wall.

Adding the Sliding Door

The remaining door to add is the sliding door on the side of the cabin. Although this is a door, the creation procedure will be closer to the windows that you've already made. Here is a synopsis of the steps:

1. Change the view to a SE Isometric view, and zoom into the patio door.

2. Make the 3D-Win-Frame layer current.

3. Create a box that is 3'-6" wide, 2" thick, and 7'-6" tall, and center it on the left edge of the patio opening.

4. Create a block-out, and center it on the window frame.

5. Subtract the block-out from the window frame.

6. Use a 3D polyline to create the boundary to the glazing, extrude it, and then center it in the frame.

7. Move the frame and glazing 1" inside the opening, not centered like the prior examples.

8. Copy the frame and glazing 3'-6" to the right and then 2" toward the inside of the cabin so that the two door frames are offset (see Figure 16.20).

9. Save your drawing as Cabin16b.dwg.

FIGURE 16.20: The completed patio door with two offset panels

Building the Balcony

You're nearly done building the cabin. The next step is to make the balcony using Booleans and the Slice tool.

1. Make a new layer called 3D-Balcony, assign it color 24, make it current, and then thaw the Balcony layer and freeze the other 3D layers.

2. Choose the Cylinder primitive tool on the 3D Make control panel to create a cylinder solid to represent the space enclosed by the balcony wall. Use the Center osnap to locate the center point of the arcs that represent the balcony wall. Select a radius of 4'-6" and a height of 5'-0".

3. Move this cylinder up 10".

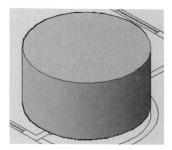

4. Draw a second cylinder using the same center point, with a radius of 5' and a height of 4'. Be sure to pick the center of the 2D balcony arcs, not the center of the 3D cylinder.

5. Start the Subtract command, and subtract the smaller cylinder from the larger cylinder to form a bowl shape (see Figure 16.21).

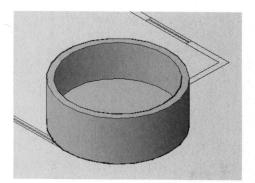

FIGURE 16.21: The beginning of the balcony

6. Expand the 3D Make control panel on the Dashboard by clicking the double arrows that appear when you place your cursor over the darker gray area to the left of the tools. The panel expands downward and makes several new tools accessible. Click the Slice button; then, back in the drawing, select the new balcony, and press ↵.

7. At the first prompt, enter yz↵. This defines the plane that you'll use to slice the balcony.

8. At the second prompt, pick the bottom corner of the cabin wall, where the bottom of the balcony meets the corner. Doing so positions the YZ cutting plane in line with the exterior wall surface against which the balcony wall butts.

9. At the third prompt, click a blank spot below and to the right of the balcony. This tells AutoCAD the side of the cutting plane where the desired objects are located. The shape is cut in half, the inside half is deleted, and the balcony is complete (see Figure 16.22).

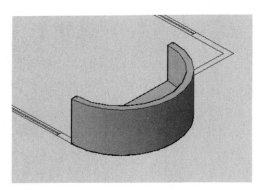

FIGURE 16.22: The balcony after using the slice tool

Putting a Roof on the Cabin

You'll finish the 3D model of the cabin by constructing a roof. The edge of the roof will be a different color from the roof surface, so you'll make them as two separate objects, each on its own layer. The edge will be a solid, and the sloping part will be a set of surfaces. Follow these steps:

1. Create two new layers: 3D-Roof-Edge with color 32 and 3D-Roof with color 114. Make 3D-Roof-Edge current.

2. Freeze all 3D layers except the two new ones, and freeze all the 2D layers except Roof. Only the roof is visible.

3. Use the Box command on the 3D Make control panel to make a box that is 6" high and sits on the four corners of the roof.

4. Move the box up 9'. Then, copy the ridgeline and hiplines of the roof up to the top edge of the box.

5. Select the objects, and use the Layer Control drop-down list to change these copied lines to the 3D-Roof_Edge layer. Then, turn off the Roof layer (see Figure 16.23).

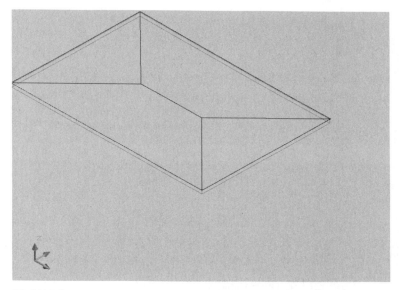

FIGURE 16.23: The solid box is made, and the copied rooflines are moved to the 3D-Roof_Edge layer

6. Start the Stretch command (on the Modify toolbar), and use a crossing window to select just the ridgeline and the ends of the four hip lines that touch the ridgeline.

7. Press ↵. Click a blank part of the drawing area for the base point, and then enter @0,0,3'↵. The roof is stretched up 3' (see the left of Figure 16.24).

8. Make the 3D-Roof layer current, and then choose Draw ➤ Modeling ➤ Meshes ➤ 3D Face.

9. With the Endpoint osnap, start at the leftmost corner of the sloping planes, and pick the four corners of the front plane of the roof. Then, at the Specify third point or [Invisible] <exit>: prompt, move

to the rightmost corner, and click this point twice. Follow the diagram on the right of Figure 16.24. Press ↵ to end the 3D Face command.

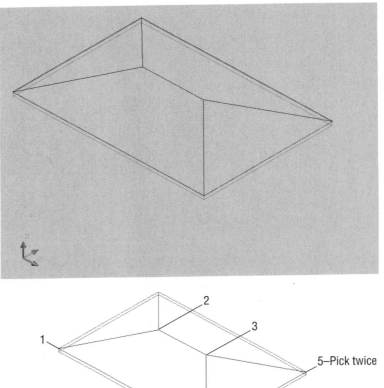

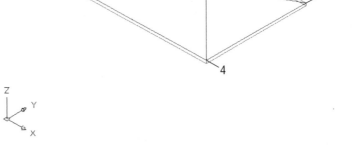

FIGURE 16.24: The ridge and hip lines are stretched up (left) and the sequence of picks for the first two 3D faces (right)

10. Repeat steps 8 and 9 for the back and left surfaces of the roof.

11. Turn off the 3D-Roof layer, and erase the ridgelines and hiplines. Turn the layer back on, and thaw the remaining 3D layers. Your drawing should look like Figure 16.25.

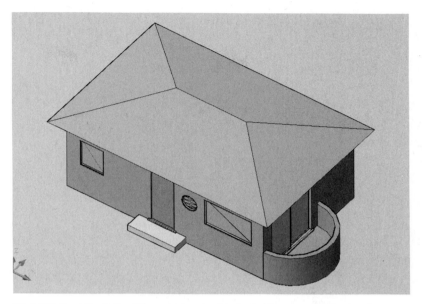

FIGURE 16.25: The completed cabin in the Conceptual visual style

12. Save this file as Cabin16c.dwg.

Using the Orbit Tools

Now that you've had a chance to set and reset various 3D views, check out the three orbit tools that are on the 3D Navigation control panel: Constrained Orbit, Free Orbit, and Continuous Orbit. You can find them on the fly-out menu that by default displays the Constrained Orbit icon. Follow these steps:

1. Make 3D-Walls-Ext current; then, freeze the 3D-Roof and 3D-Roof_Edge layers.

2. With the Visual Style set to Conceptual and the 3D View set to Southeast Isometric, click and hold the Constrained Orbit icon on the 3D Navigation control panel to open the toolbar fly-out menu; then move down to the fly-out toolbar, select the Constrained Orbit icon, and move the cursor onto the drawing area. It changes into an atom-like symbol.

3. Click and drag the cursor around in the drawing area, and note how the 3D model rotates as you move the cursor. This tool is called *constrained* because if you move the view to one of the cabin from directly overhead or directly underneath, you can't keep moving the cabin in a fashion that causes it to tumble over and over.

4. Try the other two orbiting options. Click and hold the Constrained Orbit icon to open the toolbar fly-out. Then, move the cursor down, and release the mouse button when the cursor is on one of the other two icons. Here's how they work:

▶ Free Orbit superimposes a green circle called an *arcball* over the 3D model. Smaller circles appear at the quadrant points of the larger circle. How the model moves depends on whether you click and drag inside or outside the big circle or within one of the small circles (see Figure 16.26).

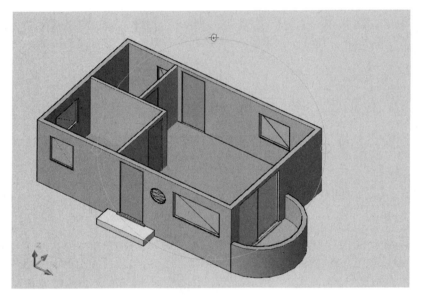

FIGURE 16.26: Changing the view with the Free Orbit tool

▶ Continuous Orbit creates an animation of the model spinning. Click and drag the cursor in a straight direction; then, release the mouse button as you're dragging. This begins the spin. The direction of your drag determines the direction of spin; and, to a degree, the speed of your drag determines how fast the model spins.

5. When you're finished, thaw the 3D-Roof and 3D-Roof_Edge layers, and reset the view to Southeast Isometric.

Getting Further Directions in 3D

Covering 3D in real depth is beyond the scope of this book, but I can mention a few other tools and features that you might enjoy investigating. First, I'll summarize a few of the solids and surface-modeling tools that I didn't cover in the tutorial on the cabin. Then, we'll take a quick look at the rendering process as it's approached in AutoCAD.

Using Other Solids Modeling Tools

You used the Box and Cylinder primitive solid tools to build up the model of the cabin. There are several other primitive shapes, all found on the top row of the 3D Navigation control panel. Four of them are shown and described here.

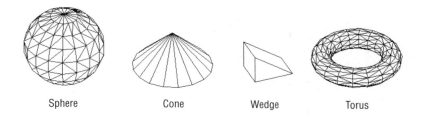

Sphere   Cone   Wedge   Torus

Sphere   You specify the center point and radius or diameter.

Cone   You specify the center point of the base, the radius of the base, and the height of the pointed tip. The base is parallel to the XY plane, and the height is perpendicular to it.

Wedge   The wedge has a rectangular base and a lid that slopes up from one edge of the base. You specify the base as you do in the Box tool and then enter the height.

Torus   This is a donut shape. You specify a center point for the hole, the radius of the circular path that the donut makes, and the radius of the tube that follows the circular path around the center point.

In the second row of the Make control panel are tools for creating solids by moving 2D shapes in the third dimension:

Extrude   Select a closed 2D shape such as a rectangle or a circle. Then, specify a height for the extrusion or a path to extrude along. If the extrusion is straight up, you enter an angle to taper the edges away from the vertical.

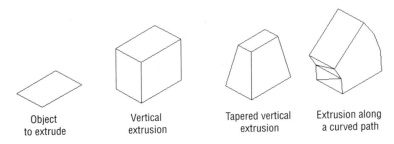

| Object to extrude | Vertical extrusion | Tapered vertical extrusion | Extrusion along a curved path |

Revolve   Select a closed 2D shape, and then define the axis and the angle of rotation.

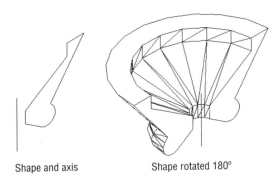

Shape and axis   Shape rotated 180°

There are many tools for modifying solids. When you formed the cabin walls, floor, and balcony, you used Union and Subtract, as well as Slice. Another solids-editing tool, Intersect, finds the volume that two solids have in common when they partially occupy the same space. Its icon is in the third row of the 3D Navigation control panel, with Union and Subtract. You select solids that are colliding, and AutoCAD creates a solid from their intersection.

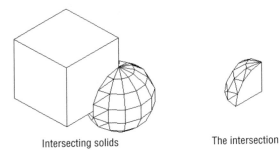

Intersecting solids   The intersection

These are only a few of the numerous tools for creating and modifying solids, but they should be enough to get you started.

Using Surface-Modeling Tools

Surface modeling has its own set of tools. Choose Draw ➤ Modeling ➤ Meshes to open the 3D Meshes menu.

You've already used the 3D Face command. Here is a brief description of a few of the other tools on this menu:

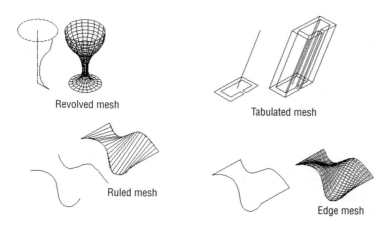

Revolved mesh

Tabulated mesh

Ruled mesh

Edge mesh

Revolved Mesh   Creates a 3D surface mesh by rotating a 2D curved line around an axis of revolution.

Tabulated Mesh   Creates a 3D surface mesh by extruding a 2D object in a direction determined by the endpoints of a line, an arc, or a polyline.

Ruled Mesh   Creates a 3D surface mesh between two selected shapes.

Edge Mesh   Creates a 3D surface mesh among four lines that are connected at their endpoints. Each line can be in 2D or 3D, and the original shape must be a boundary of a shape that doesn't cross or conflict with itself.

Most 3D models today utilize the solid-modeling tools for their basic shapes because the tools for adding, subtracting, slicing, and so forth, are easy to use and allow complex shapes to be fabricated quickly. Still, surface modeling has its uses, and sometimes a shape will lend itself to surface over solid modeling. Any serious 3D modeler will be familiar with both sets of tools.

Are You Experienced?

Now you can...

- ☑ change visual styles
- ☑ create linear 3D objects with the Polysolid tool
- ☑ extrude 2D shapes into 3D geometry
- ☑ cut holes in objects using the Subtract Boolean tool
- ☑ resize 3D objects using grips
- ☑ create 3D surface
- ☑ navigate in a 3D scene

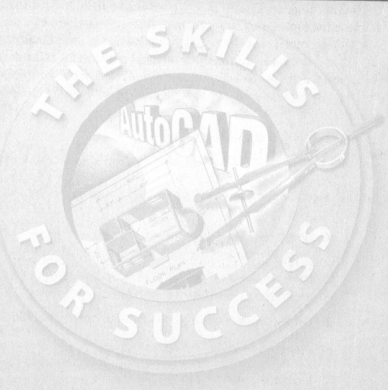

CHAPTER 17

Materials and Rendering

- Creating cameras to reproduce views
- Creating a lighting scheme
- Enabling and controlling shadow effects
- Choosing the background
- Assigning materials to surfaces
- Putting in auxiliary objects such as people and trees
- Saving setup views and lights as restorable scenes
- Outputting a rendering to a file

After developing a 3D model, you must render it. In this chapter, we'll give you a quick tour of some of these rendering steps as you set up a view of the cabin and render it. Developing a full rendering takes time and patience, but touching on a few of the many steps involved will give you a feel for the process. You've put in a lot of time working your way through this book, and you deserve to have a rendered 3D view of your cabin, however simple, to complete the process.

Creating Cameras to Reproduce Views

You'll create a rectangle to serve as the land the cabin sits on, and then you'll adjust your view:

1. With Cabin16c as the current drawing, enter **ucs**, and then press ↵ twice to return to the WCS, if you weren't already there.

2. Choose View ➤ 3D Views ➤ Plan View ➤ World UCS, or enter plan↵ w↵ to return to a plan view of your drawing.

3. Create a new layer called 3D-Land, assign it color 74, and make it current.

4. Zoom out, and create a rectangle around the cabin that is 160' wide and 140' long. To be sure the rectangle is created at ground level, don't snap to any parts of the cabin.

5. Move the rectangle to a position relative to the cabin approximately, as shown in Figure 17.1. Again, don't snap to any parts of the cabin yet.

6. Choose Draw ➤ Region, select the rectangle, and then press ↵ to end the selection process. Doing so creates a 2D object called a *region* that behaves like a 3D object. It turns opaque when the screen uses the Conceptual or Realistic visual style, and you can cut holes into it.

FIGURE 17.1: A plan view with the rectangle around the cabin

Creating the Cameras

AutoCAD uses a camera analogy to define reproducible views. The cameras and their respective targets are places in the scene and, using several available grips, are adjusted to capture the desired view.

 1. In the 3D Navigate control panel, click the Create Camera button, and then move the cursor into the drawing area. A camera icon appears at the cursor location.

2. Click below and to the right of the cabin to place the camera, and then move the cursor again. Now, the camera stays in place, and the target is moved with the cursor. The location of the target determines

the orientation of the camera, and the visible cone emitting from the camera shows the camera's *field of view*, or the angle visible through the camera's lens.

3. Turn off any running osnaps, and then click inside the cabin to place the target. The camera disappears temporarily while AutoCAD waits for input at the command line.

4. Enter n↵ to activate the Name option. At the prompt, enter **Cam Southeast**↵↵. The camera reappears in the drawing area.

 T I P   You should always give your cameras descriptive names to make it easier to find the correct view when multiple cameras exist in a drawing. You can change the camera name in the Properties palette.

5. Create another camera that views the cabin from the bottom-left corner, and name this camera Cam Southwest.

6. Use the Constrained Orbit tool to change the current view to a viewpoint from in front of the cabin and slightly above it (see Figure 17.2).

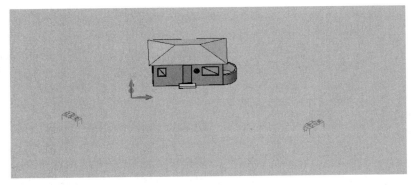

FIGURE 17.2: Viewing the cabin and cameras from above and to the front

T I P   You can access the functionality of the Constrained Orbit tool transparently (without leaving the current command) any time by holding down the Shift key and dragging the middle mouse button or scroll wheel.

7. Select the Cam Southeast camera. The field of view cone and grips are displayed, and the Camera Preview dialog box opens. This dialog box displays the view from the camera in several different visual styles (see Figure 17.3). The 3D Wireframe visual style is the default and the one you will use here.

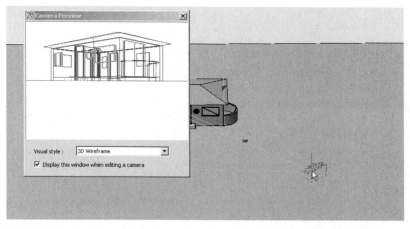

FIGURE 17.3: Selecting the camera displays its grips and the Camera Preview dialog box

8. Place your cursor over the grip at the center of the camera, and you will see a tooltip that says Camera Location. Click the grip, then enter @0,0,5'↵ to move the camera 5' up in the Z direction, to about eye level. You may need to click the grip again for the Camera Preview dialog box to refresh.

9. Press Esc to deselect the camera, and then select the Cam Southwest camera. Adjust its view, if you like, by moving the Target Location or Lens Length/FOV grips, and then move the Camera Location grip approximately 25' in the Z direction to get higher view of the structure.

10. Expand the drop-down list in the 3D Navigate control panel, and notice that the two cameras now appear in the list. Select Cam Southeast; your drawing area changes to view the scene from the selected camera, as shown in Figure 17.4.

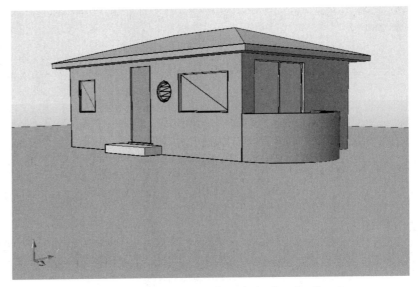

FIGURE 17.4: The cabin as seen through the Cam Southeast camera

11. Save your drawing as Cabin17A.dwg.

Creating a Lighting Scheme

Without proper lighting, the scene can look flat and unappealing. In the following sections, you will add a light to represent the sun and then an additional light to add ambient illumination to the scene.

Creating a Light Source

AutoCAD has three kinds of lighting:

Point light   All light rays are emitted from a single location and diverge as they get farther away. An incandescent lightbulb is a real-world example of a point light, even though the light does not travel toward the light's fixture.

Distant light   All light rays are parallel. Although the sun is technically a point light, at the distance the light rays travel to Earth, they are nearly parallel.

Spotlight   This is a conical representation of a spotlight.

Each has unique setup parameters. The sun is a special distant light and has its own settings. To do this, you'll use tools in the Light control panel on the Dashboard:

1. Place the cursor on the darker strip along the left side of the Dashboard's Light control panel. When the double down arrows appear, click them to open the bottom half of the control panel.

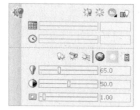

2. Focus on the three icons on the upper-right corner. The left one is a two-way toggle. Be sure User Lighting Mode is set to the User Light/Sunlight option.

3. The middle icon is an on/off toggle for Sun Status. Be sure it's toggled on.

4. Below these icons are a slider bar and a text box for the date. Use the slider bar to set the date to approximately **9/24/2007**.

5. Below that, use the time slider bar to set the time to approximately **3:35 PM**.

6. The lower half of the control panel displays a row of six icons and, below them, three more slider bars. Click the icon on the far right—the Edit the Sun icon—to open the Sun Properties palette (see Figure 17.5).

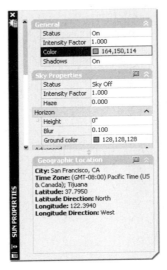

FIGURE 17.5: The Sun Properties palette

7. Make sure the General Settings at the top are the following:

▶ Status: On

▶ Intensity Factor: 1.000

▶ Shadows: On

The color value is determined by the location, date, and time specified. Close the Sun Properties palette.

8. In the same row of icons, click the Geographic Location button to open the Geographic Location dialog box (see Figure 17.6).

9. In the Region drop-down list below the map, select North America. Below that, in the Nearest City drop-down list, select Bangor, ME. A red cross appears over Bangor in the map. Because you've already set the date and time, the Time Zone drop-down list displays the accurate time zone. Click OK to close this dialog box.

TIP   If a particular city is not listed, you can uncheck the Nearest Big City option, and then click directly on the map to set the location or enter the longitudinal and latitudinal coordinates on the left side of the dialog box.

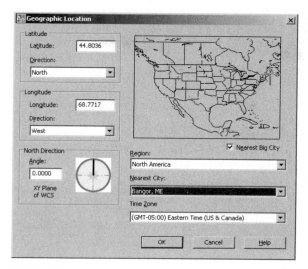

FIGURE 17.6: The Geographic Location dialog box

Enabling Shadows

To control shadows, you have to enlarge the Render control panel and make a couple of setting changes. Shadows can be soft- or hard-edged, and you can calculate them using a couple of methods. This part of the rendering process is too technical to go into in this book, but you can follow along and end up with at least one setup for shadows that will enhance the rendering of the cabin:

1. Click the double down arrows on the left, darker strip of the Render control panel to enlarge it and access more settings.

2. Click the Advanced Render Settings icon in the bottom half of the control panel to open the Advanced Render Settings palette. Scroll down to the Shadows rollout, and make sure Mode is set to Simple and Shadow Map is set to On (see Figure 17.7).

FIGURE 17.7: The Shadows settings on the Advanced Render Settings palette

3. Close the Advanced Render Settings palette.

The First Render

Let's make a preliminary render. You'll then add materials and a background and then try again.

 1. Click the Render button on the Render control panel. After a few moments, the rendering appears in the Render dialog box (see Figure 17.8).

 2. As you can see, the right side of the cabin is unlit and in total darkness. Click the Create a Point Light button in the Light control panel, and then place the light to the right of and behind the cabin. Move the light up about 30' in the Z direction. Change to a plan view if necessary and then back to the camera view when you are done.

3. Double-click the light to open its Properties palette, and make the following changes:

   ▶ Shadows: On

   ▶ Intensity Factor: 60.000

   ▶ Filter Color: 252, 250,212

   ▶ Lamp Intensity: 15,000 Cd

FIGURE 17.8: The first rendering in the Render dialog box

4. Render the scene again. As you can see in Figure 17.9, this time the shadows on the right side of the cabin are not as stark as they were previously.

FIGURE 17.9: The cabin rendering after adding the second light

5. Open the Advanced Render Settings palette again, and then click the lightbulb icon next to Global Illumination in the Indirect Illumination rollout. This will add a measure of ambient light into your scene without washing it out.

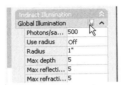

6. You can continue to tweak the lighting as you want. A good rule of thumb is to expect to dedicate 15–25 percent of a project's time to creating a good lighting scheme.

The building looks fine, but it would be nice to have something in the background other than the blank screen.

Controlling the Background of the Rendering

The following are some of the options you can set when choosing a background for the rendering:

The AutoCAD background   This is what you used for the preliminary rendering.

Another solid color   You use slide bars to choose it.

A gradient   You can use varying colors (usually light to dark) blended together.

An image   You can supply or choose a bitmap image.

You'll use the Gradient option:

1. Close the Render dialog box, and then choose Views ➤ Named Views to open the View Manager dialog box.

2. Expand the Model Views entry, and then select Cam Southeast (see Figure 17.10).

3. Expand the drop-down list for the Background Override entry, and then choose Sun & Sky. Doing so opens the Adjust Sun & Sky Background dialog box, as shown in Figure 17.11.

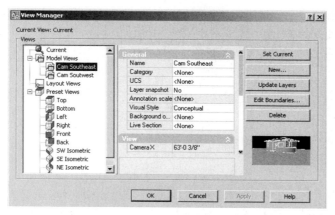

FIGURE 17.10: The Southeast camera selected in the View Manager dialog box

FIGURE 17.11: The Adjust Sun & Sky Background dialog box

4. Change the Intensity Factor to **1.5**, expand the Status drop-down list in the Sky Properties rollout, and choose Sky Background and Illumination.

5. Click OK to close the Adjust Sun & Sky Background dialog box.

6. Click Set Current in the View Manager dialog box, and then click OK to close it.

7. Render the scene. It will take a little longer to process this image. When it is done, your Render dialog box should look similar to Figure 17.12. The background image not only appears behind the cabin and ground, but it also contributes light to the scene.

 N O T E   Rendering is a processor-intensive function. It's not uncommon to experience a lag in computer performance or to hear increased cooling fan activity.

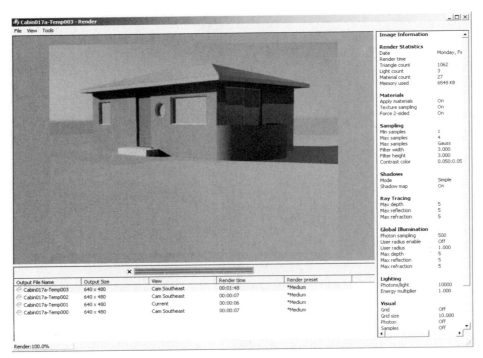

FIGURE 17.12: The cabin rendered with a Sun & Sky background

8. Save your drawing as Cabin17b.dwg.

Adding Materials

Adding the proper materials to a scene can greatly increase the realism of the drawing and convey a better sense of size and texture to the person viewing the image. This chapter assumes that you installed the material library that ships with AutoCAD 2008 with the rest of the package. You can assign materials to your drawing objects from several premade libraries, you can create materials from scratch, or you can edit materials that originate from the libraries. In the next exercise, you will apply materials from AutoCAD's libraries.

1. Choose Tools ➤ Palettes ➤ Tool Palettes to open the tool palettes.

2. Choose Tools ➤ Palettes ➤ Materials to open the Materials palette. The tool palettes contain the material libraries, and the Material palette holds the parameter controls for modifying the materials.

3. Click near the bottom edge of the tool palette tabs, where it looks as if all the tabs are bunched together. This expands a large list of the available tool palettes. Choose Doors and Windows – Materials Sample from the list (see Figure 17.13).

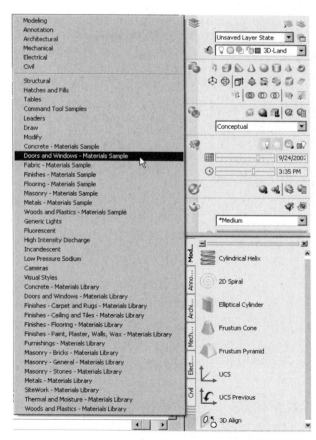

F I G U R E   1 7 . 1 3 : The list of available tool palettes including the material libraries

4. Click the Doors – Windows.Wood Doors.Ash sample sphere in the palette. The cursor changes shape to resemble a paintbrush.

5. Place the cursor over the front door, and then click to assign the ash wood material to the door. Render the drawing to see the effect.

6. Display the list of palettes, and then choose Concrete Materials Library from the list. In the palette, click the Concrete.Cast-In-Place.Flat.Grey.3, and then click the front step. Render the scene again, and you will see the concrete material applied to the step.

7. Open the Masonry – Material Sample palette. Click Masonry.Unit Masonry.Brisk.Modular.Common, and assign it to the exterior wall and balcony objects. Render the drawing one more time; it should look like Figure 17.14.

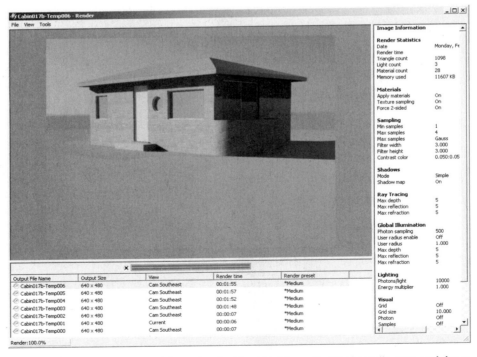

FIGURE 17.14: The cabin rendered with materials applied to the walls, step, and doors

8. Take a look at the Materials palette. At the top are sample spheres that show a representation of each material. Below the sample spheres are the controls for adjusting the appearance of the materials. The small icons in the lower-right corners of the sample areas indicate the materials are in use in the scene.

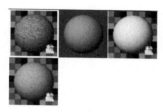

9. Open the Doors and Windows – Materials Samples palette again. Right-click the Doors – Windows.Glazing.Glass.Clear material, and choose Add to Current Drawing from the context menu. This option copies the material to the Materials palette without assigning it to an object.

10. Select the glass material in the Materials palette. In the Material Editor rollout, lower the shininess value to 95. Once you move the slider with the mouse, you can fine-tune its location using the right and left arrow keys on the keyboard. Change the Opacity value to 3 (see Figure 17.15).

FIGURE 17.15: Adjusting the glass material in the Materials palette

11. Make the 3D-Glazing layer current, and then freeze all the other layers.

12. Select all the glazing objects in the drawing. With the glass material selected in the Materials palette, click the Apply Material to Objects button below the sample area.

13. Thaw the 3D-Pivot-Doors and 3D-Win-Frame layers, make one of them the current, and then freeze the 3D-Glazing layer.

14. Select all the frames and doors in the drawing, and then click the ash wood material sample sphere in the Materials palette. Click the Apply Material to Objects button to make all the frames and doors the same material as the front door.

15. Thaw the 3D-Floor layer, and freeze all other layers. Open Flooring – Materials Samples. Click the Finishes.Flooring.Wood.Plank.Beech material in the palette, and drag it to the floor object. After a moment, the material appears in the Materials palette as well.

16. Repeat the techniques discussed in this section to apply materials to the thresholds, roof, roof edge, interior walls, the ground, and the step at the back of the building. Take your time examining the different materials available in the material libraries, and choose appropriate materials for the cabin's remaining components.

17. When you are done, thaw all the 3D layers, and render your scene. It should look similar to Figure 17.16.

N O T E   During the rendering process, I'm sure you noticed the small black squares being replaced one at a time by small areas of the rendered drawing. This indicates that AutoCAD is using bucket rendering. Before the rendering process begins, AutoCAD determines the sequence to process the squares, called *buckets*, in order to maximize the memory usage and thus increase the efficiency of the rendering.

FIGURE 17.16: The cabin rendering after applying materials to the remaining 3D objects

Rendering to a File

The Render feature by default creates a rendering in the Render dialog box only. The picture is not saved unless you explicitly tell AutoCAD to save it. You can also instruct the program as to the quality level of the rendering and the size, in square pixels, of the image. Follow these steps:

1. From the Render dialog box's menu, choose File ≻ Save to open the Render Output File dialog box.

2. Navigate to the folder you want to place the new image file, and then select a supported image file type in the Files of Type drop-down list. For this exercise, choose TIF as the file type, and name the file Cabin Rendering Small (see Figure 17.17). Click the Save button.

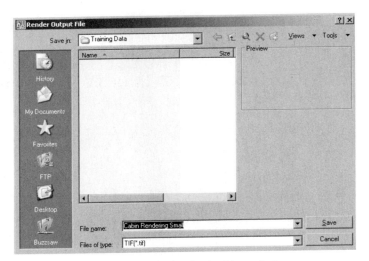

FIGURE 17.17: Saving the final cabin rendering

3. Depending on the file type you choose in the future, an Options dialog box, similar to the one shown here, will appear. In the TIFF Image Options dialog box, select 24 Bits (16.7 Million Colors), uncheck the Compressed option, and then click OK. The rendering is saved as an image file on your hard drive.

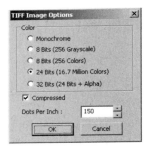

4. Expand the Render control panel. From the Select Render Preset drop-down list, select Presentation.

5. Open the Output Size drop-down list, and then choose Specify Output Size to open the Output Size dialog box.

6. Set Width to 2000 and Height to 1600, and then click OK. This is the resolution required to print a 10" × 8" image at 200 dots per inch (dpi).

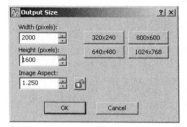

7. Click the Save Rendering to File Button to turn it on, and then click the Click to Specify Output File Name button next to the output size. Name this file Cabin Rendering Large, make it a 24-bit TIF file at 200 dpi, and uncheck the Compressed option. Click OK.

8. Save your drawing as Cabin17c.dwg, and then click the Render button again then wait a while as the new image renders. With the higher quality and larger image size, this may take considerably longer to process.

9. When the rendering is completed, look at the file size in Windows Explorer, and then compare the two images in your image-viewing software. The larger file is much crisper than the smaller image at the expense of increased rendering time.

This has been a brief introduction into the world of 3D and rendering in Auto-CAD, but you should now be oriented to the general way of doing things and have enough tools to experiment further. For a more in-depth discussion of the process, including rendering, see *Mastering AutoCAD 2008 and AutoCAD LT 2008* (Wiley, 2007) by George Omura.

Are You Experienced?

Now you can...

☑ create and manipulate cameras

☑ add sunlight to a scene

☑ place a point light

☑ specify a scene's real-world location

☑ add materials to objects

☑ render to a file

Numbers and Symbols

3D face

A triangular or four-sided flat surface that is the basic unit of a 3D surface.

3D mesh

A set of adjacent flat surfaces that together form a geometrical depiction of a three-dimensional curved surface.

3D model

An AutoCAD drawing file containing Auto-CAD objects that occupy 3D space and represent building components or geometrical objects in the real world. See also *object*.

3ds Max

A complementary product to AutoCAD, also produced by Autodesk. With 3ds Max you can create and animate 3D scenes.

A

absolute coordinates

Values for locating a point in space that describe its displacement from the *origin* (0,0,0) point of the drawing.

alias

A shortcut for starting commands. It's a short string of characters that you can enter at the *command line* instead of the full command.

aligned dimension

A linear dimension measuring the distance between two points. The dimension line for an aligned dimension is parallel to a line between the two points.

angular dimension

A dimension that measures the angle between two lines or the angle inscribed by an arc segment.

Angular unit

The unit in which angle values are displayed. The choices are Decimal Degrees, Degrees-Minutes-Seconds (listed as Deg/Min/Sec), Grads, Radians, and Surveyor's Units.

associative dimension

A dimension that updates automatically when the object being dimensioned changes size. See also *dimension*.

associative hatch pattern

A hatch pattern that updates automatically when the shape of the hatched area is modified. See also *hatch pattern*.

AutoCAD object

See *object*.

AutoSnap marker

A feature of AutoCAD that works with the object snap tools by displaying a symbol on the places in the drawing that can be snapped to. Each of these object snap modes has a different AutoSnap marker. The symbol appears when the *cursor* is near a location where you can use the active object snap. See also *Object Snap mode*.

B

base point

1. The initial point of reference for a number of modify commands, including Copy, Move, Rotate, Stretch, and Scale. 2. The insertion point for a drawing, as designated by the Base command.

baseline dimension

A dimensioning option that allows you to do multiple measurements from a designated baseline.

bearings

See *Surveyor's Units*.

bind

To transform an external reference file into a permanent part of the host file as a block. See *external reference*.

blocks

See *block reference*.

block definition

The description of an association of AutoCAD objects that is stored with the drawing file and includes a name, an *insertion point*, and a listing of objects in the association.

block reference

An instance of a grouping of objects that is inserted into a drawing and is based on the block definition for that grouping. Casually called a *block*.

Boolean operation

A series of tools that, when used with two overlapping 3D objects, result in either the two objects being joined as one (Union), one object and the overlapping volume being deleted (Subtract), or the parts of both objects outside the overlapping volume are deleted (Intersect).

Box

A 3D object consisting of a rectangular base and cap and four rectangular sides.

ByLayer

A value that can be assigned to colors and linetypes so that objects receive their color and linetype properties according to the layer they are on.

C

camera

A tool used to define and modify a view using the analogy of a real-world camera (point of view, lens length, and so on).

Cartesian coordinate system

A 2D system of locating points on a plane. It uses a horizontal (X) component and a vertical (Y) component to locate a point relative to the 0,0 point, or *origin*.

command line

A text window at the bottom of the screen that displays Command: prompts. This is where you see what you're entering through the keyboard. Also called the *Command window*.

Command window

See *command line*.

Command: prompt

The prompt at the *command line*, when no commands are currently running.

context menu

A menu that appears on the drawing area—usually as the result of a right-click—and contains options relevant to what the user is doing at that moment. Also called a *shortcut menu*.

continued dimension

A dimensioning option that allows you to place sequential dimensions that are adjacent to each other so that the dimension lines are aligned.

control panels

Any of 16 subdivisions of the *Dashboard* (some hidden by default) that house related commands and tools. Several control panels have a slide-out panel with additional tools.

crosshair cursor

A form of the *cursor* that consists of a horizontal line and a vertical line intersecting at their midpoints, resembling the crosshairs in a sighting device.

crossing window

A selection tool that selects an area defined by two points acting as opposite corners of a rectangle, which is made from right to left. All objects within or crossing the rectangle's borders are selected.

current UCS

The *user coordinate system (UCS)* that is active in a drawing. It determines the positive X, Y, and Z directions.

cursor

The pointing symbol on the computer monitor that is moved by moving the mouse. It can appear as, among other things, an arrow, a *pickbox*, and a crosshair. See also *crosshair cursor*.

cutting edge

The role certain objects can be temporarily assigned to play in a trimming operation. If an object is designated as a cutting edge, lines or other objects being trimmed are trimmed back to the point where they intersect the cutting edge.

D

Dashboard

A specialized palette that houses tools and controls for easy access. It's subdivided into one to sixteen *control panels*.

default

A value or option in a command that will be used unless you designate otherwise. In AutoCAD, default values and options are enclosed in angle brackets (< >).

dimension

A measurement, usually of distance or angularity, relating to features in the drawing. See also *associative dimension*.

dimension style

A collection of settings for *dimension variables* that is saved in a drawing under a specified name. Dimensions placed in the drawing follow the settings of the current dimension style.

dimension text

The text in a dimension. It expresses the measurement that the dimension is displaying or textual information at the end of a leader.

dimension variables

A group of settings and values that control the appearance of dimensions.

direct entry

An option for specifying the next point in a series of points, by using the *cursor* to indicate direction and the keyboard to enter the distance from the last point.

display locking

The practice of setting a floating *viewport* so that, when it is active, the scale factor does not change.

docking

Relocating a toolbar or a palette to the perimeter of the *drawing area* so it won't interfere with the AutoCAD drawing or other items on the screen.

drawing area

The portion of the monitor screen where you draw objects and view your drawing.

drawing extents

The minimum rectangular area with the same proportions as your *drawing area* that will enclose nonfrozen objects in your drawing. When you use the Zoom Extents command, the rectangular area fills the drawing area.

drawing limits

The area in a drawing that is covered by the *grid*. The user can define it. It's stored as the coordinates of the lower-left and upper-right corners of the rectangular area covered by the grid. If, on the Snap and Grid tab of the Drafting Settings dialog box, the Display Grid Beyond Limits checkbox is selected, AutoCAD displays the grid on the entire screen regardless of the limits.

drawing units

The intervals of linear and angular measurements chosen for use in a drawing.

.dwg

The file extension and format for the standard AutoCAD drawing.

dynamic block

A *block* that, after insertion, can be edited to take on a preset range of shapes and sizes to fulfill a variety of conditions in the drawing, such as windows with a multiplicity of widths and heights. It also can be set up to automatically align with geometry in the drawing.

dynamic display

A feature that, when turned on, displays coordinate, distance, angle, and Command prompt information near the *crosshair cursor* in the drawing area. The information displayed varies with the execution of the command. The Dyn button on the status bar controls whether this feature is on or off.

E

edge

1. The side of a 3D face or a *3D mesh*. 2. A command for controlling the visibility of the edges of 3D faces.

Elevation view

A view of a building that viewers get when they look at it horizontally, perpendicular to an interior or exterior wall.

entity

See *object*.

Explode

A command to undo an association of objects. It can be used on *blocks, multiline text, polylines*, and dimensions. Exploded multiline text becomes single-line text. Exploded polylines become lines and arcs. Exploded blocks become the individual objects that make up the block.

external reference

A drawing file that has been temporarily attached to another drawing for read-only purposes. Also called an *xref*.

external reference host file

The drawing file to which external references have been attached.

extrusion

1. A 2D object that has been given *thickness*. 2. A 3D solid object created with the Extrude command, by sliding a closed 2D shape along a path that is usually perpendicular to the 2D shape. If you use the Path option of the Extrude command, the extrusion doesn't need to be perpendicular to the 2D shape.

F

fill

A display mode that can be set to on or off. When it's on, it displays a solid color for shapes made with wide *polylines*, 2D solids, and *hatch patterns* using the Solid pattern. When it's off, the solid color area is invisible, and only the boundary of the fill is displayed.

floating toolbar

A toolbar that is not docked along the perimeter of the drawing area. You can move it around by dragging its title bar.

floating viewports

Openings created in the *paper space* of a drawing that allow you to view drawing components in *model space*.

font

A group of letters, numbers, and other symbols all sharing common features of design and appearance.

freeze

The off portion of a setting called Freeze/Thaw that controls the visibility of objects on layers and determines whether AutoCAD calculates the geometry of these objects during a *regeneration*. See also *layer*.

G

gradient

Similar to *hatch patterns*, gradients are filled areas with a blending of colors over the extents of that area.

graphical user interface

See *graphics window*.

graphics window

The appearance of your screen when AutoCAD is running. It consists of the *drawing area* and surrounding toolbars, menu bars, the *Command window*, and the status bar. Also called the graphical user interface. See also *menu bar*.

grid

1. A drawing aid that consists of a set of regularly spaced dots or lines in the *drawing area*. 2. A series of horizontal and vertical lines in a floor plan or section that locate the main structural elements of a building, such as columns and walls. This type is also called a column grid or a structural grid.

grips

An editing tool that allows you to perform five modify commands on selected objects without having to start the commands themselves. When grips are enabled, small squares appear on selected features, such as endpoints or midpoints. By clicking a grip, you activate the first of the available commands. To access the five commands, press the spacebar to cycle through the commands, or right-click and choose from a context menu.

H

hatch patterns

A pattern of lines, dots, and other shapes that fills in a closed area.

hatch pattern origin

A point in the drawing on which the geometry of the applied *hatch patterns* are based.

host file

See *external reference host file*.

hyperlink

An electronic connection between an Auto-CAD object and any of several places, including another drawing, a Microsoft Word document, a website, and so on.

I

icon

One of a set of small pictures on a toolbar. When the *cursor* rolls across an icon, it takes on the appearance of being a picture on a button.

insertion point

A reference point that is part of a *block* and is used to locate the block when it's inserted into a drawing. It's attached to the *cursor* while a block is being inserted. Once a block has been inserted, use the Insertion *osnap* to snap to the insertion point of the block.

Isometric view

A pictorial view of a 3D object in which all lines that are parallel on the object appear parallel in the view. See also *Perspective view*.

J

jamb

A surface that forms the side or top of an opening for a door or window in a wall.

justification point

A reference point on a line of single-line text or a body of multiline text that acts like the *insertion point* for blocks.

L

layer

An organizing tool that operates like an electronic version of transparent overlays on a drawing board. Layers can be assigned color and a *linetype*, and their visibility can be controlled. All *objects* in an AutoCAD drawing are assigned to a layer.

layout

An optional interface that serves as an aid to the user in setting up a drawing for printing. It rests "on top of" the *model space* in which the drawing of the building resides. It usually contains the title block, notes, scale, and other information. Users view a drawing through openings in the layout called *floating viewports*. A single drawing file can have multiple layouts, one for each print to be made from the file. The layout interface is sometimes referred to as *paper space*.

layout tab

A tab at the lower-left corner of the drawing area that you use to switch from a *model space* view of the drawing to a Layout view.

Leader

See *multileader*.

limits

See *drawing limits*.

linetype

The style of appearance of a line. AutoCAD styles include continuous, dashed, dash-dot, and so on.

linetype scale

A numeric value for noncontinuous linetypes that controls the size of dashes and spaces between dashes and dots. In an AutoCAD drawing, a global linetype scale controls all noncontinuous linetypes in the drawing, and you can apply an individual linetype scale to one or more selected lines.

lineweight

The value of a line's width measured in inches or millimeters.

M

material

When applied to 3D objects, materials define their appearance with color, reflection, and apparent texture.

menu bar

The set of drop-down menus at the top of the AutoCAD graphics window.

Mirror

A command that makes a copy of selected objects and flips the copy around a specified line to produce a reciprocal image of those objects.

mirror line

An imaginary line around which an object is flipped by the Mirror command.

model space

The portion of an AutoCAD drawing that contains the lines representing the building or object being designed, as opposed to the notes and title block information, which are kept on a *layout*.

Mtext

See *multiline text*.

multileader

A dimensioning tool that places an arrow at one end of a line and text at the other. Multileaders, also called leaders, are used to add textual information to the drawing and indicate the object to which it applies.

multiline text

A type of text in which an entire body of text is grouped together as one object. Casually called Mtext, it can be edited with word-processing techniques. Individual characters or words in the Mtext can have different heights, fonts, and colors from the main body of Mtext. *Dimension text* is Mtext. When exploded, Mtext becomes *single-line text*.

N

named view

A view of your drawing that is saved and given a name so that it can be restored later.

O

object

A basic AutoCAD graphical element that is created and manipulated as part of the drawing, such as a line, an arc, a dimension, a block, or text. Also called an entity.

Object Snap mode

Any of a set of tools for precisely picking strategic points on an *object*, including End-point, Midpoint, Center, and so on. It's casu-ally called *osnap*.

object snap tracking

See *tracking*.

origin

The point with the coordinates 0,0,0, where the x-, y-, and z-axes meet.

Ortho mode

An on/off setting that, when on, forces lines to be drawn and objects to be moved in a hori-zontal or vertical direction only.

orthogonal drawing

A system of creating views in which each view shows a different side of a building or an object, such as the top, front, left side, right side, and so on.

osnap

See *Object Snap mode*.

otrack

See *tracking*.

P

Pan

A command that slides the current drawing around on the drawing area without changing the magnification of the view.

paper space

A term sometimes used to refer to the inter-face for a drawing that contains layouts. See also *layout*.

path

The hierarchy of drive, folder, and subfolders where a file is stored, along with the file's name, such as C:\Program Files\Auto-CAD2008\Training Data\Cabin8a.dwg.

Perspective view

A pictorial view of a 3D object in which par-allel lines that aren't parallel to the plane of the screen appear to converge as they move farther from the viewer, similar to the way objects appear in the real world (such as rail-road tracks in the distance). See also *Isomet-ric view*.

pick button

The button on the mouse (usually the left one) that is used to pick points, buttons, or menu items, as well as to select objects in the drawing area.

pickbox

A form of the *cursor* as a small square that occurs when AutoCAD is in *selection mode*.

Plan view

A view of a drawing in which the viewer is looking straight at the XY plane in a direction parallel to the z-axis.

plot style

A group of settings assigned to a layer, a color, or an object. These settings determine how that layer, color, or object is printed.

plot-style table

A set of plot styles that controls the way in which a layout or drawing is printed.

point filters

A set of tools that allow you to specify a point in the drawing by using some of the X, Y, and Z coordinates from another point or points to generate the coordinates for the point you're specifying.

Polar coordinates

Values for locating a point in space that describe its location relative to the last point picked as defined by an angle and a distance.

polar tracking

A tool for temporarily aligning the *cursor* movement to preset angles while drawing. See also *tracking*.

polyline

A special type of line that (a) treats multiple segments as one object, (b) can include arcs, (c) can be smoothed into a curved line, and (d) can have width in 2D applications.

polysolid

A 3D object made up of rectangular segments with thickness, defined by picking the endpoints of each segment. Polysolids are commonly used to draw walls in a building.

precision of units

The degree of accuracy in which linear and angular units are displayed in dialog boxes, at the command line, or in dimensions.

prompt

The text at the command line that asks questions or tells you what action is necessary to continue the execution of a command. The *Command:* prompt tells you that no command is currently running.

R

Redraw

A command to refresh the *drawing area* or a particular *viewport*, thereby ridding it of any graphic distortions that show up on the monitor while you're drawing.

regeneration

A process in which the geometry for the objects in the current drawing file is recalculated.

regular window

A selection tool that selects an area defined by two points acting as opposite corners of a rectangle. All objects completely within the rectangle are selected, but those only partially within it are ignored. See also *crossing window*.

relative coordinates

Values for locating a point in space that describe its displacement from the last point picked in the drawing rather than from the *origin*.

render

The practice of calculating the surfaces, lights, materials, and environment to create an image file. The command to do so is also called Render.

rubberbanding

The effect of a line extending between the last point picked and the *crosshair cursor*, stretching like a rubber band as the cursor is moved.

running object snap

An *object snap mode* that has been set to be continually activated until turned off.

S

scale factor

The number that expresses the *true ratio* of a scale. For example, 48 is the scale factor for quarter-inch scale (¼" = 1'-0").

selection cycling

A procedure for selecting a particular object when it coincides with one or more other objects. To cycle, hold down the Shift key and the spacebar, and then click the line until the particular line you want becomes dashed. When that happens, release the Shift key and spacebar, and press ↵.

selection mode

The phase of a command that requires the user to select objects and thereby build up a *selection set* of objects to be modified by or otherwise used in the function of the command.

selection set

Any object or group of objects that have been selected for modification or have been selected to be used in a modification process.

selection window

A tool for selecting objects whereby the user creates a rectangular window in the *drawing area*. Objects are selected in two ways, depending on whether the selection window is a *crossing window* or a *regular window*.

shortcut menu

See *context menu*.

single-line text

A type of text *object* in AutoCAD in which each line of text is treated as an individual object, with its own *justification point*, whether it be a sentence, word, or letter.

Snap mode

An on/off setting that locks the *cursor* onto a spatial grid, which is usually aligned with the *grid*, allowing you to draw to distances that are multiples of the grid spacing. When the grid spacing is set to 0, the grid aligns with the snap spacing.

Snapbase

A command (and setting) used to reset the origin of the grid. By default, Snapbase is set to 0,0,0.

soffit

The underside of the roof overhang that extends from the outside edge of the roof, back to the wall.

solid

1. The name of a hatch pattern that fills a defined boundary with a solid color. 2. A three-dimensional object in AutoCAD that has properties similar to those of a solid block of material, such as mass, center of gravity, density, and so on.

stud

A vertical piece of lumber or metal used in framing walls. It's usually 2" × 4" or 2" × 6" in cross dimension and extends the height of the wall.

Surveyor's Units

An angular unit of direction in which the value is the angle that the direction deviates away (or bears) from true north or south, toward the east or west.

T

table

A matrix of information such as a spreadsheet, usually included in construction drawings, that contains data presented in rows and columns separated by lines.

template drawing

A drawing that has been set up to serve as a format for a new drawing. This allows the user to begin a new drawing with certain parameters already set up, because various settings have been predetermined.

text style

A collection of settings that controls the appearance of text and is saved in a drawing under a specified name. Text placed in the drawing will follow the settings of the current text style.

thaw

The on portion of a setting called Freeze/Thaw that controls the visibility of objects on layers and determines whether AutoCAD calculates the geometry of these objects during a *regeneration*. See also *layer*.

thickness

The distance that a 2D object is extruded in a direction perpendicular to the plane in which it was originally drawn, resulting in a 3D object. For a floor plan of a building, wall lines can be extruded to a thickness that is the wall's actual height. See also *extrusion*.

toolbar locking

A feature whereby a toolbar can be semipermanently fixed in a position on the screen and can't be accidentally moved.

tracking

The process by which the user sets up temporary points or angles as guides for the *cursor*, used to locate desired points in the process of drawing. *Object snap tracking* (or otrack) creates the temporary points, and *polar tracking* sets the angles. See also *Object Snap mode*.

tracking points

The temporary points that are set up for use in *object snap tracking*. See also *tracking*.

transparent command

A command that can be executed while another command is running, without interfering with the running command. Display commands, such as *Zoom* and *Pan*, are transparent.

true ratio

An expression of two numbers that defines the actual size differentiation in a scale—that is, the number of units represented by a single unit. See also *scale factor*.

U

UCS

See *user coordinate system (UCS)*.

UCS icon

The icon, usually in the lower-left corner of the *drawing area,* that indicates the positive directions of the x- and y-axes for the current *user coordinate system (UCS)*. In 3D views, the z-axis is also represented in the icon.

user coordinate system (UCS)

A definition for the orientation of the x-, y-, and z-axes in space relative to 3D objects in the drawing or to the *world coordinate system (WCS)*. UCSs can be named, saved, and restored.

V

view

A display of the current drawing from a particular user-defined perspective that is shown on the screen or in a *viewport*. Views can be named, saved, and restored.

viewport

An opening—usually rectangular, but not always—through which the user can view a drawing or a portion of it. There are two kinds of viewports: tiled viewports (used in *model space*) and *floating viewports* (used in layouts). See also *layout*.

visual style

Any of five variations of settings that control the appearance of objects to a viewer: 2D Wireframe, 3D Hidden, 3D Wireframe, Conceptual, or Realistic. You can find this on the Visual Style control panel of the *Dashboard*.

W

wireframe

A view of a 3D object that uses lines to represent the intersections of planes. The planes defined by these lines represent surfaces of building components, machine parts, and so on.

workspace

A customizable arrangement of dockable palettes, menus, and toolbars for the graphics window that can be named, saved, and made current.

world coordinate system (WCS)

The default *user coordinate system (UCS)* for all new drawing files, in which the positive directions for the x- and y-axes are to the right and upward, respectively, and in which the positive direction for the z-axis is toward the user and perpendicular to the plane of the screen.

WYSIWYG

An acronym for "what you see is what you get." It's a description applied to preview features that show you exactly what a screen will look like when printed.

X

xref

See *external reference*.

Z

Zoom

The name of a command with several options, all of which allow the user to increase or decrease the magnification of the *view* of the current drawing in the *drawing area* or in a *viewport*.

INDEX

Note to the reader: Throughout this index **boldfaced** page numbers indicate primary discussions of a topic. *Italicized* page numbers indicate illustrations.